FEMINIST
INTERPRETATIONS
OF
EMMANUEL LEVINAS

EDITED BY TINA CHANTER

THE PENNSYLVANIA STATE UNIVERSITY PRESS
UNIVERSITY PARK, PENNSYLVANIA

MW $31.60 2/8/02 (9)

Library of Congress Cataloging-in-Publication Data

Feminist interpretations of Emmanuel Levinas / edited by Tina Chanter.
     p.   cm. — (Re-reading the canon)
    Includes bibliographical references and index.
    ISBN 0-271-02113-6 (cloth : alk. paper)
    ISBN 0-271-02114-4 (pbk. : alk. paper)
    1. Levinas, Emmanuel. 2. Feminist theory. I. Chanter, Tina, 1960– . II. Series.

    B2430.L484 F45 2001
    194—dc21

                         00-064975

It is the policy of The Pennsylvania State University Press to use acid-free paper for
the first printing of all clothbound books. Publications on uncoated stock satisfy the
minimum requirements of American National Standard for Information Sciences—
Permanence of Paper for Printed Library Materials, ANSI Z39.48–1992.

DEDICATED TO THE MEMORY OF
HILLARY JOHNSON

Contents

Acknowledgments

I would like to acknowledge an exchange of letters I had with one of the contributors to this volume, Donna Brody, while the collection was in preparation, which helped me rethink some of the issues presented in the Introduction. Sandy Thatcher, director of Penn State Press, and Nancy Tuana, the series editor, have provided sound advice throughout the period of editing this book. They have both been as accommodating as possible and easy to work with and have enabled the editing process to proceed smoothly. I would also like to thank the readers for doing a fine job of advising on the final manuscript; Romaine Perin, for her painstaking copyediting, Patricia Mitchell, for her scrupulous proofreading; and Diana Witt, for preparing the index.

This volume is dedicated to Hillary Johnson. Hillary was twenty-four years old. She was a philosophy undergraduate at DePaul University, where she also studied Greek under Michael Naas, and wrote her senior thesis on Hannah Arendt, under the direction of Peg Birmingham, before she entered the M.A. program in philosophy at the University of Memphis. As she proved while she was a teaching assistant for Ronald Sundstrom, Hillary was already a great teacher, something that most of us are still working on. She already understood the importance of reaching those students who are hardest to reach, and who have the most difficulty in the writing and expression of their ideas, due to lack of preparedness.

The kind of violence that resulted in Hillary's death is something with which Levinas's philosophy is deeply concerned, and the tendency for violence and aggression to be an accepted part of male behavior in this society is something with which feminism has tried hard to bring into question. Feminism also concerns itself with addressing the questions of class and privilege that often lead individuals into feeling that their only recourse is violence. It therefore seems particularly appropriate to dedicate this volume to Hillary.

Hillary was one of those students who you knew, almost as soon as you met her, was going to be an important philosopher. Not only was she a truly exceptional student and teacher, she was also a truly exceptional person. I had the privilege of attending a memorial service for her in Chicago, where she came from, and there I heard from people who had known her much longer than I did. I have a picture in my mind of Hillary as a little girl, saying to her father, "Teach me." I have a picture of her walking to school and on the way giving her lunch to homeless people she knew, and talked to. I have a picture of her dissolving into helpless giggles, into what her best friend described as "puddles of laughter." I have a memory of her singing an Indigo Girls song, while her best friend, Lise, accompanied her on the guitar.

Everybody loved Hillary. She had an infectious, engaging energy, generosity, and love of life. I still don't understand how this could have happened. In the words of Nancy McPike, Hillary's mother, Hillary "dedicated her life to philosophy and to the search for, and love of, knowledge. She had an indomitable spirit that lives still in all of us who were fortunate enough to come into contact with her."

In the few months that Hillary was with us at the University of Memphis, she communicated her warmth, intelligence, humor, and incredible spirit. She was bright, caring, compassionate. Her death has deeply shocked the department of philosophy, and everyone who knew her.

There is, I am afraid, no easy way to say this. On November 20, 1999, Hillary Johnson was abducted. Two weeks later her body was discovered. She had been stabbed and murdered by a convicted murderer and rapist. During the two weeks in which she was missing, and after the discovery of her death, the graduate students at the University of Memphis went through something I hope none of us will ever have to go through, and many of us cannot even conceive. This is not only a testimonial for Hillary but also a testimony to the strength, courage, and fortitude of the graduate students at the University of Memphis, who are remarkable in every way.

While she was alive, Hillary made the best of her opportunities. We who still have what was taken away from her have a responsibility to learn from who Hillary was, and to try to live our lives in a better way. What Hillary's untimely death has taught me is that there is no time to lose. In the words of Hillary's stepfather, "Time is of the essence." Hillary had begun to get interested in Levinas's philosophy in the months before she died. Had she been given the chance, there is no doubt in my mind that she would have pushed forward the boundaries of philosophy.

I would like to acknowledge with gratitude permission to reprint "The Fecundity of the Caress." Reprinted from Luce Irigaray, *An Ethics of Sexual Difference*. Translated by Carolyn Burke and Gillian Gill. Translation copyright 1993 by Cornell University. Used by permission of the publisher, Cornell University Press. Rights for Europe, U.K., and the British Commonwealth were granted by Athlone Press. A portion of my introduction is refashioned from material published in my *Time, Death, and the Feminine: Levinas with Heidegger* (Stanford, May 2001). I would like to acknowledge with gratitude permission from Stanford University Press.

Preface

Take into your hands any history of philosophy text. You will find com-
piled therein the "classics" of modern philosophy. Since these texts are
often designed for use in undergraduate classes, the editor is likely to offer
an introduction in which the reader is informed that these selections represent the perennial questions of philosophy. The student is to assume
that she or he is about to explore the timeless wisdom of the greatest
minds of Western philosophy. No one calls attention to the fact that the
philosophers are all men.

Although women are omitted from the canons of philosophy, these
texts inscribe the nature of woman. Sometimes the philosopher speaks
directly about woman, delineating her proper role, her abilities and
inabilities, her desires. Other times the message is indirect—a passing
remark hinting at women's emotionality, irrationality, unreliability.

This process of definition occurs in far more subtle ways when the
central concepts of philosophy—reason and justice, those characteristics
that are taken to define us as human—are associated with traits historically identified with masculinity. If the "man" of reason must learn to
control or overcome traits identified as feminine—the body, the emo-
tions, the passions—then the realm of rationality will be one reserved
primarily for men,[1] with grudging entrance to those few women who are
capable of transcending their femininity.

Feminist philosophers have begun to look critically at the canonized
texts of philosophy and have concluded that the discourses of philosophy
are not gender-neutral. Philosophical narratives do not offer a university perspective, but rather privilege some experiences and beliefs over
others. These experiences and beliefs permeate all philosophical theories
whether they be aesthetic or epistemological, moral or metaphysical. Yet
this fact has often been neglected by those studying the traditions of

philosophy. Given the history of canon formation in Western philosophy, the perspective most likely to be privileged is that of upper-class white males. Thus, to be fully aware of the impact of gender biases, it is imperative that we re-read the canon with attention to the ways in which philosophers' assumptions concerning gender are embedded within their theories.

This new series, Re-Reading the Canon, is designed to foster this process of re-evaluation. Each volume will offer feminist analyses of the theories of a selected philosopher. Since feminist philosophy is not monolithic in method or content, the essays are also selected to illustrate the variety of perspectives within feminist criticism and highlight some of the controversies within feminist scholarship.

In this series, feminist lenses will be focused on the canonical texts of Western philosophy, both those authors who have been part of the traditional canon, as well as those philosophers whose writings have more recently gained attention within the philosophical community. A glance at the list of volumes in the series will reveal an immediate gender bias of the canon: Arendt, Aristotle, de Beauvoir, Derrida, Descartes, Foucault, Hegel, Hume, Kant, Locke, Marx, Mill, Nietzsche, Plato, Rousseau, Wittgenstein, Wollstonecraft. There are all too few women included, and those few who do appear have been added only recently. In creating this series, it is not my intention to rectify the current canon of philosophical thought. What is and is not included within the canon during a particular historical period is a result of many factors. Although no canonization of texts will include all philosophers, no canonization of texts that excludes all but a few women can offer an accurate representation of the history of the discipline, as women have been philosophers since the ancient period.[2]

I share with many feminist philosophers and other philosophers writing from the margins of philosophy the concern that the current canonization of philosophy be transformed. Although I do not accept the position that the current canon has been formed exclusively by power relations, I do believe that this canon represents only a selective history of the tradition. I share the view of Michael Bérubé that "canons are at once the location, the index, and the record of the struggle for cultural representation; like any other hegemonic formation, they must be continually reproduced anew and are continually contested."[3]

The process of canon transformation will require the recovery of "lost" texts and a careful examination of the reasons such voices have been silenced. Along with the process of uncovering women's philosophical history, we must also begin to analyze the impact of gender ideologies upon the process of canonization. This process of recovery and examination must occur in conjunction with careful attention to the concept of a canon of authorized texts. Are we to dispense with the notion of a tradition of excellence embodied in a canon of authorized texts? Or, rather than abandon the whole idea of a canon, do we instead encourage a reconstruction of a canon of those texts that inform a common culture?

This series is designed to contribute to this process of canon transformation by offering a re-reading of the current philosophical canon. Such a re-reading shifts our attention to the ways in which woman and the role of the feminine is constructed within the texts of philosophy. A question we must keep in front of us during this process of re-reading is whether a philosopher's socially inherited prejudices concerning woman's nature and role are independent of her or his larger philosophical framework. In asking this question, attention must be paid to the ways in which the definitions of central philosophical concepts implicitly include or exclude gendered traits.

This type of reading strategy is not limited to the canon, but can be applied to all texts. It is my desire that this series reveal the importance of this type of critical reading. Paying attention to the workings of gender within the texts of philosophy will make visible the complexities of the inscription of gender ideologies.

Notes

1. More properly, it is a realm reserved for a group of privileged males, since the texts also inscribe race and class biases that thereby omit certain males from participation.

2. Mary Ellen Waithe's multivolume series, *A History of Women Philosophers* (Boston: M. Nijoff, 1987), attests to this presence of women.

3. Michael Bérubé, *Marginal Forces/Cultural Centers: Tolson, Pynchon, and the Politics of the Canon* (Ithaca: Cornell University Press, 1992), 4–5.

Introduction

Reading Emmanuel Levinas is one of the most compelling and frustrating experiences I can think of. That satisfaction is elusive should come as no surprise to anyone, nor that there is a drive to continue reading, despite the diminishing returns it seems to yield: the more one reads, the less one understands, it would seem. One effect this has is to induce more reading. This structure of diminishing returns to the point of no return is reminiscent of Levinas's characterization of ethics. The more I do, the more responsible I become. This infinite call, which deepens as I try to fulfill it, draws me in, captivating me. There is no escape. I am responsible despite myself and prior to any debt I incur. As the productive outcome of ethicality diminishes, as ethics ceases to be an economy of pleasure, as I can no longer find gratification in being ethical, so the experience of reading Levinas cannot rest upon the mastering of concepts alone. Beyond the elaboration of a system, to read Levinas cannot be distinguished from responding to a call.

To what, then, are we called; what calls us to responsibility? To formulate the question in this way is already to reduce Levinas's reflections on ethics to the type of discourse that he seeks constantly to disrupt and displace. To ask what calls us to be ethical is to ask for an answer at the level of ontology; it is already to be deaf to the other. What object, what thing, what being, issues a call? What ontology of this call can be produced, what directives can be formulated in answer to the question; why should we be ethical? Such questions have their place, but this place is secondary for Levinas. These questions derive from a prior claim, a claim that has always already been heard, even if it has not always already been acted upon, acknowledged, or confirmed.

What would it mean to be a good reader of Levinas's texts? To whom does Levinas address himself? How does one read Levinas as a woman,

that is, without reading over what is said of the feminine as if it had nothing to do with being a woman? It has by now become commonplace to
point to Beauvoir's footnote in *The Second Sex* as an early feminist objection to his work.[1] But those who point to it often fail to raise the complex
issues to which it gives rise. So allow me to revisit Beauvoir's early critique of Levinas to set the scene for reading Levinas in the context of a
book that sets itself the task of taking both Levinas and feminism seriously. In a note to the introduction, Beauvoir criticizes Levinas because
he "deliberately takes a man's point of view, disregarding the reciprocity
of subject and object" (SS, xxii; DS, 1:16). Quoting a passage from Levinas's *Time and the Other,*[2] in which he seems to endorse the notion of
woman as other, thus reinforcing traditional conceptions of women,
Beauvoir seeks support for one of the central tenets of *The Second Sex*.
That is, woman "is defined and differentiated with reference to man and
not he with reference to her; she is the incidental, the inessential. He is
the Subject, he is the Absolute—She is the Other" (SS, xxii; DS, 1:15).
For Beauvoir, Levinas fits seamlessly into a long line of male thinkers
who have subordinated women to men, refused to construe the relation
between the sexes as reciprocal, denied women full subjectivity, and con-
signed them to the rank of the inessential. The quotation Beauvoir uses
from Levinas in support of her point, and the conclusion she draws from
it, bears close scrutiny, for here, in the opening pages of Beauvoir's enor-
mously influential investigation of the second sex, we can discern the
contours of the debate that follows.

   A quick glance at the quotation Beauvoir provides appears to confirm her view that Levinas's description of women, which, she says, "is
intended to be objective," can be dismissed easily. Levinas denies the
complementarity of the sexes, refuses to see them as oppositional or
correlative; indeed, he even comes close to denying consciousness to
women. Case closed, or so it would seem. The problem with Beauvoir's
straightforward dismissal of his conception of women as other is that it
fails to engage with Levinas's overall philosophical project, which is to
elevate the notion of alterity above the notion of totality. Levinas disrupts the priority of the whole, the one, or the system, on which our
notions of complementarity, reciprocity, and symmetry rest, thereby calling into question at the same time the adequacy of Beauvoir's appeal to a
model that advocates reciprocal relations. Since Levinas associates the
feminine with alterity, the feminine plays a major part in the challenge
he issues to a philosophical heritage that assumes the primacy of the

same. To take up Levinas's challenge entails that we bring into question the very standards by which Beauvoir judges Levinas's conception of the feminine wanting. Rather than requiring the feminine to conform to the canons of reciprocity and complementarity that refer ultimately to a totality, Levinas's notion of the feminine functions, on this account, to disrupt the primacy of totality, sameness, system, concept. The demands Beauvoir makes on Levinas now appear to divest his approach to the feminine of its radical potential, imposing on him precisely the restraints of a tradition that he seeks to go beyond. Could it be that Beauvoir's call for women to transcend their immanence is itself caught up in a repetition of the same, which takes shape as the implicit expectation that women should replicate or mimic the achievements of men? The terms in which this question is formulated reflect Irigaray's influence. In her interrogation of Levinas, reprinted here, Irigaray is not only concerned with the need to avoid reducing women to replicas of men, but is also alert to the danger lurking in Levinas's penchant for allowing the feminine to represent alterity. She is wary of reinscribing the feminine as subordinate to men, in a Levinasian scenario that has women facilitate men's transcendence without achieving transcendence themselves.

It hardly needs to be added that it is no small task for Levinas to short-circuit the need for reciprocity and the demands for equality that go hand in hand with it, and that even if we grant him some measure of success, there are still important questions to be asked about the implications of bringing a model of reciprocity into disrepute on the pretext of going beyond it, when it is far from obvious that reciprocity has been achieved. If women have not yet been granted the full status of their subjectivity, then what effect does the call to circumvent the model of reciprocity as untenable have on us? Whether one decides that for all the potential radicality of Levinas's celebration of the feminine in its unassimilable otherness, the feminine functions in a way that ultimately reinscribes femininity in a traditional trope that benefits men more than it does women, or whether one returns to the stalwart battle cries of feminism for equality and sameness and rejects Levinas's appeal to feminine alterity as just so much mystification, it is clear that the relation of Levinas to feminism is a complex one that demands reflection. It is clear that when Levinas associates the feminine with alterity, he cannot be unproblematically assimilated to a tradition that has figured women as other, since his entire philosophical project, contrary to the tradition, aims to establish the imperative of alterity as formative of the urge for systematicity.

In Beauvoir's defense, it should be said that the implications of Levinas's challenge to the philosophical tradition would not become fully evident until 1961, with the publication of *Totality and Infinity*, and, arguably, the radicality of his position would not widely influence the philosophical community until 1974, with the publication of *Otherwise Than Being*. *The Second Sex*, published in 1949, only eight years after the publication of *Time and the Other*, appeared at a time when Levinas's work was still relatively unknown, and his importance and originality as a philosopher was certainly unappreciated. Beauvoir was not, perhaps, in a position to recognize Levinas as someone who would bring into question some of the existential tenets, stemming from Heidegger, that she herself still held dear.

It should also be pointed out that, as in so many cases throughout *The Second Sex*, H. M. Parshley's translation helps to muddy the waters for English readers. He translates Levinas's phrase "L'altérité s'accomplit dans le féminin" as "Otherness reaches its full flowering in the feminine," thereby obscuring the term *accomplishes*, a technical term in Levinas that Parshley renders with a flourish that almost reduces Levinas's thought to the banal, rendering Levinas's ideas on women akin to stereotypical notions of femininity, and drawing Levinas back into the Romantic tradition he seeks to overturn. The notion of accomplishment carries a philosophical weight neglected both by Parshley's translation and by Beauvoir's interpretation of Levinas. It signifies a movement that cannot be fully accommodated by the language of representation, registering rather what Levinas will call sensibility, that which is expressed most often by the gestural, tonal, corporeal, materiality of bodily enjoyment, in eros, but which also resists being captured conceptually. Sensibility is both required and assumed by language; it is both taken up by representation and obliterated by it. Since this movement is recurrent and ongoing, we cannot simply say that sensibility is on the way to language, for this would impose a teleology of the concept that Levinas seeks to avoid. Since there is an ongoing fluid exchange between sensibility and representation, we cannot interpret them as if they replayed the distinction between matter and form, body and mind, or materiality and ideality. The paradoxical quality of sensibility resides in the fact that we can only gain access to it through the language of experience, and yet that very language necessarily obscures precisely the sensibility it would express. Sensibility is thus both a condition of philosophical expression and its undermining. Sensibility is an openness to alterity that does not prejudge, as a subject related to a delineated world of objects must, how alterity must conform to ideas of it.

Whether in his description of the dwelling, which the feminine facilitates, in his account of eros, a term that is used synonymously with the feminine, or in the language of maternity and obsession, Levinas's notions of sensibility and ethical affection are sexualized. The experience that is not an experience, the encounter with alterity that is not quite an encounter (for both the idea of experience and encounter would impose the requirements of preformed subjects), sensibility and obligation involve an excess, a mystery, an alterity that can never be fully recuperated by the one who suffers it. That this excess is systematically marked as feminine in Levinas's philosophy can either be ignored—which has been the typical response by Levinas's readers, or it can be taken up as a philosophically significant and politically loaded gesture. The contributors to this volume seek to take up the philosophical and political significance of the feminine in Levinas's work.

Given that Levinas, against the Western philosophical tradition inaugurated by Parmenides, claims a priority for alterity over the one, the idea that alterity is accomplished in the feminine amounts to a radical claim, which must alter the traditional association of the feminine with otherness. Levinas, it must be conceded, is in fact according the feminine a certain priority. *The feminine* is a privileged term in Levinas, since in it alterity is accomplished. Even if that priority must ultimately be rendered questionable in the light of the overall aims of his philosophy and the place it confers on women, it should at least be acknowledged that something radical might be happening here. In question, then, is whether there is a case to be made for the view that Levinas does not in fact seamlessly affirm masculine privilege, as Beauvoir represents him, but rather creates at least the potential for an overturning of that tradition. In question is whether Levinas does not so much affirm masculine privilege, as Beauvoir says he does, but rather overturns it—or at least provides resources for its overturning. Even if in Levinas's philosophy the feminine is ultimately reined in by its traditional connotations, as when the accomplishment of the feminine finds its meaning in the birth of the child, there might be scope for developing those moments in Levinas's texts where the feminine stands for absolute alterity. One of the risks to be negotiated by feminist projects that take up the feminine as a mark of radical otherness is that of coalescing with the patriarchal definitions of women that Beauvoir fought so hard to combat, confining women to the role of mysterious other, as man's muse, not quite human, incapable of rational thought or responsible action. Some of the essays included in this volume respond to this risk.

To read Levinas well would perhaps be not only to read his texts faithfully; it would be to turn away from his texts, or rather to turn his texts to what lies beyond them, and to ask what they foreclose. Refusing to accept the limits that Levinas sets for the scope of his own questioning of alterity, turning his texts inside out, could be in some sense to turn within them. It is because the world became too worldly, because it became too self-referential, because in reaching for transcendence it came up only with itself, that Levinas was moved to ask again after transcendence. Could it be that even his attempt to affirm radical alterity falls short of the very radicality that Levinas's philosophy announces? Could it be that the saying of the feminine goes beyond the said of Levinas's philosophy?

Levinas was born in 1906 in Lithuania, which he describes as one of the parts of eastern Europe in which Judaism "knew its highest spiritual development," and where Talmudic study was a way of life.[3] His father owned a bookstore in Kovno, and Levinas was steeped in Russian culture as he grew up, gaining admission at the age of eleven to the lycée in Kharkov, in the Ukraine, returning to Lithuania in 1920. The names Dostoyevsky, Gogol, Lermontov, Pushkin, and Tolstoy often find their way into his writing; indeed Levinas credits his reading of Russian novels, particularly those of Dostoyevsky, with leading him to philosophy. These are books "shot through with anxiety, by the essential, religious anxiety, but readable as a search for the meaning of life," says Levinas (Poiré, *Emmanuel Levinas*, 69). As for the 1917 Leninist revolution that brought an end to czarist Russia, Levinas says that he "didn't remain indifferent" to its temptations, but paints a picture of being largely preoccupied with his education. "It required, he says, "an immersion in the true West and perhaps in its philosophy for me to situate Russia in terms of Europe" (Poiré, *Emmanuel Levinas*, 68).

In 1923 Levinas moved to France, studying initially in Strasbourg, where he met Maurice Blanchot, who introduced him to the work of Proust and Valéry. Later, Blanchot's and Levinas's work would converge around the irremissibility of anonymous existence, which they both call "il y a," or the "there is," the notion that is so important to Levinas's work in his 1947 texts. Not only would an intellectual affinity between Blanchot and Levinas develop, but Blanchot would play a role of inestimable importance in Levinas's life: he would save his wife while Levinas was in captivity during World War II.

If Henri Bergson's work was the strongest philosophical influence on Levinas during his studies in Strasbourg, Martin Heidegger would come to dominate his thinking toward the end of the 1920s. In 1928, Levinas moved to Freiburg to take classes with Husserl. In his own words, "I had the impression that I went to see Husserl and I found Heidegger. Of course, I will never forget Heidegger's relation to Hitler. Even if this relation was only of a very short duration, it will be forever. But the works of Heidegger, the way in which he practiced phenomenology in *Being and Time*—I knew immediately, that this was one of the greatest philosophers in history, comparable to Plato, Kant, Hegel, Bergson" (Poiré, *Emmanuel Levinas*, 74).

In 1939 Levinas was drafted, having become a French citizen and having served in the military in Paris. Before the war he had published his first book, *The Theory of Intuition in Husserl's Phenomenology*, in which he wanted to "present Husserl's doctrine while finding Heideggerian elements in it. As if Husserl's philosophy already stated the Heideggerian problem of being and beings" (Poiré, *Emmanuel Levinas*, 81). In 1935 he wrote the essay "De l'évasion," in which, in Levinas's own words, "one can distinguish the anxieties of the way to come. And the whole fatigue of being, the condition of that period. Distrust in relation to being ... arose at a time in which the presentiment of the imminent Hitlerism was everywhere" (Poiré, *Emmanuel Levinas*, 82–83).[4] During his internment as a prisoner of war, Levinas began to write *Existence and Existents*, but it was not completed until after the war. It was published in 1947, the same year as "Time and the Other," with which it shares many themes.

In 1946 Levinas returned to the headquarters of the Alliance Israélite Universelle in Paris, an organization with which he had worked in a pedagogical capacity before the war, and whose aim was to emancipate Jews in countries where they were barred from citizenship. Levinas was appointed director of the École Normale Israélite Orientale, a position in which he remained until 1961, the year in which *Totality and Infinity* was published. This is the work that is generally recognized to have firmly established Levinas as a preeminent philosopher. In it, he puts forward the thesis that the face of the Other commands me ethically in a way that disrupts my selfish preoccupations. The call of the Other goes beyond being, and in this sense it is infinite. As Levinas puts it in *Of God Who Comes to Mind*, published in 1986 (twelve years after *Otherwise*

Than Being or Beyond Essence, Levinas's most important philosophical work after *Totality and Infinity*), to assume the infinite is to think the unthinkable. "This is a thinking thinking more than it thinks—Desire— a reference to the neighbor—a responsibility for the other."[5] Asked to explain what it means to be faced by an infinite responsibility to the other, Levinas often refers to everyday encounters, in which I open the door for another, or let the other person pass in front of me, or simply welcome the other with the greeting "Bonjour!" Or he will refer to the obligation to feed and shelter others, always insisting, in the words he likes to quote from Dostoyevsky's *The Brothers Karamazov*, "Each of us is guilty before everyone and for everything, and I more than all the others." Confronted with the objection that there is always more than one other, so that I am forced to choose between conflicting demands, Levinas responds that my responsibility is not diminished, only my action. Justice, he acknowledges, as the discourse that renders us equal and invests us with rights, is necessary and required. But charity, or loving the neighbor, or being answerable to the infinite, is the origin of justice, and remains necessary in another, and more important, sense, because it offers a commentary on the violence committed in the name of justice, the violence that consists in reducing the alterity of the other to an individual belonging to a group, in reducing the other to the same, or in reducing ethics to ontology.

After teaching at Nanterre, Levinas ended his official academic career at the Sorbonne in 1976, but was invited to continue teaching seminars there, which he did until 1984. He died in December 1995.

Perhaps the seduction of Levinas's work lies in its poetical, prophetic tone—he is a poet despite himself. I often think of Derrida's acknowledgment of the strange power that Levinas's language has. He observes in a note to "Violence and Metaphysics" that

> Levinas's writing ... can less than ever be distinguished from intention, forbids the prosaic disembodiment into conceptual frameworks that is the first violence of all commentary. Certainly, Levinas recommends the good usage of prose which breaks Dionysiac charm or violence, and forbids poetic rapture, but to no avail: in *Totality and Infinity* the use of metaphor, remaining admirable and most often—if not always—beyond rhetorical abuse, shelters within its pathos the most decisive movements of the discourse.[6]

The degree of self-consciousness Levinas maintains over his texts is remarkable: he is forever stepping back from his own position and providing a self-commentary, and yet his acute awareness of and meditations on the ways in which the language of his texts functions cannot prevent the breach of all formality as what Levinas calls "saying" undoes even Levinas's own reflective self-commentary. This breaching, breaking, disrupting, rupture, or interruption becomes the topic of Levinas's self-reflective comments on his own writing in *Otherwise Than Being*. "And I still interrupt the ultimate discourse in which all the discourses are stated, in saying it to one that listens to it, and who is situated outside the said that the discourse says, outside all it includes. That is true of the discussion I am elaborating at this very moment" (OB, 170; AE, 216–17).[7] In the final pages of *Otherwise Than Being*, Levinas's self-consciousness about his own writing process is supreme.

> Language would exceed the limits of what is thought, by suggesting, letting be understood without ever making understandable, an implication of a meaning distinct from that which comes to signs from the simultaneity of systems or the logical definition of concepts. This possibility is laid bare in the poetic said, and the interpretation it calls for ad infinitum. It is shown in the prophetic said, scorning its conditions in a sort of levitation.... Are the rendings of the logical text mended by logic alone?... In the writing the saying does indeed become a pure said, a simultaneousness of the saying and of its conditions. A book is interrupted discourse catching up with its own breaks. But books have their fate; they belong to a world they do not include, but recognize by being written and printed, and by being prefaced and getting themselves preceded with forewords. They are interrupted, and call for other books and in the end are interpreted in a saying distinct from the said. (OB, 169–71; AE, 215–17)

A saying distinct from a said. Herein lies an impossible yet fundamental and organizing distinction for Levinas's mature philosophical work, *Otherwise Than Being* (1974). Impossible because logically, at the level of the said, it is not a meaningful distinction, yet fundamental because it organizes everything that interests Levinas philosophically. "And I still interrupt the ultimate discourse in which all the discourses are stated, in saying it to one that listens to it, and who is situated outside the said that the discourse says, outside all it includes" (OB, 170; AE, 217) says Levinas, in a statement that thematizes in a said, and says, in a saying (*le dire*) that undoes its said (*le dit*). The saying refers to "the one that listens to it," and not to the one who says, speaks, it. The saying is not governed by the speaker, it is uttered on behalf of someone else, the Other. It derives its meaning from elsewhere, outside the system of meaning, language, and communication that unites the speaker and listener. It defies the self-referentiality of language, coming from a beyond. Saying "says to the other who is outside of themes" (OB, 169; AE, 214), and "refuses simultaneity" (OB, 170; AE, 216), inhabiting the diachronous time of philosophy (see OB, 167; AE, 213), and "not enter[ing] into the present" (OB, 170; AE, 216).

The breakup of the said in the saying is the infinite interruption effected by the other in the same. In *Totality and Infinity* (1961), published fourteen years earlier than *Otherwise Than Being*, Levinas refers to the breaking up of totality by infinity, a calling into question of the self by the other, as the face-to-face.

Ontological Difference, Sexual Difference

Before any final judgment can be made on the significance and function of the feminine in Levinas's philosophy, the radicality that Levinas claims for alterity must be appreciated. In order to properly understand the sense in which Levinas construes otherness, we need to understand his compulsion to return to Heidegger's ontological difference, but to think it as separation, rather than as a distinction, or as "an amphibology" that "does not signify the ultimate" (OB, 23; AE, 29). To understand why and how Levinas returns to the ontological difference, if only to recast it, is also to understand the extraordinary role he accords to the feminine, as an exception to the categories of being, as a way of exceeding the language of ontology. Only once we have understood the sense in which the feminine consists, for Levinas, in a departure from the landscape of ontology can we responsibly ask what possibilities Levinas's reflections open up for feminism, and in what sense they foreclose the possibility of feminist theory.

Levinas never tires of stipulating the need to rethink Heidegger's ontological difference. In *Time and the Other* he says, "One cannot ignore

[Heidegger's] distinction ... between *Sein* and *Seindes*, Being and being, but which for reasons of euphony I prefer to render as *existing* and *existent*" (TO, 44; TA, 24).[8] To appreciate both the importance of the ontological difference for Levinas and his conviction of the need to go beyond it will not only enable us to gain some perspective on the role that Heidegger plays in Levinas's philosophy. It will also demonstrate that what is at stake in Levinas's invocation of the femininity is more complicated than what Simone de Beauvoir's dismissive footnote in *The Second Sex* would lead us to believe. This is not to deny that Beauvoir's skepticism about Levinas has some validity. It is only to point out that Levinas's equation of the feminine with otherness—which in her judgment amounted to no more than the reduction of women to the inferior other of men, so characteristic of centuries of patriarchal thought—is no simple repetition of the tradition.

In raising anew the question of Being, and insisting on the difference between Dasein's way of existing and the existence of other entities, Heidegger succeeded in focusing philosophical attention on the relationship between the being that Dasein is (what Levinas calls an existent) and its act of Being (or in Levinas's terms, its existence). Having posed this relationship as decisive, according to Levinas, Heidegger approached Being or existence as if it were always possessed by someone, or as if the relationship between Being and beings is always one of belonging.[9] Levinas searches for a relationship or dialectic, or better still (since both these terms presuppose a subject-object relation), a dynamic or drama "which takes place in a hitherto unsuspected dimension" (EE, 30; DE, 42). Rather than characterizing the existent as a being who always already understands its relation to the world, albeit vaguely and in a way that is as yet unthematized, a being, that is, like Dasein, who has its Being as an issue from the start, Levinas introduces the notion of hypostasis, in order to examine the instant by which an existent takes on its existence.

Heidegger's philosophy progresses from an analysis of Dasein's involvement in the everyday inauthentic world to an analysis of Dasein's authentic, resolute, and solitary anticipation of its own death in the moment of vision. There is thus a progressive clarification that consists in the movement from the world of circumspection, in which Dasein is fallen, or immersed in the opinions of "the they" (so that I take over views that are publicly available as if they were my own; I like the music or the art that others like, and so on), to the vision that Dasein acquires when it stands alone confronting its finitude. Levinas objects to this picture on several levels. It overlooks enjoyment and materiality; it tends to denigrate the present as inauthentic, in favor of a future authenticity, and at the same time it tends to align being-with-others (*Mitsein*) with inauthenticity, while reserving authentic action for a Dasein that has divorced itself from the collectivity of "the they." Heidegger's analysis of Dasein also functions by assuming that Dasein is always already a being that essentially understands, and construing ontology as a method of drawing out explicitly that which Dasein understands implicitly by virtue of its involvement in the world. Let me briefly elaborate each of these points.

First, Levinas doesn't think that our involvement with the world can be reduced to equipmental relations, whereby we eat, or drink, or breathe in order to accomplish further ends. We do not eat simply because we are hungry, we do not take a drink merely because we are thirsty; we also drink in order to drink, we eat because we enjoy eating, Levinas insists. These activities are not to be dismissed as inauthentic, they are part of the fabric of life. In a telling observation, one that cannot fail to be informed by his own imprisonment in a labor camp, and the death of many members of his Jewish family during World War II, Levinas says, "It is in times of misery and privation that the shadow of an ulterior finality which threatens the world is cast behind the object of desire. When one has to eat, drink and warm oneself in order not to die, when nourishment becomes fuel, as in certain kinds of hard labor, the world also seems to be at an end, turned upside down and absurd, needing to be renewed. Time becomes unhinged" (EE, 45; DE, 68). It is precisely because of the horror of the Holocaust, and because Levinas is concerned to think through the implications of an ontology that failed to immunize itself against the possibility of such an event, that Levinas wants to take seriously the significance of what it means to enjoy good food and drink, to inhabit a home, and to a live a life whose meaning is irreducible to a series of means for further ends.

Second, Levinas does not think that the meaning of the present is exhausted either by the legacy it inherits from the past or by the meaning it bequeaths to the future. In other words, he thinks that the impulse that led Heidegger to avoid reducing the meaning that the present has for Dasein to presence in the sense of an object that is present-at-hand (*Vorhanden*) led him to assimilate too quickly any authentic meaning that the present could have to the significance of Dasein's temporality as a whole. Heidegger's understanding of Dasein's temporality as ecstatic leads him to overlook the possibility that there might be more to the instant than its subservient role as the resolute anticipation of one's own mortality. Levinas wants to examine the meaning of the instant outside of its function as a present that passes into a future, and he asks if the instant does not have a drama that is not immediately canceled out by virtue of its evanescence into a future. To this end he investigates phenomena such as insomnia, evasion, nausea, indolence, weariness, effort and fatigue, and pain and suffering, hoping to catch sight of the moment in which anonymous existence, or what Levinas calls the there is (il y a), turns into a subject. Levinas finds that the event by which a subject is posited, the hypostasis in which an existent arises and takes charge of its existence, is not a simple passage of the present into a future, but a complex dynamic whereby a subject encounters a duality. This duality resides both in the mastery or freedom that an existent exerts over its existence, for example in the effort of labor, and the condemnation to existence that is revealed as the pain of hard work subsides into the necessity of having to be oneself. The upsurge of an instant involves both the capacity for work that a subject discovers it has by virtue of its position, its being a base, its very materiality, and the impossibility of escaping or evading the fact that it is committed to existence. At the bottom of the irremissibility of the self lies the anonymous state of existence that Levinas describes as the there is. The I—a provisional I, as we shall see, finds itself attached to being, unable to get away from itself, unable to jump over its own shadow, and yet not without resources, not without the freedom (again, a provisional freedom) of mastery. It is tied to itself, and yet able to provide for itself, through its own labor and through the good fortune of having things at its disposal. It is free, but its freedom is both limited (it has to exist, its contract with existence is irrevocable) and available to exploitation by others (the very corporeal skills that facilitate the capacity of labor that can protect it can also become the basis of its servitude).

Third, while Levinas acknowledges that Heidegger reserves a place for being-with-others (Mitsein) in his analysis of Dasein, he suspects that the existential significance that others have for Heidegger ultimately suffers from severe attenuation and subordination to the sovereignty of a solitary Dasein. Whereas the direction in which Heidegger's analysis tends is away from Dasein's inauthentic and unreflective involvement in "the they" and toward the authentic solitude of a Dasein who has disengaged itself for the most part from its worldly entanglement, Levinas's analysis, at least in a limited sense, could be said to proceed in the opposite direction. Levinas wants to elaborate the meaning of solitude in positive terms, such that the pleasure of eating, or the curiosity of studying in order to come to know the world, are neither reducible to one another nor relegated to inauthentic experience. While the satisfaction and enjoyment of eating is not simply equivalent to the intentionality of knowledge, it does consist of converting alterity or the unknown to sameness or to the knowable. In this sense, the movement of satisfying one's needs and of rendering objects knowable is similar. In both cases, there is a reduction of otherness to the subject. I am the one who eats; I am the subject who knows. So Levinas can say that enjoyment is also knowledge and sensation. It is an encounter with alterity, but this alterity is provisional. What begins as other is incorporated into the same, and as such it follows the same movement as the light that illuminates an object, when a subject comes to know it—a reduction of alterity to sameness. Whereas ecstasis reduces the same to the other, and vision or intellect reduces the other to the same, Levinas introduces a relation from which both terms absolve themselves—the relation of the face-to-face. Here is a relation that cannot be absorbed by one term or another, a relation that overflows its terms, a relation, therefore, that cannot properly be called a relationship. It is a relationship that confers identity on its terms, rather than presupposing that they are already consolidated, before entering into relationship.

Finally, while Levinas concedes that there are certain points at which Heidegger attempts to think the very sense of existence without an existent that Levinas turns to, the decisive difference between Levinas's and Heidegger's projects that Levinas never ceases to assert is that insofar as Heidegger's thought shies away from the alterity of the other, his ontology remains in thrall to the question of Being in a way that does not allow him to give the attention to ethics that Levinas thinks it deserves. It should be added that Levinas's critique of Heidegger is based largely on *Being and Time,* and it could be argued that certain formulations of Heidegger's later philosophy come very close to Levinas. Levinas acknowledges this proximity in some of his later publications.

Now that we have reviewed some of the major ways in which Levinas departs from Heidegger, let us return to the issue of the ontological difference, in order to see how Levinas introduces the notion of the feminine. Levinas articulates in the existence of the existent a duality, as we have seen. On the one hand there is a certain mastery, and on the other hand there is the unavoidable commitment to exist that Levinas designates the there is. At issue here is Levinas's attempt to take up and rework Heidegger's construal of the relation between the being that exists (Heidegger's Dasein, Levinas's existent) and the very work of being. Heidegger stresses the impossibility of raising the question of being, in this second sense, without also occluding it, since in the very attempt to distinguish between being and beings, being withdraws, or becomes a substantive. While not disputing the fact that being or existence is concealed by the very question that tries to tease apart the meaning of Being and beings, since to thematize Being is to reduce it to something that can be grasped, Levinas asks, "Is the tie between what exists and its existing indissoluble? Can one go back to hypostasis?" (TO, 44; TA, 23), and in a passage that can be read as referring back to this question, he answers, with reference to the son: "The return of the ego to itself that begins with hypostasis is thus not without remission, thanks to the perspective of the future opened by eros. Instead of obtaining this remission through the impossible dissolution of hypostasis, one accomplishes it through the son. It is thus not according to the category of cause, but according to the category of the father that freedom comes about and time is accomplished" (TO, 91; TA, 86). The sexual specificity of this passage is by no means unique to Levinas's corpus and, far from being accidental, is in fact a structuring theme of his discourse. The entire conceptual architecture that Levinas elaborates is permeated with a sexual metaphorics. Thus, the mastery of the subject who masters existence is described by Levinas in the language of "virility," while death, eros, and ... are encounters with alterity that constitute what could be called feminized moments. Death is an encounter whereby I am "no longer able to be able," and the feminine (eros) is described in terms of modesty, hiding, and slipping away from the light. We have already seen that Levinas wants to characterize an encounter with alterity in which that alterity is not compromised, where alterity does not surrender its alterity, as it is in enjoyment, for example. In other words, alterity remains mysterious, unknowable, resistant to the power of light and illumination. So when Levinas speaks of the feminine as a mode of withdrawal, as a hiding, as modesty, and as slipping away from the light, we are already prepared for the sense in which the feminine cannot be said to be a being. The feminine, for Levinas, is a way of rendering what cannot be reduced to beings. It is, in this sense, an elaboration, or dramatization, of the ontological difference. Levinas's claim, in the preceding passage, that eros opens the future that is accomplished by the father establishes that while the feminine is associated, for Levinas, with a disruption of the ontology of being, it cannot by itself bring that disruption to fruition. Paternity is required to bring to completion the movement toward alterity that the feminine opens.

Bearing in mind that the feminine does not designate a being, but is understood by Levinas as a tendency, a way, or a regime, Levinas's commentators—and indeed Levinas himself—have tried to minimize feminist concerns. Pointing out that the feminine is not intended to designate, in Levinas's vocabulary, a being or a subject, they conclude that it would be wrongheaded to chastise Levinas for endorsing the inferiority of the feminine sex. What can be the meaning of Irigaray's objection to Levinas that the feminine lacks the face, if the term *feminine* is not intended to designate women as such?

It is true that Levinas's understanding of the feminine as a disruption of the virile categories of mastery, domination, and self-possession opens up the possibility of another way of (non)being, a different mode of existence. This feminine way of being (which is not properly speaking a way of being, but rather a slipping away from the light) interrupts the economy of being. It is an interruption of the intentional movement of knowledge, whereby a subject who seeks to know the world ends up negating the otherness of objects and reducing the world to itself. The suspicion remains, however, that while Levinas might well open up a space for the rethinking of the feminine, he does not follow through on this promise, but rather closes it down. Levinas's closure of the radical possibilities he opens up for feminism can be specified in a number of ways.

Although it is clear by now that Levinas does not intend his use of the term feminine to designate in any straightforward way empirical women, and thus can hardly be taken to be subordinating one sex to another in any simple way, it remains the case that Levinas sometimes drops his guard and resorts to language that invokes the actual empirical women that at other places in his texts he assures us he does not have in mind. So while Levinas cannot be accused of definitively or intentionally marking the inferiority of the feminine sex, there are ways in which this inferiority is marked in his texts, despite his best intentions. If there is no sense in which paternity, the father, and the son are accorded a certain priority, why are they marked in sexual, rather than neutral, terms? Even if the feminine designates a tendency, and not a being, and even if paternity and fecundity are taken to refer beyond the biological, the question remains of what significance these terms acquire. Even if, per-haps especially if (given the importance of the symbolic register of lan-guage, not to mention the care, precision, and poetic quality of Levinas's own attentive relation to language), we were to grant that Levinas always and only intends to employ these terms as metaphors, this does not mean that the resonance of these sexualized terms is not felt in the world. If Derrida is right to say that Levinas is a poet despite himself, if Levinas's almost obsessive relationship with language is not to be disregarded, and if we are to take his notion of the saying at its word, and not his, as a notion that signifies beyond and despite his said, then the metaphorical overtones of the feminine cannot be trivialized.

To give a charitable reading of how Levinas's rigorously sexualized language functions would be to credit him with having seen the radical potentiality of the feminine to break up the categories of being, and to create the possibility of ethics. A less generous reading would consist of recalling that Levinas reiterates the most traditional stereotypes when he characterizes the feminine as a dimension of silence, mystery, hiding, modesty, withdrawal, domesticity, and maternity. In *Adieu to Emmanuel Levinas*, Derrida identifies these two different readings in his discussion of Levinas's understanding of the feminine as "the welcoming one par excellence" (TI, 157; TeI, 131). One could, says Derrida, "raise concerns about a classical androcentrism," an approach he identifies with his earlier essay, "At This Very Moment in This Work Here I Am," or one could "make of this text a sort of feminist manifesto," since it defines "welcome par excellence, . . . the pre-ethical origin of ethics, on the basis of femininity."[10] The authors in the present volume adopt a variety of positions in relation to these two possibilities, some of them not wish-ing to choose between them, but maintaining that both readings can be sustained.

If, in his early work, notably in "Time and the Other" (1947), Levinas seems to acknowledge the feminine as excessive, referring to it as the other "par excellence," his characterization of femininity in *Totality and Infinity* (1961) as inhabiting the dwelling, as welcoming, discreet, and silent, appears to recoup the potentially transgressive aspect of women's alterity uncovered in the 1940s. Deprived of language, women are afforded a place in *Totality and Infinity* either as hovering in the wings of habitation—making homes habitable—or as embodying the erotic. Whatever disclaimers Levinas makes to obviate the necessity of the empirical presence of women, the figure of the feminine remains on the margins of the central ethical relation that dominates the text, the face-to-face. Neither the relationship with the discreet welcoming feminine presence nor that of eros fulfills the requirements of the face-to-face: neither qualifies as a relation to the absolutely other without return. For that, paternity, which accomplishes goodness, is required. It is not the feminine, but "the inevitable reference of the erotic to the future in fecundity [that] reveals a radically different structure," says Levinas (TI, 272; TeI, 249). Why is the reference to fecundity "inevitable," and why does it constitute "paternity" (TI, 272; TeI, 250)?

By 1974 we find Levinas in *Otherwise Than Being* championing maternity as a trope for the obsessive relation to the other, or substitution, that now describes the ethical relation previously cast in terms of the face-to-face—my unqualified response to be answerable for faults I have not committed against the other. What do we make of the apparent usurpation of the paternal by the maternal? If his references to paternity and the son are merely figures of speech, why would he allow the metaphorics of maternity to supplant them? How can we read Levinas's early acknowledgment of the feminine as excess—as the other par excellence—his subsequent apparent retraction of any transgressive aspects of feminine alterity, and finally his elevation of maternity to the apex of ethicality? Is there discernible in his acknowledgment of feminine absolute alterity or excess a saying that retracts in *Totality and Infinity* into a said, only to betray the said again in *Otherwise Than Being,* in a movement that undoes or unsays the thematization of women as silent, discreet, marginal presences, and portrays maternity as a resource for an ethic of infinite demands? No doubt such a suggestion is too schematic, since if the vacillation of the saying and the said could indeed describe the alteration of Levinas's lexicon of feminine modes, it would invade the text of *Totality and Infinity,* which could not be read as if it presented an internally consistent monotype vision, but rather as offering the feminine as a radical resource even as it also undermined or recuperated this very radicality.

Diane Perpich opens the collection with a chapter in which she documents the feminist objections raised about Levinas's characterization of women by Beauvoir and Irigaray, and tracks the concept of the feminine as it develops from Levinas's early works of 1947 up to *Totality and Infinity* (1961), suggesting that this shift is best understood as one progressing from the caress to invocation. We have already seen that Levinas wants to break out of the language of intentionality, and to invest transcendence with a meaning that goes beyond being, and that to achieve this he re-works Heidegger's ontological difference. Perpich suggests that Levinas's understanding of language as invocation accomplishes this transcendence in a way that breaks with Eleatic being, while eros ultimately falls short of plurality.

Whereas Perpich focuses on the shift that occurs in Levinas's work from 1947 to 1961, Donna Brody extends her purview to *Otherwise Than Being* (1974). In her chapter, she conveys the rich and intricate texture of Levinas's discussion of feminine, and the difficulty he faces, not only in his account of the feminine, but more generally in his effort to divorce ethics from its inevitable reduction to the phenomenal realm. How, she asks, can the feminine or ethics be articulated such that these terms do not either merely collapse into the very totality he proposes they transcend, or retreat into a nonsensical register akin to that of negative theology? Like Perpich, Brody concludes by both acknowledging the sexism of Levinas's language and maintaining that there are moments at which it affirms the feminine in ways that point beyond the economy of recuperation into which Levinas himself ties these gestures. Ewa Ziarek follows suit, finding both negative and positive aspects in Levinas, as she argues that Levinas rethinks embodiment as "prototype of an ethical experience." Ziarek suggests that the originality of Levinas's contribution to contemporary work on the body "lies in the fact that it enables the elaboration of the ethical significance of flesh and, by extension, opens a possibility of an ethics of eros. Even though this possibility is never realized in Levinas's own work, and even though his own conception of eros and femininity remain entangled in both patriarchal and metaphysical traditions, the necessary interdependence of responsibility and incarnation paves the way ... to the feminist ethics of sexual difference."

Unlike Perpich, Brody, and Ziarek, all of whom, while remaining critical of Levinas's final position of the feminine, recognize that some features of his account not only can be redeemed for feminism, but actually provide some radical resources for feminism, Sonia Sikka offers an assessment of the feminine other in Levinas that is negative. She challenges the idea that radical alterity can provide a viable model either for feminism or for ethics. Notwithstanding their differences, she points out that Levinas's conception of the feminine shares central features with those of Kierkegaard and Nietzsche. Women are associated with the finite, rather than the infinite, with the home, rather than the public sphere, and are valued for providing men with a respite, or break, from the seriousness and rigor of the higher masculine realm. Sikka calls for a feminism that recognizes women as speaking and desiring beings in their own right, and points out that "any feminism that asks men to respect the alterity of women must still, *is* still, based on a recognition of woman as *subject*." The problem inherent not just with a feminism of alterity, but also with Levinas's philosophy, Sikka suggests, is that by refusing to acknowledge the priority of recognition—or of the idea that the other is fundamentally the same as me—these celebrations of difference also deprive themselves of a nuanced appreciation of the other's difference from me. A philosophy that is based on recognition, as Sikka says, "will indeed begin by imagining the Other to be another like oneself—a subject, for instance—but can proceed, upon this basis, to take dissimilarity into account, and to respect it. It is at least capable of an ongoing and attentive dialogue with one who is dissimilar, in a way that Levinas's philosophy is not."

Ironic as it might seem, given that Levinas is known as the philosopher of the other, it is precisely Levinas's insistence upon the alterity of the other across the board, and irrespective of identity, that renders him unable to take account of the fact that different subjects are situated differently from one another, with regard to alterity. If we are all radically other, then the alterity of one other is, in some sense, indistinguishable from the alterity of all the rest![11] This makes it impossible for Levinas to allow for the significance of the fact, for example, that women have traditionally been confined to roles in which their devotion to others is expected, whereas men have not. Sikka also convincingly shows that Levinas does not leave much room for the cultural other, but rather, "has carelessly assumed his culturally engendered givens, without paying attention to any other that might question these givens."

Many of the authors in this collection refer to Irigaray, whom I have already discussed, so I will keep my comments here very brief. In "The Fecundity of the Caress," reprinted here, Irigaray objects to Levinas's association of women with profanity, infancy, and animality, tropes that exclude women themselves from the ethical and religious transcendence achieved by men.[12] Women play the role of men's "shadow" or "double," as they facilitate a transcendence from which they are nonetheless barred access. Irigaray writes, "While he, the lover, is sent back to the transcendental, she, the beloved, is plunged into the depths." In a later essay on Levinas, in which she develops and extends her critique, Irigaray writes that the "description of pleasure given by Levinas is unacceptable to the extent that it presents man as the sole subject exercising his desire and his appetite upon the woman who is deprived of subjectivity except to seduce him."[13]

Taking her cue from Levinas's claim in "Judaism and the Feminine," that "[t]he characteristics of the Jewish woman can be fixed, thanks to the charming feminine figures of the Old Testament," Claire Katz draws on, among others, Irigaray and the figure of Ruth in order to challenge the restrictions Levinas places on the feminine.[14] While Levinas credits Ruth for her faithfulness, without which "David, and the Prince of Justice who one day was to be born of him, would not have been possible" (JF, 31), Katz emphasizes Ruth's loyalty to Naomi, her mother-in-law, a loyalty between women that goes unrecognized by Levinas. Katz suggests that Levinas's conception of eros as a relationship between lovers that is "directed toward the infinite via fecundity" is grounded in Judaism in important respects. Criticizing Levinas's apparent inability to think the feminine in relation to justice, and taking note of the fact that The House of Ruth has been adopted as the name of a shelter for battered women, Katz asks, "If her only language is the cooing and laughter of lovers ... how does she ask for justice?" Taking over from the Talmud the equation of woman and the house, Levinas construes women as "mothers, wives, and daughters" who make the world "habitable" (JF, 31). Katz reads Ruth's devotion to Naomi not in terms of the secrecy and silence with which Levinas associates the feminine, but as a "public proclamation" whose significance is not restricted to the ethical realm, but is also political. Her challenge thus follows through on the suggestion implicit in Levinas's exclusion of the third party from the feminine.

Catherine Chalier's contribution to this volume was translated by Bettina Bergo (translator of Levinas's Of God Who Comes to Mind) and is excerpted from Chalier's Figures du féminin (1982). Chalier emphasizes in her reading of Levinas that his texts constitute a revolt against neutrality. She shows how Levinas's conception of the feminine, as the other par excellence, resists the framework of symmetry and opposition within which difference is usually thought. Levinas wants to think of difference not in the mode of formal logic, nor even dialectically, but as asymmetry and excess. The feminine figures in his work as that which resists essence, concept, and presence, disrupting totality and displacing the hegemonic imperialism of being. Recalcitrant, clandestine, an inversion of meaning, the feminine throws into question the dominant, systematic, and totalizing modes of thinking. Withdrawing from being, the feminine ruptures ontological categories through its anarchic saying. The Other as feminine is both discreet and exorbitant in its ultramateriality. The feminine is both profane and incomparably excellent. There is a certain lapse or failure of being signaled by the feminine, a lack with regard to being, and therefore a refusal to take on the reciprocity of symmetrical relations. The preontological status of the feminine confers on it an exceptional role with regard to totality. It is beyond, outside, before the world, and at the same time it opens onto the future, through the child. The maternal body figures in Levinas as the absolute renouncement of being for the other, and in this sense it conveys the sense of Levinas's insistence upon the extreme ethical responsibility that the I bears for the other.

Like Katz, Chalier attends, in the chapter translated here, to Levinas's characterization of the feminine in "Judaism and the Feminine," where woman expresses "the beginning of ethics" but in which "[t]he feminine welcome can not lay claim to being anything but a condition of ethics." Chalier asks, therefore, "Is it an outrage to the thinking of the philosopher to expound, in the feminine, an ethical act?" Chalier acknowledges the sense in which the feminine disturbs the order of ontology, the order of the said, when she construes the disinterestedness of maternity as a "suspension of essence," or "the interruption of the privilege accorded to the ontological question." Because of this, she even suggests that "a certain mutism in the feminine," or the fact that woman is "without words," is not necessarily to be read as "a fault or a lack," but goes on to insist that this "weakening of ontology" that Levinas figures as feminine occurs "within the space of words." That is, it also refers to a history in which "weakening, weakness, silence, and enigma were the destiny of women," a destiny that far from being broken by substituting the feminine for woman" undergoes a reinforcement, because it fails to recognize the historical context of the subjugation of women. Thus, for Chalier, the metaphorical force that the feminine acquires under Levinas's pen does nothing to exonerate him from forbidding the feminine "ethical exteriority," or the passing beyond being that the feminine facilitates. On the contrary, it allows Levinas to be equivocal—it facilitates a lack of responsibility for the historical conditions that have kept women in their place, even as Levinas rewrites that history "by associating the feminine with a site," with the home, with the dwelling that welcomes, protects, and provides rest for the masculine so that men can assume an ethical existence.

Stella Sandford argues that both commentators on Levinas who are critical of the sexist implications of his notion of the maternal and those who see it as a corrective to the bias of his earlier account of the feminine are at fault, because they fail to appreciate that the maternal "is not intended to designate something exclusively female." For Sandford, the "maternal metaphor" must be understood as "a universal model," as the "paradigmatically ethical" relation. Although Sandford resists efforts to align the feminine and the maternal, she nonetheless suggests that "maternity by itself seems to harbor the same problem previously located in eros [which, as Sandford says, is 'closely related to "the feminine"']: a tendency to exclusivity." Just as the erotic intimacy of the couple excludes the communal relationship figured in Levinas as "the third party," so the trope of the maternal duality, mother and child, "runs the risk of the exclusion of the third party." In order for the universality of the maternal to be realized, illeity, as the trace of the third party, is required, a requirement that is elaborated by Levinas as fraternity, or as "a masculine community of brothers." In this sense, for Sandford, "maternity must and does give way to paternity, that is, to the law of the father." Yet Sandford concludes with a gesture that brings into question the inevitable authority of the law of the father when she says, "In the end, as in the beginning, the 'feminine' is made to give way to the 'masculine'; the only reason one bothers to say this, the only reason one *can* say it critically, is that it need not ever be so."

Alison Ainley argues that "insofar as there are certain Kantian strains to Levinas's thinking, feminist readers of Levinas should be wary of the way in which the maternal appears as the quintessential mark of ethical exemplarity in his texts." For Levinas, maternity marks an extreme form of being-for-another "because it is a pain of the body, a corporeal undertaking that cannot be disregarded." She suggests that Kant and Levinas share a suspicion that any representation of ethical relations will be inadequate to their grandeur, and that "neither of them entirely trust philosophical language to allow" for an inquiry that they both see as necessary, namely, "whether it is possible for ethical relations with others to have some guarantee of appeal or absolute legitimacy, so that the good might be made manifest in such a way that ethics is possible." While Kant wants to ground such an inquiry in reason, Levinas deploys images that enact the pain of being obsessed by the other, an obsession that receives its most graphic formulation in maternity as extreme passivity, as substitution, as a "writhing in the tight dimensions of pain," or as "the groaning of the wounded entrails by those it will bear or has borne." As Ainley says, it remains "unclear how women philosophers and readers of Levinas are to situate *themselves* in relation to this feminine or maternal otherness." Inasmuch as such images are not meant to be converted into philosophical precepts of the experiential order, but rather to "awaken the self" to "the essential structure of ethical responsibility" through "a negative jolt of pain," women are left with the choice of identifying with the sacrifice Levinas evokes or opposing it, by somehow "making themselves other to otherness." Ainley points out, reiterating Irigaray, that "[i]n either case, it is unclear that the presence of the feminine and the relation of women to ethics and otherness has been 'thought through as such.'"

In the final chapter, Kelly Oliver presents Levinas's understanding of paternity as an alternative to the threatening authoritarian Oedipal father of psychoanalysis, who must be killed in order for the son to establish his own law. Inasmuch as Levinas defines the son's relation to the father as the promise of infinity and love that heralds an open future and a discontinuous generational time, he departs from the psychoanalytic model of paternity, in which there is a continuous symbolic repetition of the same patricidal violence that installed the masculine subject in culture. He overcomes the Freudian notion of the father-son relationship as "a virile struggle for recognition in which the son must kill the father in order to inherit his recognition, designation, and power," replacing it with a notion of paternal election, in which "the child is unique in that he is 'chosen,'" in the sense that the father responds to the child out of love, and not as a "result of a virile will." While "Levinas opens up the possibility of an alternative to this virile and authoritarian father, he ... evacuates the paternal body from the father-son relationship," and in this sense he retains the patriarchal psychoanalytic structure of paternity, in which "the authority of law demands that the father's body is always absent." Levinas's notion of paternity "leaves the body behind," thereby rejoining a tradition in which "the body [is] identified with maternity and the social [is] identified with paternity at the expense of the body." Oliver suggests that if Levinas's notion of paternity appeals to the otherness of the son, it also rests on "the sameness between father and son that allows for the father to discover himself and his uniqueness through the son." We are thus returned not only to a notion of recognition, but to one that is a masculine preserve, based on the abject ejection of the body, in which the radicality of the promise of an open future is compromised by Levinas's inability to recognize himself in the daughter rather than in the son.

By allowing women to signify otherness, Levinas continues a long tradition of male-authored texts that figure the feminine as unknowable, mysterious, ineffable, unrepresentable, and intractable. Does he thereby repeat, however unwittingly or unwillingly, the same exclusionary gesture that denies women language and confines them to a gestural, corporeal, asocial psychosis? Or does his insistent privileging of alterity over sameness, even when it suffers a relapse at certain strategically predictable points, open up a space for the radical rewriting of the feminine? Certainly there are moments in Levinas's texts in which the virile economy of philosophical logic reverts to an affection and exposure of passivity to alterity, as in eros, or in the caress. And certainly there are moments at which the most traditional edifices assert themselves, as when the subversion of the caress is recouped by a maternal trope whose telos is invariably played out in the birth of a son. As we have seen, the duality of this certainty can be read more or less generously. One could read this generously—as the achievement of the saying despite the said—in terms of the feminine exceeding the paternal logic of Levinas's texts, so that his texts catch sight of, or benefit from, an inspirational source that cannot quite be contained or disarmed even by the recuperation of its excess at the level of the said. Or one could read Levinas less generously, as consigning women to the most traditional of roles, even as he privileges—or precisely in this gesture—maternity as an ethical relationship in which I am beholden to the other to the point of substitution. Perhaps, in keeping with the vacillation of the saying and the said, a more ambivalent reading is called for, one that is both too generous, perhaps infinitely so, and one that is less than generous, perhaps necessarily so.

Notes

1. Simone de Beauvoir, *The Second Sex*, trans. and ed. H. M. Parshley (New York: Vintage Books, 1989); *Le deuxième sexe*, 2 vols. (Paris: Gallimard, 1949). Hereafter cited as SS; DS.

2. Emmanuel Levinas, *Time and the Other, and Additional Essays*, trans. Richard Cohen (Pittsburgh: Duquesne University Press, 1987), 85–88.

3. François Poiré, "Entretiens," in *Emmanuel Levinas: Qui êtes-vous?* (Lyon: La Manufacture, 1987), 64. Interview with François Poiré, trans. J. Robbins and M. Coelen, with Thomas Loebel, in *Is It Righteous to Be? Interviews*, ed. Jill Robbins (forthcoming).

4. "De l'évasion" also provides a philosophical exploration of the phenomenon that Sartre would take up as the title of his acclaimed novel *Nausea*.

5. Levinas, "God and Philosophy," in *Of God Who Comes to Mind*, trans. Bettina Bergo (Stanford: Stanford University Press, 1998), 70; "Dieu et la philosophie," in *De Dieu qui vient a l'idée* (Paris: Librairie Philosophique J. Vrin, 1982), 116.

6. Jacques Derrida, "Violence and Metaphysics: An Essay on the Thought of Emmanuel Levinas," in *Writing and Difference*, translated and with an introduction and additional notes by Alan Bass (Chicago: University of Chicago Press, 1978), 79–153, esp. 312 n. 7.

7. Derrida has also noted the importance of interruption at work in Levinas's texts: "Nearly always with him, this is how he sets his work in the fabric: by interrupting the weaving of our language and then by weaving together the interruptions themselves, another language comes to disturb the first one" (AM, 18; EM, 29).

8. See also EE, 16–17; DE, 15–17 and OB, 23; AE, 29.

9. While Levinas sometimes qualifies his judgment, acknowledging, for example, that Heidegger's notion of thrownness (*Geworfenheit*) admits that there is a meaning of existence that is irreducible to the one who does the existing, he usually assumes that existence is always possessed in some sense (however nuanced this possession might be rendered). The overall critique that Levinas issues to Heidegger therefore remains unchanged. Insofar as Heidegger's philosophy is circumscribed by his inquiry into Being, it fails to move beyond conceiving of philosophy in terms of our relationship to Being.

10. Jacques Derrida, *Adieu to Emmanuel Levinas*, trans. Pascale-Anne Brault and Michael Naas (Stanford: Stanford University Press, 1999), 44. In a footnote Derrida refers to remarks Levinas made in 1985 in the Zurich weekly *Construire* that indicate a shift in his thinking about the feminine. Levinas says that he "thought that femininity was a modality of alterity" in *Time and the Other*, but "today I think that it is necessary to go back even further and that the exposure, the nakedness, and the 'imperative request' of the face of the Other constitute a modality that the feminine already presupposes: the proximity of the neighbor is non-formal alterity" (*Adieu*, 139 n. 37). Derrida takes this as evidence for the reading that he gives in *Adieu*, and which he prefers to his earlier, more critical reading. But what does it mean to say that the feminine "presupposes" proximity, if not that the ethical relation is more original than the preethical feminine welcome? Even if Derrida's reading can be sustained here, one can point to other, later, remarks, for example those recorded in 1994, which reveal a pronounced suspicion and defensiveness against "the feminists" (*Que dirait Eurydice? What Would Eurydice Say?* Emmanuel Levinas en/in conversation avec/with Bracha Lichtenberg-Ettinger [Paris: BLE Atelier, 1997], 22). Also in evidence is a series of assertions that remain profoundly disturbing, Levinas's disclaimers notwithstanding. Woman is identified as the "category of the future," and the feminine is understood at the "deepest" level as "dying in giving life, in bringing life into the world" (27). Although Levinas tries to ward off the objections he knows his comments will provoke when he says that "it is not the 'dying'; for me, the 'dying' of a woman is certainly unacceptable. . . . I am not emphasizing *dying* but, on the contrary, *future*" (27), one must ask, whose future? Levinas's equation of the feminine and the woman here (both are the "future"); his identification of the woman with maternity; his emphasis of the maternal as the ultimate sacrifice, where "the death of the other is more important to me than my own death" (27); and his understanding of this ethicality as saintliness (28) are enough to convince me of the need for extreme vigilance and skepticism about uncritical feminist appropriations of Levinas. One simply cannot ignore the fact that throughout history, women have been systematically forced to sacrifice themselves, literally and metaphorically, for men, as if this social context were immaterial or irrelevant to Levinas's claims. The history of the systematic oppression of women makes his identification of the supreme ethical relation with dying in childbirth dangerous and unacceptable. This does not mean that I find nothing that is potentially valuable for feminism in his work, only that feminists cannot afford to be completely uncritical.

11. One might respond, on Levinas's behalf, that it is the function of politics, not ethics, to ensure equality, perhaps by recognizing how individuals are specified differently by their relations to

historical and cultural situations and traditions, but the question remains of whether Levinas's conception of ethics has not prejudged the ways in which alterity can be an issue politically.

12. Irigaray's reading of the section from *Totality and Infinity* devoted to eros was first published in translation as "The Fecundity of the Caress: A Reading of Levinas, *Totality and Infinity,* 'Phenomenology of Eros,'" in *An Ethics of Sexual Difference,* trans. Carolyn Burke and Gillian Gill (Ithaca: Cornell University Press, 1993), 185–217.

13. Luce Irigaray, "Questions to Emmanuel Levinas: On the Divinity of Love," trans. Margaret Whitford, in *Re-reading Levinas,* ed. R. Bernasconi and S. Critchley (Bloomington: Indiana University Press, 1991), 109–18; see esp. 115.

14. Levinas, "Judaism and the Feminine," in *Difficult Freedom: Essays on Judaism,* trans. S. Hand (Baltimore: Johns Hopkins University Press, 1990), 31.

1

From the Caress
to the Word

Transcendence and the Feminine in the
Philosophy of Emmanuel Levinas

Diane Perpich

Readers have found Levinas's conception of the feminine problematic from its first appearance in his 1947 works *Existence and Existents* and *Time and the Other*.[1] The first work introduced the idea that "the other par excellence is the feminine" (EE, 85), while the second added that otherness or alterity is the very "essence" of the feminine (TO, 85). In *The Second Sex*, published just two years after Levinas's essays, Simone de Beauvoir criticized Western philosophy for defining woman not in and for herself but relative to man and, moreover, in terms of what she supposedly lacks in comparison with man. Beauvoir argued that in the tradition, woman "is defined and differentiated with reference to man and not he with reference to her; she is the incidental, the inessential as opposed to the essential. He is the Subject, he is the Absolute—she is the

Other."[2] And if the feminine is the Other, this implies that the "I," or the subject, is masculine. Woman is thereby deprived of the status of a full subject and is regarded as a less than fully autonomous being. In a footnote to this discussion, Beauvoir cited *Time and the Other* as but the most recent work of philosophy to express these ideas explicitly. Remarking on Levinas's claim that "Otherness reaches its full flowering in the feminine, a term of the same rank as consciousness but of opposite meaning," Beauvoir writes, "I suppose that Levinas does not forget that woman, too, is aware of her own consciousness, or ego. But it is striking that he deliberately takes a man's point of view, disregarding the reciprocity of subject and object. . . . Thus his description which is intended to be objective, is in fact an assertion of masculine privilege."[3]

Luce Irigaray echoes Beauvoir's criticism in a text titled "Questions to Emmanuel Levinas," arguing that Levinas's description of the erotic relationship "presents man as the sole subject exercising his desire and his appetite upon the woman who is deprived of subjectivity except to seduce him."[4] Irigaray notes that in an earlier essay[5] on Levinas, she used the term *l'amante* "to signify that the woman can be a subject in love (*un sujet amoreux*)," a lover and not only a beloved (*l'aimée*), an actor and not only the passive object of desire.[6] Irigaray argues that in stripping the feminine of her active subjectivity, Levinas clings to the "rock of patriarchy," abandoning the feminine other, leaving her "without her own specific face"; she adds, "On this point, his philosophy falls radically short of ethics."[7] This charge is especially serious, of course, given that Levinas's philosophy is proposed as a re-thinking of the meaning of the ethical.

Following Beauvoir and Irigaray, readers have since objected to Levinas's descriptions in *Totality and Infinity* that portray the female beloved as "an irresponsible animality which does not speak true words," as a being "returned to the stage of infancy without responsibility," as "coquettish," "'a bit silly,'" and as having "quit her status as a person."[8] Equally disappointing and disturbing is his notion of the "Eternal Feminine" as an "incessant recommencement of virginity," "essentially violable and inviolable" (TI, 258).

Feminists who see in Levinas's ethics an important valorization of difference and a rejection of essentialist and reductive conceptions of human nature find themselves in the difficult position of having to defend, or at least account for, this notion of the feminine and for the seemingly sexist, patriarchal language in which it is expressed. This task is complicated further by the fact that the feminine is reinterpreted at each major stage of Levinas's thought, playing different roles at different times in his work. In particular, while the feminine other is the primary figure of alterity in the early works, she is replaced by a generic or neutral other, simply the other human or *l'Autrui*, in the later works. Whereas eros and the feminine are central, dominant concepts in the argument of *Time and the Other*, they are seemingly relegated to the margins in *Totality and Infinity*, where the relationship to alterity is no longer conceived as an erotic relationship occurring in the caress, but as an ethical relationship to the other accomplished "only" in language (TI, 195).

In what follows, I want to revisit the debate over Levinas and the feminine explicitly from the perspective of this shift and its significance. I will argue that the full significance of this shift is missed if it is viewed only in relation to the question of whether Levinas's philosophy subordinates the feminine and sexual difference to a neutral or masculine other and to the primacy of the ethical relationship. In the first part of the chapter, I reconstruct the two accounts of the feminine, detailing the transformations in Levinas's interpretation of this notion between 1947, the time of its first appearance, and 1961, the publication date of *Totality and Infinity*. In the second part, I argue that the shift from the earlier to the later account is motivated by certain developments in Levinas's conception of transcendence. The move from the erotic to the ethical relationship is read as a shift from the caress to language as the principal figure of transcendence, and I try to show why the shift away from the erotic is required at this stage in Levinas's thinking of transcendence. Finally, I consider what becomes of the feminine after the shift and how recognition of the link to transcendence can help to clarify the broader place of the feminine in Levinas's thought.

1. Two Accounts of the Feminine

The feminine first appears in Levinas's philosophy in the 1947 works, *Existence and Existents* and *Time and the Other*. These two short texts represent the inaugural stage of Levinas's original philosophy, in which he moves beyond the detailed, scholarly presentations of Husserl and Heidegger characteristic of his earliest publications and toward a more critical appropriation and interrogation of phenomenology. Levinas suggests in these works that phenomenological description will forever be inadequate to the task of an analysis of the relationship with the other, since "qua phenomenology it remains within ... the world of the solitary ego which has no relationship with the other qua other, for whom the other is another me, an *alter ego*" according to the Husserlian expression (EE, 83). In opposition to the conception of the other human as another ego, identical to me in essence and differentiated only by virtue of accidental features, Levinas proposes a conception of the other as an "absolute alterity" whose otherness cannot be grasped or comprehended, since to do so would be to reduce or negate it. The alterity of the other, Levinas argues, is not due to the fact that the other possesses other qualities than I do, nonessential qualities of "character, or physiognomy, or psychology" (TO, 83). Nor is this alterity "simply an effect of space, which keeps separate what conceptually is identical" (EE, 95). The alterity of the other, on this view, is not a formal, logical characteristic: it is not the reverse of identity (I and not-I), nor is it produced through negation. For Levinas, the other is not other relative to me, but *absolutely*.

In both *Existence and Existents* and *Time and the Other*, the feminine is identified with radical alterity. In a preface written for the reedition of *Time and the Other* in 1979, Levinas explains how in this early study he sought alterity starting with an "alterity-content"; that is, he sought a relation to an alterity whose difference was not incidental, but essential. "Femininity," he writes, "appeared to me as a difference contrasting strongly with other differences, not merely as a quality different from all others, but as the very quality of difference" (TO, 36). In *Time and the Other* Levinas suggests that, in the feminine, "the alterity of the other appears in its purity" because here alterity is "borne by a being in a positive sense, as essence." The feminine is presented as an exemplar or ideal figure of alterity, exhibiting a form or degree of difference that "is in no way affected by the relation that can be established between it and its correlative"; it is thus a relation that "permits its terms to remain absolutely other" (TO, 85).

This early account of the feminine contains two claims that Levinas does not explicitly distinguish, but that can be usefully teased apart. First, the feminine is not defined in terms of its opposition to the masculine; it has its own positive essence. And second, this positive essence is alterity. It is worth separating these claims because we will see that while Levinas's later accounts of the feminine maintain the first claim, they do not maintain the second. The first assertion is a direct outgrowth of the notion of absolute alterity. If the difference that characterizes the feminine were to be produced merely through opposition to the masculine, then this alterity would be relative and not absolute. Levinas's position explicitly rejects the idea that the feminine is what it is, or has its essence, only through its relation with its opposite. Concretely this means that Levinas rejects any conception that defines the feminine other through negation as the lack or absence of the masculine or of masculine characteristics.[9] Likewise, he will argue that she is not a complement to the masculine or a partial or incomplete man: "Neither is the difference between the sexes the duality of two complementary terms, for two complementary terms presuppose a preexisting whole" (TI, 86). Woman, on this view, is thus neither the helpmate of some interpretations of Genesis[10] nor the incomplete man of Freudian theory.

Consonant with this view of feminine alterity and sexual difference is Levinas's rejection of the romantic conception of love according to which love would accomplish the fusion of two persons or two souls into one. Replacing this picture, Levinas suggests that the pathos of love consists in the "insurmountable duality of beings" (TO, 86); that is, it consists precisely in the fact of being and remaining two. In eros, the ego seeks the other but finds that rather than becoming a part of himself, she remains other. Her alterity is irreducible and absolute: it cannot be bridged or diminished; it cannot be negated or reduced. Far from appearing on the stage of consciousness, the very mode of being of the feminine is defined as a "withdrawal into mystery," as "hiding" and "modesty" (TO, 87). The relation to the feminine is a relation with what "slips away from the light" (TO, 86), with what escapes comprehension and understanding.

Levinas warns that the mystery and hiding referred to here are not meant to invoke "romantic notions of the mysterious, unknown, or misunderstood woman" (TO, 86). Rather, as the mode of being of the feminine, her "mystery" indicates a structural feature that distinguishes the transcendence of the erotic relationship from the transcendence that phenomenology accords to consciousness. This is the sense of Levinas's claim that the feminine is "on the same level as, but in meaning opposed to, consciousness" (TO, 88). In early sections of *Time and the Other*, consciousness is assimilated to Plato's light, which is not itself seen but allows everything else to become visible.[11] However, Plato is not Levinas's only source here; the primary understanding of consciousness in his work derives from the Husserlian conception of consciousness as intentionality. For Husserl, intentionality expresses the fact that every consciousness is a consciousness *of something*. Every perceiving is a perceiving of something, every representing a representing of something, every desiring is directed toward the object of desire: presuming, willing, judging, loving, and hating are all *of something*. This directedness toward a content is for Husserl the essential and determining characteristic of consciousness.[12] The feminine inverts the structure of Husserlian consciousness. Hers is not a movement toward, but a withdrawal. "The transcendence of the feminine consists in withdrawing elsewhere, which is a movement opposed to the movement of consciousness" (TO, 88).

The idea that the structure of the relation to the other inverts the structure of consciousness, and that the other thus "escapes" or "overflows" comprehension, is a familiar theme from Levinas's mature works. Here we see this claim at its inception. It must be emphasized, however, that the feminine other is not unfathomable or unknowable because she is somehow too irrational, self-contradictory, or simply too vague and obscure to be understood. Rather, the import of Levinas's claim that the other escapes knowledge or understanding lies in the recognition that the relation to the other—the form of transcendence that interests Levinas—is irreducible to comprehension. It is not that the other is unknowable, but that knowledge is not the goal, nor does it provide the structure of the relationship.[13]

Levinas gives the formal structure of the erotic relationship a concrete expression in the notion of the caress. The caress is distinguished first of all from the sensation of touch and from the contact effected through touching. If the caress belonged to the sphere of sensation, Levinas claims, it would share the structure of consciousness and of knowledge. That is, the Other would be "reached" by the touched, comprehended by it with all that this implies of the grasp (*prendre*) and possession. By contrast, "what is caressed is not touched, properly speaking" (TO, 89). The difference lies in the structure of the intention. The caress is a seeking, and in that sense "on the same level" as consciousness, but it is a seeking that does not seek termination in an object. The very essence of the caress, Levinas says, "is constituted by the fact that the caress does not know what it seeks. This 'not knowing', this fundamental disorder, is the essential" (TO, 89). The caress is "like a game with something slipping away, a game absolutely without project or plan, not with what can become ours or us, but with something other, always other, always inaccessible, and always still to come" (TO, 89). Thus, even though it mimics the structure of intentionality, the erotic relationship inverts and disorders this structure. In a much later text, Levinas will remark that "the relationship with the Other can be sought as an irreducible intentionality, even if one must end by seeing that it ruptures intentionality."[14]

Shortly after *Time and the Other*, Levinas appears to abandon the feminine and the erotic relationship as the principal figures of alterity and transcendence. During the 1950s, he publishes a series of essays that continue the earlier analysis of alterity; however, they do so entirely without reference to the feminine.[15] In these essays from the fifties, the idea of absolute alterity is worked out in terms of concepts that later become familiar as the building blocks of *Totality and Infinity*—concepts such as the face of the Other, the idea of infinity, and metaphysical (rather than erotic) desire. In these new essays, the relationship to the Other is no longer sought in the caress but is said to be accomplished in *language*.

The role played by language in Levinas's philosophy is fairly well known and has been treated extensively in the secondary literature. For the moment, I want to recall only the most essential feature of this account: for Levinas, language is not only "a system of signs in the service of a pre-existing thought,"[16] it also involves a dimension of invocation and address. In Levinas's later work, these two aspects of language— invocation and representation, respectively—are captured in the distinction between the "Saying" and the "Said." In *Totality and Infinity*, this terminology has not yet emerged. However, both there and in the 1951 essay "Is Ontology Fundamental?" Levinas distinguishes the function of language as an invocation of the Other from the role of language in representation or understanding.[17] A central concern of the latter essay is to isolate the moment of invocation and to show its irreducibility to comprehension and knowledge. Levinas argues that in invoking the Other, I do not address a representation or concept of the Other, but the person him- or herself. The relationship has an unmediated quality, which renders it qualitatively different from our relations to things and which cannot be accounted for either in terms of the relation between noesis and noema (Husserl) or the description of our relation to the ready-to-hand (Heidegger). To be sure, Levinas does not deny that the Other can be given in the same manner as an object and that knowledge or comprehension of the Other is part of our aim.[18] Nor does he deny the role of language in thematization and objectification. However, he argues that every comprehension of the Other is simultaneously addressed to the Other. Every word that bears on the Other as a theme is also a word spoken to the Other. In *Totality and Infinity*, this divergence between the Other as my theme and the Other as interlocutor, exterior to every thematization, is posited as the "formal structure" of language (TI, 195). Invocation represents the possibility of a relation in which neither the ego nor the Other is absorbed or negated, in which, in other words, the terms remain "separate" or "absolute" within the relationship (TI, 195).

The irreducibility of invocation to comprehension, mirroring the earlier irreducibility of the erotic relationship, implies that invocation neither is a mode of comprehension nor presupposes or supervenes upon a prior moment of comprehension. The Other is not first of all grasped as an object of understanding and then, following this, related to as a person. Rather, Levinas says that the two relations merge or are intertwined (*se confondent*).[19] Thus, alongside the thematization that occurs in language, there is a moment that is unthematized and in principle unthematizable. Even when the Other is explicitly our theme, the language in which the theme is formulated repeats the gesture of invocation and address. It refers beyond itself to the Other.

Up to this point, the analysis of language is generally continuous with the work of the earlier texts in which the feminine and sexual difference were main points of reference. Where the analysis of invocation goes beyond the account of the erotic relationship is in the link that it constructs between language and the ethical. From the beginning, invocation is given an explicitly ethical meaning. The following passage, from a text published in 1954, is one of the very first places where this link is developed in some detail: "Language in its expressive function is addressed to and invokes the other. It does not consist in invoking him as something represented or thought, but this is just why the distinction between the same and the other, in which language occurs, is not reducible to a relation between concepts that limit one another, but describes transcendence, where the *other* does not weigh on the same, but only places it under an obligation, makes it responsible, that is makes it speak."[20] The passage is typical of the way in which Levinas's thought moves, producing new meanings and connections through the juxtaposition of terms. The first two-thirds of the passage establishes a connection, to the point of identity, between invocation and transcendence. These two terms both take place in the space or interval between the I and the Other. The distinguishing character of transcendence, as Levinas has defined it at this point in his writings, is that it establishes a relation between terms that nonetheless remain absolute or separate within the relationship. In transcendence, the terms are linked, but in a manner different from mutual determination and without the possibility of being synthesized within a larger conceptual whole or movement, such as that of a dialectic. The passage now suggests that in transcendence the other is related to me, even so closely related as to "weigh on" me, but neither as a real force that oppresses me, nor as a logical opposite where, as the not-I, the other would be the negation or limit of the I. Rather, the manner in which the other weighs upon me in transcendence will be likened to that of a moral weight, an obligation. I find myself obligated to the other, responsible to and for him. Thus Levinas can conclude that in transcendence, "the other does not weigh on the same, but only places it under an obligation, makes it responsible"; and Levinas adds, "that is, makes it speak."

Before turning to the question of how to interpret the shift described earlier from the erotic relationship of the caress to the ethical relationship accomplished in language, we need to see what happens to the feminine in the texts of this period, especially in *Totality and Infinity*. Although absent from Levinas's writings during the 1950s, the feminine is not completely abandoned, and it reappears in a new guise in *Totality and Infinity* (1961) and in an article from the same period titled "Judaism and the Feminine" (1960).[21] The discussion of the feminine is largely the same in both texts and is much richer, but also more problematic, than the earlier (1947) discussion. As in the earlier account, in the new one Levinas rejects any suggestion that woman is merely the complement of man, or that she is in any way less than fully human. However, as before, the positive possibilities of this point of departure are eroded as Levinas goes on to relegate the feminine other to those domains that have traditionally been both her purview and her lot: on the one hand, the home and domestic arrangements, and on the other, the erotic relationship and maternity. In both domains—the domestic and the erotic—the feminine will occupy an equivocal position; that is, she will be identified with a certain equivocation. This is more readily recognized with respect to the discussion of the erotic relationship, where Levinas explicitly defines the feminine as equivocation. However, it is no less true of the role Levinas assigns to her within the domestic sphere.[22]

In a section of *Totality and Infinity* titled "Habitation and the Feminine," as well as in the article "Judaism and the Feminine," the feminine is said to make the world "habitable."[23] At one level, Levinas suggests that this habitability can be attributed to the feminine insofar as she takes the raw materials of man's labor and turns them into the bread he needs to nourish himself or the clothing he needs to cover himself. However, as Levinas also points out, if it were just baking or weaving that were required, "a slave would be good enough for such tasks."[24] Levinas suggests that the world becomes habitable because the feminine creates a refuge in it, a space within which man is able to "recollect" (TI, 154) or recover himself and in which an "inner life" (TI, 158) first becomes possible. Recollection is understood here as "a suspension of the immediate reactions the world solicits"; it is a respite from the roughness of life and from the insistence and immediacy of its demands (TI, 154). As such, Levinas equates it with a certain familiarity and intimacy with one's surroundings and argues that this interiority does not accrue to the ego simply by virtue of its adapting to its world and acquiring certain habits that provide mastery over it. The "gentleness" of recollection is accomplished by "Woman": "The woman is the condition for recollection, the interiority of the Home, and inhabitation" (TI, 155).

As Catherine Chalier interprets these passages, "[T]he feminine compels the conquering and virile attitude to stop and to start thinking. She stops the project of being, a project that is deaf and blind to all that does not belong to the strength that persists. She who welcomes in her dwelling helps to find the way of interiority that stops this blind strength."[25] The world loses its threatening and unfamiliar aspect with the advent of the feminine welcome within the home. As Chalier goes on to point out, there is thus a sense in which the feminine is the condition of ethics. In producing a suspension within the spontaneous life of the masculine, the feminine welcome creates the conditions for a turn away from the self and toward the Other. But as Chalier also notes, this welcome is only a condition of ethics, it is not yet of itself ethical: "Intimacy and gentleness do not comprehend *height* which is, according to Levinas, the only authentic ethical dimension."[26]

Building on Chalier's analysis, we can add that even as a condition of the ethical, the feminine other still occupies an equivocal position. In fact, her status as condition hides an essential equivocation. Even as the intimacy and gentleness of habitation are necessary for ethics and already presuppose a certain relation with an other, they are also, and perhaps first of all, a turn *away* from the world and from others—a turn toward the self and toward the comforts of home and the security of one's own possessions. The home as refuge may contain the condition of ethics, but not unequivocally, since this refuge can also be the sight of an indifference to outsiders, to those not of this hearth. Thus, even though the relation to the feminine accomplishes the separation necessary for the ethical relation, it is not yet, of itself, ethical. Levinas acknowledges the role of the feminine in habitation as a first or initial revelation of the Other; however, he suggests that this revelation is somehow not yet equivalent to ethical transcendence: "[H]abitation is not yet the transcendence of language. The Other who welcomes in intimacy is not the *you* [*vous*] of the face that reveals itself in a dimension of height, but precisely the *thou* [*tu*] of familiarity" (TI, 155). Is this claim contradicted when just a line or two later, Levinas adds that the language spoken with this *thou* "includes all the possibilities of the transcendent relationship with the Other" (TI, 155)? We might resolve this tension, as Levinas seems to do, by suggesting that the relation to the feminine is both before and beyond the relation to the face: both more and less than ethical. In any case, what becomes clear is that even if the role of the feminine in habitation has a positive significance in accomplishing the turn toward ethics, it is an equivocal significance and accomplishment.

An even more explicit equivocality is attributed to the feminine in Levinas's discussion of the erotic relationship. The equivocation or ambiguity that Levinas refers to as explicitly feminine is not, he says, a "play between two meanings of speech, but [a play] between speech and the renouncement of speech" (TI, 260). It is the simultaneity of the "clandestine" and the "exposed" in the naked or eroticized body. Earlier in *Totality and Infinity*, Levinas develops an analysis of the face of the Other as "expression." The latter is first of all a reference not to a look on the face, but to the speech of the Other that invites or commands us to the social relation. Or, rather, *expression* is a term that consciously confounds the spheres of vision and hearing and plays these two meanings of the term against one another. At one point, Levinas remarks that the whole body is a face (TI, 262), thus the whole body is capable of expression. Now, in the discussion of the erotic, we read that in erotic nudity the body exhibits of a kind of expression, but an expression that says "less than nothing." Again Levinas appeals to the idea of the feminine as an inversion of some other order. Erotic nudity would be "an inverted signification, a signification that signifies falsely, a clarity converted into ardor and night, an expression that ceases to express itself . . . , that sinks into the equivocation of silence." Unlike the relation to the feminine in habitation, the erotic relationship is not described as prior to ethics, or as its condition, but as a degeneration of the seriousness of the face-to-face into laughter, jokes, and innuendo. It is a relation, Levinas says, "beyond the decency of words." And in a further passage, which perhaps more than any other has troubled feminist readers, Levinas describes the relation to the feminine beloved (*l'aimée*) as a relation with "an irresponsible animality which does not speak true words." The beloved is "returned to the stage of infancy" and "has quit her status as a person" (TI, 263).

2. From the Caress to the Word

I have tried to show in the preceding section that there are important and identifiable differences between the conception of the feminine advanced in *Time and the Other* and that presented in *Totality and Infinity*. A central aspect of this difference can be made more precise by our returning to the two claims about the feminine that were distinguished earlier. The first claim—that the feminine is not defined relative to the masculine but has its own positive essence—remains true of both the earlier and later accounts. For example, even though the relation to the feminine is subordinated to the ethical relationship in the 1960–61 analyses of habitation and eros, Levinas insists that this subordination does not convey a conception of woman as a mere complement to man, or of the feminine as merely the opposite or the reverse of masculinity. This is especially evident in the essay "Judaism and the Feminine" where Levinas writes: "If woman completes man, she does not complete him as a part completes another into a whole but, as it were, as two totalities complete one another."[27] However, the second claim found in the 1947 account—namely, that alterity is the essence or positive meaning of the feminine—is no longer upheld in later accounts. The feminine is no longer "the other par excellence"; rather her essence has been redefined in terms of an inherent equivocation and ambiguity.

What accounts for this reinterpretation of the feminine between 1947 and 1960? Why is the feminine abandoned as the principal figure of alterity after *Time and the Other* and what considerations guide the role subsequently assigned to this notion in *Totality and Infinity*? While it is tempting to view Levinas's reinterpretation of the feminine simply in terms of a shift in focus, from an early interest in the erotic relationship to a new concern with ethics, such an answer is ultimately inadequate. Not only is there already an invocation of the ethical in the 1947 account[28] (though this notion is not as fully developed as it will be later), but there is a thematic continuity between the earlier and later works that is dismissed by such an explanation. In both the earlier and later works, the possibility of elucidating and defending a radical conception of transcendence is central to Levinas's project, and this concern unites the two accounts of the feminine, establishing their continuity even as it accounts for their divergence. I will argue in this section that the shift in Levinas's treatment of the feminine can be read as a shift from the caress to invocation as the principal figure of transcendence. Moreover, I will suggest that the move from the caress to the word as the principal bearer of the relation to the other accompanies an advance in Levinas's conceptualization of transcendence, from an early conception that sees transcendence primarily as a flight from or break out of immanence to a more mature and complex notion in which transcendence is possible only as transcendence *in* immanence.

The notion of transcendence is introduced on the very first page of *Existence and Existents*, where it is identified with Plato's "Good Beyond Being." Levinas writes there that "the movement which leads an existent toward the Good is not a transcendence by which that existent raises itself up to a higher existence, but [is] a departure from Being and from the categories which describe it: an ex-cendence" (EE, 15). The radical ex-cendence that Levinas seeks is not a passage from one plane of being to another; rather it is a break out of existence or being altogether.[29] It is an escape or "liberation" (EE, 89) from what Levinas will describe as the weight of being.

The desire for a departure from being stems directly from Levinas's need in these early works to quit the "climate" of Heideggerian philosophy—despite the deep influence of Heidegger's ontological question on Levinas's thought, and despite the latter's conviction that there could be no returning to a pre-Heideggerian philosophy (EE, 19). It will be a matter above all in these early works of the possibility of overcoming the "Eleatic notion of being" in which multiplicity is "subordinated to the one" (TO, 92). In *Existence and Existents*, Levinas expresses this idea when he asks whether being contains "no other vice than its limitation and nothingness," and wonders whether there might not be "some sort of underlying evil in its very positivity" (EE, 20). Taking up Bergson's argument that the concept of nothingness is illusory, since even nothingness *is*, Levinas refines it by adding the Heideggerian insight that this Being (*Sein*) is not itself a being or existent (*Seiendes*). Being is not an entity, a "something" (EE, 63); it is, for Levinas, the "there is" (*il y a*), an anonymous, impersonal existing without existents.[30] In French, *il y a* is an impersonal verb form like "it rains" (*il pleut*) or "it is hot" (*il fait chaud*). Levinas remarks that the impersonal form "designates not the uncertainly known author of the action, but the characteristic of this action itself, which somehow has no author" (EE, 57). Levinas compares the "there is" to the experience of night in which all forms dissolve into darkness and nothing appears except the darkness itself. The *il y a* "involves the total exclusion of light" (EE, 58). In its obscurity and ambiguity, it is the total absence of meaning or sense and, as such, is felt as a "mute, absolutely indeterminate menace" (EE, 59).

The transcendence sought in both *Existence and Existents* and *Time and the Other* represents the possibility of an escape from the senseless rumbling of the there is. In *Ethics and Infinity*, Levinas reports that his first idea was that the there is could be transcended in the movement by which a subject takes up its own existing and posits itself in a world (EI, 51). Levinas calls this movement *hypostasis*, drawing both on the sense of this term as a sedimentation and on the ancient and medieval philosophical tradition that used this word to designate substance. However, Levinas soon came to think that the hypostasis of the subject, while it produced a certain mastery over being, did not effect an ex-cendence from being. It fails with respect to the latter because the ego in the world is burdened by its own existing. Indeed, Levinas comes to regard the existence of the ego as a solitary "enchainment" within being (TO, 56). Identity, he says, is not an "inoffensive" relation of the self to itself, but is the fact of being weighed down by one's own existing (TO, 55). "The *I* always has one foot caught in its own existence. . . . It is forever bound to the existence which it has taken up . . . riveted to its own being" (EE, 84). Moreover, even the famous freedom of thought exercised in knowing the world is incapable of breaking this enchainment: "this freedom does not save me from the definitive character of my very existence, from the fact that I am forever stuck with myself" (EE, 84). Every departure of the self toward the world, whether in enjoyment or in knowledge, inevitably involves a return of the self to itself. The objects encountered in the world are, to be sure, given as something *other* than the self, but they are so given *by* the self: "[t]he light that permits encountering something other than the self, makes it encountered as if this thing came from the ego. . . . And in this sense knowledge never encounters anything truly other in the world (TO, 68). Thus, transcendence or excendence—the departure from being—is effected neither in the hypostasis of the self (its taking up of a position within being) nor in the self's relation to the world. It will be accomplished, the early texts claim, only in the relationship to the other: "It is in eros that transcendence can be conceived as something radical, which brings to the ego caught up in being, ineluctably returning to itself, something else than this return" (EE, 96).

Given the identification of transcendence at this stage with an escape from the self and from existence, it becomes possible to see why Levinas was led to erotic desire as the figure of transcendence. In desire for the other, one is taken out of oneself; the I loses itself in desire for the other. The alterity of the other in this relationship seems decidedly different from the alterity of things, which the self gives to itself by the light of consciousness. In comprehending its objects, consciousness attains a certain mastery over them, has them in its possession and at its disposal, draws them to itself. In eros, the I is drawn to the other, given over to her, rather than the reverse; here one encounters an alterity that cannot be reduced to an object of consciousness, that does not seem to come from the self. Levinas presents the caress in these early works as an incessant recommencement of the movement toward the other. It is a seeking that is not satisfied by the presence of the other, but only renewed at a deeper level; it is a flight toward the other that does not involve a return to the self. The seeking of the caress, he says, does not degenerate into contact that would represent the ego's hold upon the other, a way of having her in his grasp. In effect, the caress is a relationship to the other in which the relationship does not diminish the distance between the terms and the distance does not prevent the possibility of a relationship. As such, it seems to offer a perfect model of transcendence. And yet we can question whether the transcendence of the caress is, as it were, transcendent enough. Doesn't the caress inevitably include the possibility of the self's return to itself in sensuous enjoyment? Doesn't it also involve the possibility that the other *does* come from the I, is a construction of the ego's fantasy?

There is evidence that Levinas himself ultimately came to the same conclusion and that this realization of the potential immanence of the erotic played a central role in his reinterpretation of the feminine in later works. A series of inversions mark the path of the erotic from 1947 to 1961, as characteristics attributed to false forms of transcendence in the earlier works are explicitly used to describe the erotic relationship in the later texts. For example, in *Existence and Existents* Levinas speaks of an "evanescence" in subjectivity, which dissipates or lightens the weight of existence, but which is nonetheless incapable of producing an ex-cendence or departure from being.[31] Ex-cendence in this case is distinguished sharply from any mere easing of the solitude of existing. Later, in the section of *Totality and Infinity* titled "The Phenomenology of Eros," Levinas not only recognizes the sensuous and evanescent character of the erotic, but makes this central to his account. The caress is there identified with a "way of remaining in the *no man's land* between being and not-yet-being" (TI, 259). This liminal position is further described as the "evanescence and swoon of the tender" (TI, 259)—both characterizations rendering it an unlikely vehicle for transcendence. Similarly, in 1947 Levinas opposes the transcendence of the caress to the dissipation of enjoyment and contact; in 1961, the caress is linked together with the dissipation of the sensuous: "The caress ... loses itself in a being that dissipates as though into an impersonal dream without will and even without resistance, a passivity, an already animal or infantile anonymity" (TI, 259). And in a final inversion, in 1947 the relation to the feminine was said to overcome the anonymous rustling and mute horror of the *there is*; in 1961, the erotic has become an extension of this notion: "Alongside of the night as anonymous rustling of the *there is* extends the night of the erotic, behind the night of insomnia the night of the hidden, the clandestine, the mysterious, land of the virgin" (TI, 257). The erotic here represents a kind of non-sense, different perhaps from the absolute lack of sense that marks the there is, but a conceptual companion to it all the same.

This last point is connected to a further feature of Levinas's original account of the feminine, a feature that in many respects is much more troubling than the ego's return to itself in sensuous enjoyment—and much more likely to put the enterprise of transcendence at risk. The silence of the feminine in the 1947 works is both noticeable and disturbing. The feminine other says nothing; she does not speak during the erotic encounter. And although this is consistent with the descriptions of the feminine as withdrawal, mystery, and absence, this silence is nonetheless eerie, even as it begins to seem all too familiar. The feminine other of Levinas's early thought is neither seen nor heard here. She is invisible and inaudible. Indeed, her silence seems more akin to muteness—not just an unwillingness to speak, but the impossibility of being heard. *Totality and Infinity* describes the language between lovers in derogatory tones as the degeneration of language into "laughter and cooing"; in the earlier accounts, the lovers' words to each other simply go unsaid or are simply not considered.

How could this complete silence, this muteness of the feminine, possibly break through the solitude of the ego, dragging it out of its concern with itself and toward the transcendence of radical alterity? In the muteness of the feminine in 1947, doesn't one already hear the distant rumbling of the there is? In order to avoid this return to silence, in order for transcendence to take on the ethical burden that it will carry in later works, will it not be necessary for the other to begin to speak?

The transcendence sought in the caress appears flawed, since, on the one hand, if the caress "reaches" the other and is faced with the presence of what it seeks, then the transcendent relation lapses into the immanence of knowledge and the sensuous. In this case, the relation between lovers becomes the "closed" or "intimate" society of two—a society that Levinas elsewhere says is "in its autarchy [or self-sufficiency] quite like the false totality of the ego."[32] On the other hand, if the caress does *not* reach the other, that is, if it preserves the alterity of the other required by transcendence, then the feminine other remains silent and withdrawn, leaving the ego solipsistically alone in his solitude. Thus, the erotic relationship fails to offer any unequivocal possibility of transcendence as Levinas defines it, and instead leaves only a choice between two forms of immanence: the immanence of the solitary ego and the immanence of the couple in love.

The shift to language in the *Totality and Infinity* discussion of alterity and transcendence reflects Levinas's ultimate recognition of this connection between the sphere of the erotic and the sphere of immanence. Here, too, we may find the reason why he abandons the feminine as the privileged example of alterity and the caress as the principal figure of transcendence. This is not to say that Levinas rejects every aspect of his earlier analysis. Quite the opposite. In the turn from the erotic to language in *Totality and Infinity*, the formal structures of the earlier analysis are conserved. In particular, the conception of absolute alterity first introduced in 1947 remains essential. Similarly, the basic structure of transcendence, first elucidated through the notion of the caress and defined as a relation whose terms remain absolute within the relationship, is retained in the descriptions of the idea of infinity, metaphysical desire, and the relation to the face. But at the same time, the formulations developed in *Totality and Infinity* mark a new departure, one in which the erotic is relegated to the realm of immanence, or quasi-immanence, since the equivocation of the erotic reflects precisely the dual possibility of this relation to exhibit and fall short of transcendence. The erotic no longer represents a pure possibility of pure transcendence; rather it shows with striking clarity just how every break with immanence is recuperable, capable of being reabsorbed within the structures of consciousness and being, or as Levinas will later say, within "the Same."

With this recognition, Levinas's understanding of transcendence undergoes a significant transformation. In the early accounts, transcendence and immanence were opposed to each other in such a way that transcendence was conceived primarily as the possibility of an escape from immanence, an exit or departure from Being in the seeking of the caress. The relation to the feminine is described "on the ontological level" as one in which the ego is "*somewhere else* than [its] self" (EE, 85; emphasis added). There is a sense in these early works that one can cheat being, finding in the relation to the feminine an "exception" to being, and even in a sense a "victory over death" when eros leads to fecundity and the relation to a son (TO, 90).[33] While this sense of transcendence as an escape or a "way outside of being" (TI, 104) persists to some extent in *Totality and Infinity*, it is qualified there by a deeper recognition of the problematic status of any "outside."

In *Totality and Infinity*'s well-known analyses of the relation to the face of the other, we find a model of transcendence in which the ego is no longer transported "somewhere else," but in which its immanence is repeatedly shattered and interrupted, disrupted by the face that calls me to goodness and responsibility. This disruption does not mark a flight from immanence, but a breach or gap within immanence. The notion of transcendence aimed at in *Totality and Infinity* is a transcendence *in* immanence, or to put this another way, it is the recognition that being is always already plural.

The plurality of being is indicated in the structure of language in a way that was impossible within the erotic relationship. Levinas argues, as we have already seen, that language is not only the communication of a theme. Apart from any theme it proposes, language is also invocation and address: "[t]he knowledge that absorbs the Other is forthwith situated within the discourse I address to him" (TI, 195). Language bears its two dimensions—representation and invocation—simultaneously and in such a way that the two are irreducible to each other. While there is in language the possibility of representing the other as an other, of grasping it and possessing it through knowledge, this possibility is also always undermined as the language in which such representation takes place also already invokes the other, addressing him or her apart from or prior to any representation. The solitude of the subject and the totality of being are thus refuted by the very words that would proclaim them. Being is always already plural; the immanence of egoistic life is always already disrupted by the transcendence of the relation to the other.[34]

While this reading accounts in large part for Levinas's abandoning his initial interpretation of the feminine, it leaves open thus far the question of how to evaluate the role subsequently assigned to the feminine in *Totality and Infinity*. And yet it is fitting that this question should be addressed here, even if only briefly. The most salient feature of the 1961 interpretation of the feminine, as found in the discussions of dwelling and eros, is its equivocal position, both more and less than the face, both before and beyond ethics. Levinas notes this manner of being between especially in relation to love, which he says is "at the limit of immanence and transcendence" (TI, 254). What does this liminality signify for Levinas? It would be shortsighted to think of the relation to the feminine merely as a degraded or fallen form of the ethical relationship, despite a certain tendency in Levinas's descriptions to present the matter in this way. Just as transcendence is not defined in a merely negative or formal manner but also has a positive significance and a concrete realization in the face-to-face relation, so too with the equivocation of the feminine.

Seeing this positive significance turns, no doubt, on seeing the unique character that Levinas ascribes to the erotic relationship. He suggests that this relationship is all too often relegated to the biological or psychological spheres, where it is treated in mechanistic terms or at the level of the search for pleasure. Levinas accuses such interpretations not only of oversimplifying the structure of the erotic,[35] but also of missing altogether the sense in which the erotic expresses or represents a "new ontological principle." "What remains unrecognized is that the erotic ... breaks up reality into relations irreducible to the relations of genus and species, part and whole, action and passion, truth and error" (TI, 276). This passage is doubly interesting because it comes from a text, titled "Transcendence and Plurality," that was published in 1949 and then included in *Totality and Infinity* with only slight modifications under the new title "Transcendence and Fecundity."[36] How was Levinas able to justify including this older text, which belongs more properly to the period of *Existence and Existents* and *Time and the Other* and to the earlier analysis of the feminine? He is able to do so insofar as that aspect of his analysis of the feminine that is emphasized in these passages remains constant: the descriptions of the feminine and the erotic relationship are not merely empirical descriptions of states or dispositions; rather they designate "essential structures."[37]

As an ontological category or mode of being, "the feminine" must be understood apart from every empirical typology. Consistent with the view that the feminine is not defined relative to the masculine, neither is it a modification or addition to an otherwise neutral or nongendered state: "The feminine is not added to an object and a Thou antecedently given or encountered in the neuter (the only gender formal logic knows)" (TI, 256). Gender in general, as the parenthetical remark suggests, is not to be thought of as derivative or ancillary, as if it were a secondary characteristic added on to a primary substance. In fact, the feminine is nowhere identified by Levinas with concrete, really existing beings.[38] It is not a set of characteristics or qualities attributed to a certain class of beings (namely, women); it is not a *type*, of which individual women would be tokens. Rather, the feminine is a principle of equivocation, introducing into being not only an essential duality or plurality, but a proliferating structure of ambiguity.

Levinas writes that the "ambiguity of love" is due to its being a relation with the other that "turns into need" even as it "presupposes the total, transcendent exteriority of the other" (TI, 254). This love that is an "enjoyment of the transcendent" is thus "almost contradictory in terms" (TI, 255). *Enjoyment* is the term Levinas uses to characterize the basic activity of the ego, its manner of existing in and *from* the elements and objects that surround it and that it constitutes as a world. Enjoyment thus designates the mode of the ego in the "Same," appropriating and reducing every other to a moment of its own egoistic life. To define love, then, as the "enjoyment of the transcendent," that is, as the appropriation of that which transcends every grasp, is to define it by an essential ambiguity and equivocation. But the point is not just that love comprises opposed tendencies or paradoxically combines contradictory elements. The problematic announced in the equivocation of the feminine and the ambiguity of love is one that increasingly occupies Levinas's thought, presenting a "special problem"[39] that is especially at issue in the later works. This problematic can be characterized in different ways; Levinas himself describes it as the problem occasioned by "the contradiction in principle that would exist in asserting the independence of ethical intelligibility relative to theoretical thought and being, and that in a discourse which is itself theoretical."[40] In *Totality and Infinity* in particular, it is the problem of how the transcendence of the ethical nonetheless *appears* without being reduced or comprehended within a theoretical framework. That this problem of appearing is precisely at issue in the equivocation of the feminine can be seen in passages in which the feminine is described as "the essentially hidden [that] throws itself toward the light," but without thereby appearing in the order of the intelligible, that is, "without becoming signification" (TI, 256) and in descriptions of the feminine as "this unreality at the threshold of the real" and as a "secret" that "appears without appearing" (TI, 257). If it were possible to use the language of contact in this context, we could say that the problem of the erotic for Levinas, and the sense in which it presents a problem "beyond the face" or beyond the strict requirements that determine the discussion of the ethical per se, is a problem about the site in which being is "touched" by ethics, in which the two come into contact. It is perhaps most fundamentally Levinas's attempt to see being as already shot through with the ethical, as already touched by the other.[41]

Does this make Levinas's account of the feminine in 1961 any more palatable to feminist readers? I suspect the answer will be "yes, and no." The sexism of Levinas's descriptions remains unchanged by this interpretation; indeed, there is no doing away with it, no way to make it disappear altogether. However, by situating the account of the feminine more directly within the fundamental problematic of Levinas's thought, readings of Levinas should no longer be able to treat the feminine and the erotic as side issues of only peripheral interest or importance for a full understanding of his thought. To be sure, this should already have been impossible after Irigaray's thought-provoking interventions, but it remains the case even today that those sections of *Totality and Infinity* dealing with dwelling and interiority and with relations "beyond the face," are given only marginal attention in the growing body of literature on this philosophy. Moreover, it may be hoped that a recontextualization or resituation of the notion of the feminine will raise new possibilities and directions both for feminist interrogations of Levinas's thought and for a Levinasian intervention in feminist considerations of the question of the other.

Notes

1. Emmanuel Levinas, *Existence and Existents*, trans. A. Lingis (Dordrecht: Kluwer, 1978); *Time and the Other*, trans. R. Cohen (Pittsburgh: Duquesne University Press, 1987). Hereafter cited in the text as EE and TO, respectively. The discussion of the feminine in *Time and the Other* is developed in much greater depth and detail and is consequently better known. However, the role of both the feminine and eros is anticipated in *Existence and Existents*. See 85 and 94–96.

2. Simone de Beauvoir, *The Second Sex*, trans. H. M. Parshley, with an introduction by D. Bair (New York: Vintage Books, 1989), xxii.

3. Ibid., xxii n. 3. On the possibility of defending Levinas against this charge, see n. 9 below.

4. Irigaray, "Questions to Emmanuel Levinas" in *Re-reading Levinas*, ed. R. Bernasconi and S. Critchley (Bloomington: Indiana University Press, 1991), 115.

5. See "The Fecundity of the Caress," in *Face to Face with Levinas*, ed. R. Cohen (Albany: State University of New York Press, 1986), 231–56.

6. Irigaray, "Questions," 115. Margaret Whitford translates *l'amante* as "woman lover," retaining the French in brackets.

7. Ibid., 113.

8. Emmanuel Levinas, *Totality and Infinity*, trans. A. Lingis (Pittsburgh: Duquesne University Press, 1969). Hereafter cited in the text as TI.

9. Herein lies a partial defense against Beauvoir's criticisms. For Levinas, the feminine other is not defined in opposition to or even relative to the masculine ego; this is the point of saying she has her own *positive* essence. Any notion of the feminine as a lack of masculine characteristics or as the non-masculine, would exhibit precisely the weak or merely negative notion of alterity that Levinas rejects. (A defense along these lines is made by Rob Manning, in "Thinking the Other Without Violence? An Analysis of the Relations Between the Philosophy of Emmanuel Levinas and Feminism," *Journal of Speculative Philosophy* 5, no. 2 [1991]: 132–43.)

There remains, however, Beauvoir and Irigaray's charge that the feminine other as Levinas portrays her is not a fully autonomous being, not a subject in her own right. Here the issues are more difficult on all sides and the rethinking of subjectivity and autonomy in each of these authors would be required to sort out the question adequately.

10. On the idea that the Genesis account does not posit woman in any simple way as the complement of man, see Levinas's commentary, originally delivered in 1972, titled "And God Created Woman" (*Nine Talmudic Commentaries*, trans. A. Aronowicz [Bloomington: Indiana University Press, 1990], 161–77). One line of interpretation pursued in the commentary suggests that there is no subordination in the text of Genesis of woman to man, or of the feminine to the masculine, but that there *is* a subordination of the sexual relationship and sexual difference to a gender-neutral human essence and to the ethical relationship between humans as such: "The meaning of the feminine will thus become clear against the background of a human essence.... The feminine does not derive from the masculine; rather, the division into feminine and masculine—the dichotomy—derives from what is human" (167–68). And later: "It is not woman who is secondary; it is the relationship with woman as woman that does not belong to what is fundamentally human. Fundamental are the tasks that man accomplishes as a human being and that woman accomplishes as a human being. They have other things to do besides cooing, and, moreover, something else to do and more than to limit themselves to the relations that are established because of the difference in sex" (169). Although it is beyond the scope of this chapter to do so, it would be interesting to pursue an extended comparison between the discussion of the feminine offered in this commentary and the analyses in *Totality and Infinity*. The Talmudic commentary may represent a subtle advance in Levinas's thinking about the feminine insofar as it pursues multiple interpretations of the feminine and is especially concerned to draw out a tension that structures the rabbinic commentaries on Genesis. This tension exists between two readings, one that posits a perfect equality between feminine

and masculine and takes sexual difference and sexual relationships as belonging "to the fundamental content of what is human" (169), and another reading, closer to Levinas's own in TI and elsewhere, according to which the sexual relationship and sexual difference are inessential and subordinate to the human, ethical relationship. Levinas purports in his commentary not to be taking sides between these two interpretations. It is not a matter, he suggests, of showing that one of these views really accords more closely with the Genesis text; rather it is a question of following "a train of thought in its multiple possibilities" (172).

11. See the sections at the end of Part II titled "Salvation Through the World—Nourishments" and "The Transcendence of Light and Reason" (62–66). Although Plato is mentioned only in the footnotes here, it is clear that Levinas is drawing on the Platonic metaphor that equates light and the conditions under which things become intelligible, and is doing so in part to link the phenomenology of Husserl and Heidegger to the long philosophical tradition that equates light and reason.

12. Two misinterpretations of this directedness might be warned against. First, as directedness toward an object, intentionality includes but is not limited to a focused attention on an individual object. Husserl emphasizes that intentionality is an inclusive title for all the ways in which consciousness "has" its objects. For example, in perception we may attend explicitly to some object or we may perceive the object in such a way that we are only more or less aware of it as a part of the background while our attention is focused elsewhere. Both cases of perception are intentional. Intentionality is not a particular type or mode of conscious activity but is the essential structure of all conscious experience. Second, 'directedness' here does not mean that intentionality functions for Husserl as a bridge between mind and world. Husserl makes it clear that intentionality is not to be understood as a relationship between a mental or psychological sphere and an extramental reality: "We must . . . be quite clear on this point that *there is no question here of a relation between a psychological event—called experience—and some other real existent—called object*" (*Ideas: General Introduction to Pure Phenomenology*, trans. W. R. Boyce Gibson [London: Collier-Macmillan, 1962/1969], 108). In his dissertation on Husserl's phenomenology, Levinas argues that to see in intentionality a bridge to the world "would amount to admitting that consciousness exists as a substance and that one of its attributes is its intentionality, which allows this substance, as subject, to enter into contact with another reality" (*The Theory of Intuition in Husserl's Phenomenology*, trans. A. Orianne [Evanston: Northwestern University Press, 1973], 41). In other words, the misunderstanding of intentionality as a bridge is possible only on the basis of a previous misinterpretation of the nature of consciousness in general.

13. This point is made explicit in *Totality and Infinity*: "For the sense of our whole effort is to contest the ineradicable conviction of every philosophy that objective knowledge is the ultimate relation of transcendence. . . . The sense of our whole effort lies in affirming not that the Other forever escapes knowing, but that there is no meaning in speaking here of knowledge or ignorance, for justice, the preeminent transcendence and the condition for knowing, is nowise, as one would like, a noesis correlative of a noema" (TI, 89–90).

14. Emmanuel Levinas, *Ethics and Infinity: Conversations with Philippe Nemo*, trans. R. Cohen (Pittsburgh: Duquesne University Press, 1985), 32. Hereafter EI.

15. See "Is Ontology Fundamental?" (1951), "Ethics and Spirit" (1952), "Freedom and Command" (1953), "The Ego and the Totality" (1954), and "Philosophy and the Idea of Infinity" (1957).

16. Emmanuel Levinas, "Ethics and Spirit," in *Difficult Freedom: Essays on Judaism*, trans. S. Hand (Baltimore: Johns Hopkins University Press, 1990), 9.

17. Emmanuel Levinas, "Is Ontology Fundamental?" in *Emmanuel Levinas: Basic Philosophical Writings*, ed. A. T. Peperzak et al. (Bloomington: Indiana University Press, 1996), 1–10.

18. Levinas, "Is Ontology Fundamental?" 6. See also Levinas's explicit claim in *Outside the Subject*: "The human being clearly allows himself to be treated as an object, and delivers himself over to knowledge in the *truth* of perception and the light of the human sciences. But, treated exclusively as an object, man is also mistreated and misconstrued" (*Outside the Subject*, trans. M. Smith [Stanford: Stanford University Press, 1994], 3).

19. Levinas, "Is Ontology Fundamental?" 6.

20. Emmanuel Levinas, "The Ego and the Totality," *Collected Philosophical Papers*, trans. A. Lingis (The Hague: Martinus Nijhoff, 1987), 41.

21. Emmanuel Levinas, "Judaism and the Feminine" in *Difficult Freedom*, 30–38.

22. An excellent and detailed discussion of the equivocation of the feminine is found in Tina Chanter, "Feminism and the Other," in *The Provocation of Levinas*, ed. R. Bernasconi and D. Wood (New York: Routledge, 1988), 32–56.

23. This view is repeated in the 1972 essay "And God Created Woman," cited earlier.

24. Levinas, "Judaism and the Feminine," 32.

25. Catherine Chalier, "Ethics and the Feminine," in *Re-reading Levinas*, ed. R. Bernasconi and S. Critchley (Purdue: Indiana University Press, 1991), 123.

26. Ibid.

27. Levinas, "Judaism and the Feminine," 35.

28. Similar claims are made by Alain Finkielkraut, *La sagesse de l'amour* (Paris: Gallimard, 1984), 77; and Tina Chanter, "Antigone's Dilemma," in *Re-Reading Levinas*, 133. The connection to ethics is perhaps clearest in the preface to *Existence and Existents* where Levinas links his own concern with transcendence (or ex-cendence) to the Platonic conception of a "Good beyond Being." The latter, Levinas says, "serves as the general guideline for this research—but does not make up its content" (EE, 15). This assessment seems accurate, since the text goes on to pursue the notion of transcendence, especially at the end of the book, but makes little or no further attempt to interpret transcendence in terms of the Good.

29. Levinas does not stick to the neologism *ex-cendence* throughout his philosophy or even throughout the text in which the term is introduced. The word *transcendence* appears in places in this text where it is clear that it is the new, Levinasian sort of transcendence that is meant. See especially 96, 100.

30. Levinas acknowledges explicitly that such a concept would be quite foreign to Heidegger's thought and could not be adopted by him, however, he vigorously defends the validity of his interpretation in both EE and TO. See especially TO 45: "I do not think Heidegger can admit an existing without existents, which to him would seem absurd."

31. On the notion of "evanescence" see EE 73, 78, 93, and 99. On the inability of the evanescence of the subject (as instant) to provide a break with being, see especially 99.

32. Levinas, "The Ego and the Totality," 30.

33. The subordination of the erotic relation to fecundity and the birth of a child at the end of *Time and the Other* is an important development and deserves more space than I can give it here. Levinas suggests in those pages that eros itself is not the relation to the future, but that it opens up this relation through fecundity: "The return of the ego to itself that begins with hypostasis is thus not without remission, thanks to the perspective of the future opened by eros. Instead of obtaining this remission through the impossible dissolution of hypostasis, one accomplishes it through the son" (TO, 91). The alterity of the son appears to supersede even that of the feminine other, since the son is more exactly both me and not-me, introducing multiplicity into the heart of being: "I do not *have* my child; I *am* in some way my child. But the words 'I am' here have a significance different from an Eleatic or Platonic significance. There is a multiplicity and a transcendence in this verb 'to exist'" (TO, 91). Interestingly enough, the analysis of fecundity does not change substantially between 1947 and 1961, even though the corresponding notions of the feminine and the erotic are significantly reworked. In fact, one might argue that the subordinate role that the feminine plays in the 1960 accounts, in which she becomes a kind of condition for the possibility of ethics, a midwife to the relations established in paternity and fraternity, is already partially prepared in the early discussions of fecundity.

34. See TI, 221: "The social relation itself is not just another relation, one among so many others that can be produced in being, but is its ultimate event. The very utterance by which I state

it and whose claim to truth, postulating a total reflection, refutes the unsurpassable character of the face to face relation, nonetheless confirms it by the very fact of stating this truth—of telling it to the Other."

35. Cf. TI, 276: "That the vital impulse propagates itself across the separation of individuals, that its trajectory is discontinuous, that is, that it presupposes the intervals of sexuality and a specific dualism in its articulation, is not seriously taken into consideration."

36. See Roger Burggraeve, *Emmanuel Levinas: Une bibliographie primaire et secondaire (1925–1985)* (Louvain: Center for Metaphysics and the Philosophy of God, 1986), 15–16, entry 41.

37. In an interview with University of Warwick graduate students, Levinas remarks that "above all" the descriptions of *Totality and Infinity* "should not be taken as psychological . . . what is described in these human states is not simply empirical, but is an essential structure" (Tamra Wright et al., "The Paradox of Morality: An Interview with Emmanuel Levinas," in *The Provocation of Levinas*, ed. R. Bernasconi and D. Wood [New York: Routledge, 1988], 171).

38. In the discussion of dwelling, Levinas remarks that "there is no question here of defying ridicule by maintaining the empirical truth or countertruth that every home *in fact* presupposes a woman. . . . The absence of the human being of the 'feminine sex' in a dwelling nowise affects the dimension of femininity which remains open there, as the very welcome of the dwelling" (TI, 158).

39. See the conversation with Levinas recorded in *Autrement que savoir: Emmanuel Levinas. Les entretiens du Centre Sèvres* (Paris: Osiris, 1988). For the discussion of equivocation and love, see especially 69–70, 74–77.

40. Levinas, *De Dieu qui vient à l'idée* (Paris: Vrin, 1992), 267.

41. For an extremely interesting attempt to develop the relationship between eros, ethics, and ontology along these lines, see Marc-Alain Ouaknin, *Méditiations érotiques* (Paris: Balland, 1992).

2

Levinas's Maternal Method from "Time and the Other" Through *Otherwise Than Being*

No Woman's Land?

Donna Brody

This chapter is divided into two sections. The first section concerns the notion of the feminine as it appears in "Time and the Other" and *Totality and Infinity*.[1] Here, I investigate the status of this word *feminine* in Levinas; does it bear a reference to empirical sex and/or gender, or is it to be read as a terminological device? Either way, as I shall show, has its repercussions for what Levinas might have to offer from a "feminist" point of view. In order to situate what we might understand by the feminine in Levinas, it is necessary to understand what "she" is doing in his texts at all. I would suggest that it is not possible to read the figure independently both of Levinas's larger ethical program and, crucially, of the methodology that seeks to articulate this program. The notions of paternity and the son will also be investigated within this horizon. Finally, having worked through this agenda, I will claim that it is not certain that women or the "feminine sex"—Levinas makes no coherent distinction between sex and gender[2]—has or could have an ethical "face."

In section 2, I claim that in *Otherwise Than Being*, Levinas extends the metaphorical limb governing a reading of the feminine.[3] The term is reconfigured as the differential notion of "subjectivity" as "substitution" of the same for the other, or "maternity." Here I argue that, far from reappearing merely as the erotically sanitized and chaste figure of motherhood—although there is certainly a case to be made for this, and Tina Chanter makes it excellently in her *Ethics of Eros*[4]—the feminine as maternity refers to and is interchangeable with a vast register of somatic experiences that fit under Levinas's umbrella term *sensibility*. I will maintain that the trope of maternity cannot be read in isolation from the suture between bodily incarnation and the transcendence of the Other. Maternity as subjectivity constitutes Levinas's most sophisticated determination of the relation between the Same and the Other—a determination that the father-son relation could not alone provide. In the twist beyond, yet "within," being, Levinas will argue that the other is already "in-the-same." But how is he to persuade us of a subjectivity that is beyond being, without leaving it as a *via negativa*, on the one hand, and without reducing it to the intelligibility of the Same, on the other hand? The answer demands an analysis of Levinas's peculiar methods of persuasion. I will show how the substitutive nature of subjectivity is textually exemplified through a substitutive maternal method.

Finally, if the feminine has regained an ethical "face" by signifying as maternity and subjectivity, what price might she have paid? Further, in conclusion, I will question whether she has indeed recovered an ethical face through the trope of maternity.

Section One

1.1 A Touch of Method

Why does Levinas use an ontological sign—*the feminine*—to describe a structure that we are pressed, even exhorted, to accede transcends its thematic significance? In the preface added in 1979 to his 1946–47 piece "Time and the Other," he explains that he began to reach toward a transcendent alterity by beginning with the "alterity-content" of the feminine. "La notion d'altérité transcendante—celle qui ouvre le temps— est d'abord recherchée a partir d'une *altérité contenu*, a partir de la féminité" (TA, 14) (The notion of a transcendent alterity—one that opens time—is at first sought starting with an *alterity-content*—that is, starting with the feminine).[5] The transcendent alterity Levinas speaks of here is that of a dimension of absolute otherness transcending being altogether, *totaliter aliter*. It signifies ethically, outside of time and consciousness, summoning responsibility toward another prior to any order of comprehension or interest. This transcending dimension is figured variously as the "face" (*le visage*), the "Other" (*L'Autre/autre; L'Autrui/ autrui*), and as a register of language he calls the "Saying" (*le Dire*). In his 1974 text *Otherwise Than Being or Beyond Essence*, he will also refer to the infinite as "subjectivity" (*subjectivité*). The contrasting register of being he terms the "Same" or the "Said" (*le Dit*). In *Otherwise Than Being* he will also call the finite being the "subject" (*sujet*). To situate ethics as an *absolute* otherness, completely exterior to being, already dictates the problems Levinas will have in articulating his claims. In order to avoid a negative theology, he must say something. But this means borrowing the intelligibility of a language and appealing to phenomenological experiences. At least in the first instance.

A similar problem of articulation besets the difficulty of describing the alterity-content of the feminine. He cannot simply invoke figures that resist phenomenality on intelligible grounds alone, as that would simply be vacuous. However, in taking the risk of talking sense, he runs the risk of reducing transcendence to immanence, to comprehension, hence betraying the exteriority of otherness and reducing it to the Same. The Parmenidean logic whereby otherness or difference can be conceived only relatively, on the basis of the Same or what is understood, thus inscribing otherness within the self-understanding of the Same (TO, 85; TA, 77), dogs his heels to the very end.

Of course, the alterity-content of the feminine is formulated as a *reaching toward* the transcending alterity of the Other. The alterity-content of the feminine is not to be conceived as radically exterior to being. This is conveyed by the oxymoronic expression of an alterity-content. How can otherness have a *contenu*? Is that not to solicit a certain modality of apprehension concerning the nature of this content? It is. The feminine in Levinas turns out to exemplify an equivocality where this consists in an alternating between transcendence and immanence, a propinquity and a proptosis: a movement folding in and out of being and an otherness constitutive of being but inaccessible to cognizance. In the feminine, Levinas discovers a "hollowing out of the fold of inwardness" (OB, 27; AE, 50)—being has a certain incognizable "fold" of otherness hollowed out within it.

Levinas's method of articulating otherness is always replete with disqualifications and negations. For example, attempting to explain the positive otherness of the feminine, he puts out of play an understanding of the term as merely the negative analogue of the "masculine" where the feminine would be conceived as the correlative, complementary, or contrary sex. Debarring this conception, he writes: "I think the absolutely contrary (*le contraire absolument contraire*), whose contrariety is in no way affected by the relationship that can be established between it and its correlative" (TO, 85; TA, 77). In this way Levinas suggests that her hyperbolic contrariety announces an alternative other than "the virility of grasping the possible, the power to be able (*'pouvoir de pouvoir'*)" (TO, 82; TA, 73).[6] The notion of "contrariety" leans on its established sense but is deepened by repetition such that it is liminally conceivable as one step beyond its conceptual measure in relation to the Same.

Levinas also firmly denies that the exteriority of feminine alterity is to be understood on the cognitive model at all: he snips off the idea that the otherness of the feminine might be a temporary occlusion to be tweaked aside or a piece of ignorance awaiting enlightenment. Rather: *the feminine is unknowable*. The essential modality of the erotic feminine is "made of alterity" (TO, 74; TA, 63). Levinas begins to snap the elasticity of an ontology that returns all experience to the knowing ego (TO, 69; TA, 56). But simply stating what the feminine is or is not remains at the level of asseveration and cannot compel. An additional measure of persuasion is required, a phenomenological method where an appeal can be made to the order of experience. Importantly, phenomenology is not a branch of casuistry for Levinas, but the very point and situation of being's vulnerability and susceptibility to an otherness irreducible to the experiences upon which it devolves.

The phenomenological context of the feminine anchors Levinas's direct claims and disclaimers with descriptive force. Do we not recognize or identify in some way with the experiences Levinas describes? Even to disagree or to correct presupposes a prior acknowledgment or tangential recognition of the phenomenology he describes. The particular revelatory context of the alterity of the feminine in "Time and the Other" is eros. Weaving between description and explanation, Levinas discursively proposes and descriptively solicits the recognition that a special mode of desire characterizes eros. This desire is for the very voluptuosity of the other (TI, 259–60; TeI, 290), a desire that feeds upon itself and does not have a correlate end.[7] Erotic desire is not to be understood on the model of a need extinguished by satisfaction. There is no ultimate teleological principle in the erotic relation; as Levinas memorably puts it, the caress "knows not what it seeks" (TO, 89; TA, 82).

But are the lovers not also beings? The aimless caress plainly does not exhaust the erotic situation. By *Totality and Infinity*, Levinas adjusts the emphasis on the elusive "feminine" component of erotic desire with its ontological intrication. He writes that the love peculiar to eros can be reduced to the side of being, to immanence, "be divested of all transcendence" (TI, 254; TeI, 285). Strictly speaking, the essential modality of eros consists in this oscillation where desire twists in and out of need, "the simultaneity of need and desire, of concupiscence and transcendence, tangency of the avowable and the unavowable, constitutes the originality of the erotic which, in this sense, is the *equivocal* par excellence" (TI, 255; TeI, 285–86). Levinas's interlacing of the thematic and the avowable with an unavowable dephasing and attenuation of significance textually exemplifies the equivocal movement of the one into the other characterizing the erotic relation. His writing could be considered, in this sense, as itself erotic.

To gain a peep at the erotic "nudity" of the feminine—an essential nakedness, a fundamental laying bare of a virginal alterity impregnable to consciousness—Levinas describes the phenomenology wherein the feminine snatches herself away from being. However, insofar as Levinas wishes to suggest an alterity belonging to the feminine—in her erotic incarnation she elusively withdraws from the light (a metaphor of disclosure and knowledge)—there is a sense in which the experience of the feminine is inassimilable to consciousness and hence irreducible to phenomenological experience or recognition. Indeed, it is this character of feminine elusiveness that is central to the erotic experience itself. But this means that Levinas's analysis, as he quite rightly points out in "Time and the Other," "is not phenomenological to the end" (TO, 78; TA, 67).[8]

While Levinas's phenomenology in "Time and the Other" cannot be "phenomenological to the end" (ibid.; if it could, the caress would be no more than grasping and emprise), he also warns us that he is only going to "touch" on a phenomenology of voluptuousness (TO, 89; TA, 82). It is difficult to know how much significance to attach to that warning: might any feminist objections meet with this evasion? Further, a "dialectical" method formally ties together the "touchings" on phenomenology into a certain trajectory. He writes, "I began with the notions of death and the feminine, and have ended with that of the son. I have not proceeded in a phenomenological way.... The concrete situations that have been analyzed represent the accomplishment of this dialectic. Many intermediaries have been skipped" (TO, 92; TA, 87). Levinas thus only "touches" on a phenomenology of the voluptuous, he does not proceed in a phenomenological way, and he skips intermediaries. A triple bypass of feminist objections? But matters are more complex and equivocal.

1.2. Whose Phenomenology?

Let us begin by problematizing Levinas's phenomenology of eros from a feminist perspective. A double-sided problem exists: Levinas examines the erotic feminine from the point of view of the subject whose "masculine" grasp she eludes. His address to the reader also supposes that the reader occupies the position of subject. Assuming that "the feminine" refers to a woman or "the feminine sex," then straightaway it becomes possible to remark on the exclusory and one-sided nature of this phenomenology. Can a *woman reader* identify or recognize herself in Levinas's descriptions? Are his accounts of the erotic feminine in any way what she experiences in the erotic relation? Does she have a counterpart whose mode of being consists in slipping away from the light? It is difficult to see how she could recognize herself as an alterity-content: is she then a dark continent unable to understand herself?

Further, *to whom* does this phenomenology appeal? Whom is Levinas addressing? When, for example, he writes that the voluptuosity of eros is "a game absolutely without project or plan, not with what can become ours or us, but with something other, always other, always inaccessible, and always still to come [à venir]" (TO, 89; TA, 82), it is necessary to wonder at this collusive address to "ours" and "us." As Irigaray protests, in her "Questions to Emmanuel Levinas," is the woman a subject in the act of love? Can a woman become a subject in love (un sujet amoureux)?[9] She objects that the woman is obliterated as a subject desiring *along with man* as subject.[10] I would add, is the woman *reader* not also obliterated? It could certainly be argued that Levinas's descriptions of the erotic feminine occlude the woman from participation in the game: that she figures as a mute pole of resistance to the active (male) lover without her own point of view. If a point of view belongs to a knowing subject, or male lover (following these equations for the moment), and the feminine constitutes an inverse movement "opposed to the movement of consciousness" (TO, 88; TA, 81), the *reductio ad absurdum* is that she is not even to be counted as a being. Superficially, it would seem that this species of objection depends upon tying the notion of the feminine to empirical sex or gender. Levinas simultaneously denies and suggests the connection.

Disclaiming the reading that would refer the feminine to the woman/ female sex, he abruptly notes, for example, in the course of discussing the home or habitation as feminine in *Totality and Infinity*, "Need one add that there is no question here of defying ridicule by maintaining the empirical truth or countertruth that every home [and every erotic relation?] in fact presupposes a woman?" (TI, 157–58; TeI, 169; my insertion). Still on the topic of the home, he is at pains to point out, "The feminine has been encountered in this analysis as one of the cardinal points of the horizon in which the inner life takes place—and the empirical absence of the human being of the 'feminine sex' in a dwelling in nowise affects the dimension of femininity which remains open there, as the very welcome of the dwelling" (TI, 158; TeI, 169).[11] Perhaps, then, the term the *feminine* is just that: a term, a procedural device, a mucilaginous metaphor.

In places Levinas explicitly assigns a purely formal level to the term of the feminine. He calls the erotic relation a "situation" (TO, 85; TA, 77). An "event" (TO, 87; TA, 80). A "category" (TO, 88; TA, 81). However, even if this situates how we are to read the figure of the feminine in Levinas, the most pertinent feminist consideration would be that it loses the specificity of an irreducible alterity belonging to the feminine sex. Thus, either one reads the phenomenology as indeed referring to the feminine sex (following Levinas's conflation of sex and gender) and hence one might follow Irigaray's objections. Or, one reads the feminine as a figure, indifferent to sex, in which case irreducible sexual difference is lost. Either way poses problems from a feminist point of view that seeks to put into question the identity of the feminine sex.

However, as mentioned, Levinas equivocates between the two possibilities. Countering those places where he denies that the feminine need refer to an empirical woman, he slips in observations such as the following: in the midst of explaining the epiphany of the feminine, he continues "at the same time interlocuter, collaborator, and master superiorly intelligent, so often dominating men in the masculine civilizations it has entered, and woman having to be treated as a woman, in accordance with rules imprescriptible by civil society" (TI, 265; TeI, 295–96). Here Levinas makes the move of connecting the figure of the feminine to empirical men and women. In *Totality and Infinity* he calls the feminine "the other refractory to society" (TI, 265; TeI, 297). If indeed the feminine is to be read in accordance with a factical reference to biological sex or gender, then Levinas himself appears at times not only to believe in the nuisance value of Antigone to civil society—in the power of the woman/feminine to subvert the Proper domain of civil order—but also that the feminine/woman/female is intrinsically "other" or "refractory" to "masculine civilization" and essentially unfit for it.

The ambivalence of Levinas's own standpoint on the *status* of the feminine is not clarified when he equivocally gestures toward the "legitimate" claims of feminism by writing: "I do not want to ignore the legitimate claims of the feminism that presupposes all the acquired attainments of civilization" (TO, 86; TA, 79). Again, it is difficult to know how to read this remark. Given that he has previously commented on the masculine nature of civilization, it is a rather backhanded acknowledgment since it suggests that the legitimate claims of feminism necessarily ride on the back of possibilities opened up by masculine civil society. The word *legitimate* is also ambiguous. It might mean rightful or just, but it might also mean no more than the legitimating conditions provided by masculine civil society. As if we should be thankful. Returning to the tentative connection between the feminine and factically existing women, however, and taking into account the notion that she is a refractory other to civil society, this leaves the legitimate claims of feminism without a point of purchase. She can make no claim if she is essentially outlawed from and other to society—her claims are unintelligible; she so often "dominates society" "in accordance with rules imprescriptible by civil society" (TI, 264; TeI, 295).

The importance of the equivocal status of the feminine concerns not only feminist questions we might put to Levinas depending on how we might read this word, but the internal logical dynamics of Levinas's own texts. The double allegiance to the feminine both as a trope and as carrying empirical referentiality not only threads the confusion through with certain "patriarchal" premises concerning the characteristics of the idea of the feminine, it also has certain *ethical* consequences. I want to raise at this stage the further question of whether the feminine, prior to *Otherwise Than Being*, has an ethical face. I shall discuss this in the context of the father-son relationship, which Levinas argues transcends the erotic feminine, leaving her behind on the hearth rug at home.

1.3. Maternity for Paternity

For at least two reasons Levinas believes that the erotic relation must be transcended. First, in "Time and the Other" he poses the double-sided question of how the ego can be preserved in transcendence and not simply crushed or absorbed by the other (see TO, 77; TA, 65). "How can the ego that I am remain myself in a you?" (TO, 78; TA, 65). Correlatively, how can the ego that returns to itself be preserved in transcendence: "How can the ego become other to itself?" (ibid.). This is one of Levinas's earliest engagements with the problematic of how there can be a "relation which is not a relation," a *rapport sans rapport* between absolutely separate terms. One wonders, initially, if Levinas has not already solved the dilemma in the equivocality of the erotic relation where "in voluptuosity the other is me and separated from me" (TI, 265; TeI, 297). However, this turns out to be crucially limited. The reason for the inadequacy of the erotic relation as a *terminus ad quem*, which Levinas gives in *Totality and Infinity*, turns on distinguishing between two types of love. The love peculiar to eros is "supremely non-public" (TI, 265; TeI, 297), a "dual egoism" (*égoïsm a deux*) (TI, 266; TeI, 298), a "non-signifying" (TI, 265; TeI, 297). Love in the erotic relation is "love of the love of the other" (TI, 265; TeI, 297).

To break open the "closed society" (*société close*) (TI, 265; TeI, 297) of the lovers, therefore, involves a further movement involving another, or other others. The erotic relation is not yet language, sociality, the sphere of intersubjective commerce and the possibility of justice.[12] Nor, we might note, does the feminine have language when conceived as the welcome of habitation, "But habitation is not yet the transcendence of language. The Other who welcomes in intimacy is not the you (*vous*) of the face that reveals itself in height, but precisely the thou (*tu*) of familiarity" (TI, 155; TeI, 166). The intimacy of the feminine, as a cardinal point of inner life, the home,[13] and in her erotic elusiveness, does not have a face: only the publicly avowable *vous* (of masculine civilization?)

allows the rectitude of the face to signify itself for it is coeval with the recognition of "other others" or the "third party" (*le tiers*). And hence to any meaningfulness that the responsibilities of the face oblige: without other others and shared systems of intelligibility and recognition, there would be no way of putting bread in the mouths of widows and orphans. It is imperative for Levinas, then, to move from the *tu* of femininity to the *vous* of the face. To transcend the familiarity of the feminine, the biological male must have a son: he insists that paternity is the *only* possible transcendence of the erotic relation (*d'une seule manière: par la paternité*) (TO, 91; TA, 85).

He writes, controversially, "I do not *have* my child, I am in some way my child" (TO, 91, TA, 86). The caress is fecund: ideally it issues in the child. In this way the father, at least, manages to be both himself and other than himself. The mother does not appear to have a relation to transcendence. Levinas talks of the child as a son, not a daughter. A momentous biological essentialism is at work: the principle of identity and difference—necessary as opening onto the subject's relation with infinity—is reserved to the male sex. The mother does not have such a relation with her son, because he is not the same sex. As Irigaray hotly notes, the mother-daughter relation is not thematized. In fact, it is not even mentioned. A question mark already hangs over whether the feminine—or the woman—has any correlative movement of self-preservation and self-transcendence. Is ethical responsibility confined to the otherness of a male other? Whereas it was possible to wonder whether the term of the feminine was reserved to the female sex, there seems no such equivocality haunting the unambiguous notions of paternity and the son. If the fecundity of the caress resulted in a daughter instead of a son, would this be a failed dialectic? An *aborted* dialectic? An incidental intermediary to be skipped? Would a couple who were unable or did not want a son be *miscarried* moments of the dialectic? Alternative voluptuous arrangements are ignored, and a matrilinear dialectic excluded from any significance.

If Levinas had reserved the transcendence of the egoic intimate economy of the erotic relation to fatherhood, that would have been bad enough. But it is further conserved to fathering a son, not a daughter. The daughter thus has no entry into language. She is caught in a hopeless double bind. On the one hand, she has no intrinsic bond to or "sameness" with the father; on the other hand, she is not "other" than him either: she has no face. Without a face, she is once more wholly reducible to the male order of the Same. This heterologous movement debars the female from language for which she would need to enter masculine civilization. Without the intersubjective horizon of language, there are no faces. She is doomed on this logic to circulate endlessly through the "supremely non-public" (TI, 265; TeI, 297) economy of the home, eros, and nonsignifying motherhood. The circle is closed. The trap is intensified when we look at just what Levinas means by "non-signifying" (ibid.).

1.4. Feminine Facelessness

"Non-signifyingness," Levinas explains in *Totality and Infinity*, is not equivalent to a brute materiality or "the stupid indifference of matter" (TI, 264; TeI, 295). Rather, although the erotic relation "excludes the third party" (TI, 265; TeI, 297) and is "without language" (ibid.), nonetheless, "as the reverse expression of what has lost expression" the feminine "thereby refers to the face" (TI, 264; TeI, 295). Similarly, "disrespect" (TI, 262; TeI, 294) presupposes a face, whereas things do not. In the context of eros, Levinas writes, "It is necessary that the face have been apperceived for nudity to be able to acquire the non-signifyingness of the lustful" (TI, 262, TeI, 294). In this way, the argument goes, the "asocial" relation of eros has a "negative" reference to the social. But *for whom* does the "reverse expression" of the lustful negatively implicate and refer to sociality and the face? Is she not without language? How is it possible for her to have apperceived the expression of the face that her carnal nudity reverses? Again, the meaning of nonsignifyingness is only available to and from *his* point of view. The feminine lacks the resources to understand her own erotic significance as nonsignifying. The "disrespect" conveyed by her "immodesty" (ibid.) tangentially refers to and presupposes the face only *for him:* he who has language. The feminine falls outside of this logic of complementarity: is she not then, as regards herself and with respect to his respect for her, precisely—ethically—at the level of elements and things? (ibid.). Her dead face is shown but does not let *her* see.

Minimally, whether the feminine has a face in either "Time and the Other" or *Totality and Infinity* is obscure. Maximally, it is possible to make the stronger case that she does not have a face. The closest Levinas gets to giving her a face is when he writes, having pronounced on the necessity of having apperceived the face in order to appreciate the nonsignifyingness of the lustful, "The feminine face joins this clarity and this shadow" (ibid.). What shadow? Here we must note the negative influence of the concept of the feminine in Levinas, briefly untrammeled from a patriarchal net of assumptions in the promise of an alterity-content, but reensnared at an even greater metaphysical depth. For Levinas proceeds to explicate this shadowland. Apparently, feminine epiphany "laughs under the cloak of its own expression" (TI, 264; TeI, 296), where voluptuosity discovers the hidden as hidden (TI, 260; TeI, 291), and "this mode of 'saying' or of 'manifesting' itself hides while uncovering, says and silences the inexpressible, harrasses and provokes" (ibid.). Here Levinas seems to be attributing to the feminine a certain self-consciousness that delights in subverting the signifying of the face. She hides her mockery under the cloak of uncovering herself for him.[14]

Levinas proceeds to give the feminine a face only to take it away again in the next breath. He continues, "In the feminine face the purity of expression is already troubled by the equivocation of the voluptuous. Expression is inverted into indecency, already close on the equivocal that says less than nothing, already laughter and raillery" (ibid.). If she shows a face to him, it is already a face that troubles through erotic elusiveness: itself on the edge of a taunting equivocation which says less than nothing. And laughs at him. Profanes. Less than nothing? That is the unsaying voice of the horrifying indeterminate menace that Levinas explores in *Existence and Existents*. He calls it the *there is* (*il y a*). The feminine face is proximal to the monstrous and ungraspable squeaking and rumbling of the indeterminate *il y a*. "Alongside the night as anonymous rustling of the *there is* extends the night of the erotic" (TI, 258; TeI, 289). Along with the alterity-content of the feminine the *il y a* is similarly situated to "introduce a duality into existence, a duality concerning the very existing of each subject. Existence itself becomes double" (TO, 53; TA, 88). If this seems to be going too far, it is worth noting that in at least two places Levinas puts the feminine at an even deeper subterranean level of darkness than the disturbing monstrosity of the *il y a*. He writes that *she weighs heavier even than the "weight of the formless real"* (TI, 257; TeI, 287; my emphasis): another formulation for the *il y a*. Again, the feminine is "behind" the night of insomnia or the *il y a* (TI, 258; TeI, 289).

The disturbing aspect of Levinas's discourse in particular on the feminine in "Time and the Other" and in *Totality and Infinity* is that it is impossible to remove the cloak of the feminine as a cultural or historically defined gender construct that might be nonfixed, fluid, and susceptible to change. On the contrary. He indemnifies these qualities to change by making them part of her essential alterity-content. Worse still: on the strong reading I have suggested, she has no face, for she has no language. It is not even certain that she is to be recognized as a being. Always assuming that we connect the notion of the feminine to empirical sex and gender. However, even if it is possible to doubt that connection, it is not possible to doubt that Levinas does not only take out interest on the loan of the term of the feminine: he pays it back by redoubling it; at the very least, the notional term of the feminine is returned to the patriarchal economy of desire. If it takes Levinas toward a "transcendent alterity," it is only because the feminine is functionally subordinate and instrumentally reducible to the entry of the male into the masculine preserve of language and the face.

1.5. The Fatherly Future

In *Totality and Infinity*, the relation between father and son hinges more emphatically on the element of time. The future of the son is "[b]oth my own and non-mine, a possibility of myself but also a possibility of the other" (TI, 267; TeI, 300). It is this future, irreducible to the power over possibles—for the son has his "own" future—that Levinas calls fecundity. He denies that the future of the father within the son is, however, a new avatar, "[a]nd yet it is my adventure still" (TI, 268, TeI, 300). Clearly, Levinas is protesting against the notion of the social relation as ontological and reducible to relations of consciousness and power (TI, 276; TeI, 308–9). Rather, he is attempting to show that the social relation is predicated upon a movement of transcendence. The relation with the son establishes a "relationship with the absolute future or infinite time" (TI, 268; TeI, 300).

Levinas is claiming that the identity of the "I" is both maintained in the son and also discontinuous, for the son articulates the time of the Other rather than affirms and renews the substance and time of the "I" or the father. The relation between father and son thus provides a generational account of being "produced as multiple and split into the same and the other. . . . It is society, and hence it is time" (TI, 269; TeI, 301). Put differently, fecundity accounts for why a concern for the Other is at once concern for the future of the Other. In that sense it "goes beyond the face"—it goes beyond the temporal immediacy of a historically localized sea of faces, as it were. It is a complex and dubious disquisition, for it might be argued that Levinas has said no more than that fecundity and fraternity are tendentially grounded upon kinship relations, and the denial that this is a new "avatar" of self amounts only to a difference between beings that could be accounted for in intramundane terms. It is also unclear with what *necessity* he moves from the futurity exhibited by the feminine where "[t]he caress is the anticipation of this pure future without content" (TO, 89; TA, 82) to the claim that this erotic future is "resolved" in paternity (TI, 271; TeI, 304). Why should the temporal movement be continuous in *this* way? That aside, what concerns us here is that, once again, the feminine does not enter into this "infinite" time of sociality. If the "fecundity of the I is its very transcendence" (TI, 277; TeI, 310), and this is limited to paternity and filiality, then the feminine is not fecund, or only fecund to the extent that she is necessary for sexuality to result in the fecundity and transcendence of the father-to-be. Talking of paternity as the production of an innumerable future, where the "I" in the son is both the unique son and also nonunique, brother among brothers, Levinas writes, "The human I is posited in fraternity" (TI, 279; TeI, 312–13). Is she a human being? The father always to be, through his son: she has no future, no time to be otherwise, no time for a face.

When Levinas writes that the biological origin of fecundity does not neutralize the paradox of its meaning, and "delineates a structure that goes beyond the biologically empirical" (TI, 277; TeI, 310), it could be argued that a great deal "goes beyond the biologically empirical"—phenomenology, for example. One wonders if he has succeeded in arguing for the father-son relationship as "a relation of rupture and of recourse at the same time" (TI, 278; TeI, 310) in a way that is immune from an alternative explanation of this relation and this continuous discontinuity. It is not clear that the metabolic transcendence Levinas describes is necessarily *ethical*. Without pressing the argument further, the model (if it is one) of the father-and-son relation does not directly lead onto or explicate the absolute ethical transcendence of the Other. Paternity goes beyond the face in an ever-recommencing infinition of time. *It does not do the work of showing how the I is "open" to or always already receptive to the ethical appeal of the face*. It does not show how the otherness of the Other can sneak into the sameness of the I and summon it to responsibility. Levinas does not return to the relation of paternity, but he does return to address the question of how the Other can smuggle itself into the Same. In *Otherwise Than Being*, the feminine returns to displace the primacy of the father-son relation as the prototypical structure of the relation between the I and the Other.

Section Two

2.1. A Sensible Feminine

Why am I not simply deaf to the Other? How is it that the Other can summon me toward ethical responsibility? By the time Levinas writes *Otherwise Than Being*, he is concerned to show how being is "open" to or already intricated with the otherness of the Other. His accounts in this text shatter out from one chapter, on "substitution," the centerpiece of the book that will describe the nature of "subjectivity" as a transfer for the other. The feminine that reversed the movement of consciousness in a hollowing out of the fold of inwardness is further elongated, more deeply vulnerable, becoming "an inversion in the process of essence" (OB, 107; AE, 168).

Just as Levinas could not carry the sense of the feminine using a language inadequate to the task, so the same problem will beset his attempts to articulate the nature of subjectivity. It is not enough that he declaim, for example, that subjectivity is a "nameless singularity" (OB, 106; AE, 168) and "not statable in terms of consciousness, discourse, and intentionality" (OB, 106; AE, 169). Strictly speaking, then, and cauterizing the possibility of justifying his argument in advance, "It is unsayable, and thus unjustifiable" (OB, 107; AE, 169). To persuade us that subjectivity is a substitution of and for the Other, then, it is not sufficient simply to assert as much. The method of *Otherwise Than Being* will repeat and transform the erotic phenomenology of "Time and the Other." To show how being has the other in its skin, as it were, Levinas substitutes the term of the feminine with a deliberate linguistic register of tactility, of materially dense somatic terms immediately replete with their recurrence or reversion into phenomenological significance. To say something about that "nameless singularity," Levinas appeals to a certain experiential modality carried by his words. Recalling the feminine in contrast to the "light" of being, and the susceptible "passivity" of the subject with respect to the unmasterable feminine, Levinas writes, "The tropes of ethical language are found to be adequate for certain structures of the description:

for the sense of the approach in its contrast with knowing, the face in its contrast with a phenomenon" (OB, 120; AE, 192).

The "tropes of ethical language" in *Otherwise Than Being* fall under the category of "sensibility," which Levinas defines as "being affected by a non-phenomenon" (OB, 75; AE, 121). The immediacy of bodily sensations and experiences is not only phenomenological, but, Levinas wants to say, primarily a "contact," an exposure or proximity to the signifying of the Other as "the-other-in-the-same" before they turn into a cognition. He argues that previous philosophical determinations of sensibility (especially that of Husserl) do not exhaust the signifying of the sensible and of immediacy. Rather, first and foremost, sensible experience is an obsession by the other, or a maternity; "immediacy is this vulnerability, this maternity" (OB, 76; AE, 76), "the subject is affected without the source of the affection becoming a theme of representation" (OB, 101; AE, 159). Indeed, Levinas argues that the whole of being "signifies only on the basis of the one-for-the-other of substitution of the same for the other" (OB, 26; AE, 80). He writes, "[T]he sensible—maternity, vulnerability, apprehension—binds the role of incarnation into a plot larger than the apperception of self" (OB, 76; AE, 123). This "larger plot" is subjectivity, a substitution of the self for the other.

Paralleling the equivocality of the erotic relation, folding in and out of transcendence and immanence, "maternity, vulnerability, responsibility, proximity, contact—sensibility can slip toward touching, palpation, openness upon ... consciousness of ..." (OB, 76; AE, 122; see also OB, 79; AE, 127). The equivocal erotic relation is a prototype of ambiguous sensibility where sensibility hesitates and passes between being and transcendence, where "[p]henomenology defects into a face, even if, in the course of this ever ambiguous defecting, of appearing, the obsession itself shows itself in the said" (OB, 90; AE, 144). In sensibility Levinas seeks a subjectivity "independent of the adventure of cognition, and in which the corporeality of the subject is not separable from its subjectivity" (OB, 78; AE, 125).

Levinas finds the trope of maternity appropriate for signifying the sense of "bearing par excellence" (OB, 75; AE, 121). It also operates as a figure conveying both the notion of the "other-in-the-same," at once an immemorial and irrecuperable attachment already made (e.g., OB, 78; AE, 126). Tropes of enjoyment remain, but in addition, Levinas shifts and broadens his emphasis to include those of pain and suffering, for example, "Is not the restlessness of someone persecuted but a modification of maternity, the groaning of the wounded entrails by those it will bear or has borne? In maternity what signifies is a responsibility for others" (OB, 75; AE, 121). The feminine, it seems, has already lost her carnality, which has been substituted for the unexciting and erotically purified trope of maternity. By the end of this chapter, I hope to have brought this reading into question.

The most remarkable transformation, however, is from a feminine without a face in "Time and the Other" and *Totality and Infinity*, to the elevation of the feminine as nothing but a face: she becomes the signifying par excellence of otherness, of subjectivity, pure Saying. Her carnal nakedness becomes a stripping beyond nudity (OB, 15; AE, 31), a denuding even of the skin (ibid.), "stripped to the core" (OB, 49; AE, 84). Her "dark side," shadowland of the less-than-nothing, the laughter, the cloak of raillery, and sisterhood to the sinister *il y a* is vertically and dramatically reversed: Levinas writes that subjectivity "is being torn up from oneself, being less than nothing, a rejection into the negative, behind nothingness; it is maternity, gestation of the other in the same" (OB, 75; AE, 121). From the depths of taunting erotic seduction to the very acme of responsible ethical motherhood? Undeniably. But not completely. When Levinas writes, "The one-for-the-another has the form of sensibility or vulnerability, pure passivity or susceptibility, passive to the point of becoming an inspiration, that is, alterity in the same, the trope of the body animated by the soul, psyche in the form of a hand that gives even the bread taken from its own mouth. Here the psyche is the maternal body" (OB, 67; AE, 109), it is clear that the maternal is the trope both of the body and of the Saying soul or psyche: subjectivity. However, it is also the "form of sensibility"—and interchangeable with an enormous itinerary of somatic terms that, taken together, Levinas calls the "tropes of ethical language" (OB, 120; AE, 192).

We constantly move through, among others, skin, persecution, breathing, irritability, obsession, possession, susceptibility, nakedness, exposure, wounding, trauma, psychosis, shock, vulnerability, wounding, outrage, and even shivering, panting, and shuddering. Part of the suasive appeal of these terms concerns the automicity and sensorial "undergoing" of bodily incarnation. The phenomenological force concerns the irrefusability of the somatic order, which Levinas further transmutes into "pure undergoing"/"pâtir pur"[15] when considered as being affected by a non-phenomenon. He also expropriates terms from a psychic order: the subject is equally unfree to decline an "obsession" or a "possession." I would suggest that the manifold dimensions of "sensibility" would not exclude the voluptuosity of the erotic relation, although the emphasis has shifted and expanded into a larger repertoire of sensation.

Of course, simply invoking and appealing to even these "passive" experiences cannot quite take us to an inapprehensible sense of subjectivity—here, too, the method cannot be "phenomenological to the end" (TO, 78; TA, 67). To push the phenomenology to eclipse itself on the edge of intentionality, "below the openness of the feeling upon the felt, of a consciousness upon a phenomenon",[16] another method is required to supervene upon and interrupt even a liminal phenomenological purchase. This method is metaphysically indebted: Levinas will textually insinuate and linguistically duplicate, as it were, the torsion between the Saying and the Said, between subjectivity and the subject. He works from both sides at once: from the "this" side of a concupiscent phenomenology, deliberately twined around and between the "Saids" of thematic discourse and from the "hither-side" under the aegis of the infinite where subjectivity as substitution is already "presupposed." Through a recombinative method where one term, metaphor, syntax, or figure of speech is constantly substituted, and recentered in a "recurrence" to others, Levinas's ultimate methodological accomplishment is to present his text as itself a face. This method at once reflects the correlation between subjectivity and the intentionality of consciousness (OB, 71; AE, 115).

2.2. Hostage to Maternity

Levinas defamiliarizes what we might ordinarily understand by these sensible experiences, as he did with the exaggerated contrariety of the feminine: he will paleonymically displace this vocabulary. He begins to displace these terms by putting all of the tropes into play simultaneously rather than systematically developing any one of them. Between these terms are collisions, collusions, confusions, and infusions, made possible not just through the proximity of some of these terms to others—an obsession might be a persecution; a nakedness might be an exposure; a wounding might be traumatic—but also through a curiously equivocal syntax where these terms are sometimes held apart and sometimes conflated or identified with one another. For example, sometimes Levinas refers one term to another. "In one's skin" is referred to "a recurrence in dead time or the *meanwhile* which separates inspiration and expiration, the diastole and systole of the heart" (OB, 109; AE, 172). But this reference recurs to a previous reference where recurrence has itself been referred to the "dead time" (*temps mort*) as an accusation in one's skin (OB, 107; AE, 170). From the one to the other and back again. Sometimes a term defects in favor of analogy—"as though" defecting from an appraisal of its monstrative significance. Only to slither into coincidence, dispensing with an "as if" or an "as though": for example, "Persecution is not something added to the subjectivity of the subject and this vulnerability: it is the very movement of recurrence" (OB, 111; AE, 176).

Levinas textually insinuates the notions of substitution and recurrence through the way in which his tropes both recur to one another and substitute for one another. Meaning is both composed and decomposed. His method here is an exiled method, splitting up, hemorrhage, pseudonymic, in "masks" and "borrowed names" (OB, 106; AE, 168), expelling significance through a restless respiration as one term is sucked into another and passes through its membranes as an exhalation. Only to be pulled in again by another name, another mask. As for the notion of subjectivity itself, this is "[n]ot a reference from one term to another, as it appears thematized in the said, but substitution as the very subjectivity of the subject" (OB, 13; AE, 29). Referring one term to another again, he writes, "Animation can be understood as an exposure to the other, the passivity of the for-the-other in vulnerability, which refers to maternity, which sensibility signifies" (OB, 71; AE, 114).

The alterity-content of the feminine was contrasted with the knowledgeable comportment of being in "Time and the Other." But this entailed that Levinas also deploy that language of being in order both to point to this elusive modality of the feminine, and to situate that to which it was exterior. The term "of the feminine" was also a name borrowed from being, shifting between immanence and pronominally designating an alterity-content. In a parallel movement, Levinas interweaves his delirious ethical tropology with the language of being, for example in contrasting the notion of subjectivity with that of the egoic subject. Ontological concepts are twined around and between the vocabulary of sensibility. The strategy of diremption where the tropes of sensibility become only vestigal reminders or remainders of their customary significance is repeated with respect to an ontological order of signs. For example, the term *subjectivity* is itself clothed in a borrowed costume of being, taken from the realm of ontology even if marks a breakage with ontology. As a mark of the break these terms become pronominal. Levinas also uses the terms of *I, me, ego, subject,* and *self* in double configurations and slippages as his displacements of "ethical language." These terms displace their presumptive referents, becoming pronominal. Nor can subjectivity be situated or positioned or located without further pronominal gestures.

He also duplicates the same word to mean both thematically and athematically. The notion of "skin," for example, a favorite with Levinas, is re-centered to mean conceptually and as a "surplus over meaning"/ "surplus de sens" (TI, 128; TeI, 135). The persecuting other will insinuate itself into the same. "In a caress, what is there is sought as though it were not there" (OB, 90; AE, 143–44). An analogy. But to have a skin is also to be too tight in one's skin, persecuted, altogether traced through by the other, *mal dans sa peau* (OB, 106; AE, 167). The term *skin* shifts about, first a Said, and then a Saying. The skin is very thin, quasi-transparent, "It is a thinness already reduced to the alternating of sense, the ambiguity of a phenomenon and its defect" (OB, 90; AE, 143). This movement is a "reversion of thematization into ethics."[17] It is also, we might note, a parabolic and paralogical extension of the erotic feminine's inverse movement of consciousness in "Time and the Other." The carnality of the feminine reappears in *Otherwise Than Being* as the caress or the skin. This time, the caress is not limited to the elusive alterity-content of the feminine, but has already taken the step toward a transcendent alterity as one of the modes of sensibility; "[t]he caress is the not coinciding proper to contact, a denuding never naked enough" (OB, 90; AE, 144); "[t]he skin caressed ... is the divergency between the visible and the invisible" (OB, 89; AE, 143). Again, "[s]ignifyingness, the one-for-the-other, exposedness of self to another, it is immediacy in caresses and in the contact of saying" (OB, 85; AE, 135).

2.3. About Face

The startling aspect to this method is that it never takes place without a dissimulation of the possibility of accomplishing it. The method of trying to lift the Saying out of the Said is inscribed in the singularity of the Saying that describes the event of subjectivity itself, where subjectivity "can indeed appear in an indirect language, under a proper name ... and therefore refer to essence. But it is first a non-quiddity, no one, clothed with purely borrowed being, which masks its nameless singularity by conferring on it a role" (OB, 106; AE, 168). The purely Saying moment of Levinas's discourse, therefore, is also a nonquiddity, the explicit project of showing us the Saying without a Said (and even this word "Saying" must be *said*) constitutes Levinas's own conferring of a role upon this method. And with a role reversal, an inversion, a double inversion, for Levinas will refer essence to the nameless singularity that, once stated, refers to essence: "An alternating rhythm of the said and the unsaid, and the unsaid being unsaid in its turn, will have to be substituted for the unity of discourse."[18]

Again and again, and this is implied in Levinas's repetition of ontological terms to mean first the Said and then the Saying, he wishes to doubt that the "opposition" between ontology and ethics "constitutes an alternative."[19] It is not difficult to appreciate the efficacy of Levinas's metaphors of mediastinum. The ontological Saids become, in Levinas's measures of *démesure*, a "Saying otherwise." Enigmatically, Levinas's words are to carry an ethical resounding within themselves "like the echo of sound that would precede the resonance of this sound" (OB, 111; AE, 175). The concepts he arranges are de-ranged in a recurrence to or substitution for the "hither-side"; an ethical *sens* is substituted for an intelligible sense. Yet these paleonymically displaced concepts work also through their coherence as themes. Levinas *over*determines ontological categories. Deliberately, superlatively, "which transforms them into ethical terms" (OB, 115; AE, 181).

In *Otherwise Than Being*, the feminine has left the zone of being and the voluptuosity reserved to eros to signify the skin of sensibility or corporeality: a knot with being as well as a denouement of being (OB, 77; AE, 123). Both phenomenal and at once a collapse of phenomenality, "more naked than nudity" (OB, 88; AE, 141). From facelessness in "Time and the Other" and *Totality and Infinity*, she may be read as the face par excellence. The trope of maternity is not one term among others with a detachable univocal significance, but a very reference to the density of sensibility as the one-for-the-other: sensibility as the skin, contact, the caress—all forms of sensation where this somatic logic would not exclude the carnality of the voluptuous feminine. The figure of maternity is not to be read as somehow sanitized of all bodily incarnation—on the contrary. It is the very figure of embodiment, flesh and blood, and sensorial contact.

However, if the feminine in *Otherwise Than Being* could be read in one way as recovering a face, becoming the very Saying itself as sensibility and subjectivity, she might also be read in another way as a consequence of the troubled dialectic that previously ended in paternity and the son. Is "maternity" not one of the "tropes of ethical language" (OB, 120; AE, 192)? Do any of these tropes bear a reference to the empirically feminine sex? Was she not exiled from language? Is the neighbor not the "brother," a "fraternity" (OB, 87; AE, 138; see also, for example, OB, 152; AE, 238) rather than a sorority? It might be objected that she forsakes sexual difference and an irreducible alterity-content (problematic though it is in Levinas) for a multivalent subjectivity. It might also be objected that the female capacity for child-bearing is poached, colonized, and substituted from her to him where it figures as a kind of agamic or parthenogenic reproduction of the other-in-the-same. In other words, she may be read as redetermined according to the most eminent meaning—or she may be read as *altogether* obliterated, exiled even from the significance of maternity.

Conclusion

When Levinas writes that "the coveting of the child, both other and myself—takes form in voluptuosity" (TI, 266; TeI, 298), he is speaking and writing as a man for himself, for other men, and for the male reader. When Levinas writes, "The tender designates a way, the way remaining in the *no man's land* between being and not-yet-being" (TI, 259; TeI, 290), it is entirely a man's land where the tender, the feminine, operates as the way. The way away from himself and back to himself. She has no way. The tender way is, on the contrary, *no woman's land*.

When Levinas writes, "The subjectivity of sensibility, taken as incarnation, is an abandon without return, maternity, a body suffering for another" (OB, 79; AE, 127), this giving and this abandoning, this body suffering for another, is the dignity of the denuded feminine as face giving and given without return to herself. This giving and this subjectivity is given from her, as her, by her, but one hesitates, finally, over whether it is given *to* her.

Notes

1. "Time and the Other," in *The Levinas Reader*, ed. S. Hand (Cambridge, Mass.: Basil Black-well, 1989), 38–58; and *Le temps et l'autre* (Paris: Presses Universitaires de France, 1989). Referred to in the text as TO and TA, respectively. *Totality and Infinity*, trans. A. Lingis (Pittsburgh: Duquesne University Press, 1969); and *Totalité et infini*, Le Livre de Poche edition (The Hague: Kluwer Academic, Martinus Nijhoff, 1990). Referred to in the text as TI and TeI, respectively.

2. I shall follow Levinas's conflation of the distinction between sex and gender throughout. In this way the equivocal dual-referentiality of the notion of the feminine to either sex or gender—or possibly both or neither, as will be seen—is sustained. While a distinction between biological sex (female) and gender "construct" (feminine) should not be ignored, and while it would be interesting to unpack Levinas's notion of the feminine precisely in terms of that distinction, my concern here is to offer a reading that does not depart from Levinas's ambiguous running together of sex and gender. This is important if we are to understand the nature of his equivocalites concerning the term of the feminine, for much ambiguity, and the conclusions that might be drawn from it, depend upon this blurring. Had Levinas distinguished between sex and gender, then the term of the "feminine" would tend to fall into the category of gender rather than sex, but in his texts the term—at times—carries a sexually "essentialist" reference as well. The ambivalence, the muddle even, is crucial, for it determines a certain undecideability over whether the term of the "feminine" is a trope or a construct, or whether it does indeed carry empirical reference. I would also suggest that the distinction is in any case not as watertight as has often been assumed. See Tina Chanter's excellent discussion of the 'problematic nature' of the distinction in her *Ethics of Eros: Irigaray's Rewriting of the Philosophers* (New York: Routledge, 1995).

3. *Otherwise Than Being or Beyond Essence*, trans. A. Lingis (The Hague: Martinus Nijhoff, 1974); and *Autrement qu'être ou au-delà de l'essence*, Le Livre de Poche edition (The Hague: Martinus Nijhoff, 1990). Referred to in the text as OB and AE, respectively.

4. See *Ethics of Eros*, esp. chap. 5.

5. "Time and the Other," in *Time and the Other (and Additional Essays)*, trans. R. A. Cohen (Pittsburgh: Duquesne University Press, 1987), 36.

6. The analysis of the feminine in "Time and the Other" is foregrounded by those of death and time. There, Levinas contests the Heideggerian notion of being-towards-death by insisting upon the "feminine" thought of death as a stoppage or seizing up of activity and freedom, an abrupt impossibility of further possibilities. Levinas considers that Heidegger's notion of being-towards-death, as the possibility of impossibility or of ceasing to be, opens up a span of life possibilities that, for Levinas, amounts to an active appropriation and mastering of the alterity of death. Levinas rethinks death as "the end of the subject's virility and heroism" (TO, 41; TA, 59), where the "existence" of death is "made of alterity" (TO, 43; TA, 63). He moves from death to the modality of the future which is similarly "in no way to be grasped" (TO, 43; TA, 64). Plainly, the alterity of the feminine is proximal to the notions of death and time—and much could be said about the historical identifications of the feminine with death—but death and the event of the future is also associated with the face-to-face relation (TO, 45; TA, 68–69).

7. In the nonintentionality of the caress where one desires *per impossible* the very voluptuosity of the other, Levinas provides an erotic mode of what he calls Metaphysical Desire for the Other that similarly goes beyond any *intentum* and is animated by its "object." See, for example, TI, 2; TeI, 33.

8. We might add to the list with the experiences of effort, indolence, insomnia, fatigue, and the *there is* (*il y a*) that Levinas charts in *Existence and Existents*, a work that is in many ways a sister set of essays to "Time and the Other." These experiences also comprise moments of alterity within being counterposed to the "hypostatic" upsurge of a being in time where the self exerts a mastery, consciousness, and order over the world. The structural modality of these experiences is not, however,

the always-yet-to-come future, but a gap or a lapse in time, a time lag. The same theme occupies him in *De l'évasion*. In various essays, including "Time and the Other," Levinas also utilizes the structure of pain and suffering to show the passivity of pure undergoing where the point is similarly that the subject is "in relation to what does not come from itself" (TO, 40; TA, 56).

9. Luce Irigaray, "Questions to Emmanuel Levinas: On the Divinity of Love," in *The Irigaray Reader*, ed. M. Whitford (Oxford: Blackwell Publishers, 1994), 204.

10. Ibid. Luce Irigaray presents a rather different phenomenology of the caress in her "The Fecundity of the Caress," in *Face to Face with Levinas*, ed. R. A. Cohen (Albany: State University of New York Press, 1986), 231–56, a critique of "he"—Levinas, and, positively, a phenomenology of eros from "her" point of view. It is a remarkable piece of work, but Irigaray's rapturous phenomenology of the caress is not necessarily every woman's experience, just as Levinas's description is arguably not necessarily every man's (or woman's) experience. Especially not when viewed in certain localized cultural contexts. Notably missing from Irigaray's account is Levinas's inclusion and insistence upon an element of erotic attraction arising from insurmountable difference, whereas Irigaray's essay inclines toward a notion, beatific in places, of union or fusion between the lovers: a cozy absence of a little bit of "fire and ice" (ibid., 237). However, it could be argued, the desire for union does not amount merely and flatly to the narcissistic seeking of a sister soul, as Levinas claims. No doubt any complete phenomenology would account for erotic desire in terms both of union and the pathos of separatedness.

11. Structurally, the home is a midway point in Levinas's analysis in *Totality and Infinity*. It is situated between sheer "living from" the elements or enjoyment (*jouissance*)—an analysis that challenges the primacy of representational thought—and reflective and self-reflective engagement with the world. The home is presented as a kind of "recollection in tranquility," suspended between the agreeableness of the elemental and the immediate reactions the world solicits (TI, 154; TeI, 164–65).

12. If the face summoned me to responsibility for only one Other, there would not be a question of responsibility for other Others. As Levinas puts it, "If proximity orders me only to the other alone, there would not have been any problem . . . a question would not have been born, nor consciousness, nor self-consciousness" (OB, 157; AE, 245). But my neighbor has neighbors too. What are they to one another, and what is that relation to me? This is a question of a relationship with *le tiers*, or the "third party": other Others. However—and to condense a rather complex argument—it is a sophistry to consider that I am responsible for a singular Other. Levinas writes, "it is not that there would first be a face, and then the being it manifests or expresses would concern himself: the epiphany of the face qua face opens humanity" (TI, 213; TeI, 234). The face is at once both a reference to the "third" where "[t]he others concern me from the first" (OB, 159; AE, 247), and the "latent birth" (OB, 157; AE, 244) of consciousness, contemporaneousness, intentionality, and the intellect. The face is thus a double origin, both a reference to other Others and the production of representational thought and consciousness; "consciousness is born as the presence of the third party" (OB, 160; AE, 249).

13. See also Levinas's "Judaism and the Feminine Element," trans. E. Wyschogrod, *Judaism* 18 (1969): 30–38. The first three pages refine and echo his earlier discussion in *Totality and Infinity* concerning the notion of the feminine as "habitation."

14. In "Judaism and the Feminine Element," Levinas, in the context of tracing through the feminine in relation to Judaism, writes, "The feminine will never take on the aspect of the divine. . . . The dimension of intimacy is opened by woman, not the dimension of loftiness." He also echoes the thought that there is an ambivalence about the feminine. "Woman is complete immodesty, down to the nakedness of her little finger. She is the one who, *par excellence*, displays herself, the essentially turbulent, the essentially impure. Satan, says an extremist text, was created with her" (35). However, it is unclear throughout whether or to what extent Levinas's exegetical commentary or interpretations could be read as either endorsement or criticism.

15. "Useless Suffering," in *The Provocation of Levinas: Rethinking the Other*, ed. R. Bernasconi and

D. Wood (London: Routledge, 1988), 157; and *Entre nous: Essais sur le penser-a-l'autre* (Paris: Bernard Grasset, 1991), 108.

16. "Language and Proximity," in *Collected Philosophical Papers*, trans. A Lingis (Dordrecht: Martinus Nijhoff, 1987), 117–18; and *En découvrant l'existence avec Husserl et Heidegger* (Paris: J. Vrin, 1982), 227.

17. Ibid., 124 and 234, respectively.

18. "God and Philosophy," in *Collected Philosophical Papers*, 173, and *De Dieu qui vient a l'idée* (Paris: J. Vrin, 1982), 127.

19. Ibid., 155 and 97, respectively.

3

The Ethical Passions of Emmanuel Levinas

Ewa Płonowska Ziarek

[The] memory of flesh as the place of approach is ethical fidelity to
incarnation.

—Luce Irigaray

The originality of Levinas's later work on ethics, still insufficiently discussed, lies in his elaboration of ethical responsibility in terms of embodiment, passion, or even delirium. Levinas's inquiry in *Otherwise Than
Being or Beyond Essence* into ethical responsibility prior to the subject's
commitment and intentionality opens a reflection on the coincidence
of responsibility, passion, and embodiment.[1] As Simon Critchley writes,
"[T]he entire phenomenological thrust in *Otherwise Than Being* is to
'ground' ethical subjectivity in sensibility and to describe sensibility as
proximity to the Other, a proximity whose basis is found in substitution."[2] Indeed, Levinas argues that the aim of the book is to "disengage

For a longer version of this essay, see my *Ethics of Dissensus: Postmodernity, Feminism, and the
Politics of Radical Democracy* (Stanford University Press, 2001), 47–62.

the subjectivity of the subject from reflections on truth, time and being . . . borne by the said; it will then present the subject, in saying, as sensibility" (OB, 19). This achievement of Levinas's ethics, which makes the question of passion and corporeality central to ethical experience, is at odds, however, with the parallel development in *Otherwise Than Being*, namely, with what Tina Chanter calls "an eclipse of Eros and femininity" and the corresponding privilege given to maternity purified of sexuality. As Chanter asks, "Why is it that the only aspect of eros responsible enough to gain admission in *Totality and Infinity* is that of fecundity? And by 1974, in *Otherwise than Being*, why does maternity occlude paternity, while eros is abandoned altogether?"[3] By exploring the tensions between these two mutually incompatible developments in Levinas's work, I would first like to ask how the perspective of ethics changes the relation between embodiment and language. Second, I would like to examine whether Levinas's reformulation of responsibility as passion and his emphasis on embodiment allows us to rethink his earlier formulations of eros and femininity in the direction indicated by Luce Irigaray's work on the ethics of sexual difference.

What is remarkable in Levinas's later work is that the possibility of ethical responsibility is located not in consciousness or free will, but specifically in incarnation, defined as "the extreme way of being exposed." For Levinas the philosophical privilege granted to reflection and consciousness, that is, to the "for itself," signifies freedom and the coincidence of the self with itself at the price of the negation of both alterity and the body. As Levinas writes, the for itself of consciousness "is always a self-possession, sovereignty, *arche*" (BPW, 80). Associated with will, spontaneity, and mastery, consciousness can grasp responsibility only in terms of its own freedom. By contrast, Levinas's ethics posits responsibility prior to the will and the intentionality of consciousness— a responsibility that befalls or summons the ego before any initiative or choice of the subject: "Irreducible to consciousness, even if this relation overturns consciousness and manifests itself there—obsession traverses consciousness contrariwise inscribing itself there as something foreign, as disequilibrium, as delirium undoing thematization, eluding *principle*, origin, and will. . . . This movement is, in the original sense of the term, an-archic" (BPW, 81). Coming from an unknown exteriority, from an unknown origin, responsibility is experienced as something foreign to the subject rather than as a commitment the subject assumes freely for herself: "It is *already* a summons of extreme exigency, an obligation which is *anachronistically* prior to every engagement" (BPW 81). As such, obligation is experienced as the breakdown of intentionality, or, as Lyotard puts it, as a displacement of the I from the position of enunciation to the position of the addressee.

In answering the question of how an ethical responsibility can be reflected in consciousness, Levinas argues that consciousness—the for itself—does not exhaust the meaning of the subject. What persists alongside consciousness, and yet is not encompassed by it, is the "living flesh," the embodied ego—or what Levinas calls ipseity. Thus, for Levinas the initial instance of the displacement of the consciousness from the position of enunciation is to be found in the body itself. In a movement evocative of Merleau-Ponty's critique of the primacy of the negativity and transcendence of consciousness (for itself) over the inertia of the body (in itself), Levinas rethinks embodiment not only as the condition of relations to objects but also as a prototype of an ethical experience. In contrast to the transcendence of the body in self-reflection, "oneself," or ipseity, signifies for Levinas an embodied self—a prelogical, presynthetic entwinement of thought and extension, or what Levinas calls "being in one's skin." Following Susan Handelman, we might describe "oneself" as "'the materialist' interruption of the consciousness,"[4] but that designation confronts us with a task of working out the relation between the materiality of the body and language.

The emphasis on embodiment makes it impossible to limit Levinas's theory of discourse to the familiar contrast between the saying and the said. The said, let us recall, represents for Levinas the unity and systematicity of propositional discourse, aiming at synchronizing and establishing relations between different terms. On the philosophical level, the said, with its correlation of the subject and object, structures the discourse of knowledge. On the linguistic level, the said can be approximated to the symbolic order, to the provenance of the signifier and the abstractness of the linguistic code. The saying, on the other hand, reveals a unique ethical dimension of signification that is a precondition of every communicative situation. To disclose the signification of the saying, one needs to shift the analysis of language not only from the notion of the system to what speech-act theorists call the linguistic act, but also from the spontaneity of enunciation to the originary receptivity of the speaking subject. As a condition of communication, the saying signifies an exposure to the other, a possibility of being addressed by the other prior to any intention, need, or demand of the subject. It is a modality of address and contact, a turning toward the other that produces an inversion of the I prior to the narcissistic identification with one's own image. The saying reveals that the original position of the subject qua subject is in the accusative "me" rather than the nominative "I" of enunciation. Although the saying is always already mediated by the said, it nonetheless interrupts and transcends the symbolic order, preserving in this withdrawal the trace of the ethical relation to alterity, the nonthematizable exposure of the subject to the other. It marks a radical displacement not only of philosophical reason, but also of language as system.

Levinasian scholars usually stress an insurmountable dislocation (both temporal and spatial) of these two significations of the said and the saying. Yet, in order to understand Levinas's claim that language is already incarnation, the disjunction between the saying and the said has to be reworked in the context of embodiment and sensibility. While the incarnation of language exposes for Levinas the structuring role of the said in sense perception, the saying allows him to redefine sensibility beyond vision and sight. In its "pre-ontological weight," the said is not merely a system of signs representing reality, but has a constitutive role in perception—"it already bears sensible life" (OB, 35). In its double function of verbalization and nominalization, the order of the said both structures and resolves the ambiguity of sense perception—the ambiguity of the sensed and the sensing, identity, and duration. Verbalization allows the sensible qualities of the perceived things to be transformed into the time of consciousness, whereas nominalization constitutes in this temporal flow the identities of the perceived qualities and endows them with meaning. Although the said reveals the ambiguity of sense perception, at the same time, it synchronizes perception, time, meaning, and consciousness and thus designates the sensible as always already intelligible.

The saying, by contrast, reveals a different sense of sensibility and describes it as the capacity for being affected by the other: "to be in one's skin is an extreme way of being exposed" (OB, 89). By situating the act of enunciation in the context of a response to the other, the saying contests not only the spontaneity but also the disembodied character of enunciation. As Levinas repeatedly argues, the saying, in its corporeal form, is the very signification of sensibility. In contrast to the epistemological significance of sense perception, the saying reveals an ethical sense of sensibility as exposure and vulnerability: "in the form of corporeality, whose movements are fatigue and whose duration is ageing, the passivity of signification, of the one-for-another is not an act, but patience, that is, *of itself sensibility*" (OB, 55; emphasis added). It is a prereflective sensibility characterized by touch rather than by vision: "In starting with *touching*, interpreted not as palpation but as caress, and *language*, interpreted not as the traffic of information but as contact, we have tried to describe *proximity* as irreducible to consciousness" (BPW, 80). Influenced by the late work of Merleau-Ponty, the figure of the touch signifies, as Elizabeth Grosz argues, not the mastering spontaneity of vision, but contiguity, contact, and exposure to the outside.[5] Given the fact that the significance of touch has been elaborated in *The Totality and Infinity* almost exclusively in the context of erotic love, the recurrence of this figure to describe the ethical structure of sensibility will prompt us to ask in the second part of this essay whether ethical passions are separable from eros and sexuality, as Levinas seems to suggest.

By elaborating the ethical import of the sensible, Levinas departs from his earlier insistence in *Totality and Infinity* that the ethical experience transcends the sensible life, although it should be stressed that even in that text he already contests the primacy of vision in order to redefine sensibility as enjoyment: "Sensibility is not a fumbling objectification. Enjoyment, by essence satisfied, characterizes all sensations whose representational content dissolves into their affective content" (TI, 187). And yet, as Levinas argues, since perception reduces the other to the order of knowledge, whereas the complacency of enjoyment reduces the world to the consumption and possession of the subject, ethical relation with the other in *Totality and Infinity* has to transcend both these forms of sensibility: "Total alterity, in which a being does not refer to enjoyment and presents itself out of itself, does not shine forth in the *form* by which things are given to us.... The relation with the Other alone introduces a dimension of transcendence, and leads us to a relation totally different from experience in the sensible sense of the term, relative and egoist" (TI, 192–93). It is precisely this separation of ethical responsibility from the sensible life that Levinas contests in *Otherwise Than Being*. In so doing, he overcomes, as Tina Chanter suggests, a certain formalism of the ethical relation that still persists in *Totality and Infinity*.[6] This new development in Levinas's ethics means not only that the disjunction of the said and the saying does not transcend the order of the sensible, but also that it creates a similar noncoincidence between the epistemological and the ethical forms of sensibility. As Alphonso Lingis, among others, suggests, it is a noncoincidence between the epistemological function of sense perception and an ethical significance of the exposure to exteriority.[7]

It is this inseparability of body and language, of expression and sensibility, I argue, that opens a productive engagement between Levinas's ethics and feminism. Like much of contemporary feminist theory, Levinas's ethics contests the disembodied subject of enunciation and the corresponding reduction of language to formalism. In particular, we can see here parallels between Levinas and Luce Irigaray, who likewise rejects those accounts of the linguistic constitution of the subject that ignore the function of embodiment. As she writes in An Ethics of Sexual Difference, "[T]he subject who enunciates the law is, they tell us, irrelevant, bodiless, morphologically undetermined ... the net of a language which he believes he controls but which controls him, imprisons him in a bodiless body, in a fleshless other, in laws whose cause, source, and physical living reason he has lost."[8] For both Levinas and Irigaray, the intersection of embodiment and language does not entail a reduction of the body to the passive surface of inscription and the corresponding abstraction of language from the body, but, on the contrary, exposes the ambiguity inherent in the constitution of the body.

For Levinas this ambiguity of constitution emerges already in the phenomenological reduction of the body. In an attempt to constitute the flesh as the objective body, consciousness finds itself already dependent on incarnation: "Flesh then, as objective body, is thus constituted for consciousness out of 'powers' that are already tributary to this body. Consciousness turns out to have already called upon what it is only just supposed to be constituting" (OS, 97). For Levinas as for Merleau-Ponty, this anachronism is not a vicious circle, but a revelation of "the original incarnation of thought" (OS, 97). Although it can be belatedly grasped by consciousness as the objective body, embodiment reveals a prior "intimate" exteriority on which consciousness and language themselves depend[9]: "The irreducible circumscribed here does not come from a non-interiorizable outside, an absolute transcendence. In constituting consciousness itself ..., a paradoxical ambiguity appears; the texture of constituting is stitched with threads coming also from the constituted, without that provenance having had to answer to any 'intentional aim.'"[10] This ambiguity of the constituted and the constituting means that embodiment cannot be confused with either the biological body or the passive receptivity of matter: "The fundamental concept of ipseity, while tied to incarnation, is not a biological concept" (BPW, 87). Yet, and this might be even more important, it also means that the significance of embodiment cannot be reduced to its historical constitution—

it is not "a uniqueness of natural or historical conjuncture" (BPW, 84). As Levinas argues, embodiment is already "the inaugural event of culture': "Culture does not come along and add extra axiological attributes, which are already secondary and grounded, onto a prior grounding representation of the thing. The cultural is essentially embodied thought expressing itself, the very life of flesh manifesting ... original significance of the meaningful or the intelligible" (OS, 110). Thus, the ambiguity of incarnation—the anachronism of the constituted and the constituting—cannot be resolved into the classical oppositions of nature and history, body and language, passivity and activity, but makes both sides of these oppositions undecidable. Instead of privileging one side of these oppositions over the other, Levinas elaborates the chiasmic inversion of the body and language: the obverse side of the incarnation of language is the linguistic constitution of the bodily self and vice versa. Just as language for Levinas cannot be abstracted from the body, so too the singularity of the embodied self cannot be indicated except through catachresis, through the improper borrowing of the personal pronoun: "As an original non-quiddity—no-one—clothed as a being by a pure borrowing that masks its nameless singularity by bestowing it with a role, the fulcrum of a mind is a personal pronoun" (BPW, 85).

The most productive engagement between Levinas's ethics and feminism can occur in the context of the ethical interpretation of embodiment. This turn toward the ethical significance of the body that I try to elaborate in this essay does not deny the fact that the materialization of the body occurs, as the work of Michel Foucault and Judith Butler has shown us, in the matrix of the discursive power relations. This insight is consonant not only with a mediation of embodiment through the order of the said, but also with Levinas's critique of the internal relation between discourse and domination. Exposing the inherent connection between knowledge and power, Levinas claims that "it is in the association of philosophy with the State and with medicine that the break-up of discourse is surmounted. The interlocutor that does not yield to logic is threatened with prison or the asylum or undergoes the prestige of the master and the medication of the doctor" (OB, 170). By extending Levinas's claims about power and language to the constitution of the bodies, we can say that this constitution reveals the *political character of all logical rationalism, the alliance of logic with politics*" (OB, 171; emphasis added). And yet the very ambiguity of the bodily constitution also means that the linguistic materialization of the body in Levinas's philosophy cannot be limited exclusively to the political order of the said; it also implies an anarchic ethics of embodiment, which interrupts and retreats from the said. Thus, perhaps the most original contribution of Levinas's work to the contemporary debates on the body lies in the fact that it enables the elaboration of the ethical significance of flesh and, by extension, opens a possibility of an ethics of eros. Even though this possibility is never real-ized in Levinas's own work, and even though his own conception of eros and femininity remains entangled in both patriarchal and metaphysical traditions, the necessary interdependence of responsibility and incarna-tion paves the way, thanks to Luce Irigaray's intervention, to the feminist ethics of sexual difference.

The ethical significance of the body is, indeed, what is at stake in Levinas's redefinition of corporeal schematism. Given the chiasmic structure of body and language, it is not surprising that Levinas argues in *Otherwise Than Being* that "the concept of the incarnate subject is not a biological concept. The schema that corporeality outlines submits the biological itself to a higher structure" (OB, 109). What is this schema that makes embodiment a "condition" of an ethical experience of uncon-ditional responsibility? In what way does the corporeal schematism make the lived body already an effect of substitution, of one being for the other? Levinas redefines here the notion of corporeal schematism elabo-rated by Merleau-Ponty in the *The Primacy of Perception*, where the body schema, modeled on Lacan's notion of the mirror stage, both guarantees the coherence of the embodied ego and provides a map of the possible relations to objects and to others: "A 'corporeal or postural schema' gives us at every moment a global, practical, and implicit notion of the relation between our body and things, or our hold on them."[11] More evocative of Merleau-Ponty's later work on the dehiscence of the flesh elaborated in *The Visible and Invisible*, Levinas's schematism does not stress the unifica-tion of the embodied ego but exposes disproportion or constriction char-acteristic of bodily "identity." One can see here a certain parallel between Levinas's revision of schematism and Irigaray's redefinition of the psycho-analytic concept of the imaginary, also inspired by Merleau-Ponty's *The Visible and The Invisible*. Although for Levinas the schematism of the body makes the constitution of the body already dependent on the relation to the outside, this relation is no longer understood, as it is still the case in Merleau-Ponty, in terms of the subjective mastery over things, but, rather, as the "hold" of exteriority on the subject. Preceding the identification with the visual schema, which, indeed, guarantees the mastery of the ego and the unification of the body, the bodily schematism Levinas briefly outlines has the structure of torsion, or constriction, rather than that of the visual container: "The body is not merely an image or a figure; above all, it is the in-oneself and contraction of ipseity" (BPW, 87).

Understood as torsion and constriction, the schematism of embodiment unhinges the classical relation between matter and form. Unlike the materiality of matter, which is defined in terms of the unity with its form, the materiality of embodiment is characterized by a disproportion or noncoincidence with form, which, nonetheless, does not imply a disjunction between different terms. It is the movement of contraction, or the spasm of matter, that traces the knot of ipseity: "The ego is *in itself* not like matter is in itself, which perfectly wedded to its form, is what it is. The ego is in itself like one is in one's skin, that is to say, cramped, ill at ease in one's skin, as though the identity of matter weighing on itself concealed a dimension allowing a withdrawal this side of immediate coincidence, as though it concealed a materiality more material than all matter" (BPW, 86). This schematism of embodiment does not unify the ego but, on the contrary, inscribes the noncoincidence with oneself within the very heart of bodily identity and makes it the basis of the ego's relation to the others. It is as if the exposure to the radical exteriority were coextensive with the constitution of the lived body.

Enabling and preceding the movement of loss and recovery characteristic of the identification of consciousness with itself, this paradoxical structure of embodiment signifies an irremissible attachment to oneself, which, at the same time, coincides with the radical exposure to the outside. If one can still preserve the term of identity for such a knot in which exposure to exteriority constitutes what is most intimately one's own, it is, as Levinas reminds us, an identity of nonessence. That is why Levinas prefers the term *singularity*, which for him precedes the opposition between the particular and the general. As Levinas writes in an extremely suggestive passage, evocative of Luce Irigaray's language of mucous and elemental passions, "[T]hat this unity be a torsion and a restlessness, irreducible to the function that the oneself exercises in the ontology . . . presents a problem. It is as though the atomic unity of the subject were exposed outside by breathing, by divesting its ultimate substance even to the mucous membrane of the lungs, *continually splitting up*" (OB, 107; emphasis added). The decisive difference between Irigaray and Levinas lies, however, in the fact that for Irigaray such a schematism of embodiment enables an ethical redefinition of both female embodiment—her being neither one nor two—and cros, while for Levinas it is tied to the anguish of the unsexed subject.

The negativity of constriction marks the singularity of the lived body in contradictory terms of the withdrawal from consciousness and the impossibility of slipping away from one's body. Similarly, this negativity reveals the anarchic withdrawal of the body from the order of the said while at the same time maintaining the impossibility of abstracting language from the body. The materiality of embodiment, its paradoxical identity without essence, signifies the impossibility of taking distance from one's body, the impossibility of transcending one's skin: "Unlike consciousness, which loses itself so as to find itself again in the retentions and protensions of its time, the oneself does not slacken the knot attaching it to the self only to tie it once more.... The oneself is the irremissible identity that has no need to prove or thematize this identity" [BPW, 85]. This is another sense in which the materiality of embodiment is more "material" than matter because the opacity of the body withdraws from the immediate coincidence with consciousness, form, and language. Always already mediated and yet withdrawn from the said, incarnation indicates a paradoxical exile, or even the splitting of the ego, without, however, being a cause of alienation or separation of the self from itself. As Levinas writes, "[I]t is ... a withdrawal *in itself*, an exile *in itself*, without foundation in anything else, a noncondition. It is withdrawal without spontaneity, and thus always already over, always already past" (BPW, 85). Despite this retreat, the "oneself" does not become ecstatic, but, in Luce Irigaray's terms, remains an "in-stant." The inability of the ego to flee from one's own skin, despite the fact that the body is always already withdrawn from the ego, becomes for Levinas a paradigm of ethical responsibility that befalls the subject prior to any initiative. Interpreted in ethical terms, being in one's skin signifies an exposure to accusation, the impossibility of fleeing responsibility.

"More material than matter," the constriction of embodiment does not signify for Levinas a mere limitation or "excidence" of being, but is already an effect of a prior ethical relation to the other—an effect, as Levinas puts it, of "having-the-other-in-one's-skin" (OB, 115). Drawing on the Latin etymology of the word *anguish* (*angustia*), Levinas describes this constriction in the following way: "Here are we obliged to speak of the irremissibility and the anguish (in the etymological sense of the term).... This anguish is not the existential 'being toward death' but the constriction of an 'entry within,' which is not a flight into the void

but a passage into the fullness of anxiety of contraction" (86). By referring to the Latin (rather than the Greek) etymology of the word anguish,
Levinas dissociates the movement of constriction from the Heideggerian
"being toward death" and describes it instead as the exposure to the
other, a passage into responsibility up to the point of substitution for
another. Susan Handelman suggests that the inspiration for this redefinition of constriction might come from the Jewish kabalistic tradition of
tzimtzum: "[T]here is an interesting analogy here to the kabalistic idea of
God's creation ... through God's self-contraction—tzimtzum—rather
than expansion.... for Levinas, the emptying out or contraction of the
subject is what opens it to the positivity of ethical relation, not the negativity of the abyss."[12] It is perhaps this Jewish sense of constriction as
creation that allows Levinas to rethink the relation between body
schematism and negativity: Being in one's skin' could certainly be called
negativity (albeit a negativity prior to discourse as the indisputable
homeland of dialectical negativity)" (BPW, 86).

In order to distinguish the negativity of embodiment both from the
dialectical negation and from the existential void of being, Levinas interprets constriction as both the possibility and the effect of the relation to
the other: "[N]egativity without the void of nonbeing, negativity entangled in its own impossibility, outside of all initiative, an incredible withdrawal into fullness, without any detachment from self, is an impossibility
of slipping away" (BPW, 87). In her reading of Levinas, Luce Irigaray
redefines this ethical relation to the other in terms of sexual desire. For
Irigaray, the constriction of embodiment creates an interval between
matter and form as the very place of desire between the sexes: "Desire
occupies the place of the interval.... Desire demands a sense of attraction: a change in the interval, the displacement of the subject or of the
object in their relations of nearness" (ESD, 8).

Although Levinas wishes to separate sexual relations from ethics, he
nonetheless locates the ethical import of embodiment in the anarchic
susceptibility to obsession and passion: "All the transfers of sentiment ...
could not take root in the ego were it not, in its entire being, or rather its
entire nonbeing, subjected not to a category, as in the case of matter, but
to an unlimited accusative" (BPW, 91). An ethical body is, in other
words, a passionate body. Such a passionate body is a condition of being
in the accusative, of responsibility, and of substitution: "Obsession ... is
anarchic. It accuses me on the hither side of prime matter seized by the
category" (BPW, 78). For Levinas, carnality and passion are in fact the
only analogues capable of conveying the anteriority of responsibility to

freedom: "[T]his formulation expresses a way of being affected that can in no way be invested by spontaneity: the subject is affected without the source of the affection becoming a theme of re-presentation" (BPW, 81). Only the notion of passion verging on delirium can capture the inversion of intentionality and the disturbance of consciousness without converting this disturbance into representation: "Consciousness is thus afflicted before entertaining an image of what reaches it, afflicted in spite of itself" (BPW, 82).

The originality of Levinas's emphasis on the ethical significance of passion, sensibility, and embodiment is particularly striking in the context of his departure from the Kantian legacy: Levinas contests not only the symmetry between responsibility and freedom, which means that responsibilities cannot be freely chosen or assumed by the ethical subject, but also the purification of ethical imperatives from all "pathological passions." In his *Critique of Practical Reason*, Kant attempts to curtail the anarchic force of the categorical obligation by maintaining the interchangeability between obligation and freedom on the one hand, and obligation and the law, on the other. The reversed deduction of the categorical imperative—the moral law taken as a premise for the negative deduction of freedom—aims to establish the equivalence between a specific obligation ("act in such as way") and the universal norm ("so that the maxim of your will can always be valid as the principle of a universal legislation also"). By rewriting obligation as the universal principle, Kant, as Lyotard points out, reduces prescriptive to the metalanguage of norms, and, thus, to descriptive statements: "[I]t is in this metalanguage of norms that, according to Kant, the maxim of a particular action can be declared the principle of a universal legislation."[13] Yet, as Levinas's ethics implies, another consequence of this reduction of responsibility to the metalanguage of the law lies in the separation of duty from the body and passions. Levinas's intervention thus destroys the series of equivalences set up by the categorical imperative: between obligation and law, between obligation and freedom, and finally, between the addressee of the prescriptive and the subject of enunciation. For Levinas the scandal of these equivalences betrays not only "the ego's infatuation with knowledge," but also the suppression of the body and passion. As Alphonso Lingis suggests, Levinas "reverses the Kantian position; for him responsibility, sensitivity to others, does not conflict with, mortify, sensibility for mundane beings, but makes it possible."[14] No longer mediated by the universal law, ethical obligation finds its form in sensibility.[15]

Yet this radical potential of Levinas's work is undercut at the moment it confronts sexuality. Levinas's fidelity in *Otherwise Than Being or Beyond Essence* to the ethical significance of incarnation, sensibility, and passion should have led him to discuss what Luce Irigaray calls an ethical encounter "in embodied love." What prevents Levinas from taking this decisive step? While Levinas admits passions into the realm of ethics, he himself repeats the classical Kantian gesture of purification and dissociates those passions from any relation with sex. I would argue that such a purification assumes in Levinas's work two forms: ethical masochism and sublimation. In good Kantian fashion, Levinas can maintain the separation of ethics from sexuality at the price of reducing the ethical significance of passion to pain. In so doing, Levinas's work remains vulnerable to the critique of the Kantian ethics advanced by Lacanian psychoanalysis. As Slavoj Zizek observes, for Lacan Kant's "very renunciation of 'pathological' enjoyment (the wiping out of all 'pathological' content) brings about a certain surplus enjoyment" in pain itself.[16] And if in Kant's case, this surplus of obscene enjoyment in the very stringency of the law can be compared to the sadism of the superego, what does guarantee that in Levinas's work the anguish of the ethical subject does not collapse into a secret enjoyment of the pain itself, into an original ethical masochism? To forestall such a possibility, is it not necessary to elaborate an ethics of sex rather than to exclude eroticism from of the domain of ethics?

The other way Levinas avoids an ethics of eros is through the process of sublimation associated in his work with the idea of divine creation. For Levinas, the ethical character of embodiment ultimately finds its expression not in sexuality, but in God's creation: "Does not this thought, in its absolute diachrony, in the noninstant of creation, where the self called to being is not there to hear this call it obeys, conceive an unlimited and anarchic passivity of the creature?" (BPW, 89). This turn to divine creativity, and to its earthly counterpart, the passionless motherhood, suggests not so much a suppression of sexuality as its idealizing sublimation, which exists side by side with a certain hostility (in Levinas's terms, "violation" and "disrespect" [TI, 260, 262]) to the nonsublimated form of eros represented by femininity. As the obverse side of sublimated love, femininity in Levinas's work is relegated to animality, profanation, shame, indecency, irresponsible infancy, and so on, and thus associated with all terms that evoke and justify the Kantian exclusion of "pathological passions" from the domain of ethics.

In her critique of Levinas, Irigaray is particularly attentive to the violence inherent in this oscillation between sublimation and debasement of eros in Levinas's work. Unable to imagine the ethics of sexuality, Levinas's male lover eventually turns toward the transcendent God, while the woman is plunged back into the abyss of the nonhuman—"the not yet of the infant" or no longer that of animal. As Irigaray claims, this masculine sublimation of eroticism prevents Levinas from seeing an expression of divinity in woman's sensibility and in the act of love itself. As she points out, "[T]he loved one would be relegated to the abyss so that the lover might be sent back to the heights. The act of love would amount to contact with the irrationality of discourse, in order to send the loved one back to the position of fallen animal" and man to the ecstasy in God.[17] Yet, if the turn to God justifies, like an alibi, the disrespect for eros and femininity, then this conception of divinity is itself at fault. According to Irigaray, "[I]f some God obliterates respect for the other as other, this God stands as the guarantee of a deadly infinity."[18]

To exit this deadly circle of sublimation and debasement, and to prevent the disjunction between the spiritual creation and degraded eroticism of the flesh (in Irigaray's terms, the split between the Angel and the mucous), Irigaray shifts Levinas's discussion of passion, embodiment, and sensibility in the direction an ethics of sexual difference. Consider, for instance, Irigaray's redefinition of ethical passion as erotic wonder:

> Who or what the other is, I never know. But the other who is forever unknowable is the one who differs from me sexually. This feeling of surprise, astonishment, and wonder in the face of the unknowable ought to be returned to its locus: that of sexual difference. The passions have either been repressed, stifled, or reduced, or reserved for God.... But it is never found to reside in this locus: *Between man and woman.* Into this place came attraction, greed, possession, consummation, disgust, and so on. But not the wonder which beholds what it sees as if for the first time, never taking hold of the other as its object. (ESD, 13)

For Irigaray, the redefinition of wonder as an erotic passion escapes the pitfalls of both moral masochism and disembodied sublimation. In her reading of Descartes, Irigaray argues that wonder, the astonishment provoked by the totally other, is the ethical passion par excellence. Her point is that wonder, as the first passion, precedes the very opposition of pleasure and unpleasure, and by implication, Levinas's distinction between narcissistic enjoyment and ethical anguish. As Irigaray writes,

"This passion has no opposite or contradiction and exists always as though for the first time" (ESD, 12). Consequently, despite its privileged position in Levinas's and Kant's ethics, pain for Irigaray is a secondary emotion, already dependent on a judgement whether the encounter with the other is agreeable to the subject or not.

When returned to the locus of sexual difference, wonder does not compromise the ethical alterity of the lover, but on the contrary, registers the fact that this erotic encounter is wholly different form all expectations, demands, or knowledge. Rather than being an expression of egoism, eroticism, Irigaray argues, suspends our schemas and definitions, enabling us to encounter "the other not transformable into discourse, fantasms, or dreams, the other for whom it is impossible that I substitute any other, any thing, any god."[19] The eroticization of wonder prevents, therefore, the degradation of sexuality, still evident in Levinas's work, either to "the complacent pleasure of dual egoism" (TI, 266) or to the sublime "coveting" of the son.

The ethical significance of eroticism suggested by Irigaray, I argue, does not do violence to Levinas's concept of embodiment, but revises his discussion of passivity and temporality. For Irigaray, the ethics of eros is a peculiar act of desublimation, which restores to sexual pleasure its status of creation, reserved in Levinas's work for God. As she writes, "[E]ither pleasure is a mere expenditure ... or else it is a unique and definite creation."[20] This creativity of erotic pleasure complicates Levinas's claim that ethical passions reveal the anarchic passivity of the body. We have to dwell for a moment on Levinas's paradoxical formulation of the anarchic passivity. As we have already seen, for Levinas the ambiguity of the constituting and the constituted make the classical opposition between the passive matter and active form untenable. The anarchic character of passivity—the inversion of the imperialism of consciousness—is another example where this opposition breaks down. Levinas launches a twofold objection against the ways the concept of passive matter has been theorized in the philosophical tradition. First, the notion of passive matter implies "the pure submission" to a form or category and thus guarantees the privilege granted to logos and meaning: "Things as "prime matter" bear the weight of the kerygmatic logos, which gives this matter its characteristics.... The logos that informs prime matter in calling it to order is ... a category" (BPW, 87). Furthermore, despite the submission to form, matter in the philosophical tradition is still envisioned as an obdurate power: "As a potential being, prime matter remains a power which form takes into account. It is not by chance that Plato speaks of the indestructibility of matter or that Aristotle views matter as a *cause*" (BPW, 87). To depart from this tradition, Levinas claims that the ethical passivity of embodiment lies not in the submission of matter to form, or matter to discourse, but in the anarchic susceptibility to pas-sion. For Irigaray, however, the passionate erotic body is never passive. As she insists, erotic passion, prior to any procreation or "coveting" of the child, is already a creation in itself: "having to create, give birth to, engender, the mystery she bears—prior to any conception of a child."[21] Rather than transcending the sexed body, as does sublimation, the erotic creation consists in the transformation of the flesh itself, in the rebirth of the lovers bestowing life on each other.

In such an act of creation, lovers give each other time and the future. Irigaray's emphasis on time in erotic pleasure further complicates Levinas's discussion of the temporal structure of embodiment. What is absolutely crucial for Irigaray is that Levinas does not discuss embodiment primarily in spatial terms as the location of perspective, but elaborates the tem-porality of the body. For Irigaray, however, the time of flesh cannot be limited exclusively to Levinas's "diachrony of aging."[22] Levinas focuses on aging in order to suggest a correspondence between the temporality of the body and the diachrony of the trace of the other. According to Levinas, the temporality of the body is irreducible to the mastery of the past in memory or the projects for the future: it is not "the flux of time bit-ing into the future while conserving a past.... [It] does not lend itself to either a synthetic activity or recollection, or anticipation" (BPW, 84). In the aging process, the temporality of the body presents itself as a passive synthesis, as the very lapse of time irretrievable by memory. In a similar way, the trace of the other also signifies for Levinas an "utterly bygone past," which nonetheless troubles the present. As he writes, "[N]o memory could follow the traces of this past. It is an immemorial past" (TO, 355). Although in "The Trace of the Other" Levinas argues that such an im-memorial past can only be experienced in the encounter with the other, in "Substitution" he locates such temporality already in the withdrawal of the body from the time of consciousness. Just as the trace of the other is incommensurate with the order of the said, so too the recurrence of the flesh, the passive synthesis of aging, evades the time of consciousness.

In her critique, Irigaray claims that this limitation of the recurrence of flesh to what Levinas calls "the dead time" of aging is already a symptom of the exclusion of sexual pleasure from ethics. The darker side of this exclusion lies in the fact that the male lover invariably seeks to recover from the passive synthesis of aging through the procreation of the son. As Levinas admits in *Totality and Infinity*, "[T]he relation with the child … establishes relationship with the absolute future, or infinite time. … In fecundity the tedium of … repetition ceases; the I is other and young. … Fecundity continues history without producing old age (TI, 268). The juxtaposition of *Totality and Infinity* with *Otherwise Than Being* demonstrates that aging and procreation are structural counterparts, and one cannot revise one without challenging the other. That is why Irigaray's emphasis on the time of sexual pleasure is decisive, because it opens another ethical dimension of temporality, irreducible either to the dead time of aging or to the future announced by procreation. What lovers create in sexual love is a future prior to the procreation of the child: "a future coming, which is not measured by the transcendence of death but by the call to birth of the self and the other. … Searching for what has not yet come into being, for himself, he invites me to become what I have not yet become."[23] This relation with the future in sexual pleasure is not transformed into a power, anticipation, or project of the subject, but resembles very closely the Levinasian idea of infinity. To use and displace Levinas's own description of fecundity, we can say that the time of sexual pleasure, "both my own and not-mine, a possibility of myself but also a possibility of the other," simply does not enter "into the logical essence of the possible" (TI, 276).

In the end I would like to suggest that even though Levinas fails to address the question of ethics of sexual difference, his work in fact does reconfigure the masculine side of this difference. As Levinas himself puts it, his work suspends the "virile and heroic" conception of masculinity in the Western philosophical tradition, by exposing the masculine subject to the constriction of embodiment, passivity of aging, vulnerability, and passion. What the feminine side might look like in the light of Levinas's ethics liberated from the restrictions of the patriarchal thought—well, the answer to this question is still very much a matter of invention.

Notes

1. The following abbreviations of Levinas's texts will be used in this chapter: BPW: *Basic Philosophical Writings*, ed. Adriaan T. Peperzak, Simon Critchley, and Robert Bernasconi (Bloomington:

Indiana University Press, 1996); OB: *Otherwise Than Being or Beyond Essence*, trans. A. Lingis (The Hague: Martinus Nijhoff, 1981); TI: *Totality and Infinity*, trans. A. Lingis (Pittsburgh: Duquesne University Press, 1969); TO: "The Trace of the Other," in *Deconstruction in Context: Literature and Philosophy*, ed. Mark Taylor (Chicago: University of Chicago Press, 1986).

2. Simon Critchley, *The Ethics of Deconstruction: Derrida and Levinas* (Oxford: Blackwell, 1992), 179.

3. Tina Chanter, *Ethics of Eros: Irigaray's Rewriting of the Philosophers* (New York: Routledge, 1995), 207.

4. Susan A. Handelman, *Fragments of Redemption: Jewish Thought and Literary Theory in Benjamin, Scholem, and Levinas* (Bloomington: Indiana University Press, 1991), 254.

5. Elizabeth Grosz, *Volatile Bodies: Toward A Corporeal Feminism* (Bloomington: Indiana University Press, 1994), 98.

6. Chanter, *Ethics of Eros*, 198.

7. Alphonso Lingis, "The Sensuality and Sensibility," in *Face to Face with Levinas*, ed. Richard A. Cohen (Albany: State University of New York Press, 1986), 220–21.

8. Luce Irigaray, *An Ethics of Sexual Difference*, trans. Carolyn Burke and Gillian C. Gill (Ithaca: Cornell University Press, 1993), 133. Subsequent references to this text will be marked parenthetically in the text as ESD.

9. Susan Handelman writes that for Levinas "the body itself is a paradigmatic example of an exteriority not constituted by my consciousness." Levinas's discussion of the anachronism of bodily constitution is, however, more complex: the body can always be constituted by consciousness (and reduced to the status of the objective body) but it is this act of constitution that reveals the prior embodiment of consciousness itself.

10. Emmanuel Levinas, "In Memory of Alphonse de Waelhens" in *Outside the Subject*, trans. Michael B. Smith (Stanford: Stanford University Press, 1993), 108. Subsequent references will be marked in the text as OS.

11. Maurice Merleau-Ponty, "An Unpublished Text," trans. Arleen B. Dallery, in *The Primacy of Perception and Other Essays*, ed. James M. Eddie (Evanston: Northwestern University Press, 1964), 5. Merleau-Ponty stresses his indebtedness to Lacan's "Mirror Stage" in the essay "The Child's Relations with Others," 136.

12. Handelman, *Fragments of Redemption*, 259.

13. Jean-François Lyotard, "Levinas's Logic" in *The Lyotard Reader*, ed. Andrew Benjamin (Oxford: Basil Blackwell, 1989), 294.

14. Alphonso Lingis, "The Sensuality and Sensibility" in Cohen, *Face to Face with Levinas*, 224.

15. This point is also stressed by Critchley, in *The Ethics of Deconstruction*, 180.

16. Slavoj Zizek, *For They Know Not What They Do: Enjoyment as a Political Factor* (New York: Verso, 1991), 231.

17. Luce Irigaray, "The Fecundity of Caress," trans. Carolyn Burke, in Cohen, *Face to Face with Levinas*, 241.

18. "The Fecundity of the Caress," 247.

19. Irigaray, "The Fecundity of the Caress," 255.

20. Luce Irigaray, "Questions to Emmanuel Levinas," in *The Irigaray Reader*, ed. Margaret Whitford (Oxford: Basil Blackwell, 1991), 181.

21. "The Fecundity of the Caress," 242.

22. For an illuminating discussion of the temporality of the body in Levinas's ethics, see Handelman, *Fragments of Redemption*, 253.

23. "The Fecundity of Caress," 232–33.

4

The Delightful Other

Portraits of the Feminine in Kierkegaard, Nietzsche, and Levinas

Sonia Sikka

I would guess that most scholars of Levinas are by now acquainted with Simone de Beauvoir's brief critical remark, in *The Second Sex*, regarding Levinas's description of the feminine as absolutely other.[1] Among those who have addressed themselves to this remark, the most common position seems to be that, although there are indeed some problems with Levinas's depictions of the feminine in a number of his works, Beauvoir's criticism, directed toward *Time and the Other*, is founded on a fundamentally mistaken interpretation of the basic role of the feminine qua other within the overall structure of Levinas's thought. R. J. S. Manning, for instance, defends Levinas against Beauvoir while acknowledging that at points his patriarchal language demonstrates how "even Levinas's ethico-philosophical project of 'ethics as first philosophy' still is not

ethical enough."² Manning's main claim is that Levinas is not opposing
an exclusively feminine object to an exclusively masculine subject, nor is
he "asserting masculine privilege by labeling and naming women," as
Beauvoir supposes (133). On the contrary, Levinas's philosophy challenges all such violent appropriations of the other, and is therefore "an
ally in the ethical struggle against the oppression of women which is feminism" (137).

Manning is doubtless right to maintain that, in *Time and the Other*,
"the alterity and mystery of the feminine" in the erotic relation indicates,
for Levinas, "the absolute alterity of every Other" (136–37), an alterity
that ethics, as first philosophy, is supposed to respect. Nonetheless, there
is a disturbing continuity between Levinas's portrayals of the feminine
other, in *Time and the Other* and elsewhere, and the portrayals analyzed
critically by Beauvoir. This continuity should make one wary, I believe,
of seeing in Levinas a friend of feminism.

In this chapter, I intend to support Beauvoir's negative appraisal of
Levinas on the feminine other. To do so, I will examine three forms of
feminine otherness that can be located in Levinas's writings and will com-
pare these with similar and parallel themes in Kierkegaard and Nietzsche.
Kierkegaard and Nietzsche are two other relatively recent thinkers whose
remarks on the feminine and on women are on the surface clearly sexist—and particularly from the point of view of a feminism such as Beauvoir's—but who have been the objects of some qualified feminist defense.
With respect to the feminine, all three of these authors—Kierkegaard,
Nietzsche, and Levinas—clearly emphasize and value alterity, of one
form or another. In criticizing their accounts, I want to vindicate what is
likely to be a twentieth-century feminist's first, primarily negative, reaction to these portraits of women. I thereby also want to question the
notion of alterity, or at least of *radical* alterity, as a model for either ethics
in general or feminism in particular.

On this last point, I should admit from the beginning that I recognize
myself in the conception of subjectivity presupposed by Beauvoir as
applying to both men and women, and do not recognize myself in the
accounts of women's consciousness proposed by feminisms that focus on
radical alterity. I do not therefore assume that the latter are simply
wrong, since I understand that the feminism that suits me will not suit
every woman, given that not every woman is just like me. However, one
cannot accuse Beauvoir, and those of us sympathetic to her analysis, of
not wanting to be, or of refusing to be, "women" without begging the

question in a highly illegitimate fashion. And there are good reasons, I will argue, to be nervous about Levinas's use of the motif of feminine alterity, and about feminist appropriations of this motif.

Woman as Break

An important aspect of feminine alterity in the portraits of woman painted by Kierkegaard, Nietzsche, and Levinas consists in the representation of her as a "break" from everyday masculine existence. The senses of *break* that I have in mind here are well expressed by the *Concise Oxford Dictionary* (seventh edition) in its definitions of the term as "gap" or "interruption of continuity" as well as "short spell of recreation or refreshment between periods of work." These definitions aptly describe one element of the way Judge William portrays woman, for example, in Kierkegaard's *Either/Or II*.[3] The parable of the classical scholar, whose wife blows away the dot that he had taken to be an unknown vowel marking but that is in fact just a grain of snuff that has fallen onto the page (E/O II, 309), provides an excellent illustration. The scholar is engrossed, to the point of obsession, in the seriousness and abstractness of his daily work, which is connected with the larger world outside the home. His wife, whose concern lies with concrete existence of the domestic variety, provides for him a break from the difficulty and the unending drive toward accomplishment that characterize his own masculine existence, thereby rooting him back in the finite.

According to Judge William, this orientation toward the finite constitutes woman's fundamental nature. As opposed to man, who restlessly aspires toward the infinite, woman is supposedly happy in the finite and is therefore "in harmony with existence as no man can or ought to be." This makes her, unlike any man, "exquisite" and "lovely" (E/O II, 311). His own wife exemplifies these characteristics. "What she does I cannot explain," he says, "but she does it all with a charm and graciousness, with an indescribable lightness, does it without preliminaries and ceremony, like a bird singing its aria" (E/O II, 308). This putative nature also indicates the function of woman, and ultimately Judge William describes woman in terms of this supposed function, which is in turn defined in terms of her value for man. She is said to have first approached man as a "child," wishing only "to be a solace to him, to alleviate his need" (E/O II, 311), which she does presumably through her charming and birdlike graciousness. Through her "absolute virtuosity for explaining the finite" (E/O II, 310) and for dignifying the minutiae of life, which are her domain, woman prepares an abode for man, who otherwise would have none, being ever restless through his relation to the infinite (E/O II, 313).

Judge William has no mean estimation of the value of this function, calling woman "man's deepest life" (E/O II, 310). But it remains true that she is defined in terms of her value to man, and this relation is not reciprocal. That is, while woman and man certainly need one another, his definition, although it includes a relation to her as a necessary condition for him, does not include being a means for her own accomplishment of herself. Moreover, given that, for Kierkegaard, the highest possibility of human existence consists in achieving a synthesis of the finite and the infinite,[4] one cannot avoid drawing the conclusion that man is finally capable of a higher existence than woman is. She is, after all, allegedly happy in the finite, while he, through the anchorage she provides on the one hand and his own relation to the infinite on the other, may attain an ideal of spiritual maturity that surpasses her own.[5]

These criticisms do not, however, reach the essence of what makes Judge William's portrayal of woman fundamentally objectionable. The deepest problem with this portrayal is also the most obvious one: namely, that it is simply not true, and this is because it has been constructed through an inner conversation of man with himself, rather than through any genuine dialogue in which women are allowed to say, for themselves, who they are and what they wish to be. By this point in the nineteenth century, it was certainly possible for a man, like Kierkegaard, to entertain the thought that a woman might prefer to be, and therefore have found it in her nature to be, a scholar rather than a much-needed break for a scholar, or that she might not experience her own activity as charmingly birdlike, or that she might find it incredible to find herself described as happy in the finite, having never experienced any such happiness. Kierkegaard does not entertain this thought because he does not wish to. Judge William believes that emancipation would result in a corruption of woman (E/O II, 311–13) because she would thereby lose her enchantment as the ideally different. She would then no longer be able to fulfill her role—which he of course values highly—as a lovely and exquisite break from the troubled seriousness of masculine existence. The monologue underlying this portrait of the feminine is a monologue of desire.

However highly it esteems women, the estimation is ultimately rooted in self-centeredness and tyranny.

Nietzsche's treatment of the same theme, for all its patent misogyny, at least has the virtue of recognizing that the vision of woman as the ideally different is based on a lie. He, too, extols the value of woman as break in no uncertain terms: "When a man stands in the midst of his own noise, in the midst of his own surf of plans and projects, then he is apt also to see quiet, magical beings gliding past him and to long for their happiness and seclusion: *women*. He almost thinks that his better self dwells there among the women, and that in these quiet regions even the loudest surf turns into deathly quiet, and life itself into a dream about life."[6] But this dream is an illusion. It requires distance (the title of this passage is "Women and their action at a distance") and is destroyed by familiarity with the real beings upon whom the ideal is projected. To be sure, Nietzsche almost always describes the reality of these beings in predominantly negative terms, here commenting that "even on the most beautiful sailboat there is a lot of noise, and unfortunately much small and petty noise" (124).

He often also claims that women themselves promote the illusion that attracts men to them. In *Beyond Good and Evil*, he says of woman that "her great art is the lie, her supreme concern is appearance and beauty," adding, "Let us confess it, we men: it is precisely *this* art and *this* instinct in woman which we love and honour: we who have a hard time and for our refreshment like to associate with creatures under whose hands, glances and tender follies our seriousness, our gravity and profundity appear to us almost as folly."[7] As in Judge William's parable of the scholar, the value of the feminine resides here in its providing, for "we who have a hard time," meaning "we men," a break, a relief and release, from the supposedly masculine world characterized by difficulty and effort. The status of this break is more trivial than it is in Judge William's description, and Nietzsche's account, in contrast with Kierkegaard's, is full of pejorative clichés about the reality behind the veil. But on occasion Nietzsche does recognize, as Kierkegaard seems not to, that these constitutions of the feminine are created by a disguised will to power, where men project their desires into an ideal form that they name "woman," and then ask that actual women conform to this ideal. "For it is man who creates for himself the image of woman," Nietzsche writes in *The Gay Science*, "and woman forms herself according to this image" (GS, 126). An aphorism in *Twilight of the Idols* repeats this claim with a variation on

Genesis: "Man created woman—but what out of? Out of a rib of his God, of his 'ideal.'"[8] And even the pages in *Beyond Good and Evil* which arguably contain Nietzsche's harshest polemic against women (BGE, 143–50) are prefaced by a moment of skepticism, where Nietzsche acknowledges that the "truths" about "woman as such" that he is about to relate are to a great extent "*my* truths" and therefore may say more about him than they do about women themselves (BGE, 144).

This acknowledgment does not, however, prevent Nietzsche from going on to demand that women continue to conform themselves to masculine ideals. His opposition to emancipation in *Beyond Good and Evil* explicitly rejects women's right to speak for themselves with the absurd statement, "I think it is a true friend of women who calls on them today: *mulier taceat de muliere!* [let woman be silent about woman]" (BGE, 232). While the general tenor of Nietzsche's remarks in these pages is far removed from that of Kierkegaard's depiction of women in *Either/Or II*, he shares Judge William's fear that through emancipation woman may be "deprived of her *enchantment*" (BGE, 150). The basic themes are the same, and contain nothing novel: woman is defined and valued in terms of male desire; she is refused the right to speak for herself; and any movement that would release her from this definition is resisted on the grounds that it would reduce her value.

If Manning is right to claim that Levinas's philosophy is an ally of feminism, then it should stand fundamentally opposed to any such definition of woman. It is true that, as a relation in which the alterity of the other is maintained, the erotic relation in *Time and the Other* prefigures the ethical relation, as Levinas understands it. It is also true that Levinas's philosophy purports to be against all violent attempts to grasp the Other, and this should include attempts to subsume that Other under a definition that is an extension of oneself. But the other of the erotic relation as Levinas describes her simply is not the Other of the ethical relation as Levinas describes him. And although Levinas's account of the former is more sympathetic in *Time and the Other* than in *Totality and Infinity*, in neither work is she respected as one who must be allowed to speak for herself.

In fact, in *Totality and Infinity*,[9] the erotic relation is in important respects the antithesis of the ethical one. In the section titled "Phenomenology of Eros," Levinas does emphasize tenderness before the vulnerability of the beloved. But given some of the terms he employs in this section—"profanation" (TI, 259/TeI, 241), "animality" (TI, 259/TeI,

236), "violation" (TI, 260/TeI, 237), "indecency," (TI, 260/TeI, 238) the "wanton" (TI, 261/TeI, 238), "lasciviousness" (TI, 263/TeI, 241)—and given that *eros* is for him redeemed not by its own nature but by the engendering of the "son," it would seem that the erotic relation is here also depicted as a form of intercourse, less than fully human and bordering on the shameful, with a faceless other in order to reproduce oneself. This does not strike me as being in any sense a prefiguration or indication of, much less a model for, the ethical relation, however conceived. It is, however, an all too common reality in the history of men's treatment of women.

The "epiphany of the feminine" in *Totality and Infinity*—equivocal, dissimulating, and nonsignifying (TI, 264/TeI, 241–42)—is essentially distinct from the epiphany of the face that obligates and commands attention to its speech. With reference to the descriptions of the feminine in *Totality and Infinity*, therefore, Craig Vasey is right to note that "the reason why women are not serious others in Levinas's work is precisely that they are 'unfaced' (de-faced?)—at any rate faceless."[10] The feminine as object of *eros* is one place in which this effacement of woman occurs in *Totality and Infinity*. Another place is in the identification of the feminine with dwelling and habitation, where woman is not the *vous* that speaks and to whom one owes respect, but the intimate *tu* that is supposedly a condition for "the interiority of the Home" (TI, 155/TeI, 128). There are clear similarities between Levinas's descriptions, in these pages, of feminine alterity in relation to dwelling and Judge William's remarks on woman as the one who prepares an abode for man and anchors him in the finite. Dwelling, to which the feminine, "the welcoming one par excellence" (TI, 157/TeI, 131), is essential, is described as "a retreat home with oneself as in a land of refuge" (TI, 156/TeI, 129). It is for Levinas pervaded by "those silent comings and goings of the feminine being whose footsteps reverberate the secret depths of being" (TI, 156/TeI, 129). This silent woman is experienced as "a delightful lapse in being, and the source of gentleness itself" (TI, 155/TeI, 129).

She is, in short, a break, an interruption in the continuity of "virile" existence, and therefore a first initiation into the good beyond being. She does still provide refuge for "we who have a hard time," but for Levinas, in contrast with Nietzsche (whose value system, promoting the "masculine" virtues of self-assertion and hardness, is the reverse of Levinas's), this refuge is no mere relaxation; it is also a source of education. Like Kierkegaard, Levinas does not view woman as a trivial addition to man.

She—or at the least the dimension of the feminine—breaks the obses-
siveness of his self-assertive concern with his own projects and, through
the gentleness of her welcome, points him toward the possibility of the
ethical. However, just as, for Kierkegaard, it is in the end the man who
is finally capable of the higher destiny with the help of woman, so for
Levinas the ethical relation, for which the feminine is a preparation, is
a fundamentally masculine one. Once again, the feminine is described
in terms of its function in the life of man and prized as a necessary condition for the achievement of his highest possibility. And in any case the
description ascribes to woman a nature that she may not recognize (that
I do not recognize) as her own, and a function that she may have no
desire to fulfill. Far from maintaining her in her alterity in the sense of
granting to her the right to define herself, these portraits of woman
define her as the other who is needed for oneself. She is needed for both
the reproduction of oneself, as in Levinas's description of the erotic, and
for the spiritual progress of man. Admittedly, the latter consists not in
being for oneself but in being for the other. Nonetheless, it remains true
that, far from leaving blank the space titled "woman" and inviting her
to fill it in herself, Levinas writes all over this space, inscribing it with his
desires, his needs, his mission, in terms of which the feminine is never
a for-the-sake-of, but always an in-order-to, a means rather than an end.
Whatever tenderness or pity he might feel for her, however much
he might appreciate the radiance of her discreet presence within the
home, under such descriptions she remains, in the very depths of her
essence, Zeug.[11]

I would therefore again agree with Vasey that Levinas's description
of the feminine in *Totality and Infinity* "seems fairly straightforwardly an
expression of good old-fashioned masculine privilege and arrogance"
("Faceless Women," 324–25) and that "*chez* Levinas the innovative concept of feminine otherness has little to do with any challenge to the
sociopolitical traditions of patriarchy" (325). Moreover, I think it cannot be emphasized strongly enough that it will not do to say at this juncture, as some people want to, that Levinas deliberately adopts a male
point of view out of respect for the alterity of the feminine one, which
he does not pretend to be able to assume. Manning, for instance, says:
"Levinas's philosophy is a male philosophy, written from a man's point
of view (how could it be otherwise?), but perhaps it is the best kind of
male philosophy in that in opposing all relations of power with every
Other, it opposes every relation of power and oppression between men

and women" ("Thinking the Other Without Violence," 137). Levinas's concrete descriptions of woman are unethical, though, and do not even begin to live up to the nonviolent relation to the Other that he advocates. To say, against this, that he can only write from a "man's point of view" is to legitimize these descriptions, and the experiences underlying them, as the only ones of which that view is capable. But surely feminism, if it speaks to men as well as to women, asks men to see women differently from how they have in the past. It asks them not to constitute women within the horizon projected by their own desires, but to see them *in some sense* more as they see themselves and other men, at least to the point of acknowledging that women, too, look out at the world rather than merely being looked at, that they, too, desire rather than being merely desired, that they, too, speak rather than being merely spoken about, that they, too, are individuals with differing characteristics rather than a homogenous group possessing a simple and common essence. And it asks them to become acquainted with women more in the way that they would become acquainted, *ideally*, with other men: through a respectful, attentive, and considerate dialogue.

This is to say that any feminism that asks men to respect the alterity of women must still, *is* still, based on a recognition of woman as *subject*, in the above-listed senses. If a description of "woman" does not properly acknowledge her subjectivity in at least these senses, it is violent, however one might want to challenge and modify the notion of the subject, shared by Sartre and Beauvoir, as a *pour-soi*(for-itself). Unless men are intrinsically and irrevocably incapable of treating women ethically (which I do not believe), such an acknowledgment is possible for them. From *Levinas's* point of view, in a "phenomenology" that often does little more than delineate the contours of a highly particular experience, "woman" is the interiority of the home as opposed to the exterior public world. She is the darkness of *eros*, as opposed to the light of signification and speech. In both cases, her very essence is constituted as being a break from—and with, and in—the *primary* world, the world in which men stand face-to-face with one another. This constitution is not inevitable for men. For one thing, it is entirely possible for a man to refrain from defining the essence of "woman" purely on the basis of a highly limited, partial, and specific experience of some woman. Men are quite capable of acknowledging the relativity and finitude of such experiences, and so of not making the move—the essence of all violence in the realm of definition—that says: "this is how $x(1)$ affects me; therefore, this is the nature of *x* as such." It is also not necessary for a man to experience the specific woman with whom he dwells as essentially, and nonreciprocally, responsible for the accomplishment of habitation, nor is it necessary for him to experience her, within the erotic relationship, as an infantile, coquettish, and slightly silly Other, an Other with whom one plays "as with a young animal" (TI, 263/TeI, 242). If I were to be wrong about this (which I do not think I am), the conclusion I would draw is not that such experiences of the feminine are not unethical after all, but that men's relationships with women, at least in these domains, are intrinsically unethical, and that therefore lesbianism is the only real option for a woman who wishes to maintain her integrity within a committed sexual relationship.

Ironically, then, I am claiming that the problem with Levinas's portrait of the feminine, as with those of Kierkegaard and Nietzsche, is that he, like them, fails to imagine this Other as another like himself. He fails to recognize her as a subject, and to constitute her alterity on the basis of this recognition. This is of course a peculiar criticism to level against an ethics whose originality is supposed to reside, as Ewa Ziarek puts it, "in its obstinate refusal to think the other."[12] In raising it nonetheless, I am implying that Levinas's failure to be just to the feminine does not merely constitute a lapse or hypocritical moment within his thought, but indicates a problem at the very heart of it. I will now develop this implication further in examining two other forms of feminine otherness that Levinas's portraits share with those of Kierkegaard and Nietzsche.

Woman as Being for Another

"It is a woman's nature to pray for others," writes Kierkegaard as Judge William, whereas "man by nature prays for himself" (E/O II, 314). Another aspect of the otherness of woman's nature consists in this dedication to the other that supposedly differentiates her from man. According to Judge William, man "has his specific task, his specific place" (E/O II, 314), implying that the contrasting essence of woman involves her giving herself over to preserving and advancing the tasks and places of others, that is, of other men.

Nietzsche also, in his own way, sees unqualified devotion to another as characteristic of woman's nature. For him, it differentiates feminine from

masculine love: "What woman means by love is clear enough: total devotion (not mere surrender) with soul and body, without any consideration
or reserve, rather with shame and horror at the thought of a devotion
that might be subject to special clauses or conditions" (GS, 363). "A man
who loves like a woman becomes a slave," he adds, "while a woman who
loves like a woman becomes *a more perfect woman.*" There is no doubt
which of these Nietzsche judges as superior in itself. Given his table of
values, this allegedly feminine love would have to rank close to the bottom, expressing a way of being that he generally despises in his writings.
Moreover, given his analysis of life as will to power, such devotion, like
all apparent dedication to another, is ultimately self-seeking. While
"women's love and sympathy" appears to involve total sacrifice to a
man, in truth it is profoundly "egoistic"[13] and while "the mother represents altruism convincingly," in truth through her "religion of weakness" she achieves her true goal of "overcoming the strong" (WP, 423–24,
no. 817).

Kierkegaard does not despise or denigrate feminine devotion to the
other in any way. He does, however, see it as a characteristic confined to
the ideal type of woman and does not suggest that it is something men
should emulate. What seems to set Levinas's portrayal of the feminine
as essentially for the other apart from accounts such as these is that he
not only does not denigrate or seek to exploit this figure, but uses it as a
symbol for the original asymmetry of the protoethical relation. In the
maternal body in particular, he sees a sign of such a relation, reading this
body as a condition in which one is responsible for the Other with the
very substance of her being, prior to any acquaintance with him or her,
prior to any knowledge of his or her characteristics, and prior to any
choice, but in a subjection that is election rather than enslavement.
Maternity is thus an apt symbol for the way Levinas understands ethical
vulnerability, in which one is wholly exposed to the Other. Indeed, he
says in *Otherwise Than Being:* "Maternity in the complete being 'for the
other' which characterizes it, which is the very signifyingness of signification, is the ultimate sense of this vulnerability. This hither side of
identity is not reducible to the for-itself, where, beyond its immediate
identity, being recognizes itself in its difference."[14] It would seem, therefore, that as opposed to the feminine figures identified with domesticity
and the erotic in *Totality and Infinity,* the figure of the mother in *Otherwise Than Being* does not represent the feminine as a secondary sex.

For this reason, Craig Vasey, whose critical remarks on *Totality and*

Infinity I have already cited, says that in the figure of the mother, Levinas "makes a more legitimate use of feminine imagery" ("Faceless Women," 329), and that one can even conclude, from an examination of this figure, that Levinas's basic categories "define a theoretical position that is practically indistinguishable from feminism" (317). However, this statement is questionable in its assumption that "feminism" could be equated with a single theoretical position, one that, for instance, would be happy to exalt and approve the figure of the mother as intrinsically being for another, and to see in this figure an ethical ideal, presented by the feminine, for women and others. There is not this measure of agreement among feminists about what the "feminine" consists in, and attempts to define the feminine that claim universality for themselves (a claim one can avoid through one's style, as well as by explicitly qualifying one's account) cannot help but fall into essentialism. Unsurprisingly, that fall is mainly, and sometimes only, visible to those who do not agree with the particular definition being proposed, to those who identify themselves as an example of what is being defined but not with the definition given, so that the latter seems to them an alien constraint, a deformation of their being. One must always take note that universal definitions of this sort leave the person who does not recognize herself in them with the unpalatable choice of either submitting to such a deformation or admitting she is not a "genuine" instance of the category after all. But she may ask why she is not allowed to challenge and broaden the definition by presenting herself as a counterexample, and by what authority another—Levinas, for example, or Kierkegaard or Nietzsche, but in principle another woman, too—could possibly claim to have a more intimate acquaintance with her "essence" than she herself does. In any event, some women are certainly likely to experience an unwelcome deformation in an account that views maternity as the highest destiny of the feminine and that exalts motherhood as total dedication to another.

Historically, accounts such as these have not been allies of feminism, but have tended to promote the subjugation of women. The uniqueness of Levinas's variation is supposed to rest in the fact that the mother, as a trope, expresses not merely the ideal of woman but the ethical dignity of the human in general. The maternal body is, after all, a metaphor. The problem is that metaphors matter, and sometimes the concreteness of the letter—speaking, as it always does, of particular entities—signifies more than the superior spirit it is meant to convey. One suspects that, in Levinas's usage of the maternal figure, the particular entity who bears the significance, the woman, remains a vehicle or vessel for a spirit that is, from the beginning and in the end, man. Her role, literal and spiritual, is to gestate him, to give birth to an excellence that she may come to share but that is in itself masculine and has always been masculine.

Levinas's "Et Dieu créa la femme"[15] confirms this suspicion, affirming the spirituality of the masculine, of which the feminine is merely a "corollary" (141), an "appendix" (142), a "minor articulation" (141). To his spirit, she is the body that both tempts him to eros and is ideally shaped to bear him (144). The feminine body thus figures the concupiscence that stands in tension with the law (129), but that may be redeemed through its capacity to produce the masculine face. Her being for another is then not the being for the other of the ethical face-to-face; it is the being for another constituted by that other's anxiety and desire. It is functionality rather than obligation, and to be a function is inescapably to be the second sex. This difficulty is not eliminated by Levinas's statement that it is not the woman who is secondary, but the relation with her (DCF, 135), since to suggest that the human prior to sexual differentiation is nonetheless somehow masculine is to say, and not so subtly, that she achieves her humanity in the transcendence of her gender, while he achieves his humanity in the fulfillment of his. The fact is that Levinas says "the feminine" when he could say, exclusively, "the erotic relation," and this choice is significant. It seems unlikely that he would assent to a description, from a woman's point of view, of the masculine as secondary. No woman, however, would give such a description, except as a deliberate reaction. She would say "the erotic relation," not the "masculine"; she would say, "the object of eros," not "man." Levinas could do likewise, but does not. This is not because he writes from "a man's point of view," but because he writes from a deeply patriarchal one, which is not necessary for man as such. It is from that patriarchal point of view that the subordination of woman to man is seen not as a form of manmade injustice, but as a necessary part of the divine plan (DCF, 142), instituted by the god of a religion whose superiority to all others supposedly lies in its refusal to locate the divine anywhere other than in ethics (!).

Levinas's feminine metaphors actually arise out of, and legitimize, the status of woman as secondary in her being for another as much as do the accounts of Kierkegaard and Nietzsche. In so doing—because metaphors matter—they in fact preach that she, the other to him, be sacrificed to another even though, in *Otherwise Than Being*, he states unequivocally that "to say that the other has to sacrifice himself to the others would be to preach human sacrifice!" (OB, 126/AE, 162). A serious shortcoming with the type of feminine tropes that Levinas employs is that they, in contrast with self-sacrificing masculine figures, involve no relation to justice. In Levinas's thought, the original asymmetry of the ethical relation, in which I owe the other everything, is modified with the development of justice, but equations of justice, where goods are calculated and distributed, requires the presence of a third. Unfortunately, for woman, neither in the interiority of the home nor in the interiority of the maternal body is there a third who would limit the demands made on her and guarantee her safety. Furthermore, Levinas himself never depicts her as one who is owed; she is always the one who gives, except when she is the object of desire. Leaving aside the question of whether Levinas's description of the original ethical relation is accurate in the first place, surely an ethics emphasizing the infinite obligation of this relation over the calculations of justice said to evolve from it is not an ideal ethics for women, who have in many cases been encouraged to discount themselves for far too long. Surely, given the historical situation of woman, she should be encouraged to count herself in rather than out, to place the relations of justice, where her own interests are taken into account, higher than an asymmetrical relation in which they do not count.

Notice what happens, in this regard, if one introduces, into the portrait of ideal maternity painted by Levinas, the image of a woman who, in order to secure her own well-being, chooses to eject the other whom she harbors within her body. From the perspective of Levinas's ideal mother, must not this latter woman, whether or not her choice is guaranteed by the law of the land, be judged as monstrous? It must, I think; and at the risk of sounding prosaic, this suggests to me (since I find such a judgment monstrous) that feminism may be better served by an old-fashioned discourse of rights in which alterity is predicated on the basis of a recognized identity, and by an even more old-fashioned metaphysics in which being is judged as in itself good, evil consisting in a deprivation of it and so, in the case of moral evil, in the act whereby one unjustly deprives another of his or her fair share of it.

Although I will want to qualify the preceding suggestion eventually, I do wonder if, given that Levinas in practice fails to recognize the face of woman (and in fact the face of other others as well, a point I will take up later), it could even be that an ethics emphasizing alterity and asymmetry, an ethics that deliberately refrains from imagining the Other as another like oneself, might contribute to a failure to recognize and respect that Other, and precisely in his or her very difference from oneself. Can the other really speak to you, for herself, against your anticipations and expectations, if you do not first come to meet her with the presupposition that you two are at some level alike in your being? Can you engage in a dialogue with her that modifies your preconceptions unless you continue to imagine and reimagine, in an ongoing, complex interplay of analogy drawn from yourself and receptivity to the saying of the other? In the absence of such imagination, which takes knowledge as a regulative ideal, does not the supposed alterity of the other—her alluring feminine mystery, his exotic cultural foreignness—become an excuse for the opposite, for writing oneself—in the particularity of one's gender, one's tastes, one's tradition, one's religion—upon the space of the other? Through such writing, one ends up encountering, ironically, never the other, but only oneself, only the other painted in the image of oneself. In the case of Levinas, it is neither coincidence nor mere hypocrisy that a philosophy emphasizing radical alterity nonetheless produces a figure of woman as entirely constituted and looked at, an object of male vision rather the subject of any self-expressive speech. This would tend to vindicate Beauvoir's belief that male talk of the radical otherness of woman, her mystery and indefinability, is always rooted in, and serves to excuse, masculine appropriations of her.

Woman as Indefinite

Kierkegaard's treatment of the essence of woman certainly supports this conclusion. Judge William is not given to romantic flights of fancy about the mystery of woman, since such flights belong to the aesthetic temperament to which he is responding critically. But he does see in the essence of woman something shifting and paradoxical, "simultaneously more perfect and more imperfect than the man":

> If we wish to characterize the most pure and perfect, we say "a woman"; if we wish to characterize the weakest and most fragile, we say "a woman"; if we want to convey a conception of the spirituality elevated above the sensuous, we say "a woman": if we want to convey a conception of the sensuous, we say "a woman": if we wish to characterize innocence in all its uplifting greatness,

wc say "a woman": if we wish to characterize the depressing feeling of guilt, we say "a woman." (E/O II, 92)

As Wanda Warren Berry notes, in this passage "not only is the 'essence of woman' defined simply in terms of her relationship to man, she has her meaning only in men's various perceptions of valuational opposites."[16] Judge William's sense of woman as the intrinsically different other, then, does not lead to a perception of her as impossible to define through the essence of man, but to a perception of her as entirely constituted in relation to man.

Nietzsche does occasionally wax rhapsodic about woman, or about what woman represents, but he is usually aware that he is speaking of an illusory projection, a dream of man rather than the reality of woman as such. Most often, this dream is of an indefinite future, rich with possibility. As such, it is the dream of life itself: "But perhaps this is the most powerful magic of life: it is covered by a veil interwoven with gold, a veil of beautiful possibilities, sparkling with promise, resistance, bashfulness, mockery, pity, and seduction. Yes, life is a woman" (GS, 272). As already pointed out, Nietzsche sometimes claims that woman participates in the manufacture of this dream, in order to enhance her own value in the eyes of man, and his comments on the waking reality behind the dream are almost always pejorative. He does understand, though, that the mystery of woman, her apparently unfathomable depth, consists in the infinite promise of what is in fact pure appearance, lacking all depth.[17] On the whole he tends to be aware, moreover, that the reason woman is pure appearance, the reason there is nothing to her but beautiful surface is that man, as her lover, does not want to know what is under her skin (see GS, 122). He wants to know only the object transfigured by eros, but this object, being constituted—like everything else in man's world that he pretends to be other than himself—by his perspective, can be maintained only by not wanting to know. Since this object is only made to be by the vision of desire, the hidden depths of its "in itself" cannot be fathomed. The "in itself" of a projection, after all, lies not in the projected object, but in the one who projects. To seek it in the object is therefore to seek what does not exist.

In *Time and the Other*, Levinas, like Kierkegaard under the persona of Judge William, does not intend his notion of the otherness of woman in a romantic sense.[18] In what he describes as the "modesty" and "mystery" of the feminine, he sees "a mode of being that consists in slipping away from the light" (TO, 87/TA, 79). This "hiding" (TO, 87/TA, 79) is a being intrinsically refractory to all attempts to grasp and know, to wrest from hiddenness and bring into the light: to make appear as a phenomenon. It gives the feminine its irreducible alterity, and in the darkness of this alterity Levinas finds a shadow of the relationship with the other in general, which he also describes in terms of mystery: "The relationship with the other is not an idyllic and harmonious relationship of communion, or a sympathy through which we put ourselves in the other's place; we recognize the other as resembling us, but exterior to us; the relationship with the other is a relationship with a Mystery" (TO, 75/TA, 63). While the ethical relation has its own kind of light, however, the light not of knowledge but of speech, the erotic one remains in itself within the darkness of desire, being redeemed into the light not by the face of the woman but only by the face of the son obscurely coveted through her. The experience of feminine mystery as such within the erotic relationship is not an experience of an Other who interrupts the incessant forward movement of the soul's desire for succession that Plotinus identified as the source of time.[19] On the contrary, this mystery is a reification of that desire, and therefore quite similar to the mystery of "woman" as life in Nietzsche's tropology, where she is identified with the indefiniteness of the future. The similarity can be clearly seen in Levinas's description of the "caress":

> The seeking of the caress constitutes its essence by the fact that the caress does not know what it seeks. This 'not knowing', this slipping away, a game absolutely without project or plan, not with what can become ours or us, but with something other, always other, always inaccessible, and always still to come (à venir). The caress is the anticipation of this pure future (avenir) without content. It is made up of this increase of hunger, of ever richer promises, opening new perspectives onto the ungraspable. It feeds on countless hungers. (TO, 87/TA, 82–83)

This is not the alterity of the one who refuses to appear within the phenomenological horizon projected ultimately by self-concern. It is the alterity of the one who is nothing but that concern, of the purely phenomenal being that in relation to itself is, as Nietzsche says, not even shallow, because, being nothing but the skin that is wanted in desire, it has no depth at all. Unfortunately, unlike Nietzsche, Levinas tends not to recognize explicitly that the "other" he is dealing with here is not woman as such but only eros as a dimension of his own existence.

As with Kierkegaard and Nietzsche, then, the mystery of woman within Levinas's portrait is the mystery of the apparent object. This is once again an inversion of the ethical relation. The feminine other is the inverse of the ethical other who is supposed to disrupt all phenomenological constitution, thereby disrupting myself in the continuity of my concern with the world made by me and for me. While the ethical other is presented as a rejoinder to the thought that would consider its own *Dasein* (existence) to be the final for-the-sake-of of all involvements, the feminine other, portrayed as the dark womb of man's future, is quite continuous with such a thought.

Strangely, therefore, in the figure of woman, Levinas encounters not the genuinely other but only himself. He encounters only the other that he himself constitutes, and constitutes in its very otherness. As I have suggested already, I believe that, peculiar as it may seem, a tendency toward such constitution belongs to the very nature of Levinas's thought. One can see a distinct failure genuinely to encounter the other in Levinas's treatment of the cultural other as well. For the most part, Levinas does not think much about this other, but scattered references suggest that he is not inclined to have much respect for his otherness, if "otherness" means dissimilarity to oneself. His reaction to an African custom in the following exchange provides a telling example:

LEVINAS: I always say—but privately—that in humanity the only serious things are the Greeks and the Bible; everything else is dancing. I think this welcomes everyone; there is no racism in it.

CHRISTOPH VON WOLZOGEN: "Everything else is dancing"—one could here naturally think of Nietzsche.

LEVINAS: Yes, but you know: on the television one shows these terrible things in South Africa. And there, when they bury men, they *dance*. Have you seen this? This is supposed to be a manner and fashion of expressing sadness.

VON WOLZOGEN: It is *also* an expression.

LEVINAS: Yes, certainly, to that extent I am still a philosopher. But it communicates the impression of a dancing civilization; they weep differently.[20]

One cannot help noticing in Levinas's words here an unthinking complacency about his own cultural vantage point, complete with all of its presuppositions. One also cannot help noticing that Levinas rarely hesitates in his assumption that Judaism is the highest type of religion. When this assumption is taken together with the claim that "everything which comes to us"—meaning presumably "to us Jews"—"from India, everything that comes to us from China" is "idolatry" (DCF, 146), it seems likely that Levinas is not much interested in a dialogue with cultures or religions significantly different from his own. In criticizing him on this point, I do not mean to defend cultural relativism. My problem with what I see as Levinas's failure to respect anything genuinely other is not that he reaches a certain conclusion, as if, given sexual and cultural differences, it were always wrong to reach a conclusion, a thesis I absolutely do not want to maintain. The problem is that he has not *reached a conclusion* at the end of some process of dialogue and reflection. He has carelessly assumed his culturally engendered givens, without paying attention to any other that might question these givens. In fact, Levinas is so deeply embedded in what is his own that he almost never even entertains the thought that the truly other might have something to be said for it, let alone something to say to *him*. [21]

On these points, a reader's experience of Levinas's thought cannot help but be affected by his or her own situation in relation to, or among, the others of whom Levinas implicitly or explicitly speaks. For a reader whose identity belongs unequivocally to the "same" of the Western tradition—male, European, and Greco-Christian—Levinas's thought can perhaps easily be taken at face value as announcing an interruption of this same by another. However, for a reader with a different identity—for instance an identity such as mine, which includes being female, Asian, and Hindu—that thought also asserts itself, in significant respects, as a recurrence of the same: the same old patriarchal mono (I almost want to say with Nietzsche monotono-) theism, the same old imperialism, the same old absence of hospitality towards the foreigner, lacking even the decency to suspend judgment when faced with one who is unknown.

This lack of attention to the genuinely different could be explained in part by the prophetic style of Levinas's thought. Such a style is not very conducive to maintaining the caution and restraint that are necessary conditions for any just approach to the Other who is not similar to oneself.[22] But the problem is not simply a matter of style, nor does it only indicate a blind spot in Levinas's thinking. It is the direct result of a tendency that one should not be surprised to find in Levinas. There is a link between Levinas's suspicion of any emphasis on *enracinement* (rootedness) on the one hand,[23] and his lack of suspicion about his own *enracinement*

within a historical tradition on the other. His disregard of cultural specificity, that is, leads to a naive position where, in his relation to the cultural other—neither Greek nor Christian nor Jew—Levinas exemplifies
unthinking rootedness rather than opposing it.

In truth, appearances to the contrary notwithstanding, respecting the
dissimilarity and specificity of the Other is not the central concern of
Levinas's thought. This is a philosophy of the Other that, although it
claims to be based on difference, is in another sense indifferent to difference. It is a philosophy that says: beyond all identity and difference and
prior to them, there is this Other who challenges my self-absorption, and
to whom, whoever (s)he may be, I, whoever I may be, owe bread and water
and warmth and shelter. It is the face of *this* Other that forbids violence,
a face naked of any of the differentiating and specifying characteristics
that would identify it as a member of one group rather than another. This
is perhaps the only kind of ethics that could come out of the Holocaust,
and it is deeply right on its central point, and also right to privilege this
point above any other. Although I have elsewhere defended Heidegger
against Levinas,[24] I do see in the latter's thought an essential corrective to
any philosophy that would set something above the "ought" of what one
owes to the Other qua Other, meaning here not the one who is dissimilar, but the one who is face, beyond all difference. The ethical relation,
then, is actually a being for the Other that is indifferent to difference.

The thought of this relation emphatically sets itself against the temptation to think, even for a moment, let alone for ten months (the length
of Heidegger's active political engagement with Nazism), that it might
be permissible to support a regime that would make the ethical value of
a human being contingent upon some definite ethnocultural identity,
some set of specifying characteristics. Levinas's true opponent is not a
subtle cultural imperialist, but someone tempted to think that *ethos* is
prior to ethics, and to see the latter as dependent upon and derived from
the former. This is someone who overemphasizes *enracinement*, setting it
above the demand for a justice that does not care about roots and soil.

Having said this, however, one should also acknowledge that there is
a level, resting on the basic and universal one of physical pain and enjoyment, at which justice requires attention to specificity. By its very nature,
Levinas's indifference to the differences between faces results in a tendency not to do justice to faces that are specifically other, a tendency
exacerbated, not diminished, by his "obstinate refusal to think the other."
Justice to these others is not well served by the Levinasian notion of

radical alterity. It is better served, I think, by the grammar of "recognition" (*reconnaissance*) even with all of its attendant difficulties. Although *recognition* literally means "knowing again" and so suggests matching the perceived characteristics of an entity with some prior representation, its actual usage can include granting the validity of someone's claim to difference, or acknowledging his or her right to speak. Recognition will indeed begin by imagining the Other to be another like oneself—a subject, for instance—but can proceed, upon this basis, to take dissimilarity into account, and to respect it. It is at least capable of an ongoing and attentive dialogue with one who is dissimilar, in a way that Levinas's philosophy is not.

To say this is not necessarily to claim that Levinas is wrong about the *basis* of ethics. As Stephen Watson points out: "Notwithstanding the poverty of his own claims for the immediacy of the ethical, surely Levinas is right in this respect—one cannot deduce peace from war. We will need an account of rationality in the realm of the political otherwise than the strictly demonstrative, or all 'recognition' will be dissolved. And we will need an account of the recognized otherwise than all 'mediation,' or means, or powers, or will, or forces and their calculations."[25] Levinas may be right that, prior to recognition and necessary for it, there is the original recollection of responsibility to the Other, which has already assumed the obligation to recognize. This responsibility, the essence of the ethical relation, *is* immediate at least in the sense that it cannot be deduced from any other type of relation. It would be possible to claim that this point constitutes the actual centre of Levinas's thought, and that therefore, contrary to some of my claims, such critiques as the one I have given really only touch the margins. I do not mind accepting this judgement, as long as it is acknowledged that margins, like metaphors, do matter. However, I also want to concur, finally, with Irigaray's judgment that this ethics does not know its limits.[26] In that case, perhaps what it needs most are precisely critiques that, by concentrating upon its peripheral concerns, help to define those limits.

Notes

1. See Simone de Beauvoir, *The Second Sex*, trans. H. M. Parshley (New York: Alfred A. Knopf, 1957), xvi n. 3. Beauvoir views Levinas's account of the feminine as typical of those masculine

representations of man and woman wherein "He is the Subject, he is the Absolute—she is the Other."

2. R. J. S. Manning, "Thinking the Other Without Violence? An Analysis of the Relation Between the Philosophy of Emmanuel Levinas and Feminism," *Journal of Speculative Philosophy* 5 (1991): 132–43, 133. In his own criticisms, Manning singles out "Lévinas's use of the masculine language 'paternity' and 'father' and 'son' within his concept of fecundity" (138). He concludes that Levinas's usage of this language does involve violence, noting that, as someone who is "deeply informed" by Judaism, Levinas "writes out of a profoundly sexist and patriarchal tradition" (140).

3. Søren Kierkegaard, *Either/Or, Part II*, ed. and trans. Howard V. Hong and Edna H. Hong (Princeton: Princeton University Press, 1987); hereafter E/O II. My analysis of Kierkegaard will be confined to Judge William's comments about women in this work, which can be fairly closely identified with Kierkegaard's own views on the subject. Beauvoir, by contrast, frequently attributes remarks made from the aesthetic point of view in Kierkegaard's works to Kierkegaard himself, mistakenly assuming that they can be counted among the opinions that Kierkegaard holds. See, for example, *The Second Sex*, 186–87.

4. This ideal emerges in, for instance, Kierkegaard, *The Sickness unto Death*, trans. Alastair Hannay (London: Penguin, 1989).

5. For a more detailed and qualified assessment of this point, see Wanda Warren Berry, "Judge William Judging Woman," in *International Kierkegaard Commentary: Either/Or, Part II*, ed. Robert L. Perkins (Macon: Mercer University Press, 1995), 33–57, esp. 39–40.

6. Friedrich Nietzsche, *The Gay Science*, trans. Walter Kaufmann (New York: Vintage, 1974), 124. Hereafter GS.

7. Nietzsche, *Beyond Good and Evil*, trans. R. J. Hollingdale (London: Penguin, 1972), 149; hereafter BGE.

8. Nietzsche, *Twilight of the Idols/The Anti-Christ*, trans. R. J. Hollingdale (London: Penguin, 1990), 33.

9. Emmanuel Levinas, *Totality and Infinity*, trans. Alphonso Lingis (Pittsburgh: Duquesne University Press, 1969); hereafter TI. *Totalité et Infini* (The Hague: Martinus Nijhoff, 1961); hereafter TeI.

10. Craig R. Vasey, "Faceless Women and Serious Others: Levinas, Misogyny, and Feminism," in *Ethics and Danger: Essays on Heidegger and Continental Thought*, ed. Arleen B. Dallery and Charles E. Scott (Albany: State University of New York Press, 1992), 318.

11. This term, which Heidegger uses in *Being and Time*, can be translated variously as "equipment," "tool," or simply "stuff." Heidegger applies it to all entities whose nature is determined by their use.

12. Ewa Ziarek, "Kristeva and Levinas: Mourning, Ethics, and the Feminine," in *Ethics, Politics, and Difference in Julia Kristeva's Writing*, ed. Kelly Oliver (New York: Routledge, 1993), 64.

13. Nietzsche, *The Will to Power*, trans. Walter Kaufmann and R. J. Hollingdale (New York: Vintage Books, 1967), 407, no. 777; hereafter WP.

14. Levinas, *Otherwise Than Being or Beyond Essence*, trans. Alphonso Lingis (The Hague: Martinus Nijhoff, 1981), 108; hereafter OB. *Autrement qu'être ou au-delà de l'essence* (The Hague: Martinus Nijhoff, 1974), 137; hereafter AE.

15. In Levinas, *Du sacré au saint: cinq nouvelles lectures talmudiques* (Paris: Éditions de Minuit, 1977); hereafter DCF.

16. Kierkegaard, "Judge William Judging Women," 37.

17. Cf. Nietzsche *Twilight*, 35: "Women are considered deep—why? because one can never discover any bottom to them. Women are not even shallow."

18. Levinas, *Time and the Other, and Additional Essays*, trans. Richard A. Cohen (Pittsburgh: Duquesne University Press, 1987); hereafter TO. *Le temps et l'autre* (Paris: Presses Universitaire de France, 1991), 78; hereafter TA.

19. See Plotinus, *The Enneads*, trans. Stephen MacKenna (London: Penguin, 1991), 227–28.

20. Christoph von Wolzogen, *Humanismus des anderen Menschen*, trans. Ludwig Wenzler, in *Mit einem Gespräch zwishen Emmanuel Levinas und Christoph von Wolzogen* (Hamburg: Felix Meiner, 1991). Cf. Levinas in *French Philosophers in Conversation:* "I often say, though it's a dangerous thing to say publicly, that humanity consists of the Bible and the Greeks. All the rest can be translated: all the rest—all the exotic—is dance." Raoul Mortley, *French Philosophers in Conversation: Levinas, Schneider, Serres, Irigaray, Le Doeuff, Derrida* (New York: Routledge, 1991), 18. If one were looking for an exemplary definition of how not to read the other, one could hardly do better than the statement, "All the rest can be translated."

21. I have inserted the word *almost* in this sentence out of deference to the following statement by Levinas, which at least acknowledges ignorance: "For me, certainly, the Bible is the model of excellence; but I say this while knowing nothing about Buddhism." *Entretiens avec Le monde: 1. Philosophies, Introduction de Christian Delacampagne* (Paris: Éditions la Découverte, 1984), 147.

22. On this point, see Stephan Strasser, *Jenseits von Sein und Zeit* (The Hague: Martinus Nijhoff, 1978), 372.

23. See, for example, Levinas, "Philosophie, justice et amour," in *Entre nous* (Paris: Bernard Grasset, 1991), 136–37.

24. In "Questioning the Sacred: Heidegger and Levinas on the Locus of Divinity," *Modern Theology* 14 (1998): 299–324.

25. Stephen Watson,"The Face of the Hibakusha: Levinas and the Trace of the Apocalypse," in *Writing the Future*, ed. David Wood (London: Routledge, 1990), 166.

26. Luce Irigaray, "Questions to Emmanuel Levinas: On the Divinity of Love," trans. Margaret Whitford, in *Re-reading Levinas*, ed. Robert Bernasconi and Simon Critchley (Bloomington: Indiana University Press, 1991), 113.

5

The Fecundity of
the Caress

A Reading of Levinas, *Totality and Infinity*, "Phenomenology of Eros"

Luce Irigaray

On the horizon of a story is found what was in the beginning: this naive or native sense of touch, in which the subject does not yet exist. Submerged in *pathos* or *aisthesis*: astonishment, wonder, and sometimes terror before that which surrounds it.

Eros prior to any *eros* defined or framed as such. The sensual pleasure of birth into a world where the look itself remains tactile—open to the light. Still carnal. Voluptuous without knowing it. Always at the beginning and not based on the origin of a subject that sees, grows old, and dies of losing touch with the enthusiasm and innocence of a perpetual beginning. A subject already "fixed." Not "free as the wind." A subject that already knows its objects and controls its relations with the world and with others. Already closed to any initiation. Already solipsistic. In charge of a world it enjoys only through possession. With no communion and childlike acceptance of that which is given. A consumer who consumes what he produces without wonder at that which offers itself to him before any finished product occurs.

Sensual pleasure can reopen and reverse this conception and construction of the world. It can return to the evanescence of subject and object. To the lifting of all schemas by which the other is defined. Made graspable by this definition. *Eros* can arrive at that innocence which has never taken place with the other as other. At that nonregressive in-finity of empathy with the other. At that appetite of all the senses which is irreducible to any obligatory consumption or consummation. At that indefinable taste of an attraction to the other which will never be satiated. Which will always remain on the threshold, even after entering into the house. Which will remain a dwelling, preceding and following the habitation of any dwelling.

This gesture, which is always and still preliminary to and in all nuptials, which weds without consum(mat)ing, which perfects while abiding by the outlines of the other, this gesture may be called: the touch of the caress.

Prior to and following any positioning of the subject, this touch binds and unbinds two others in a flesh that is still and always untouched by mastery. Dressing the one and the other without and within, within and without in a garment that neither evokes, invokes, nor takes pleasure in the perversity of the naked but contemplates and adorns it, always for a first time, with an in-finite, un-finished flesh. Covering it, uncovering it again and again, like an amorous impregnation that seeks out and affirms otherness while protecting it.

In that place, nothing attests to the subject. The ever prolonged quest for a birth that will never take place, whose due date still and always recedes on the horizon. Life always open to what happens. To the fleeting touch of what has not yet found a setting. To the grace of a future that none can control. That will or will not happen. But while one waits for it, any possession of the world or of the other is suspended. A future coming not measured by the transcendence of death but by the call to birth of the self and the other. For which each one arranges and rearranges the environment, the body, and the cradle, without closing off any aspect of a room, a house, an identity.

The fecundity of a love whose most elementary gesture, or deed, remains the caress.

Before orality comes to be, touch is already in existence. No nourishment can compensate for the grace or work of touching. Touch makes it possible to wait, to gather strength, so that the other will return to caress and reshape, from within and from without, a flesh that is given back to itself in the gesture of love. The most subtly necessary guardian of my life is the other's flesh. Approaching and speaking to me with his hands. Bringing me back to life more intimately than any regenerative nourishment, the other's hands, these palms with which he approaches without going through me, give me back the borders of my body and call me to the remembrance of the most profound intimacy. As he caresses me, he bids me neither to disappear nor to forget but rather to remember the place where, for me, the most intimate life is held in reserve. Searching for what has not yet come into being for himself, he invites me to become what I have not yet become. To realize a birth that is still in the future. Plunging me back into the maternal womb and beyond that conception, awakening me to another birth—as a loving woman.

A birth that has never taken place, unless one remains at the stage of substitution for the father and the mother, which gestures toward an act that is radically unethical. Lacking respect for the one who gave me my body and enthusiasm for the one who gives it back to me in his amorous awakening.

When the lovers, male or female, substitute for, occupy, or possess the site of those who conceived them, they founder in the unethical, in profanation. They neither construct nor inhabit their love. Remaining in the no longer or the not yet. Sacrilegious sleepers, murderous dreamers— of the one and of the other in an unconscious state that might be the site of sensual pleasure? Sterile, if it were not for the child.

Which explains the closure, the sealing up of the society of couples: barren—if it were not for the child? And the abandonment of the beloved to the anonymity of love. To that touching vulnerability of a woman who can only be mortal. At least for him and in this place.

The caress does not seek to dominate a hostile freedom. However profaning. Transgressing the freedom of God? Sensual pleasure may be nourished by this transgression. Whence its ever-increasing avidity. Its unending deferral of its own potential? While he, the lover, is sent back to the transcendental, she, the beloved,[1] is plunged into the depths. The caress does not attain that more intimate dwelling place where something gathers itself in from a more secret consummation? In and through a mucous shelter that extends from the depths to the heights? From the most subterranean to the most celestial? A circulation from the one to the other that would happen in lovemaking?

Profanity always designates a threshold: the one where the simultaneity of what is hidden and what is revealed is in operation. The passage from mucous membrane to skin? But also, the presentiment of the first dwelling place where, now, there is no one, only the memory and expectation of amorous fecundity. No nudity brings back to light the intimacy of that first house of flesh. It is always nocturnal for a certain gaze—which wishes for clothing in order not to see that it cannot see everything?

The evanescence of the caress opens on a future that differs from an approach to the other's skin here and now. Stopping at that point risks relegating the beloved to the realm of animality once the moment of seduction, of penetration beyond anything visible, has passed. Always alien to the intimacy of the mucous, not crossing the threshold, still remaining outside, the lover continues to caress until he founders in some abyss. He does not attain communion in the most inward locus of the feeling and the felt, where body and flesh speak to each other.

In this moment of ultimate sympathy, the feeling and the felt go so far as the vertigo of "getting in over their heads," of immersion in that which does not yet have an individualized form, until they are returned to the deepest level of elementary flux, where birth is not yet sealed up in its identity. There, every subject loses its mastery and method. The path has been neither made nor marked, unless in the call to a more distant future that is offered by and to the other in the abandonment of self. Causing the possibles to recede, thanks to an intimacy that keeps unfolding itself more and more, opening and reopening the pathway to the mystery of the other.

Thus a new birth comes about, a new dawn for the beloved. And the lover. The openness of a face which had not yet been sculpted. The bloom that comes of flowing to the depths of what nourishes it again and again. Not a mask given or attributed once and for all, but an efflorescence that detaches itself from its immersion and absorption in the night's most secret place. Not without sparkling. The light that shines there is different from the one that makes distinctions and separates too neatly.

Does this mean that the beloved—and the lover—find their positions thus reversed, from inside to outside? It does not. Rather, that together, what is most interior and what is most exterior are mutually fruitful. Prior to any procreation.

The son does not resolve the enigma of the most irreducible otherness. Of course, he is not engendered without having had his place in the crypt of the beloved's womb. Where the lover falters, and whence he returns, without any possible recognition or vision of this terrain. Does the son appear to the father as the impossible image of his act of love?

But, before the appearance of the son, the beloved's fulfillment tells him, shows him, the mystery of fecundity. Looking again at the woman he has loved, the lover may contemplate the work of fecundation. And, if the surrender of the beloved woman—and of the female lover[2]—means a childlike trust, an animal exuberance, it illuminates the aesthetics and ethics of the amorous gesture, for those who take the time to reopen their eyes.

The beloved's beauty announces the fulfillment of the flesh. She is more beautiful, or differently beautiful, when she makes love than when she parades around in all her finery. The most intimate fecundity of love, of its caress, of its transcendence of all restraints on this side of the other's threshold, is proffered in this parousia—silently. Wonder at what is reborn from the heart's depths through a new conception. She would be regenerated by returning, with him, to a time before the fixed, mortal due date of her birth? Taken back to the acceptance of her life by the lover and accompanied on this side of, and beyond, a given day of reckoning.

Prior to any procreation, the lovers bestow on each other—life. Love fecundates both of them in turn, through the genesis of their immortality. They are reborn, each for the other, in the assumption and absolution of a definitive conception. Each one welcomes the birth of the other, this task of beginning where neither she nor he has met—the original infidelity. Attentive to that weakness which neither one could have wanted, they love each other as the bodies they are. Not irremediably diminished by having been born in different times and places nor by having lived prior to their mutual union and generation.

The mystery of relations between lovers is more terrible but infinitely less deadly than the destruction of submitting to sameness. Than all relationships of inclusion or penetration which bar the way to that nourishment which is more intimate than all others, which is given in the act of love.

Sameness, which quarrels about how much room it is due, occupies my flesh, demarcates and subdivides my space, lays siege to and sets up camp on my horizon—making it uninhabitable for me and inaccessible to the lover.

Porosity, and its fullest responsiveness, can occur only within difference. A porosity that moves from the inside to the outside of the body. The most profound intimacy becomes a protective veil. Turns itself into an aura that preserves the nocturnal quality of the encounter, without masks. Distance of the impenetrable in the clarity of daylight, of that which perceives but never beholds itself. Sometimes it crosses itself like a threshold, while touching and being touched by the other, but is forgotten and then recollected.

How to preserve the memory of the flesh? Above all, for what is or becomes the site that underlies what can be remembered? Place of a possible unfolding of its temporality? Burial ground of the touch that metabolizes itself in the constitution of time. Secret fold stitched into the time of the other. Eternity of the Other?

While there remains this mystery of the touch that goes beyond touching, the intention of every gesture, how can one recall this permanence? Become it as one recollects it? Make time of this source of time? Arrive at this nocturnal temporalization of touch?

Without a face? The face swallowed up by the nocturnal experience of touching, touching self and other, re-touching. Veiled by that which is situated only beyond the project. Invisible because it must defend itself unceasingly from the visible and the night. Both.

Beloved, the female lover emerges from all disguises. No longer frozen in a deadly freedom but permitted growth, which is still possible, and a face without any habits, which lets itself be seen in order to be reborn beyond what has already appeared. And in a state of imperfection, the unfinished condition of every living being.

In that place, there is no discovery to scrutinize. That which lets itself go in the most intimate touch remains invisible. Touch perceives itself but transcends the gaze. And the issue of nakedness. Touch never shows itself, not even if its precision could thus be made manifest. Reaching the other, or not. But it remains palpable fresh on this side of and beyond the visible.

Spelled out in images and photographs, a face loses the mobility of its expressions, the perpetual unfolding and becoming of the living being. Gazing at the beloved, the lover reduces her to less than nothing if this gaze is seduced by an image, if her nudity, not perceived as endlessly pulsating, becomes the site of a disguise rather than of astonishment at something that moves, unceasingly and inwardly. The beloved's vulnerability is this unguarded quality of the living, revealed in a form that is never definitive. If he thinks he leaves her like a dead body, cold it be that the lover discovers in her what is terrible about the limits of nudity, or dredges up what he needs to move on to some place beyond the realm of the living?

The face, or at least a certain conception, idea, or representation of it, can be swallowed up in the act of love. A new birth, which undoes and remakes contemplation by returning to the source of all the senses—the sense of touch. There is no longer any image there, except for that of letting go and giving of self. Among other ways, with the hands. Sculpting, shaping, as if for the first time, on the first day. The beloved would be engulfed in infancy or animality only to be reborn from there as flesh reshaped inside and out. Innocent of absorption in self and of self? Encounter across a threshold that differs from the irreversible one of mortal birth. Approach, communion, and regenerating fecundation of the flesh that touches itself on an ever more distant horizon, repeating and transcending the original conception.

Also surpassing the corruption of what has already been seen. Return to a certain night whence the lovers can arise differently illuminated and enlightened. They give themselves to each other and give up what has already been made. Of themselves and of reason. Opening to an innocence that runs the risk of folding back on itself in defense of the past. In this gesture, each one runs the risk of annihilating, killing, or resuscitating.

Lovers' faces live not only in the face but in the whole body. A form that is expressed in and through their entire stature. In its appearance, its touch. A *morphé* in continual gestation. Movements ceaselessly reshaping this incarnation.

The lovers meet in one moment of this incarnation. Like sculptors who are going to introduce themselves, entrust themselves to one another for a new delivery into the world.

And all the senses share in the nature of the caress, the hand serving, in its way, as the most intimate means of approach.

There the female lover is not subjected to alternations of fire and ice— mirror or frost that the male lover would have to pass through to reach the beloved. Given back to her own movements, to the demonstration of her charms, the female lover also revives herself in the flame and does not simply receive it from the other. Waiting without becoming rigid, she does not close herself off or enclose herself in some sepulchre of images or some project that denies her dynamism. She tends toward her own fulfillment, already unfolds herself to gather in more.

Thus, neither the one nor the other will take the initiative of plucking the bloom in order to contemplate it. Both contemplate and bloom. Opening and closing themselves in order to keep giving each other that which they could never have brought to life. Regenerating, renewing each other, in memory and in anticipation of the moment of their mutual fecundation. Each one moving along the path to some in-finite which trembles in the encounter without closing itself up or making decisions according to the limiting dimensions of some transcendental value to be attained.

The beloved woman falls back into infancy or beyond, while the male lover rises up to the greatest heights. Impossible match. Chain of links connecting, from one end to the other, a movement of ascent in which neither is wed, except in the inversion of their reflections.

When the male lover loses himself in the depths of the beloved woman's sensual pleasure, he dwells within her as in an abyss, an unfathomable depth. Both of them are lost, each in the other, on the wrong side, or the other side, of transcendence.

Beloved woman. Not female lover. Necessarily an object, not a subject with a relation, like his, to time. She drags the male lover into the abyss so that, from these nocturnal depths, he may be carried off into an absolute future.

The beloved woman sinks into the abyss, founders in a night more primeval than the night, or finds herself dispersed in the shards of a broken mirror. Do the pearls of ice or frost of her reflection put up a screen to love? Made from the brilliance of her finery? Of the beloved man, desired in and through her, who banishes her from the place of greatest tenderness. Calling her to freeze into the shapes that separate her from herself. She who is deprived of the suppleness of her loving mobility, torn away from her source of respiration, which is also cosmic, where she moves in harmony with the fecundity of nature. For her, a living mirror. Tuned differently to the rhythm of the earth and the stars. Intimately tied to universal circulation and vibration that go beyond any enclosure within reproduction. Turning in a cycle that never resolves back to sameness. Continual and patient engendering of an obscure labor. More passive than any voluntary passivity, yet not foreign to the act of creating/procreating the world. Within her something takes place, between earth and sky, in which she participates as in a continual gestation, a mystery yet to be deciphered. Heavy with her destiny.

When the lover relegates her to the realms of infancy, animality, or maternity, one aspect of this mystery, the relation to the cosmos, is not brought to light. What is left out is participation in the construction of a world that does not forget natural generation and the human being's role in safeguarding its efflorescence. A gestation in which the subject as microcosm is not given to nourishing, sheltering, and fecundating itself at the expense of a macrocosm for which it no longer shows any concern, believing that it is given once and for all, to be exploited endlessly, carelessly, irretrievably. Cultivating one's already enclosed garden. The work of a landowner who shows no regard for the natural world that makes fucundity possible, or for the God's concern with this universe of incarnation and the harmony of its attractions.

Separating her off into the subterranean, the submarine, stone and airborne flight lacking the sparkle of light and fire. Dismissing her to a perpetual future. Forgetting that which is already insistent here and now—already hidden or still buried. Uprooting the female lover from her fundamental habitat.

Annexing the other, in all his/her dimensions and directions, in order to capture him/her, captivate him/her within a language that possesses as its principal and internal resources only the consummation and speed of its contradictions. Deployment of a network that takes in the whole and deprives it of its most intimate breath and growth. A garment that first and foremost paralyzes the other's movement. Protecting it, like the shield of the hero who defends the beloved woman from some conquering rival?

But thus shielded, how does one live? For the woman who is so protected, what future remains? Inside this male territory, even if she plays at disguising herself in various showy and coquettish poses which he "strips away" in the act of love, she still lacks both the identity and the passport she needs to traverse or transgress the male lover's language. Is she some more or less domesticated child or animal that clothes itself in or takes on a semblance of humanity? Takes on the subject's unconscious and involuntary movements, veils them in softness, in folds, in spaciousness to give him back some room. Wraps herself up in the remainder of what he has taken in and from love. But what of her own call to the divine?

About this he has little to say. And since it is not her place to speak when he renders her profane in sensual pleasure, is he not also sacrilegious vis-à-vis God? The "God" of lightness, of "incarnation," the God of life—of the air, of blood, and of the maternity of the son who appears in the "form" of the cloud that accompanies the tablets of the law. The male lover would take this God into his discourse and beyond, refusing him the freedom of some future manifestation. He invokes this God but does not perceive him in the here and now, where God is already to be found and lost; in the sensibility of the female lover. In the creation that she perpetuates while preserving her intimacy, her inviolability, her virginity. God of the universe, God of the fecundity of a future coming, which is also preserved in the female lover.

When he does not reduce, or seduce, her to his needs, the male lover also summons her to God. This is just as regressive. Is she like a child or an animal in his eyes? Irresponsible, so that he can regain his freedom.

The very lightness of loving gestures and deeds makes one forget that when the female lover is also beloved, her abandon is inspired by the most absolute trust in the transcendence of life. Still in the future, always being reborn. Allowing herself to sink into the night, she calls forth from there a new morning, a new spring, a new dawn. The creation of a new day? From the source of a light that precedes and surpasses the limits of reason.

The first act of creation of the God? Before peopling the sky and the earth. Illumination that precedes any part in the organization, the ordering of a world. Contemplation prior to any vision. Opening to that less-than-nothing which is not nothing—light. Ultimate incorporation of the newborn man. The first discovery outside the womb, or in regeneration.

The matter without which no creation of form is possible, light is the chance for emergence out of chaos and formlessness.

Returning to the depth of night, the female lover waits for light—the light that shines through discourse, that filters through words, that bestows a sense of the cosmos, but also that which is illuminated in the grace of regeneration and transfiguration? Giving herself to nature to be reborn from there, made fertile—within herself. Pregnant with a son, perhaps (but shy a son and not a daughter, her other self?), but also with herself, by him. Fecundity of a love that gives itself over, on this side of and beyond reason—to the source of light. There where things have not yet taken their places but remain possible. In the future. Still germinating, growing, being revealed. The female lover will have to cultivate the intimacy (the seed?) of this fecundity and the path from the most hidden part of the night to the efflorescence of the day.

When the beloved woman presents herself or appears to the male lover as a paradise to be referred back to infancy and animality, then the act of love leads not only to profaning, but also to a destruction, a fall. The beloved woman would be cast down to the depths so that the male lover could be raised to the heights. The act of love would amount to reaching the inordinate limits of discourse, so that the woman is sent back to the position of fallen animal or child, and man to ecstasy in God. Two poles that are indefinitely separate. But perhaps the beloved woman's secret is that she knows, without knowing, that these two extremes are intimately connected.

Beneath her veils, she keeps secret watch over a threshold. A slight opening onto the depths or abysses of all language, birth, and generation. It is up to the male lover to find there or to perceive the fall into amorphousness or the astonishment of what has not yet been given form or revealed from above. To bring about *with* her, and not through or in spite of her, the assumption of the flesh. Instead of leaving her to her own profanation and despoiling, to reconstitute again and again only her virginity. To re-envelop herself in a *something more than* all humanity? Whereas the male lover leads her back to the *not yet* of the child, the *never like him* of the animal—outside human destiny. Separating himself from her with this gesture, to return to his "ethical responsibilities."

In this sense, the beloved woman, she who renounces her responsibility as a lover, succumbs to the temptation of being seduced by the male lover. She divests herself of her own will to live in order to become what is required for his exercise of will. Which assigns her to the place of non-willing in his ethics. Her fall into the identity of the beloved one cancels out any real giving of self and makes her into a thing, or something other than the woman that she needs to be. She lets herself be taken but does not give herself. She quits the locus of all responsibility, her own ethical site. She is placed under house arrest, lacking the will and movements of love. Except for the waiting and the healing of profanation? Falling into the depths? She gathers round herself and wraps herself with what was secretly entrusted to her—without his knowledge. Barely moves at all, but unfolds round herself the garments of protection and display. Of paralysis where dance is concerned, even running the risk of resigning from the creative part of love, except for remaining desirable, guarding the source and secret of her appeal. With no responsibility for bringing to life that something more than man's strategy of seduction which lies hidden within him? For unveiling a difference that remains obscurely connected to him.

If she comes back to herself, to herself within herself, to him within herself, she may feel responsible for another parousia. She may need to create, engender, give birth to the mystery she bears—prior to any conception of a child. No longer standing in the shadow of the one who draws on the mystery, taking charge—she herself—of bringing it to light. Engendering some love prior to, as something more than, a son. And a daughter.

Generating the dwelling, her site, with the male lover. Remaining on the threshold that is always receding and in the future of a mystery she must reveal under pain of ethical dereliction? The lover would assist her in this parturition, provided he does not simply send her back to the depths. The one for the other, messengers of a future that is still to be built and contemplated. The one for the other, already known and still unknown. The one for the other, mediators of a secret, a force, and an order that also touches on the divine.

Occasionally going their separate ways, meeting again, linking up again, in order not to lose their attentiveness to what transcends their already actual becoming. Listening to what has never taken place or found its place yet, to what calls to be born.

This simultaneity of desire and transcendence is traditionally represented by the angel—the divine messenger. Who is not foreign to desire and anger in some dimension that would not be one of need.

But here, sensual pleasure would hold fast to the fate of an exorbitant ultramateriality that has fallen away from discourse. That has never been brought to fruition or fulfilled in its transcendence. Captive of a destiny, without remission. Of an original sin without possible redemption? Manifesting itself outside language, outside and in spite of reason. Beyond all measures.

For the male lover, the transcendence of the Other justifies this infidelity to love. Returning to his God in a discontinuity of *eros*. If it were not for pardon.

And what of the female lover? Grace for what has not yet gone far enough into the future or been faithful enough to the moment, for what remains unfinished, left over. Remission of deprivation, of the distress of waiting, which punctuates the chronology of the lovers' unions and separations. Both fulfilling the cycles of their solitude to come back to the other, wounded perhaps, but free for a possible return because of the pardon that each gives. Allowing each to become detached from self and from the other. Renewal of the attraction that is also nourished in the suspense of reconciliation. There, sacrifice is neither sacrifice of nor mourning for the one or the other but absolution for what was not perfect. A marker in time that opens on to infinity, without sending it back to an origin or a goal deprived of an access, a threshold.

The flesh of the rose petal—sensation of the mucous regenerated. Somewhere between blood, sap, and the not yet of efflorescence. Joyous mourning for the winter past. New baptism of springtime. Return to the possible of intimacy, its fecundity, and fecundation.

But time enters in. Too closely connected with counting and with what has already been. And how can an evil that has lasted for such a long time be repaired in a second? Call to the other from a starting point of virginity, without any trace of scars, marks of pain, and self-enclosure? Love the other above and beyond any work of healing.

And when others continually interfere with this expectation of union, what can be done to maintain a candor that neither cries out for remission nor burdens the male lover with the task of healing wounds?

But doesn't the male lover keep asking the beloved woman to efface an original wound of which she would be the bearer? The suffering of an open body that cannot be clothed with herself, within herself, unless the lover is united with her in the joy—not the sacrifice—of the mucous, the most intimate part of the dwelling. Where crossing the threshold is no longer a profanation of the temple but an entrance into another, more secret, space. Where the female lover receives and offers the possibility of nuptials. Rapture unlike that of the conqueror who captures and dominates his prey. Rapture of return to the garden of innocence, where love does not yet know, or no longer knows, nudity as profane. Where the gaze is still innocent of the limits set by reason, of the division into day and night, the alternation of the seasons, animal cruelty, the necessity of protecting oneself from the other and from the God. Face to face encounter of two naked lovers in a nudity that is more ancient than and foreign to sacrilege. That cannot be perceived as profanation. The threshold of the garden, a welcoming cosmic home, remains open. There is no guard but love itself, innocent of the knowledge of display and of the fall.

Intuition without a goal, intuition that does not mark out but inscribes itself in an already insistent field. A prehensive intuition, which inhales from the air something of what is already there to come back to itself?

The beloved woman would be she who keeps herself available in this way. Offering to the other what he can put to his own use? Opening the path of his return to himself, of his open future? Giving him back time?

When the beloved woman perceives the male lover in this way, does she inscribe herself in a moment of her own trajectory as he arrives at a moment of his own? He believes that she is drawing him down into the depths; she believes that he is cutting himself off from her to constitute his transcendence. Their paths cross but achieve neither an alliance nor a mutual fecundation. Except for the male lover, whose double is— the son.

The beloved woman is relegated to an inwardness that is not one because it is abyssal, animal, infantile, prenuptial, while the lover is left a solitary call to his God. Withdrawn to the opposite poles of life, they do not marry. They occupy the contrapuntal sites of human becoming. The one watches over the substrate of the elementary, of generation, but the act of love scatters her among the archaic elements of earth, sea, and airborne flight. Caressing her to reach the infinity of her center, the male lover strips or divests her of her tactility—a porosity that opens onto the universe—and consigns her to a regression of her womanly becoming, which is always in the future. He is forgetful of the fucundity, here and now, of lovemaking: the gift to each of the lovers of sexuate birth and rebirth.

The one who takes the other into the self during lovemaking is inordinately cut off by this act. There is no opportunity to mourn an impossible identification. Attraction in union, and the chance of its fecundity.

Revealed only in the son, fecundity continues to disguise itself as the fecundation of the lovers in difference. As the fruit of communion between lovers, male and female, the son becomes the male lover's ornament and display of the same as himself, the position of his identity in relation to, and through, paternity.

If conceived in this way, the son does not appear as love's fulfillment. Perhaps he bars the way to its mystery? The aspect of fecundity that is vouched for only in the son obliterates the secret of difference. As the male lover's means of return to himself outside himself, the son closes the circle: the path of a solitary ethics that, for its own need, lacking the fulfillment of nuptials, will have intersected with the female lover who fails to take responsibility—the beloved.

When recognized only in the son, love and sensual pleasure bespeak the male lover's vulnerability on the threshold of difference. His retreat and appeal to his genealogy, his future as a man, his horizon, society, and security. Turning around in a world that remains his own. Contained within and by himself, with no dwelling for the female lover, except for the shelter she gives to the son—before his birth.

If the male lover needs to prove himself in sensual pleasure, he does so in order to sink down into the other of himself. To put down the night side of himself, which he covers up in the reasonable habitat of his life and from which he gains, as he emerges, the form of his highest ascension. The body of the beloved, male or female, which has been approached through caresses, is abandoned on the threshold of the nuptials. There is no union. The seduction of the beloved woman serves as a bridge between the Father and the son. Through her, who is only an aspect of himself, the male lover goes beyond love and pleasure toward the ethical.

"In this frailty as in the dawn rises the Beloved One, who is the Beloved Woman [l'Aimé qui est Aimée]. An epiphany of the Beloved, the feminine is not added to an object and a Thou antecedently given or encountered in the neuter (the sole gender formal logic knows). The epiphany of the Beloved is but one with her regime of tenderness."[3] The fragility and weakness of the beloved woman are the means by which the male lover can experience love of self as of a beloved who is powerless. Flesh of which he would remain the actual body.

Touching that which is not contained within the limits of his flesh, his body, the male lover risks an infinite outpouring into some dead being. He who has no connection to his own death puts the other at permanent risk of loss of self in the wrong infinity.

Touching can also place a limit on the reabsorption of the other in the same. Giving the other her contours, calling her to them, amounts to inviting her to live where she is without becoming other, without appropriating herself.

But does one who encounters only self in the beloved woman caress himself under the guise of a greater passivity? Adorning and inhabiting her with his own affects? If necessary, endowing her with some sense of touch as impersonal, a tactile *there is* adopted from his own subjectivity. Aporia of a tactility that cannot caress itself but needs the other to touch itself.

The threshold is still missing. The point of access to the most mucous part of the dwelling.

The abyss is circumscribed by the unavoidable alterity of the other. Its absolute singularity. Which should be protected prior to any positioning or affirmation of another transcendence? The transcendence of the "God" can help in the discovery of the other as other, a locus where expectation and hope hold themselves in reserve.

A dwelling place which becomes the matrix of the male lover's identity. Does she have no place anywhere? Hiding her dereliction in terror or irony, she calls for complicity with something other than profanation, animality, infancy. She calls—and sometimes in her dispersed state—to the feminine that she already is, secretly. Wanting to give herself over without giving up or violating her intimacy.

Modesty is not found on one side only. Responsibility for it should not belong to only one of the lovers. To make the beloved woman responsible for the secret of desire is to situate her also, and primarily in the place of the beloved man [*l'aimé*]—in his own modesty and virginity, for which he won't take ethical responsibility.

Would the task of the female lover be to watch over at least two virginities? Her own and the son's, to whom the male lover delegates the part of himself that is still virginal. A move toward interiority, of course. The male lover also seeks himself in this passage where he cannot cross the threshold from what is not yet to what is still in the future. Searching in infancy and animality for some moment whose obscure attraction remains insistent within himself. Call to an obscure night that is neither a return to immersion in the mother nor profanation of the beloved woman's secret, but the weight of his own mystery.

But, if some God obliterates respect for the other as other, this God stands as the guarantor of a deadly infinity. As a resource of life and love, the divine can only aid and further the fulfillment of the relation with the other. Provide the audacity of love. Encourage the risk of encountering the other with nothing held in reserve.

The fecundity of God would be witnessed in the uncalculating generosity with which I love, to the point of risking myself with the other. A loving folly that turns back the other's ultimate veil in order to be reborn on another horizon. Together, the lovers becoming creators of new worlds.

One should say, the lovers. Since to define the loving couple as a male lover and a *beloved woman* already assigns them to a polarity that deprives the female lover of her love. As object of desire, of the desirable, as call to the alterity of the night or the regression to need, the woman is no longer she who also opens partway onto a human landscape. She becomes part of the male lover's world. Keeping herself on the threshold, perhaps. Allowing the limits of her world, her country, to founder, to be swallowed up. But remaining passive within the field of activity of a subject who wills himself to be the sole master of desire. Leaving him, apparently, the whole of sensual pleasure, leaving him to a debasement without recourse to herself. What remains for him is reliance on the son as the continuation of his path.

Thus, the God, like the son, would serve as a prop in the ethical journey of man, who forgets to safeguard for the female lover the light of her return to self. He looks at her before plunging her into the night of his jouissance, his infantile or animal regression. But isn't it in the space between God and son that he takes her and annuls her as other? And renders her profane through his transcendence and relation to the divine?

Sensual pleasure would remain that which does not know the other. Which seduces itself, through her, to go down to the depths and return to ethical seriousness. Not coming face to face with an other who is responsible, especially for pleasure. But shirking this responsibility in the thoughtlessness of pleasure. An indifferent shore where he finds respose from ethical integrity?

Wouldn't the most terrible ethical demand be played out in that scene? Because it is a confrontation, here and now, with the mystery of the other. Because it is tied to a past and a future of incarnation. Modesty being a sign of an intimacy that demands, even begs for, a return. A supplication that calls wordlessly to reappear beyond immersion, in a light that has not yet been seen.

To give or give back to the other the possible site of his identity, of his intimacy: a second birth that returns one to innocence. A garment that isn't one, a kind of an envelopment that keeps continual watch over a space for birth—becoming other than a return to self. A becoming in which the other gives of a space-time that is still free. In which he re-entrusts me to a genesis that is still foreign to what has already taken place.

This gesture is more modest than the caress. A caress that precedes every caress, it opens up to the other the possible space of his respiration, his conception. Greeting him as other, encountering him with respect for what surrounds him—that subtle, palpable space that envelops each of us like a necessary border, an irradiation of our presence that overflows the limits of the body. Capable of more than the "I can" of the body itself.

This caress would begin at a distance. Tact that informs the sense of touch, attracts, and comes to rest on the threshold of the approach. Without paralysis or violence, the lovers would beckon to each other, at first from far away. A salutation that means the crossing of a threshold. Pointing out the space of a love that has not yet been made profane. The entrance into the dwelling, or the temple, where each would invite the other, and themselves, to come in, also into the divine.

Not divided into their alliances between highest and lowest, the extremes of day and night, but summoning these ultimate sites at the risk of union and fecundation of each by the other. A passage through the loss of the individual body, through the surrender of the "I can" that opens up a future without the sacrifice of the one to the other. Creation of love that does not abandon respect for the ethical.

This union does not ignore sensual pleasure; it sounds out its most plummeting and soaring dimensions. Not divided into elements belonging to different domains, the lovers meet as a world that each reassembles and both resemble. Inhabiting it and dressing it differently. The male lover's and the female lover's horizons being irreducible.

The beloved woman—when called a child or an animal—is also she who holds the highest note. Whose voice carries the farthest, is the finest, and the strongest.

Her fall into the depths would mean that her voice was lost. Her song unheard. Her vocalism forgotten. The beloved woman would be mute or reduced to speaking in the spaces between the consonants of the male lover's discourse. She would be relegated to his shadow as his double, that which he does not yet know or recognize in himself, presenting itself to him under the guise of the beloved woman. Disguising for him the space of the present. An engulfment of his in-stance in the present, which clings to memory, and the song of the female lover. Which he sends down to the depths so that he can rebound into the transcendent. Manifested in and through writing. Absent and awaited in spirit. Whose voice would have been silent for a long time. A seriousness that is hard to maintain, which history would try to rediscover, re-uncover through the text.

Neither wanting nor knowing how to see himself in this body that he is no longer, the male lover would appear to himself in a female other, mystery of the site of his disappearance. In order to keep the secret, she must keep quiet, no song or laughter. Her voice would give her away. Reveal that she is not what the male lover thinks or searches for. That she is only a cover for what he is seeking, through and despite her.

Before parousia occurs, silence happens. A silence that rehearses oblivion and is only filled by music. There, the voice of the woman who sings and calls to the lover is still missing. It has been stifled by the noise of instruments and of nature running wild or abandoned to prostitution.

Unless she, too, disguises herself, in the guise of angels? Who perhaps have no sex? An interval that speaks between the bride and the spirit? Neither the one nor the other expressing themselves, unless it is through the mediation of the orders of the angels.

The expectation of parousia would also mean the death of speech between the sexual partners of the scene. Which foretells the terrible aspect of a new cosmic chaos and the disappearance of the gods. The hope of a new pentecost? Of the spirit's coming to the bride in the joy of a different union.

The feminine would remain in search of its cause and sought out as a cause, but never thought through as such. Always relegated to another kind of causality. At best, defined qualitatively. Women the adjectives or ornaments of a verb whose subject they can never be.

The logos would maintain itself between the verb and the substantive. Leaving out the adjective? A mediation between the act and its result. The place of attraction? In between loving and love would be the place of the beloved—man or woman. The one who is lovable. Approachable in his/her tenderness.

The two philosophical gestures would come down to grounding, unfolding, and surrounding that which founds itself: acting and constituting the substantive of the act. Closure of an age. The partly open would be remembered in the qualities of the beloved woman. Her already passive appearances or attributes? Over which she keeps watch, however, as they resist being taken up into substance.

Does the beloved woman's appeal convey a sense of that which has not yet solidified into the hardness of a name or noun or the seal of a signature? Between the act and the work would be situated that which reveals a future that the male lover understands not as the work of love but as the lightness of sensuality. As the repository of certain characteristics which the male lover does not retain when he is a beloved, the beloved woman's significance derives from this less than nothing, a substitution that does not disclose itself as such. She is brought into a world that is not her own so that the male lover may enjoy himself and gain strength for his voyage toward an autistic transcendence. In his quest for a God who is already inscribed but voiceless, does she permit him not to constitute the ethical site of lovemaking? A seducer who is seduced by the gravity of the Other but approaches the female other carelessly, he takes her light to illuminate his path. Without regard for what shines and glistens between them. Whether he wills it or not, knows it or not, he uses this divine light to illuminate reason or the invisibility of the "god."

In the meantime, he will have taken from the beloved woman this visibility that she offers him, which strengthens him, and will have sent her back to darkness. He will have stolen her gaze. And her song. Her attraction to a divine that becomes incarnate—in light, in the contemplation of the universe and the other. The divine revealed in those of its dimensions that are also accessible to the senses. Having already appeared and still to come, and which beauty would call to mind? A partial opening. A threshold. Also between past and future. The male lover steals her desire from her to adorn his world—which predates love—to spark his pleasure and aid his ascent following the lightness of a fulfillment that will not occur in the encounter between them. A union, or wedding, that is broken off at least twice. No "human" flesh is celebrated in that *eros*.

Failing to take into account his own limits, the male lover penetrates into flesh that he consumes and consummates without attention to the sacrificial gesture. He "takes communion" without benefit of rites or words. He is absorbed into nothing—unless it is his Other? Without detectable transition. Without a trace of this rape. If it were not for the exhaustion and suffering of the beloved woman, who is reduced to infancy, left to herself or to animal savagery.

Confounding the one and the other, bending them to the same logic, the male lover ignores the irreducible strangeness of the one and the other. Between the one and the other. He approaches the other to reduce it to that which is not yet human in himself. Sensual pleasure that does not take place in the realm of the human and will not be its creation. Neither ethical nor aesthetic.

When the female lover trusts the other beyond the limits of his possibilities, she is cast down and utterly forsaken. When she opens herself to the most intimate point of her being, to the most profound depths of her inwardness, but is not touched and returned to the most sublime part of herself, she is overcome by a night without end. Her invitation to inhabit this dwelling is a call for communion in the secret depths of the sensible realm and not for a defloration of herself as a woman.

The beloved woman's face illuminates the secret that the male lover touches on. Shining with a new light, bathed in a horizon that goes beyond intention, her face expresses what is hidden without disposing of it in a meaning. It is full of what cannot be said but is not nothing— thanks to the already and the not yet. A taking shape of matter that precedes any articulation in language. Like vegetative growth, animal anticipation, a sculptor's roughcast. An aesthetic matrix that has not yet produced results but is recognized as a prerequisite to the completion of all gestures.

The caress seeks out the not yet of the female lover's blossoming. That which cannot be anticipated because it is other. The unforeseeable nature of contact with otherness, beyond its own limits. Beyond the limits of its

"I can." The irreducible nature of the other's presence, which is put off to a time always in the future, which suspends parousia indefinitely. The other, because it is still to come, would only maintain the male lover in his love of self, as he makes himself beloved. He thus resigns from the woman's ethics, which is an opening of and to another threshold.

The act of love is neither an explosion nor an implosion but an in-dwelling. Dwelling with the self, and with the other—while letting the other go. Remembering while letting the other be, and with the world. Remembering the act not as a simple discharge of energy but for its characteristic intensity, sensation, color, and rhythm. The intensity would be or would constitute the dimensions of the dwelling, which is always in process. Never completed. Unfolding itself during and between the schedule of encounters.

If the beloved woman is relegated to infancy and animality, love has no dwelling. Nor does the male lover, who desires the ethical in a return to some Transcendent. Who bases this site on nostalgia for an inaccessible here and now of love and sensual pleasure?

Pleasure is never conceived as an instance of power in the act. It is said to be a way out, an exit from itself, as if tied to the instant, dispersing or rarefying our being—while overseeing an evasion. It is presented as an amputation of the being's ecstasy and not as a fulfillment that surpasses its destiny in the past and in the future. A liberation of being through the affective. Rather it is conceived as a break, a paroxysm whose promises cannot be kept, a disappointment and a deception in its internal becoming. Doomed to shame through its inability to measure up to the exigencies of need. Never up to what is expected of it. Never in the realm of the ethical.

Before the clamorous display of a presence that tells of nothing but its own emptiness, one should remain impassive in order to turn toward new values and horizons, without falling into the trap of a relapse into what has already been seen and known. The impatience of one who wants something else is not of the same register, musically, as the noise of one who cries out that he wants me not to want any longer. I am to want what he wants or to nourish myself on his desires, in that place where I can only do so at the cost of renouncing my incarnation.

An aggressive appeal by the other, who lets me know that he can no longer bear the suspension of his will. That he is hungry for my hunger.

He is ready to destroy it in order to ignore the place where his hunger might take place—his appeal to the infinite, the unappeasable, the always more. He must bear its weight in separation, if I am to communicate with him in a dimension that guards the mystery of the absolute without abolishing it. In a demand for regressive nurturing, for example.

The lives of both the one and the other are at stake. A future is only possible if this respect for limits is admitted, also in the instant. If my hunger is not always turned back into uncertainty about the other's hunger. If he leaves me to the openness of my quest without absorbing me into his desire for nothing, unless it is to stifle what I am silently. In order to exist by himself?

One might as well say, to die? To produce, to produce himself in my place? This impossibility, which is both ridiculous from the start and insistent in its manifestations, can cut off my inspiration through its violence. For all that, however, he does not discover its source.

Forgetting that I exist as a desiring subject, the other transforms his need into desire. Desire for a nothing—the abolition of the other's willing, which would become a not-willing. Unless it is desire for a Transcendent—an Other of the same.

In this way, sensual pleasure finds itself set adrift, permanently. The distraction of transfiguration, transmutation, resurrection. An infinite substitution and spelling out of appearances, the masks falling without parousia? An illumination capable of being buried beneath displays, but not signifying a return to animality or infancy.

Does the male lover not impose upon the beloved woman that which he cannot see in himself? That which keeps him from becoming what he is, and from being able to encounter her, herself? Wrapping her up in what he cannot bear of his own identity, he secretly places her in the maternal position. A destiny, or maya, hidden in its identifying strata. A net which he cannot pass through again, which he imposes upon her, in order to rend it—figuratively. He discovers nothing. And if she surrenders as a child or animal, her finery fallen, the God becomes even more transcendent, inaccessible. Out of touch.

Might not the infinitesimal but impassable distance in our relation to death then be that which would take place in the touching of the female sex? Whence the assimilation of the feminine to the other? And the forgetting of a vital threshold—the tactile.

This locus of my concentration and of his opening out without futile dispersion constitutes a possible habitation. Turning back on itself and protecting me until the next encounter. A kind of house that shelters without enclosing me, untying and tying me to the other, as to one who helps me to build and inhabit. Discharging me from a deadly fusion and uniting me through an acknowledgment of who is capable of building this place. My pleasure being, in a way, the material, one of the materials.

Architects are needed. Architects of beauty who fashion jouissance— a very subtle material. Letting it be and building with it, while respecting the approach, the threshold, the intensity. Urging it to unfold without a show of force. Only an accompaniment? It only unfolds itself from being unfolded. It is in touch with itself from being touched while touching itself. It must be able to inhere. To continue to live in itself in order to live with. One must reach the heart of one's habitation in order to cohabit. This heart is always in motion and, at the same time, does not lack a dwelling. A qualitative threshold makes it possible for love to ensure. For the lovers to be faithful? When they do not obey, the threshold wears out. The house of flesh, which lets them remember each other, call to each other—even at a distance—is destroyed.

Letting go and dwelling in the strength of becoming, letting the other go while staying contained and insistent, such is the wager that the female lover must make. Not holding back, but dwelling in that which wraps itself around a nonforgetfulness. That which is reborn, again and again, around a memory of the flesh. Flourishing again around what, in herself, has opened up and dispersed itself in sowings. Sowings that are fecund if she, the one who is unique, recalls this impossible memory. Is attentive to a time that is always consecrated to the depths. To drifting. To an infinite substitution.

There remain only the immemorial intrauterine abode and trust in some Other. Between blind nostalgia and ethical tension, the male lover loves and despises himself through the beloved woman—who is the beloved man. He attracts and rejects himself through this other, while he takes on neither infancy nor animality.

Is the memory of touching always disguised by senses that forget where they come from? Creating distance through a mastery that constitutes the object as a monument built in place of the subject's disappearance.

The memory of touching? The most insistent and the most difficult to enter into memory. The one that entails returning to a commitment whose beginning and end cannot be recovered.

Memory of the flesh, where that which has not yet been written is inscribed, laid down? That which has no discourse to wrap itself in? That which has not yet been born into language? That which has a place, has taken place, but has no language. The felt, which expresses itself for the first time. Declares itself to the other in silence.

One must remember this and hope that the other remembers. Lodge it in a memory that serves as its bed and its nest, while waiting for the other to understand. Make a cradle for him inside and out while leaving him free, and keep oneself in the memory of the strength that revealed itself, that acted.

But leaving free, giving an invitation to freedom, does not mean that the other wants it to be so. And lives in you, with you.

Far away, potentially. Avoiding encounters, approaches that convey the limits of the flesh. Remaining at a distance, in order to destroy the possibility of us?

A sort of abolition of the other, in the loss of the body's borders. A reduction of the other—even if it means consuming the flesh for the Other? Between the memory that preserves in expectation and respects the advent or the eventuality of the other and the memory that dissipates itself in assimilation, something is lacking—that memorial in which the flesh survives in its mobility, its energy, its place of inscription, its still-virginal power.

Must one have a certain taste? One that does not exist or inhere in any nourishment. A taste for the affective with and for the other. This taste that ought not to remain in an obscure nostalgia but rather ought to attend to that which always forgets itself. As impossible to gratify? Which does not exclude the enjoyment of whoever feels without wanting to absorb or resolve. Between the body and the subtlety of the flesh— bridge or place of a possible encounter, unusual landscape where union is approached?

It is not a matter of the preciosity of a fetish or of the celebratory perfume of some sacrifice. Prior to any construction of words, any enshrinement or destruction of idols or even of temples, something—not reducible to the ineffable aspect of discourse—would keep itself close to the perception of the other in its approach.

The other cannot be transformed into discourse, fantasies, or dreams. It is impossible for me to substitute any other, thing or god, for the other— because of this touching of and by him, which my body remembers.

To each wounding separation, I would answer by refusing the holocaust while silently affirming, for myself and for the other, that the most
intimate perception of the flesh escapes every sacrificial substitution,
every assimilation into discourse, every surrender to the God. Scent or
premonition between my self and the other, this memory of the flesh as
the place of approach means ethical fidelity to incarnation. To destroy it
is to risk the suppression of alterity, both the God's and the other's.
Thereby dissolving any possibility of access to transcendence.

Notes

1. (At this point, the text begins to set up the differential positioning of the lover [amant] as a
masculine subject and the beloved [aimée] as his feminine object. Henceforth, whenever the effects
of this positioning are emphasized, amant is translated as "male lover" and amante as "female lover";
similarly, to underscore Irigaray's point that the object position is also gendered, aimée will be translated as "beloved woman," and aimé as "beloved man" or "beloved one."—Trans.)

2. (Henceforth, the distinction between woman as beloved [aimée] and woman as lover [amante]
receives increasing emphasis.—Trans.)

3. Emmanuel Levinas, Totality and Infinity: An Essay on Exteriority, trans. Alphonso Lingis
(Pittsburgh: Duquesne University Press, 1969), 256. (The translation is modified in accord with present usage [e.g., aimée is here translated as "beloved woman"].—Trans.)

6

Reinhabiting the House of Ruth

Exceeding the Limits of the Feminine in Levinas

Claire Elise Katz

> A man's home is his wife
> (The house is Woman)
> —The Talmud

In a footnote to her introduction to *The Second Sex*, Simone de Beauvoir takes Levinas to task for what she sees as his attempts, like those of others who come before him, to posit woman as Other. She cites from *Time and the Other* the following passage:

> Is there not a case in which otherness, alterity [*altérité*], unquestionably marks the nature of a being, as its essence, an instance of otherness not consisting purely and simply in the opposition of two species of the same genus? I think that the feminine represents the contrary in its absolute sense, this contrariness being in no wise affected by any relation between it and its correlative and thus remaining absolutely other. Sex is not a certain specific

difference ... no more is the sexual difference a mere contradiction.... Nor does this difference lie in the duality of two complementary terms, for two complementary terms imply a pre-existing
whole.... Otherness reaches its full flowering in the feminine, a
term of the same rank as consciousness but of opposite meaning.[1]

To understand de Beauvoir's criticism of Levinas, one must realize that
de Beauvoir interprets this relationship of subject/other in its most disparaging form. To be Other to the male subject is to be incidental, to be
inessential to the essential.[2] De Beauvoir takes issue with what she sees as
Levinas's disregard for reciprocity and his masculine privilege disguised as
an objective position. According to de Beauvoir, Levinas assumes a masculine privilege when he maintains the subject/object dichotomy where
he, Levinas qua male, occupies the position of subject, and the feminine,
the "mysterious" feminine, occupies the position of object.

In a translator's note to *Time and the Other*, Richard Cohen takes de
Beauvoir to task and defends Levinas by claiming that de Beauvoir has
misunderstood Levinas's analysis and simplified the relationship between
the subject (he) who is absolute, and the feminine other. Cohen's defense
of Levinas reminds us that, for Levinas, the other has priority over the
subject, and, thus, de Beauvoir was too quick to chastise Levinas for sexism. However, each of these notes—Beauvoir's criticism, which assumes
the other as antagonistic, and Cohen's defense of Levinas—represents
an extreme position, neither of which is accurate. De Beauvoir is right to
raise this question to Levinas; that is, she is right to ask after the way in
which the feminine is conceived by him. However, by attacking him
for casting woman as other, she reveals her misunderstanding of what
Levinas means by the other and the position the other holds in his analysis.[3] As a result, she also does not see the way Levinas's project radically
departs from the philosophies that precede him.

Luce Irigaray is also critical of the conception of the feminine in
Levinas's project, though her criticism differs from de Beauvoir's.[4] Where
de Beauvoir worries that the Other is the feminine, Irigaray worries that
Levinas, like the philosophers who precede him and despite appearances,
did not take sexual difference into account with his conception of the
Other. In addition, Irigaray is concerned that the role in which the feminine is cast, that is, as the Beloved, is a disparaging one. As the Beloved,
the woman plays a transcendental role: she makes possible the man's
transcendence to the ethical, while she is cast downward. Thus, Irigaray

claims, the feminine in Levinas's project perpetuates the dominant story in the history of Western philosophy: the claim of neutrality in one's analysis, without acknowledgment of the sexual difference at work in the background.

I claim that Levinas's efforts to define and situate the feminine are differentiated from those of his predecessors, and even his contemporaries, in two significant ways: (1) the feminine plays a significant if not indispensable role in his philosophical work, and (2) his view of the feminine is informed by the strong influence of the Judaic on his philosophical thought. That the feminine is other is not the problem; rather, it is the particular role that the feminine plays, and what it means, specifically, for the feminine to be other, that is in question in Levinas's work. So while de Beauvoir's concerns are legitimate, and to be taken seriously, it is Irigaray's criticisms, which recognize Levinas's positive formulation of the Other, that are far more penetrating. Moreover, because the role of the feminine is so intrinsic to Levinas's project, to criticize the way in which Levinas conceives the feminine opens up the possibility that an examination could, in the end, undermine the analysis, or put into jeopardy the project itself, a project that is not necessarily antifeminist, or antiwoman, in its aim. The significant role of the feminine and the Judaic influence on Levinas's thought, if taken together, reveal within Levinas's work a rich and complex view of the feminine, one that is both philosophically and religiously based, and one that can be read with both affirmative and negative attributes.

My focus in this chapter is twofold: (1) to examine the conception and work of the feminine in *Totality and Infinity* found in the sections titled "The Dwelling" and "The Phenomenology of Eros,"[5] and (2) to explore how the influence of Jewish thought on Levinas's work motivates this conception.[6] I turn first to Levinas's conception of the feminine, where I argue that he uses the feminine as a transcendental structure.[7] The feminine creates the dwelling, the welcoming, and habitation, thus providing the means of enjoyment and sensuality that are interrupted by the ethical. The dwelling provides the place from which the man transcends, in order to attend to his more important duties, but to which he returns for refuge. One of my primary goals in this section of the chapter is to problematize the easy characterization of the feminine as a metaphor. Although I admit that the feminine is used metaphorically, my claim is that the feminine is not merely a metaphor. I then turn to Levinas's discussion of love, as he describes it in the "Phenomenology of Eros," and to

Luce Irigaray's comments on this discussion. I interrogate not only the way Levinas conceives love, but also the way Irigaray interprets Levinas on love. Finally, I turn to the biblical story of Ruth to illustrate Levinas's themes of love, fecundity, and the ethical. But it is through this examination of Ruth that I also offer a means to disrupt the Levinasian analysis. That is, I raise the question of the feminine not only as a transcendental condition for the ethical but as a figure of the ethical itself. Thus, my goal in this chapter is to draw out the Judaic elements of Levinas's thought and to use this influence in order to reexamine the feminine as conceived in *Totality and Infinity*.[8]

A. The Work of the Feminine

Housework

Levinas says in *Totality and Infinity* that in order for the ethical to arise, or for it to be possible, there must be an intimacy, a familiarity, an enjoyment that is disrupted. In habitation the "I" takes pleasure in the handling of a tool (over and against the mere instrumentality of tools as we see in Heidegger). Unlike the tool, however, habitation provides the condition from which the man[9] "enters" the world. The man goes into the world as someone who is at home with himself and who can return to his home. The home, which provides the place to which the man can return for refuge, is thus characterized by intimacy. Hence, the man has a life that is both inside (his life of enjoyment), and outside (the ethical) the home.

The gentleness of habitation is the feminine presence.[10] The relation of I to the Other in the face-to-face is identified by language; and the face-to-face, though always eluding my grasp, is not hidden. In contrast to the Other, woman who is "discreetly absent" and "silent" accomplishes the task of making the home hospitable; the woman [*la Femme*] makes possible the "condition for recollection ... and inhabitation" (TI 155/128).[11] Levinas tells us, "The Other who welcomes in intimacy is not the *you* [*vous*] of the face that reveals itself in a dimension of height, but precisely the *thou* [*tu*] of familiarity: a language without teaching, a silent language, an understanding without words, an expression in secret" (TI, 155/129).[12] Thus, the feminine makes possible the subject, or the man's, participation in the ethical; however, it does so without participating in the ethical relation itself.

Thus, to talk about the feminine as the condition for the possibility of the ethical raises a question about who is, or who can be, the ethical subject, and who is or can be the Other. The confusion that arises from Levinas's use of the feminine has its roots in its ambiguous reference: does feminine refer to empirical women, or is it being used metaphorically throughout his work to refer to what would be taken as sex-stereotyped feminine attributes such as gentleness? And Levinas himself in this section equivocates between the uses of these two terms. Certainly, one could argue for the latter position, namely, that Levinas's account of the feminine is merely metaphorical. Here, in *Totality and Infinity*, Levinas's own claim to use metaphor is illustrated when he writes: "Need one add that there is no question here of defying ridicule by maintaining the empirical truth or counter truth that every home *in fact* presupposes a woman? . . . [T]he empirical absence of the human being of the 'feminine sex' in a dwelling nowise affects the dimension of femininity which remains open there, as the very welcome of the dwelling" (TI, 157–58/131). Commentators of Levinas also claim that the feminine is used by Levinas metaphorically. Adriaan Peperzak, for example, insists on interpreting Levinas as using the feminine metaphorically by equating "man, woman, and child" with Levinas's use of "the stranger, the widow, and the orphan," thus concluding that Levinas is not excluding woman (or women) from the ethical relationship.[13] Although I acknowledge the metaphorical use of this phrase, I also think that to interpret the feminine metaphorically may occlude the nuance of the text. Thus, I want to dwell on the biblical significance of this reference, since it is precisely the way that this reference appears in the Hebrew Bible[14] and the midrash that makes the phrase so powerful.[15]

In Malachi and Job, references are made to the stranger, the widow, and the orphan—a phrase Levinas appropriates—as those who are most helpless and exposed to possible injury. Levinas employs the biblical command to be responsible to those who most need our help: "the stranger, the widow, the orphan, and the poor,"[16] in order to impress upon us the extremity of the ethical command of the other. All these individuals are for Levinas examples of the Other par excellence, and this view is supported by rabbinic interpretation. A rabbi in the midrash asks, "Why does God love the orphans and the widows?" "Because," he answers, "their eyes are raised to none but him."[17] The answer the rabbi gives is an interesting one, for it tells of the aloneness that characterizes the widow and the orphan. There is a special connection between the orphan and the widow, for they are defined in the absence of a male protective figure in the household.[18] They are both without a male person anchoring them to the home. And so, in the rabbi's view, they are left in God's care. But although the widow has a place in Levinas's conception of the ethical relation, we cannot ignore her status as such: she is defined in the absence of a man. Merely mapping "man, woman, and child" onto this biblical phrase covers over the nuance of the biblical expression. Moreover, the possibility that it refers to concrete women, a possibility that arises from Levinas's own equivocation of these terms, must be addressed.

Although the ambiguity of the "silent," feminine presence in "The Dwelling" is not resolved, we can see resonances of a more determinate position in Levinas's views on Judaism. In his essay "Judaism and the Feminine,"[19] Levinas tells us that "[t]he characteristics of the Jewish woman are fixed thanks to charming feminine figures of the Old Testament" (DF, 31/DL, 52). After listing the various wives of patriarchs and prophetesses, with their respective virtuous traits and noble deeds, Levinas claims: "But the world in which these events unfolded would not have been structured as it was—and as it still is and always will be—without the *secret presence, on the edge of invisibility,* of these mothers, wives and daughter; without their *silent footsteps* in the depths and opacity of reality, drawing the very dimensions of interiority and making the world precisely inhabitable" (DF, 31/DL, 53; emphasis mine).[20]

Throughout this essay, just as in *Totality and Infinity,* there is an equivocation between the 'feminine' and 'woman' that would indicate that *feminine* is not a mere adjective for female traits but also signifies the female sex. Here, as in *Totality and Infinity,* woman is described as a "strange flow of gentleness" and as "the one 'who does not conquer'" (DF, 33/DL, 55). The Talmud further tells us that "'[t]he house is woman'" (DF 31/DL 53), and Proverbs tells us it is through woman as a keepsake of the hearth that the public life of man is possible" (DF, 32/DL, 53). Talmudic law, which excludes women from being judges and witnesses,[21] in effect keeps women from participating in the public realm. The Orthodox strains of Judaism affirm the public-man/private-woman opposition; that is, these branches affirm the traditional historical roles of men and women, where men were assigned roles that dealt with public life, while women were confined to those roles that were associated with the home.[22]

Thus, I want to stress the possibility that the characterization of the relationship between the feminine, or woman, and the home, as described in this essay in particular and in Judaism in general, is parallel to the description we find in "the Dwelling." This similarity may confirm two points for us: (1) there is indeed a relationship between the ideas in Levinas's confessional writings and the ideas in his philosophical writings; and (2) there is evidence to support the interpretation of the "feminine" as a reference to concrete woman.

For Levinas, the role woman plays in making possible man's transcendence extends beyond the dwelling and into the erotic relationship. Moreover, even if we allow that Levinas is using the feminine metaphorically in the dwelling, he is clear that the erotic relationship is excluded from the ethical. As such, the beloved in the erotic relation is not an ethical other. It is at this point that we can raise questions not only about how Levinas understands the erotic relationship, that is, the love relationship between the man and woman, but also about how his conception of eros has been understood.

The Labor of Love

According to Levinas, the erotic, conjugal relationship between a man and woman is not an end in itself; "[t]he meaning of love does not, then, stop with the moment of voluptuousness, nor with the person loved" (DF, 36/DL, 60). Further, he says, "[t]his dimension of the romantic in which love becomes its own end, where it remains without any 'intentionality' that spreads beyond it ... is foreign to Judaism" (DF, 36–37/DL, 60). Levinas's view of the erotic relation follows the Talmud. In Judaism the erotic relationship is not merely an end in itself; the relationship between lovers is directed toward the infinite. Yet, while fecundity is important insofar as it signifies the continuation of the Jewish people,[23] Judaism also emphasizes the role of sexual pleasure for its own sake.[24] Thus, these two view of sexuality, views Levinas himself accepts, need to be reconciled if we are to have an accurate conception of Levinas's position. My intention is not to be an apologist for Levinas. Rather, I want to present him in the strongest light possible, so that whatever criticism I offer might provide leverage to rehabilitate some of his central insights, rather than forcing us to abandon them.[25]

Levinas identifies the love relationship, in contrast to the ethical relationship, as a return to the same. Following a structure that we also find in Sartre, Levinas describes the love relationship as a relationship wherein what the lover wants is not just to love the other, but to have the Beloved love him back.[26] The erotic relationship is not a relation of infinity in itself; the erotic fulfills the ethical, the reaching out toward infinity, through fecundity; specifically, through the birth of a son.[27] The erotic, or the relationship with "the Other as feminine, is required in order that the future child come to pass from beyond the possible, beyond projects" (TI, 267/245).[28] Since, for Levinas, the erotic relationship culminates in fecundity, specifically in the birth of a son, and since Levinas, as the writer, assumes the position of the "I," one must conclude that the other is the "feminine sex", in other words, a woman.

According to Levinas, ambiguity characterizes the erotic. The relation with the other in love turns into a relation of need, while also transcending such a relation. Love both presupposes the exteriority of the other while also going beyond this exteriority of the other, of the beloved. Taking up the Aristophanes myth in Plato's *Symposium*, Levinas sees love as a mixture of immanence and transcendence (TI, 254/232). Although Levinas disagrees with the implication of fusion signaled by the myth,[29] he does find compelling the ambiguous notion of love as a relation in which there is a return to the self, but also as a relation in which the self is transcended. Love "is an event situated at the limit of immanence and transcendence" (TI, 254/232). The face of the other, of the beloved, reveals within it what is not yet. It reveals the future that is never future enough, a future that is "more remote than possible" (TI, 254–55/232–33). The ambiguity of love lies, finally, in the possibility of the Other to appear as an object of need and yet still retain its alterity, "the possibility of enjoying the Other, of placing oneself at the same time beneath and beyond discourse—this position with regard to the interlocutor which at the same time reaches him and goes beyond him, this simultaneity of need and desire, of concupiscence and transcendence, tangency of the avowable and the unavowable, constitutes the originality of the erotic which, in this sense, is *the equivocal* par excellence" (TI, 255/233). The beloved—who is situated both before the ethical, as a transcendental figure, and beyond the ethical, in the form of eros and the possibility of fecundity—appears as both need, or the present, and desire, or the future, that is, the exterior or the beyond. But regardless of how we situate the beloved in relation to the ethical, as either below, before, or beyond the ethical, the beloved remains outside the ethical. This view of the beloved as outside the ethical, as that which draws the lover "down," is further explicated in Levinas's "Phenomenology of Eros."

Levinas begins his phenomenology of eros by declaring that "[l]ove aims at the other; it aims at him in his frailty [*faiblesse*]" (TI, 256/233).[30] Love aims at the tenderness of the Beloved. For Levinas, the tenderness is not something added to the Beloved; rather, the Beloved "is but one with her *regime* of tenderness" (TI, 256/233).[31] Levinas's analysis continually uses language that presents the image of the Beloved cast below, while the lover is taken to new heights. The Beloved is "dark," "nocturnal," "clandestine," "deep in the subterranean dimension" (TI, 257/234). The Beloved equivocates between virginity[32] and profanation, between modesty and immodesty (TI, 257–58/234–35). The lover's movement before this frailty, which Levinas terms *femininity* (TI, 257/234), is "absorbed in the caress" (TI, 257/234). The caress, though it is like sensibility, transcends the sensible. It seeks the not-yet, a "future that is never future enough, in soliciting what slips away as though it *were not yet*" (TI, 257; 258/235).[33] The caress both expresses love, and yet is inadequate to do so (TI, 258/235). The Beloved, characterized as "the virgin," is at once "violable and inviolable," the "Eternal Feminine" (TI, 258/236), "the future in the present" (TI, 258/236). That at which the caress aims is neither a person nor a thing (TI, 259/236). The future is an intangible, it is a *not yet*.

The relation with the Beloved resembles a relationship with a child, a child who does not have responsibility, who is carefree, coquettish, and "a bit silly" (TI, 263/241). To play with the Other in eros, resembles how one plays with a young animal (TI, 263/241). In this erotic relation, Levinas casts the woman, the Beloved, as somehow not human, and whatever the case, not an adult person engaged in the all-important task of ethical responsibility. She profanes because she does not participate in the ethical. Yet it is because of her that he, the lover, the man, can transcend. It is the woman who makes such transcendence possible. In the name of sexual difference and the preservation of alterity, Levinas has cast each player in this love scene in a different role. Thus, unlike the man, the woman is cast down into the abyss, into the darkness, into that which suggests a void of God and religion. But it is the *not yet*[34] with which Levinas is really concerned. The description of the feminine, of the Beloved, of voluptuosity in love, only serves to indicate the way in which the face in eros distinguishes itself from the face in the ethical relation. The couple, the lovers, are sealed as a society of two. Love excludes the third party. It remains outside the political, secluded in its intimacy, its dual solitude. It is closed; it is nonpublic (TI, 265/242–43).[35] While the language of justice identifies the ethical relationship with the other, language turns to cooing and laughter in the erotic relationship. The language that marks the ethical relation is absent from the erotic. Thus, for Levinas, the child, the future, the transcendence of love, redeems voluptuosity, the concern with itself, the sealed society the lovers construct. According to Levinas, love escapes itself, escapes a return to the same, when it is directed toward the future, when it engenders the child.

The focus on the future, on fecundity, frames "The Fecundity of the Caress,"[36] Irigaray's remarkable essay on Levinas's conception of love. Irigaray, though indebted to Levinas for the influence his ethics has had on her work,[37] still takes issue with the way in which Levinas's ethics, radical as it might be, nonetheless remains blind to its own faults. In particular, Irigaray takes Levinas to task for, and criticizes his conception of, the erotic, on the grounds that he frames voluptuosity within the confines of its utility—that it engenders a child. Irigaray takes issue with this problem on two counts: if she satisfactorily undermines the necessity of procreation as the end of voluptuosity, she (1) establishes the significance of eros as something that goes beyond the mere physical, as something other than that which leads to maternity; and (2) she undermines the heterosexual framework Levinas assumes.[38] Irigaray's style of writing, her repetitive use of key phrases, serves to underscore the way in which these same themes, though inverted for her own use, play a significant role in Levinas's description of the erotic relation. In Irigaray's view, Levinas characterizes voluptuosity such that it can be redeemed only in the marriage bed with the intent to produce a child. And yet Irigaray also undermines this assumed relation, or unification, by recalling that when the erotic relation comes to an end, or rather, is fulfilled temporarily,[39] the lover is "left to his solitary call to his God," while "the beloved woman is relegated to an inwardness that is not one because it is abyssal, animal, infantile, prenuptial" (FC, 202). In Irigaray's analysis, the lovers are "withdrawn to opposite poles of life, they do not marry" (FC, 202). Thus, in spite of themselves, lover and beloved are not unified in life. Each plays a different part in the erotic drama. He, as lover, is the subject who acts on the beloved, the passive woman who waits and receives him. And while the woman gives to the man a son, it is he, the lover, who achieves transcendence. The birth of the son renders this return incomplete, but incomplete only for the man. The beloved woman, through eros, maternity, and birth, makes the son possible, but it is the man who reaps this benefit as "the seduction of the beloved woman serves as a bridge between Father and son.[40] Through her, the beloved, who is only an aspect of himself, the male lover goes beyond love and pleasure toward the ethical" (FC, 203). Thus, here again, the woman provides the means that make possible the man's entry into the ethical world. But, according to Irigaray, the entry comes at the expense of the woman. She is left without subjectivity, without access to the ethical, and outside any relation to God.[41] For the man to engage in voluptuosity and bring about the birth of a son, he, the lover, must mingle with the wrong side of transcendence (FC, 194); he must risk the "loss of self in the wrong infinity" (FC, 204).

We can take the focus of Irigaray's general project—the ethics of sexual difference[42]—as a clue to understanding her approach to Levinas. According to Irigaray, Levinas, in spite of himself, fails in his attempt to conceive radically enough an ethics that would take into account sexual difference but not reinscribe the same secondary role generally attributed to women in the history of Western philosophy. Why is the erotic relation, love, exempt from the ethical? It is clear that the beloved woman in Levinas's love scene plays a role that serves to aid her lover while she is cast back down into the abyss. With the emphasis on maternity and the birth of the child as the end of the voluptuosity, Levinas puts woman back into the one place that has always been assured her.[43] By making only the woman responsible for modesty, for profanation, for the secret of desire, Levinas assigns her to a place and to an unfair responsibility, both of which, he maintains, are outside the ethical. Thus, woman's relation as a sexual being, as lover and as mother, keep her confined to the erotic relation, a relation outside the ethical.[44] At the very least, Levinas's framework explicitly excludes the erotic from the ethical relation—the wife is not the ethical other to her husband.

In "Questions to Emmanuel Levinas,"[45] Irigaray echoes the critique found in "The Fecundity of the Caress" when she tells us, "[T]his non-definition of the other, when the other is not considered to have anything to do with sexual difference, gives rise to an infinite series of substitutions, an operation which seems to me non-ethical."[46] However, in "Questions to Emmanuel Levinas," Irigaray also attacks Levinas's conception of love at the core of its structure, something she does not do in "The Fecundity of the Caress." To critique Levinas's conception of love, it may not be enough merely to say he privileges the erotic relation that ends in fecundity over voluptuosity. It is significant that we recall how Levinas set up the ethical relation, that which is not a return to the same. The love relationship, according to Levinas, risks this return that is rendered incomplete by the birth of a child—a son. Thus, from Irigaray's analysis we can glean three ways in which to question Levinas's analysis: (1) through the structure of the ethical relation itself, as that which is projected toward the infinite; (2) in Levinas's claim that the love relationship is a return to the same; and (3) even if we grant that the love relationship is a return to the same, we can question if the birth of a child is the only way to render this return incomplete.[47]

Irigaray is correct, in my view, to claim that the Other cannot be thought of without thinking it in terms of sexual difference.[48] But I am less inclined to say that Levinas is unsuspecting of what he is doing, even though he does claim to want an ethics that will be neutral with regard to sexual difference.[49] By assuming the position of the 'I' and assigning the feminine to the role of the beloved, Levinas accords a place to woman—though this place is squarely within the traditional space allotted her as lover and mother.[50] In light of her focus on Levinas's conception of love, I think Irigaray is right to point out the negative place in which Levinas has cast woman—the beloved, namely, that she is passive, without God, and unable to transcend (which Levinas, clearly, privileges). And I would even go so far as to say that Levinas is not aware of, or has not made explicit, the amount of work the feminine does for him in his analysis.

Irigaray's essay is at once philosophically compelling and aesthetically beautiful, and my remarks on Levinas are indebted to, among other things, her insight into the absent feminine voice and the question of sexual difference within Levinas's analysis of love. But while I am indebted to Irigaray's work, I also approach Levinas from a different perspective, a perspective that raises questions within Irigaray's reading of Levinas and leads to my second divergence from Irigaray's critique. There is no doubt that Irigaray's criticism that Levinas privileges the erotic relation ending in fecundity over the erotic relation ending in voluptuosity is warranted. But I also think elements of Levinas's analysis could be regarded as positive, even within the context of Irigaray's compelling critique. Thus, I want to push Irigaray's critique of Levinas in order to show the limitations of her critique but also to deepen it. I claim that Irigaray is right when she accuses Levinas of reinscribing a traditional belief about eros, but I also think that his position is more complicated than one of merely reinscribing the traditional role of women. This complexity derives from the Judaic influence on Levinas's philosophical thought, which provides a larger context within which his work can be interpreted.[51]

In "Judaism and the Feminine," Levinas recounts a rabbinic commentary on love and conjugal relations:

> [M]aternity is subordinate to a human destiny which exceeds the limits of "family joys": it is necessary to fulfil Israel, "to multiply the image of God" inscribed on the face of humanity. Not that conjugal love has no importance in itself, or that it is reduced to the ranks of a means of procreation, or that it merely *prefigures* its fulfillment, as in a certain theology. On the contrary the ultimate end of the family is the actual *meaning* and the joy of this present. It is not only prefigured there, it is already fulfilled there. This participation of the present in this future takes place specifically in the feeling of love, in the grace of the betrothed, and even in the erotic. The real dynamism of love leads it beyond the present instant and even beyond the person loved. This end does not appear to a vision outside the love, which would then integrate it into the place of creation; it lies in the love itself. (DF, 37/59)

This passage provides us with a point of a departure by adding a dimension to Irigaray's analysis that is, for the most part, absent. There are two issues at stake here: (1) the significance of sexual relations in themselves; and (2) assuming an end to those sexual relations, it is not clear to what one is giving birth. Irigaray's criticism holds firm insofar as Levinas prioritizes one erotic relation—the one that ends in the birth of the child, over another—the one that seeks pleasure in itself. Yet Levinas makes explicit his view that conjugal relations are important in and of themselves. It is clear that in "Phenomenology of Love," the section on which Irigaray focuses, Levinas does emphasize the fecundity of the event. But I think it is important to distinguish between the priority Levinas gives to the erotic relationship that ends in fecundity, and the view that his analysis is blind to, or rejects, an erotic relationship that is, itself, its own end. For Levinas, there is no question, at least in his analysis in *Totality and Infinity*, that voluptuosity is redeemed, or rendered legitimate, if it issues in a child. Thus, we must reconcile these two analyses, the one in

Totality and Infinity and the other in "Judaism and the Feminine," which, if read together, reveal a tension in Levinas's own view on love: on the one hand, the analysis in *Totality and Infinity* indicates that voluptuosity is redeemed only through the birth of the son. On the other hand, his remarks in "Judaism and the Feminine" indicate that he wants to affirm the value of the erotic relation independently of the birth of the son. Thus, the disparity in his view necessitates that we investigate why Levinas might hold these two apparently opposing positions, and how these two positions might be reconciled with each other.[52]

As I mentioned earlier, according to Levinas, love desires the other such that the relation becomes a return to the same. This return is, in part, what distinguishes the erotic relation from the ethical. Thus, by adding the dimension of fecundity to the erotic relation, Levinas characterizes love as something that could aim at the future, as that which could aim at something beyond itself.[53] Fecundity, then, transforms the love relationship into an ethical relationship; voluptuosity is redeemed when it aims toward the future and issues in a child, a son. So, insofar as Levinas needs a discussion of fecundity, this discussion must take place within the context of a discussion of the erotic relation.[54] Nonetheless, we must remember that a transformation is required for the erotic to become ethical.

There is a sense in which Levinas sees each birth of the child as a birth of another member of Israel. In "Judaism and the Feminine," Levinas characterizes the birth of a child as that which signifies a projection toward the future in terms of fulfilling Israel, fulfilling a commandment that is older than history itself. Thus, here we get the religioethical significance of fecundity, and one cannot help but wonder what happens to the analysis if this part is excised from the analysis as a whole. What happens to the analysis if we remove that one feature? Can we still have a Levinasian ethic? What would it mean if woman did not occupy the place Levinas carved out for her? Is it possible for woman to occupy a place other than the one Levinas prescribes? Could woman be an ethical Other? Could she be an ethical 'I'? The biblical story of Ruth, where we find a touching, intimate relationship between two women, Ruth and Naomi, opens a space for these questions to be explored. The narrative illustrates the lack in Levinas's analysis, a lack that recalls Irigaray's concerns about the place Levinas defines for woman; but by revealing this lack, we also show how woman exceeds the boundaries that define her. That is to say, the story of Ruth helps to illustrate how woman, as the very figure of hospitality and welcoming, exceeds her own limits outside the ethical relation and, thus, puts into question Levinas's analysis. In the section that follows, I turn to the Book of Ruth in order to illustrate further the way in which these Levinasian themes of alterity, the ethical, and fecundity are both demonstrated and disrupted. The story of Ruth opens a space for us in which to consider what it might mean to alter the role of woman and, thus, disrupt the whole.

B. Dwelling in the House of Ruth

As the Book of Ruth opens, we learn that it is the time of the judgment of the judges, and there was a great famine in Bethlehem in Judah.[55] Elimelech, fearing that his family would starve, took his wife, Naomi, and their two sons, Mahlon and Kilion, to Moab. After some time, Elimelech died, leaving Naomi widowed; Naomi's sons each eventually married Moabite princesses: Orpah and Ruth. That Elimelech took his family to Moab and that his sons married Moabite princesses is significant. Scripture tells the Jews that "an Ammonite and a Moabite may not join the congregation—or the assembly—of God." The commandment stems from a previous time in history when both of these nations were inhospitable to fugitive Jews who were in the desert. Living in Moab did not promise to be easy. After ten years of living there, Naomi's sons died, leaving their wives—Naomi's daughters-in-law—widowed, as she was. Some time later, Naomi hears that the Lord has come to the aid of the Jewish people by providing them with food. A stranger in Moab, Naomi, with no blood ties to the country, is uncomfortable there. So, she and her daughters-in-law prepare to go back to Judah. After a short time into their journey Naomi turns to her daughters-in-law and tells them to return to their home in Moab, where they may be more likely to find a husband. Each refuses, though Orpah eventually gives in and returns home.[56] Ruth, however, in her stubbornness and her loyalty to Naomi refuses to go back, and in her famous proclamation tells Naomi, "Where you go I will go, and where you stay I will stay. Your people will be my people and your God my God. Where you die I will die, and there I will be buried. May the Lord deal with me, be it ever so severely, if anything but death separates you and me."[57] Ruth travels to Judah with Naomi, and she takes it upon herself to glean in the fields, in order to feed both herself and Naomi. While Ruth is gleaning in the field, Boaz sees her and asks who she is. The foreman describes Ruth to Boaz as someone who "worked steadily from morning till now, except for a short rest in the shelter."[58] Boaz tells Ruth she must not glean in any other field, for he will take care of her and see that she drinks when she is thirsty and that none of his servants bothers her. "Why," Ruth asks him, "have I found such favor in your eyes that you notice me—a foreigner?"[59] Boaz answers her: "I've been told all about what you have done for your mother-in-law since the death of your husband—how you left your father and mother and your homeland and came to live with a people you did not know before."[60] Later, Ruth marries Boaz and gives birth to Obed, who becomes the father of Jesse, who is the father of David.[61]

The story of Ruth presents us with interesting questions for Levinas. How do we characterize the relationship between Ruth and Naomi? Is it ethical? Is it familial? Is it a friendship? Can it be discussed within the parameters of Levinas's analysis? Ruth, like Naomi, is both widow and stranger, and so in a more literal fashion we can say that both Ruth and Naomi fit squarely into the place of ethical other—each is a woman who only has God to look out for them. But if we only see Ruth and Naomi as two women who are otherwise helpless, we fail to see the richness of the relationship between them. Is Ruth's loyalty to Naomi to be forgotten so that all we remember or take notice of is the great-grandson, David, who is her descendent? Is the significance of Ruth's actions limited to fecundity, to her destiny as David's great-grandmother? Let us begin by looking at Ruth, who is both the widow and the stranger.

Repeatedly in the Bible, the Jew is told of his obligation to the poor, the stranger, the widow, and the orphan.[62] *Stranger* is translated from the Hebrew *ger*, which can mean "convert," or simply "one who resides." Initially, according to the story, Elimelech and his family are the strangers, for not only are they living in a place that is not their original home, but it is a place that was inhospitable to Jews in the past. The stranger relation is reversed when Ruth, the Moabitess, marries one of Naomi's sons. Inhospitality of the past is transformed to hospitality through Ruth, that is, through the feminine. The focus here is on the family of Ruth's in-laws, not her own family, and by putting Naomi in the position in which she does, Ruth is putting her in-laws—her husband's family—above her own family. She is seen as part of Naomi's family both from the narrator's perspective and from Ruth's own perspective; hence, there is no question in Ruth's mind that she should leave Moab and go with Naomi back to Judah.

Whether Ruth has converted at this point is not clear, especially in light of the biblical injunction against such a conversion; nor is it clear what this conversion would mean. Nevertheless, Ruth is viewed and cited as the first convert. As such, who she is as stranger or convert is a complex problem.[63] In the land of Judah, Ruth is a stranger, but her *strangeness* is complicated by her presumed act of conversion. If we grant that Ruth's speech to Naomi constitutes a conversion, her alterity is eradicated.[64] Conversion can be seen as a drawing of the other into the same, not seeing the other as other. Since the stranger is the one to whom the Jew is most responsible, the conflicted identification of the convert, an individual who still retains some *strangeness*, or *otherness*, while having also been drawn into the same, problematizes the ethical relationship with the rest of the Jews. The convert raises a question for the Jew who is wholly obligated to the stranger. How is the born Jew to think of the convert: as Jew or as stranger? This question is raised again by Ruth herself, who, when wondering why Boaz has treated her so kindly, refers to herself as a foreigner. We do not know if Boaz was following the biblical command to the Jews that they "refrain from molesting the stranger or oppress him, for [they, the Jews] lived as strangers in the land of Egypt," or if he was abiding by the command that widows are to be allowed to glean in the fields. We do know from Boaz's own statement that he noticed the way in which Ruth treated Naomi after Ruth's husband (Naomi's son) died. Ruth's *strangeness* is further complicated by the midrash commentary on David. David asks God, "How long will they rage against me and say, 'Is he not of tainted descent? Is he not a descendent of Ruth the Moabitess?'"[65] The implication of David's question is that even David, King of the Jews (and maybe even those who descend from him) is touched by the strangeness of Ruth.

Can we not look at Ruth's response to care for Naomi as ethical? It is clear from Ruth's actions that the bond is actually quite strong. It is Ruth who goes out to find work, who gleans in the fields, and who brings home the food. Ruth and Naomi are, quite literally, two widows and two strangers who live together in their own dwelling. Ruth's choice to leave her mother, father, and homeland in order to follow Naomi and Naomi's God is seen as an act of loyalty by Kristeva, who describes Ruth's decision to follow Naomi as "show[ing] a devotion to Yahweh, but even more so a loyalty—that one might call passionate—between the two women."[66] Kristeva's view is supported by Elie Wiesel, who sees Ruth as "stubborn in her loyalty and her resolve."[67] Ruth, though she is now the stranger in the land of Judah, is the one who cares for Naomi. Ruth sees in the eyes of Naomi the other others. She recognizes that there are others who make a claim on her and to whom she is responsible. Ruth's act of conversion is ethical, but not only ethical. In the words of her own proclamation, her act of conversion reveals its political component. Ruth's response is not just to Naomi, but also to God and to a nation. Could we not say that it is precisely because of the character that Ruth embodies, that Judaism holds Ruth up as the first convert and that makes her worthy of being the ancestor of David? Moreover, is this character not the character that exemplifies the very attributes Levinas describes in "Judaism and the Feminine," and "The Dwelling"? That is, one might say that Ruth's behavior, while characteristically, or stereotypically, feminine, is also the exemplification of the ethical response to the Other. Thus, we can ask if there is not still an element of the relationship between Ruth and Naomi that exceeds Levinas's categories of the woman, or of the feminine. That is, the conception of the feminine, as the welcoming of habitation and the beloved, was understood to make the ethical possible, while not participating in the ethical. Yet it is precisely these attributes, which make the feminine a transcendental condition for the possibility of the ethical, that also appear to drive the feminine to participate directly in the ethical. One might even ask if the narrators of this story, in their efforts to put Ruth back into a traditional role of women by marrying her off to Boaz, are not aware of this excess.[68] One might say that Jewish culture could not incorporate into its thinking this family of two women.[69]

Conclusion

As a result of Levinas's exclusion of the erotic from the ethical, the relationship between the feminine, the erotic, and the ethical remains problematic in his analysis, and the problematic of this relationship arises regardless of how we interpret the term *feminine* in "The Dwelling." The exclusion of the erotic from the ethical raises questions about the relation and responsibility between a husband and a wife. In the section of *Totality and Infinity* titled "Ethics and the Face," Levinas tells us that "[t]he Other is the sole being I can wish to kill" (TI, 198/173). Thus, we can, and should, ask, "To whom does the commandment Thou shalt not kill, apply?" To whom need it apply? If the beloved is not an ethical other, then is Levinas claiming that the face of the beloved never poses a threat? Is it really the case that a man never wishes to kill his spouse, his lover, his beloved? Surely this cannot be true, given the numerous accounts of wives—those who are beloved—who are killed by their husbands and lovers. Surely these categories cannot be so exclusive of each other. If the beloved is not the ethical other, what ethical claim is made on her husband? What obligation is owed to her? If she is excluded from the discourse of the ethical and, thus, excluded from the action of the political, if she is silent but for her "laughter and cooing," how does she protest the violence that is done to her? If her only language is the language of lovers, how does she tell the public of such violence; how does she ask for justice? Clearly Levinas does not mean that women do not actually speak. Nonetheless, we must examine what relationship the erotic can have to the ethical within the analysis he gives us.

Levinas's Hebrew roots give him profound insight into the obligation and responsibility for the other, for those who are most vulnerable. And yet it is his Judaism that precisely allows his inadequate view of women to emerge and take hold. But we must bear in mind that Levinas's analysis is not just about the ethical. The feminine plays a fundamental role as the condition for the possibility of the ethical; and if that role is altered, we are required to investigate how, or in what ways, that alteration disrupts the analysis. Levinas has put women—both as a figure in his analysis and those who would read him—in a precarious place: the feminine is essential to his position, thus to disrupt its place is to disrupt the analysis. To read his text and question the place of women, raises questions about the entire analysis itself. At what point do we risk upsetting the whole analysis so that there is little left of what Levinas has said? Thus, Irigaray's criticisms are ultimately not just about the conception of the feminine; they go to the heart of Levinas's work.

There is a sense in which Ruth's actions indicate an excess that is present in the feminine. Within a Levinasian analysis, Ruth so fulfills the definition of hospitality that she exceeds the traditional definition of a woman and transforms her activity in the dwelling. By gleaning in the fields she feeds Naomi. Thus, one might say, if taken to its extreme within, and pushed to the limit of, the boundaries of the description Levinas gives us, the feminine has no choice but to become ethical, to respond to the Other ethically. That is, in spite of himself, Levinas, while using the feminine as a condition for the possibility of the ethical relation, creates the conditions by which the feminine itself can and must participate in the ethical. As a result of this formulation, woman, inevitably, participates in the ethical, a role I believe he explicitly gives to the feminine in *Otherwise Than Being*.

Notes

1. Simone de Beauvoir, *The Second Sex*, trans. H. M. Parshley (New York: Random House, 1952), xix. *Le deuxième sexe* (Paris: Gallimard, 1949), 15.

2. *The Second Sex*, xix/15.

3. De Beauvoir uses *feminine* and *woman* equivocally. This equivocation is problematic and is precisely what is at issue in Levinas's work.

4. Irigaray looks at both *Time and the Other*, trans. Richard Cohen (Pittsburgh: Duquesne University Press, 1987); *Temps et l'autre* (Montpellier: Fata Morgan, 1979), hereafter cited as TO/TA followed by the respective page numbers, and *Totality and Infinity*, trans. Alphonso Lingis (Pittsburgh: Duquesne University Press, 1969); *Totalité et infini* (The Hague: Martinus Nijhoff, 1961), hereafter cited as TI followed by the English translation and then the original French page numbers. De Beauvoir wrote *The Second Sex* prior to the publication of *Totality and Infinity*.

5. One might even find the format of the text interesting. The two sections that focus on the feminine "sandwich" the long discussion of the ethical relation. Thus, the feminine is not included *in* the discussion of the ethical, just as it is excluded from the ethical relation itself; the feminine is prior to the ethical in the sense that the feminine presence and the dwelling give rise to, or make possible, the ethical; and the feminine is after, or beyond, the ethical. The ordering of the discussions in this text is reminiscent of Hegel's structure in *The Philosophy of Right*, trans. Allen Wood (Cambridge: Cambridge University Press, 1991), where the home gives rise to, or makes possible, the political. I think there is a strong resemblance to Hegel here, but I also want to claim that Levinas's conception of the feminine, the dwelling, and the erotic suggest that his Orthodox Jewish roots are at work in the background informing his description.

6. In an interview with Richard Kearney, Levinas tells us he wants to keep his philosophy and his confessional writings separate (Emmanuel Levinas and Richard Kearney, "A Dialogue with Emmanuel Levinas," in *Face to Face with Levinas*, ed. Richard Cohen [Albany: State University of New York Press, 1986]). Levinas's wish could indicate that, on the one hand, he does not want his religious writings subjected to philosophical interrogation, while, on the other hand, he does not want his philosophy to be thought of as mere religious musings. But Levinas's intention to keep these writings separate does not preclude his Judaism from influencing his approach to philosophy. In fact, Levinas's view of the feminine provides one point of contact where we can see the impact of Judaism on Levinas's philosophy. So, while the goal of this article is not to show, definitively, the relationship between Judaism and its influence on Levinas's philosophy, I do wish to draw on the Judaic influence that is present in his work. See, for example, Levinas's essays in *In the Time of the Nations*, trans. Michael Smith (Bloomington: Indiana University Press, 1994).

7. My claim here is that the feminine in *Totality and Infinity* continues a use that Levinas began in *Time and the Other* and anticipates a conception of the feminine found in *Otherwise Than Being or Beyond Essence*, trans. Alphonso Lingis (The Hague: Martinus Nijhoff, 1981); *Autrement qu'être ou au-delà de l'essence* (The Hague: Martinus Nijhoff, 1974). Hereafter cited as OB and AE followed by the respective page numbers in English and French. In *Time and the Other* the feminine plays the role of radical alterity and, as such, provides the motivation for the analysis itself. Levinas writes: "I think

the absolutely contrary [*le contraire absolutement contraire*], whose contrariety is in no way affected by the relationship that can be established between it and its correlative, the contrariety that permits its terms to remain absolutely other is the *feminine*" (TO, 85/TA, 77). So, here the feminine is described as absolutely other. But is this because the feminine is the ethical other, or merely because Levinas recognized the radical differences between the sexes? The feminine is then reconceived in *Totality and Infinity* to play the role of both the dwelling and eros, a transcendental condition for the man to participate in the ethical relation. In *Otherwise than Being* the feminine can be found within the metaphor of maternity—"the gestation of the other in the same" (OB, 75/AE, 121). To examine the feminine in *Time and the Other* and *Otherwise than Being* within this same chapter would be to do an injustice to these two other texts. However, I want to claim that the feminine in *Totality and Infinity* provides a bridge between the feminine in *Time and the Other* and Levinas's conception of maternity in *Otherwise Than Being*.

8. To draw out this relationship, I look not only at Levinas's own writings on Judaism, for example, those in *Difficult Freedom: Essays on Judaism*, trans. Seán Hand (Baltimore: Johns Hopkins University Press, 1990); *Difficile liberté*, 2d ed. (Paris: Albin Michel, 1976), hereafter cited as DF/DL followed by their respective English and French page numbers, but also at the rabbinic writings found in the *Midrash Rabbah*, translated under the editorship of Rabbi Dr. H. Freedman and Maurice Simon (New York: Soncino Press, 1983), hereafter cited as *Midrash*, followed by biblical book; and the Talmud, translated under the guidance of Rabbi I. Epstein (New York: Soncino Press, 1935). The reference is to the Babylonian Talmud. Hereafter cited as Talmud, followed by the tractate.

9. I am retaining this language because I think the gendered language is significant.

10. For an extended discussion of this theme see Catherine Chalier, "Ethics and the Feminine," in *Re-reading Levinas*, ed. Robert Bernasconi and Simon Critchley (Bloomington: Indiana University Press, 1991), 119–29.

11. This point marks the change in the conception of the feminine from *Time and the Other* to *Totality and Infinity*. In the former, the feminine is conceived as Absolute Other, or radical alterity, hence the problem Simone de Beauvoir has with this text. However, in *Totality and Infinity*, the feminine is no longer the other, or at least not the Absolute Other, here referring to the ethical other. Moreover, we can also already see Levinas's equivocation between *feminine* and *woman*—he uses the latter explicitly in this section.

12. Woman's silence is also emphasized by the rabbis, in response to their wonder about why Eve was created from Adam's rib: they surmise that God's other choices would have led to nonvirtuous traits in women. The midrash commentary tells us that woman was not created from God's eye, "lest she [woman] be a coquette; nor from the ear, lest she be an eavesdropper; nor from the mouth, lest she be a gossip." Despite all God's efforts to create a woman who had only virtuous traits, and much to the dismay of the rabbis, woman still managed to acquire all the qualities God tried to prevent. Besides giving us examples of the biblical woman who possess these nonvirtuous traits, the Talmud relates the less than positive view that "Ten measures of speech descended to the world; women took nine and men one" (Kid. 49b). Although woman, concrete woman, obviously, speaks, her silence is preferred.

13. Adriaan Peperzak, *To The Other* (West Lafayette: Purdue University Press, 1993), 129.

14. See Deut. 10:18 and 16:11, for example.

15. My aim here is not to insist on the literal over the metaphorical; rather, I want to emphasize the *possibility* of the feminine as something other than metaphor, a possibility that many wish to ignore. As we will see when we get to Levinas's discussion of love and fecundity, it is difficult to have a son without a concrete woman!

16. See Levinas's discussion of this theme in his essay "Judaism," in *Difficult Freedom*, trans. Seán Hand (Baltimore: Johns Hopkins University Press, 1990), 24–26; *Difficile liberté* (Paris: Albin Michael, 1976)]. Hereafter cited parenthetically in the text as DF followed by the English page number and DL followed by the French page number.

17. The rest of the reply is "A *father of the fatherless and a judge of the widows* (Ps. 68:6); hence he who robs them is like one who robs God." *Midrash Rabbah*, Exod. 30:7–8.

18. Levinas uses the French *l'orphelin* (orphan); the biblical passage translates the Hebrew as "fatherless," and the Hebrew root used in the Hebrew text also means fatherless.

19. Levinas, DF, 30–37/DL, 50–62.

20. Here Levinas's emphasis is both ambiguous and provocative. By emphasizing the silence of women's footsteps Levinas could be accused of reinscribing the sexist idea that women ought to be seen and not heard. Yet there is a sense in which Levinas is trying to reveal the power these women had to move history and destiny, even though that power was, and could only be, displayed through silent means. Rebecca, for example, is the manager of her household who deceives Isaac into giving the blessing intended for the firstborn to be given to her favorite—Jacob, the second born.

21. Talmud, Joma 43b.

22. In Judaism this split between public and private, man and woman, is emphasized so much that women are exempted from the positive precepts, namely, the timed commandments (commandments that must be done during certain times of the day, for example, the prayers in the morning), which may interfere with their obligations to the home. This exemption gives rise to the prayer men say in the morning when they thank God for not being born a heathen, a slave, or a woman. The prayer is not supposed to be inherently disparaging to women. The intended emphasis is that men were given the honor of the obligation to uphold all the 613 commandments. Positive or not, this view is similar to the one we find in ancient Greece. For example, in the ancient Greek vision of the world, women were responsible for burial rights while men are responsible for the state. See, for example, Sophocles' *Antigone*, trans. Elizabeth Wyckoff, in *Sophocles I* (Chicago: University of Chicago Press, 1954).

23. For a more detailed discussion of this topic, see David Biale, *Eros and the Jews* (New York: Basic Books, 1992).

24. Although not commanded by the religion, the Talmud tells us that divorce is acceptable if a child is not born within ten years of marriage (Talmud, Jeb. 6:6). The relationship between the Jews and the erotic is a puzzling one, and it risks being characterized too simply by the passage cited earlier. It is not the case that sexual activity is always, at every moment, to be directed at having a child. There is a great emphasis on sexual pleasure in Judaism—the *Ketubah* (the marriage contract) explicitly states that the husband is responsible for the sexual gratification of his wife, and interestingly enough, some rabbinic commentaries do not reverse the obligation to extend to the husband. I think that Levinas and Talmudic law understand the romantic relationship in much broader terms. See David Biale, *Eros and the Jews*.

25. Ironically, use of the Judaic influence, while giving us a different framework in which to understand his position and appreciate the positive features of his analysis on the erotic, simultaneously opens up other avenues through which to criticize Levinas's work. Thus, this approach yields an account that further illustrates the complex relation between the feminine and the ethical.

26. Jean-Paul Sartre, *Being and Nothingness*, trans. Hazel Barnes (New York: Washington Square Books, 1953). *L'être et néant* (Paris: Gallimard 1954). Specifically, this theme can be found on page 491 of the English text, although the theme is present in the entire subheading "First Attitude Toward Others: Love, Language, Masochism" contained within the larger section "Concrete Relations with Others."

27. Although we can wonder if the birth of a son is a reflection of the fecundity of a male writer, it seems more than coincidental that Judaism has a less than positive attitude toward the birth of a daughter. Even filial piety is more often talked about as that of a son to his parents, as if there is no daughter present.

28. It is ironic that Levinas, in light of his complaint that Heidegger overlooks the enjoyment of things as an end in themselves, would, in his phenomenology of love, gesture toward love as something directed toward a future (though it is a future that is "not yet") rather than allowing for love

to be valued solely as an end in itself. Levinas does allow for the presence of pleasure—"voluptuosity"—for the sake of itself; however, he does so with a conditional insofar as he emphasizes the futural aspect of the relation. But I want to point out that it is precisely this ambivalence between pleasure for the sake of itself, something Levinas allows for explicitly, and the privileging of the love relation that ends in fecundity, that creates a tension in Levinas's analysis of love. On the one hand, Levinas should be lauded for recognizing the pleasurable element of eros; but on the other hand, he does privilege the erotic relation that, ultimately, ends in the birth of a son. It is this tension that I want to exploit in my exploration of his analysis.

29. For Levinas separation is actually better than the initial fusion, for it is only with the separation that one can be in relationship with another. See Levinas's discussion in *Time and the Other*.

30. It is not clear to me why Levinas writes with a masculine pronoun here. This section seems very clearly to be about erotic love, love that culminates in the birth of a child, and thus, for Levinas, the author, a love that is with a woman. There are places in the essay where he specifically refers to the feminine, and where language to describe the beloved seems to be feminine language. Thus, the ambiguity makes unclear whether Levinas intends this discrepancy.

31. We should be sure to note the similarity in the descriptions of the lover in the "Phenomenology of Eros" and the Feminine in "The Dwelling."

32. Although "virgin" and "virginity" are certainly correct translations of *vierge* and *virginité*, I think we could also think of these words in terms of their connotation of purity rather than of sexual inexperience.

33. This discussion of love resonates with the analysis Levinas gives of the feminine and the erotic in *Time and the Other*.

34. Levinas, reiterating Sartre, tells us that "if to love is to love the love the Beloved bears me, to love is also to love oneself in love, and thus to return to oneself" (TI, 266/244). Voluptuosity in love does not transcend itself. It is in this description, that we see what Levinas means by a return to the self. As a dual solitude it remains sealed unto itself. The love relationship in Levinas's analysis is directed toward a future. Levinas makes this point repeatedly. We find a similar analysis in *Time and the Other*: the love relation is the juncture between present and future. It is being that is also a "being not yet" (TI, 257/234). "It manifests itself at the limit of being and non-being" (TI, 256/233).

35. This characterization further removes the erotic from the ethical. Levinas is specific, even in *Totality and Infinity*, that the third, a signification of the political, always accompanies him. That is, though Levinas needs to separate the ethical from the political for purposes of the analysis, he acknowledges the intimate relationship that the ethical has to the political. In his description of the erotic, he is clear that the erotic is closed off from public space. As such, it would be difficult then to make the case that it, by itself, without the birth of the child, the son, is ethical.

36. Luce Irigaray, "The Fecundity of the Caress," in *An Ethics of Sexual Difference*, trans. Carolyn Burke and Gillian Gill (Ithaca: Cornell, 1993). Hereafter cited as FC followed by the page number.

37. For a detailed discussion of Irigaray's relationship with and debt to Levinas, see Tina Chanter's book *Ethics of Eros: Irigaray's Rewriting of the Philosophers* (New York: London, 1995).

38. Chanter, *Ethics of Eros*, 218.

39. Irigaray also underscores the ambiguity of the erotic as a relation that is at once sated and insatiable and therefore resembles both finite need and the infinity of ethics.

40. One cannot help but notice, with the capitalization of *Father*, the allusion to Christianity's trinity and the role Mary played as bridge between God, the Father, and the birth of Jesus Christ. And it is precisely this reading of Levinas, one that implicitly assumes a Christian perspective, that I want to confront. That is, I do not claim that Irigaray is necessarily mistaken in her criticism of Levinas. Rather, I want to call attention to the way Irigaray might be overlooking elements of Levinas's thought by viewing him through a Christian lens, even if this lens is unintended.

41. One theme in Judaism claims that women are not required to study Torah because they are already ethical; they are already closer to God. (See Franz Rosenzweig, *The Star of Redemption*, trans.

William Hallo [Notre Dame: University of Notre Dame Press, 1970], 326.) One can see both the positive and negative in this view. Historically, women have been denied both rights and privileges because they (women) were thought to be more moral. Ironically, women were initially denied the U.S. vote because politics was deemed too dirty for them to touch; women then acquired the vote because it was thought their moral character would improve the lot of politics. Unfortunately, the nonrequirement to study Torah was transformed into a prohibition among the more Orthodox segments of the Jewish religion. One cannot help but wonder how the view that women are more ethical than men, are closer than men to God, informs Levinas's analysis. For a similar claim and women and the ethical, see Chalier's chapter, "Exteriority and the Feminine," from *Faces and the Feminine*, translated by Bettina Bergo and published in this volume.

42. We could take Chanter's title, *Ethics of Eros*, also as a cue.

43. Alison Ainley takes issue with this interpretation. She argues that the dwelling Levinas calls forth here is a more like a community of reconciliation. However, as I mentioned previously, one must still account for Levinas's explicit exclusion of the erotic from the ethical. As long as woman is in the role of the beloved she is excluded from the ethical—at least in relationship to her lover. See "Amorous Discourses: 'The Phenomenology of Eros' and Love Stories," in *The Provocation of Levinas*, ed. Robert Bernasconi and David Wood (London: Routledge, 1988), 70–82.

44. I would actually claim that woman as mother is, for Levinas, the ethical relation par excellence, but this relation does not appear until *Otherwise Than Being*. However, I think the seeds of this relationship or this possibility are already present in his construal of the feminine in *Totality and Infinity*.

45. In *The Irigaray Reader*, ed. Margaret Whitford (Oxford: Blackwell, 1991), 178–91.

46. Luce Irigaray, "Questions to Emmanuel Levinas," in *The Irigaray Reader*, 182.

47. Although I am in agreement with Irigaray's concerns and with her criticisms of Levinas's phenomenology of love, I also want to acknowledge the dilemma in which we find Levinas. He must write from his own point of view, that of a man, lest he be accused of trying to presume to know what love would be for a woman. So his analysis of love will clearly be lacking; if nothing else, it lacks the woman's point of view. In spite of this shortcoming, as well as others in his analysis, I do commend Levinas for recognizing the significant role women play in the birth of a child and for attaching that role to a concrete, intimate relationship with another human, rather than giving us an analysis that either describes women in terms of mere utility, that is, as someone who is only a vessel for the man's progeny, or that presumes that children just suddenly appear as if no mother was present or needed. That latter view is illustrated in Hobbes's comment that "men spring up from the ground like mushrooms." Cited from Seyla Benhabib, *Situating the Self* (New York: Routledge, 1992), 156. For the full citation, see Thomas Hobbes, "Philosophical Rudiments Concerning Government and Society," in *The English Works of Thomas Hobbes*, ed. W. Molesworth (Darmstadt: Wissenschaftliche Buchgesellschaft, 1966), 2:109.

48. And Derrida is correct that Levinas left us little choice but to think the Other as not woman—or at least not a woman anchored to a home and a man. See Derrida, "At This Very Moment in This Work Here I Am," in *Re-reading Levinas*, ed. Robert Bernasconi and Simon Critchley (Bloomington: Indiana University Press, 1991), 19–48, an essay devoted primarily to a discussion of *Otherwise Than Being*, though this problem is also commented on in *Totality and Infinity*.

49. For example, in *Time and the Other*, the feminine is claimed as radical alterity, and it is as the feminine, as this radical alterity, that the subject moves out of the *il y a* and contracts its existence. Sexual difference plays a fundamental role in providing the motivation for the ethical relation.

50. In Derrida's view, the assumed sexual difference, and demarcation, in this text is striking (Derrida, "At This Very Moment"). Derrida essentially asks, with regard to fecundity and the birth of a son, in particular, "Why should a 'son' better represent, in advance, this indifference? This unmarked difference?" Essentially, he is asking, why can the future not be a daughter? By organizing the analysis as he has, Levinas has assumed sexual difference and made it work as such. The future

cannot be a daughter because the author writing the analysis is a man. In his own response to the question, Derrida notes parenthetically his comment, cited in a footnote to "Violence and Metaphysics," his essay on *Totality and Infinity*: "'Let us observe in passing that *Totality and Infinity* pushes the respect for dissymmetry to the point where it seems to us impossible, essentially impossible, that it could have been written by a woman. The philosophical subject of it is man'" (Derrida, "At This Very Moment," 40). In Derrida's view, Levinas assumes the stance of the male subject without acknowledging this position. Moreover, that Levinas subordinates an alterity marked by sexual difference indicates that Levinas thinks of himself as presenting a neutral Other, one not marked by sexual difference. Levinas claims in an interview with Bracha Lichtenberg-Ettinger that he is not subordinating woman, but sexual difference, to alterity (*Que dirait Eurydice? What Would Eurydice Say?* Emmanuel Levinas en/in conversation avec/with Bracha Lichtenberg-Ettinger [Paris: BLE Atelier, 1997]). However, in light of the stance Levinas takes as author, the other is marked by sexual difference and then disguised as a neutral other. The wholly other who is not supposed to be marked by sexual difference, is found already to be marked by masculinity (Derrida, "At This Very Moment," 40).

51. We cannot know for sure if Levinas accepts the Judaic view of love and sexuality, nor can we know for sure if this view is in the background of Levinas's analysis. I do think it is safe to say that Levinas would have been aware of these views. Levinas is no ordinary man, and he is certainly no ordinary Jewish man. He is heavily steeped in the Talmudic tradition. He was not merely raised in it, but he also actively studied it himself. Sexual relations within the Jewish tradition is not an obscure topic, not a topic that Levinas would have had to seek out in order to come across writings on it. Because the Talmud governs all aspects of life, discussions on marriage and family are not only included, but are discussed at length.

52. Given Levinas's own use of the word *conjugal*, one can presume, at least given the time he was writing, that he is referring to marriage; given Levinas's attention to fecundity, Irigaray's insight that Levinas focuses on a specifically heterosexual framework is affirmed. I do not think Levinas will be able to escape that charge against him. However, I do want to reexamine the erotic relation with an eye toward acknowledging two things that, for Levinas, are implicated in each other: (1) the role of pleasure in the relationship, and (2) the attention paid to the presence of a woman in the discussion of fecundity. Alison Ainley also takes up this point. She claims that while Levinas wants to give us an account of love that contains within it the "beyond it" and makes maternity possible, he does not want to make it a determining factor (Ainley," Amorous Discourses," 76). However, Ainley also realizes and takes issue with the heterosexual framework Levinas assumes by taking such a position (Ainley, "Amorous Discourses," 78).

53. The *Ketubah*, the Jewish marriage contract, states that a husband is responsible to his wife for three things: food, clothing, and sexual gratification. Although a marriage that results in no children after ten years is grounds for granting an annulment, a childless couple is not required to dissolve their marriage. Levinas writes, "[L]ove [that] becomes its own end, where it remains without any 'intentionality' that spreads beyond it, a world of voluptuousness or a world of charm and grace, one which can coexist with a religious civilization, is foreign to Judaism" (DF, 36–37/60). This point, according to Levinas, is not intended to mean that woman is to be pregnant and confined to the home; nor is it about Judaism's prudish attitude toward sexuality. Rather, Levinas tells us, this view of love is due to "the permanent opening up of the messianic perspective—of the immanence of Israel, of humanity reflecting the image of God that can carry on its face" (DF, 37/60).

54. But Levinas's connection should not necessarily be an indication that he thinks every sexual act *ought* to *end* in maternity, or even be *intended* to *end* in maternity. We must be careful to avoid a logic that reverses the necessary relation between sexuality and fecundity. Factually, fecundity requires sexuality, though sexuality does not require fecundity. In terms of his ethical analysis, however, Levinas does privilege sexual activity that ends in fecundity. Yet, even if we acknowledge the privilege Levinas gives to love that results in a child, we must, also, acknowledge that Levinas allows

for a sexuality that intends pleasure for its own sake; if we are to pay heed to Levinas's Jewish roots, then we must contend with the remarks that Judaism itself makes about sexuality.

55. I want to note here that there are shelters for battered women in Baltimore and in Washington, D.C., called The House of Ruth. They take their name from Ruth's character as a helper, particularly of other women. I also want to note that Ruth's name in Hebrew means "friend."

56. Midrash speculates that Goliath is the descendent of Orpah. Thus, the two grandsons meet as antagonists. Although Orpah is not viewed in the story as a traitor, to claim that her descendent is Goliath, who is eventually slain by David, the great-grandson of Ruth, does leave us wondering about Ruth's destiny.

57. Ruth 1:16–17.

58. Ruth 2:6.

59. Ruth 2:10.

60. Ruth 2:11.

61. It is interesting, in light of the Jewish view of sexuality, that it is not Boaz who approaches Ruth, but Ruth who seeks Boaz out, while he is sleeping. Moreover, it is Naomi who encourages her to do so.

62. "How," it is asked in the midrash, "can one rob from the poor?" The answer is given that one robs from the poor when we do not give them what we are obliged to give them—gleanings, the forgotten sheaves, the corner of the field, and the poor man's tithe. We rob them when we fail in our obligation to them.

63. I am tracing a theme that can also be found in the work of Julia Kristeva, for example, "The Chosen People and the Choice of Foreignness," in *Strangers to Ourselves*, trans. Leon S. Roudiez (New York: Columbia University Press, 1991); and Elie Wiesel, in his essay "Ruth," in *Sages and Dreamers* (New York: Touchstone, 1991), gives us an interesting discussion of the relationship between alterity and conversion.

64. The words of Ruth's speech, "I'll go where you go, your people will be my people, your God will be my God," are the words that all converts to Judaism say.

65. *Midrash Rabbah*, Ruth 8.

66. Kristeva, "The Chosen People and the Choice of Foreignness," 71.

67. Wiesel, "Ruth," 53. Loyalty, according to Jewish faith, is a strong ethical duty See, for example, George Fletcher, *Loyalty: An Essay on the Morality of Relationships* (New York: Oxford, 1993), 37. It is why the law forbids fathers from testifying against their sons in a court of law. It is precisely because of the role partiality plays, that of knowing someone, that gives rise to the ethical call to loyalty. We can see even in the Jews' relationship to God that the relationship is one of loyalty. Although it is questionable that the term *chosen people*, as it is applied to Jews, reflects the voluntary choice the Jews made to enter into the covenant, it seems clear that the fact they did enter into the covenant gives rise to their loyalty to God. God proclaims, "I am the Lord thy God which have brought thee out of the land of Egypt, out of the house of bondage" (Exod. 20:2).

68. If Irigaray is right, then Levinas's analysis does not allow for a relationship between women— sexual or otherwise. Although Ruth appears to be in an ethical relation to Naomi, though she appears to have responded to Naomi, it is not clear that we can use such terminology in regard to that relationship. How, then, is it possible to think of woman as ethical other to woman, as in the relationship between Naomi and Ruth; and how can we account for the ethical within the family? What kind of space is there for woman outside the erotic? If the passage from the ethical to the political is immanent—that is, if the ethical and the political are inseparable such that the latter always already accompanies the former—and if woman is not part of the ethical, then what space is she accorded in the political?

69. For a detailed analysis of this theme, see *Reading Ruth: Contemporary Women Reclaim a Sacred Text*, ed. Judith A. Kates and Gail Twersky Reimer (New York: Ballantine Books, 1994).

7

The Exteriority of the Feminine

Catherine Chalier

Translated by Bettina Bergo

What has humanly taken place has never been able to be confined in its site.
—Emmanuel Levinas, *Otherwise Than Being or Beyond Essence*

I. The Unsituatable

The interpretation of subjectivity as a substitution breaking with essence, which desituates the subject, produces signification in a movement of turning toward the other person [*autrui*],[1] which is a movement without reserve or postponement. If "that which has humanly taken place has never been able to be confined in its site," this is because what is human is inscribed nowhere else than in the break with every private locale, every residence or homeland, every space upon which consciousness

This essay first appeared as part of chapter 3, "L'extériorité au féminin" (Exteriority in the Feminine), in Catherine Chalier, *Figures du féminin* (Paris: La Nuit Surveillée, Collection Questions, 1982).—Trans.

would affix its seal. The human, or the nomad, has left without reserves for the future, without even knowing whither he goes and whether he is going to some place, his mind made up by hearing the summons of the other man. The demand for a response to the other's word cannot be reconciled with any sort of private privilege. The human thus pronounces the interval of a space that is oriented from the Same toward the Other [l'Autre]. The human expels subjectivity from its premises, in order that it Say substitution or the time of the Infinite in the finite. Like a name with no essential guarantee, subjectivity is this hearing of the Other, eponymous with the human. It is also a statelessness.

The unsituatable, or the human, is experienced in the break with the categories by which the I reflects on itself and attempts to comprehend the other person [autrui]. No existent is a positivity. The human is heralded in the ever new instant of a practical rationality, namely, the disquieting of the Same by the Other; the enucleation of oneself. Like the unsituatable movement toward the Other [l'Autre], [such is] the word addressed to him, which causes one to be born to oneself. "[It is] as if, in going toward the other [l'autre], I rejoined me and implanted myself in a ground, henceforth my native one, unburdened of all the weight of my identity."[2]

Nevertheless, just as one speaks of a bad infinity, there also exists a bad unsituatable, or a utopia that does not raise itself to the human and produces no native ground. "This world, in which reason recognizes itself more and more, is not inhabitable. . . . There lies the spirit in its *masculine* essence, which lives *outside* exposed to the violent sun that blinds; . . . out of place, solitary and wandering, and already thereby alienated by the products that it created, and which stand before it dauntless and hostile to it."[3]

This bad unsituatable and this uninhabitable outside find themselves thus related to "the spirit in its masculine essence." The alienation of man from his creations results from "the very virility of the *logos* as universal and triumphant, which hunts even into the shadows that could have sheltered it" [*Difficile liberté*, 50; Eng., 33, my translation]. This is to say that the spirit in its masculine essence appears on the order of an absolutely alienating category of being, as the source of an errancy or wandering that forbids manifestation of the orientation toward the Other [l'Autre], because subjectivity [here] gets lost in its creations.

The masculine creates works but is incapable of defending them. These works are speechless, abandoned to whomever would seize hold of them. They form something like a "world of realities or results, a world of 'complete works,' inherited from dead wills."[4] The work, produced by the masculine spirit, always fails. History well bespeaks this reign of reality-results, this injustice done to those who believed they could say they were part of it by creating. The violence and the constant dispossession of the meaning that subjectivity believes it places in its works are masculine effects. In this spirit is thus lacking the moment of the extra-territoriality that comes from the attention to the other person [*autrui*]; too taken up with its works, this spirit has not the time [for such an attention]. And believing that it expresses itself in this way, this spirit in fact denies itself expression, for "it is only in approaching the other [*autrui*] that I am present to myself" [*Totalité et infini*, 153; Eng., 178, my trans.].

What role, then, should one give to the feminine? Does it have an ontological function relative to this violent disorientation accruing to the masculinity of the spirit? Is there a "vocation of the one that does not conquer" [*Difficile liberté*, 50; Eng., 33, my trans.], of the one that does not lose herself in her own productions, since creating is not her lot?[5]

The function of the feminine consists in "surmounting" [ibid.] such an alienation, in permitting the masculine to break with this uninhabit-able outside and with its solitude, which subsists "despite the presence of God" [ibid.]. For this, it is necessary that the feminine make a *site* appear in space. "In order that the inevitable uprootedness of the thinking that dominates the world accommodate a rest—a return to its home—it is necessary that there be produced, in the geometry of infinite and cold spaces, the strange weakening [*défaillance*] that is gentleness. Its name is *woman*" [*Difficile liberté*, 50, our italics; Eng., 33, my trans.]. Or, "the gentle in-itself" [*Difficile liberté*, 51; Eng., 33, my trans.]. Without woman, without her weakness and the intimacy of her home, man would know "nothing of what transforms his natural life into ethics" [*Difficile liberté*, 51; Eng., 34, my trans.].

The reception [given] by woman in the home suggests a halt to the masculine spirit assaulted by history, and to his self-dispossession in his works. Although it be ephemeral, the birth of detachment and concentration in woman's presence is a condition of the passage from the natural existence that is lost in its productions into an ethical life.

Woman would therefore express, in her gentleness, the beginning of ethics. The residence, considered in the feminine—whoever it might be who receives us there—would determine the conversion of the bad unsituatable into an ethical unsituatable.

Without the "secret presence" and the quality "at the limits of evanescence" [*Difficile liberté*, 48; Eng., 31, my trans.] of the feminine, the world would not escape a life both spontaneous and rude, one characterized by a force ongoing. Wheat would not be ground, nor flax woven. The uninhabitable world would leave every possibility for an ethical life in suspense. The silent voice of the one who receives and the dimension of the intimate that she opens are thus not sociological, or psychological, evidence, but a moral paradigm and a category of ontology. They are the response—without words—to the virility of the universal and triumphant *logos*. Detachment and concentration with a view toward the ethical.

Nevertheless, woman is not capable of more than this. Her intimacy and gentleness do not open the dimension of height where the ethical unsituatable lives. The "swooning of the inner life" saves the human from its disorientation, but it also stands "at the limit of relaxation or interruption" [*Difficile liberté*, 56; Eng., 37, my trans.], thereby forbidding all height. The feminine welcome can not lay claim to being anything but a condition of ethics. In the speech [*la parole*] of the one who continually escapes, of the one who is "the essentially impure" [*Difficile liberté*, 56; Eng., 37, my trans.], it is not fitting to hear the beyond of ethics.

To be sure, a person's feminine quality "could neither deform nor absorb her human essence" [*Difficile liberté*, 51; Eng., 34, my trans.], qua human she remains capable of an ethical existence, but not as a feminine being.[6] The feminine remains closed to the height that announces transcendence. It saves the human from violence, but because it is essentially impure and weak in its gentleness, it does not assume responsibility for another person.

Would speaking, then, of an exteriority in the feminine [mode] contradict this? Is it an outrage to the thinking of the philosopher to expound, in the feminine, an ethical act?

II. A Grammatical Error

In the Hebrew language the word *woman*, *Ishah*, is formed from *Ishe*, or *man*. Levinas takes hold of this etymology for which "woman derives quasi-grammatically from man" [*Difficile liberté*, 52; Eng., 34, my trans.], to assert a common identity of destiny and dignity for man and woman.

Yet this derivation would have it that the masculine keep "a definite priority," that it "remain the prototype of the human and determine eschatology relative to which maternity itself is described: the salvation of humanity" [*Difficile liberté*, 53; Eng., 35, my trans.]. A derivation is always that, even in the absence of any certainty about the first term.

As the prototype of the human, the masculine determines eschatology relative to which maternity is described—how shall we understand this claim? What conclusions shall we draw about those who have always existed between the name and the body?

The masculine defines eschatology because it opens the dimension of height, where this metaphor indicates that which is beyond history, the encounter with the absolutely other. Eschatology is not thought as the laborious finality of history, but much more as that which tears us out of history. "Without hope for oneself or liberation with respect to my time" [*En découvrant l'existence avec Heidegger et Husserl*, 192], eschatology is the passage into the time of the other [*autrui*]. Salvation thus comes about in a liberation in regard to one's own time and that of finitude. One must not speak of being-for-death,[7] but of "being for-the-beyond-of-my-death" [*Humanisme de l'autre homme*, 42]. For if man posits himself in being in such a way that the other person counts more than he does, if he is good, he is not for-death [*pour-la-mort*]. He is for-another [*pour autrui*] and infinite like the time envisaged in the discontinuity that separates time of the one, from that of the other [*l'autre*].

Now, such an orientation is that of paternity. His work. "In paternity, where the I [*Moi*] is prolonged in the Other [*l'Autre*], across the definitive permanence of an inevitable death, time triumphs by its discontinuity over old age and destiny" [*Totalité et infini*, 258; Eng., 282, my trans.]. In this sense, the masculine is the prototype of the human and determines eschatology for an ethical humanity; the same humanity that does not seek to express itself by productions, but by its approach to the other man. Paternity, whether biological or not, is this "original effectuation of time"[8] [*Totalité et infini*, 225; Eng., 247, my trans.]. It is therefore appropriate to describe maternity in relation to paternity.

Would maternity be a lesser generosity such that it be paternity that determines ethical disinterestedness and eschatology? Why differentiate between the masculine and the feminine to speak of the surpassing of one's time, or the attention that leads to the time of the other [*l'autre*]?

If generosity is envisaged, it is inappropriate either to quantify it or to debate priorities in its regard. Arguments would not prevail over conviction, and it is not a matter of pleading the cause in order to win it. Yet because generosity is associated with disinterestedness, it is necessary to understand the latter term. It is literally "dis-interested-ness," or the suspension of essence. That is, the interruption of the privilege accorded to the ontological question. The putting in question of the interrogation concerning what is "proper" or "own." Now, if maternity, as integrally for-the-other [pour-l'autre], states such a disinterestedness, or absolute patience for the other person, it does not utter this with words. This is not a fault or a lack, to be sure, since what is thus signified is that woman lives, integrally, this for-the-other-person [pour l'autrui]. When the substitution of the one for the other is absolute, there is no longer place for the word, "the persecuted one can not defend himself by language, for the persecution is a disqualification of the apology. Persecution is the precise moment in which the subject is affected or touched without the mediation of the logos."[9] The exceptional quality of woman must leave her without words. And yet, in the fact of disinterestedness, paternity remains unsurpassable, while maternity is the more anarchic knowledge thereof.

The justification of this is found when dispossession is experienced in the extreme, in the investiture of the body, condemning one to silence. Such a perfection cannot be said. Paternity has, for this, a priority over this dispossession or perfection. Since paternity is not an embodied knowledge of disinterestedness, but rather a knowledge that is spoken, it has the advantage of words although it produces a less excellent substitution. Paternity knows the apology, teaching; it names those things that it engenders.

To establish a distinction between the masculine and the feminine in their relation to eschatology, to subordinate the second to the first, is not to discern a greater or a lesser degree of generosity, but rather to distinguish between the modalities of its Saying [Dire] and to privilege the name relative to the body. In accomplishing too well the substitution—in their bodies—women, without the position for or quality of speech, see themselves referred to a derivative position. Only the one who can write and say eschatology, in words, and who can give his or her name, is entitled to state the human [décliner l'humain].

The identity of destiny and of dignity, of man and of woman, does not abolish the order of precedence which associates disinterestedness with the work of paternity. The Hebrew grammar understands this preference. Thus the feminine continues to be written, in its derivation.

To write grammar otherwise, to invent a few novel errors, is not to will the reversal of this determination. This is not a challenge that ranks with pride, but the taking into consideration that language is not a simple modality of thinking, and that the *logos* is not neutral. In this sense the difficulty encountered by Levinas in his choice of a Greek site, which for him was unsurpassable—as that from which to cause a thought come from elsewhere to be heard—is perhaps not foreign to a certain mutism in the feminine. It is as if the utter novelty of another syntax were lost in this necessity of borrowing the path of a unique or singular *logos*. For such a syntax there would no longer be priorities in the order of derivation.

This is not the excess of an heretical thinking, but an allusion to the exigency that thinking accord with the body. And that thinking be accomplished in the verb. In passing up such an assistance, women have not so much known the excellence of a maternal ethic as they have the effect of a violence come from the masculine, from the very prototype of the human.

III. A Necessary Weakening

The metaphors about the feminine, and the feminine as metaphor, give account of a weakening of ontology; they put in question whomever pretends to exist in positivity. The idea of the incognito, moreover, to which these metaphors are tied—for example, manifestation without manifestation, hearing without words, silent language—underscores the dimension of the secret afferent to them. Beyond the phenomenon and being, the feminine thus sustains an enigma, that of the proximity of the other qua other. In its discretion, the feminine heralds "the intervention of a meaning that disturbs the phenomenon, but is wholly disposed to withdraw like an undesirable stranger unless one lends an ear to those steps growing remote" [*En découvrant l'existence*, 213]. This meaning, this enigmatic and reserved transcendence, which escapes themes and concepts, is on the side of a pure experience.

The feminine "evanescence" is not other than that of all proximity, since the latter makes light of the "sciences [*savoirs*] and truths which present themselves as the essence";[10] it ruins all representation and makes us anxious about the neighbor encountered therein, without our being able to say who he is. If proximity is the event of the face-to-face encounter with the other person [*autrui*], then the feminine is, itself, the paradigm of its enigma, of its "original language, its language without words or propositions, its pure communication" [*En découvrant l'existence*, 228]. The feminine "by which a hinter-world prolongs the world" is the "Other par excellence" [*De l'existence à l'existant*, 145; Eng., 85, my trans.].

Is it only that, however? Can one say, indifferently, the neighbor, the Other, and the feminine?

Thus, when it is asserted that the other person is revealed in "the original phenomenon of gentleness" [*Totalité et infini*, 124; Eng., 150, my trans.], and that "the welcome of the face ... is produced, in an original manner, in the gentleness of the feminine face" [Ibid.; my Eng. trans.], it is suggested that if the feminine par excellence is Other [*Autre*], it is nevertheless inappropriate to speak of every Other in the feminine. Such a gentleness keeps a memory of an encounter with the Other who has a woman's face.

Similarly, the feminine specificity of welcome within the home, the intimacy that it protects so that the masculine might rest before assuming an ethical existence, signifies a role of woman and not that of any Other at all.

The metaphors, the figures of the feminine, engage the empiric of an encounter with the Other within the space of words. Yet the Other, under the circumstances, has the face of a woman. Feminine every Other is not. This is why the weakening necessary to "pass beyond being" also refers to a history in which weakening, weakness, silence, and enigma were the destiny of women. And not an excellence of metaphors that signify the Other without ever imitating a model. Now this destiny, tied to the violence of all that is undergone, cannot be broken by substituting the feminine for woman. Quite to the contrary, that would reinforce this destiny without recognizing it, since it is thereby said that feminine is not the attribute of someone [*de quelqu'une*].[11]

Ethics, as the beyond being, would nonetheless demand that we have done with those words that consecrate a role by attributing it to an essence. To name the silence, the home, and the weakening, and this by a term so scarcely neutral as that of the feminine, is an attitude that is too equivocal. It is astonishing as well, since, by associating the feminine with a site, the same attitude seems to forbid it ethical exteriority.

Notes

1. Throughout this chapter, I translate *autrui* as "another person" or "the other person," since it arose in Old French simply as the object case—or the case of the direct object—of *l'autre*, "the other." I translate *l'autre* and *l'Autre* as, respectively, "the other" and "the Other," following the capitalization in the original. Although a certain indistinction between these two arises in the text, the "other," or *l'autre*, underscores the alterity of the other person in contrast with *autrui*, and the "Other" denotes, generally, the concept of the other qua other. The French terms are preserved throughout between brackets.—Trans.

2. Emmanuel Levinas, *Noms propre* (Paris: Fata Morgana, 1976), 64.

3. Emmanuel Levinas, *Difficile liberté: Essai sur le judaïsm*, 3d ed., revised and corrected (Paris: Albin Michel, 1976), 49, our italics; Eng., 32, my translation.

4. Emmanuel Levinas, *Totalité et infini: Essai sur l'extériorité*, 3d ed. (The Hague: Martinus Nijhoff, 1980), 203; Eng., 228, my trans.

5. The French text reads, "Y a-t-il une 'vocation de celle qui ne conquiert pas,' de celle qui ne se perd pas dans ses productions puisque en créer n'est pas son lot?" Setting the demonstrative pronoun in the feminine, *celle*, Chalier is referring here to the one whose role has been that of a welcomer and keeper of the home. While the pronoun comprises women, here, Chalier does not mean that a woman might not have other roles and, as she makes clear at the end of the chapter, it is not her intent to assimilate the concepts *the feminine* and *women*. Despite this, a certain slippage occurs between the senses of these terms as her remarks on Levinas unfold.—Trans.

6. Levinas is speaking about those human beings of whom the essential quality of "feminine" is predicated. It is unlikely that he means, thereby, women and men with feminine qualities. —Trans.

7. Levinas writes Heidegger's *Sein zum Tode* in French as "être-pour-la-mort," which I feel is better rendered "being-unto-death" or "being-for-death" than the conventional English translation, "being toward death." He thus shifts the sense of *zum* from a directional sense to a more attributive one: being, and especially the being whose most peculiar possibility is its death, is *for* -death. Conceived without eschatology, that being is mere finitude and stands within death's sphere.—Trans.

8. The sense of "*originelle* effectuation du temps" must here be understood in the sense of that which dates, or comes, from the origin of something. By contrast, the French adjective *original* denotes, instead, that which comes directly from the hand of its author, as would a work of art, and from which copies are made. The English *original* leaves this distinction to context.—Trans.

9. Emmanuel Levinas, *Autrement qu'être ou au-delà de l'essence*, 2d ed. (The Hague: Martinus Nijhoff, 1978), 156; Eng., 121, my trans.

10. Emmanuel Levinas, *En découvrant l'existence avec Husserl et Heidegger* (Paris: J. Vrin, 1982), 235.

11. The French text reads, "puisqu'est dit que féminin n'est pas nécessairement l'attribut de quelqu'une." One could translate "quelqu'une" as "some female" or "someone who is female." As Chalier (and first Levinas) has argued, all Others are not feminine, rather the "experience" of gentleness carries with it the memory of the feminine face. However, the feminine, and what Chalier calls the destiny of women, is but an extreme—and a silent—degree of alterity. Thus the argument, here, against substituting feminine for woman: women may be feminine, silence and enigma have been their destiny, but she argues that the weakness reminiscent of the feminine, by which one passes beyond being, is not women's affair par excellence—Trans.

8

Masculine Mothers?

Maternity in Levinas and Plato

Stella Sandford

In *Otherwise Than Being*, Levinas makes an interesting and somewhat unexpected return to two of the themes of *Totality and Infinity*:[1] *jouissance* and sensibility. This is unexpected for two reasons. First, in the earlier text both themes appear in section 2, "Interiority and Economy," where they are articulated in terms of the atheistic ego, or the apparently preethical subject who seems no longer to play a part in Levinas's work by the time of *Otherwise Than Being*. Second, the notions of *jouissance* and sensibility, when read into section 4 of *Totality and Infinity*, would seem to be most readily associable with *eros*, and eros—essentially ambiguous but ultimately compromised by immanence and concupiscence (TeI, 298; TI, 266)—is, increasingly, opposed to or contrasted with ethics.[2] In *Otherwise Than Being*, however, one finds *jouissance* and sensibility integral to the elaboration of (ethical) proximity. Clearly, then, the terms are not being used in exactly the same way in the two different texts, but there is nevertheless a striking similarity. It is as if the *nature* of *jouissance* and sensibility remains the same, while their role(s) in relation to the subject, or their significance vis-à-vis the very ethical subjectivity of the subject, are radically rethought.

In *Totality and Infinity* the relation between *jouissance* and sensibility is not entirely clear, and at times Levinas seems almost to equate the two terms. (TeI, 144; TI, 136). More often, he speaks of sensibility as "the instance," "the fact," or "the mode" of *jouissance*, to be described "starting with the *jouissance* of the element" (TeI, 143, 144; TI, 135, 136), as if sensibility is the very affectivity of the ego, or the way in which *jouissance* is lived. In fact, though, in the subsection titled "Sensibility" Levinas's main concern seems to be to emphasize the nonrepresentational nature of *jouissance*, and its elaboration as sensibility works as an affirmation of this assertion through the implication of a perhaps conventional distinction between the sensible (*jouissance*) and the intellectual (thematizing consciousness).

It is the nonthematizing nature of *jouissance* and sensibility that *Otherwise Than Being* shares with *Totality and Infinity*, as well as an emphasis on the physicality—and hence the vulnerability—of the subject as sensibility. The difference between the two texts with regard to these two themes is then partly one of accent. Both share the description, its details albeit more explicit in *Totality and Infinity*, of *jouissance* and sensibility as connected with bodily need, but in the earlier text the emphasis falls on pleasure, while in *Otherwise Than Being* Levinas stresses pain and suffering. This perhaps also explains the preference for the word *jouissance* in *Totality and Infinity* and for *sensibility* in *Otherwise Than Being*. The major difference, though, is the description of sensibility in *Otherwise Than Being* as the sine qua non of ethical subjectivity. Although this is presented under several aspects, I want here to concentrate on just two: sensibility as the need and enjoyment of food, and sensibility as maternity.

For Levinas, the fact that the human being, as much as the animal, needs to eat is the condition for the relation with the neighbor (*le prochain*), in which the very humanity of the human is inscribed. In the earlier work this "transcendental" structure was already signaled in the identification of other conditions. In *Totality and Infinity* the ethical relation, the welcome of the Other, was said to be impossible with empty hands and closed doors (TeI, 187; TI, 172), hence the analysis of dwelling, work, and possession. In "The Trace of the Other" the word *liturgy* in its nonreligious sense was evoked in order to express the idea that in the ethical relation (or in the *oeuvre*, the "good work") one must have something to lose.[3] In *Otherwise Than Being* these conditions are reduced to their most basic instance: "To give, to-be-for-another, despite oneself, but in interrupting the for-oneself, is to tear the bread from one's own mouth, to nourish the hunger of another with one's own fasting" (AE, 94; OB, 56). Even more than this, "one has first to *enjoy one's bread*, not in order to have the merit of giving it, but in order to give it with one's heart, to give oneself in giving it" (AE, 116; OB, 72). The connection with *Totality and Infinity* is particularly interesting here. In both texts nourishment is connected to *jouissance* in an essential way. In 1961, in Levinas's characterizing all *jouissance* as "alimentation," the transmutation of the other into the same (into me), its nonethical, egoistic nature was also stressed (TeI, 113; TI, 111). In *Otherwise Than Being* the nature of *jouissance* is fundamentally the same, and now "ethics" is more explicitly thematized as the *foregoing of nourishment*. The literal ingestion of food is still the model of egoism, but now its reverse also—tearing the bread from my mouth—plays a significant role.

Levinas expresses this thought in an even more visceral way: "Only a subject that eats can be for-the-other, or can signify. Signification, the-one-for-the-other, has meaning only among beings of flesh and blood" (AE, 119; OB, 74). Conventionally, of course, the reference to the composition of the human as "flesh and blood" implies susceptibility, vulnerability even unto death, and this is just what Levinas intends. In a complex way, however, for him the vulnerability of sensibility is also, or makes possible, vulnerability to proximity, to *le prochain*. Thus proximity will also be described as *trauma*,[4] and in *Otherwise Than Being* the themes of pain and suffering come to the fore (AE, 102; OB, 63). In a connected manner, the epitome of sensibility is, however, characterized as *maternity*, and the figure of the maternal body becomes the privileged case of substitution.[5] In a sense, the choice of the metaphor of maternity is an obvious one for Levinas. At the beginning of chapter 2, "the knot of subjectivity" is described as "the torsion of the Same and the Other ... Intrigue of the Other-in-the-Same," which is or which accomplishes itself in proximity. More simply, "subjectivity is the other-in-the-Same" (AE, 46; OB, 25), and given these explanations, it is not difficult to see, in a rather literal way, how prenatal maternity could become the paradigm case of "the Other in the Same," or of passive (and perhaps unchosen) responsibility.

References to *"the gestation of the other in the same"* (AE, 167; OB, 105), used metaphorically but also as a description of maternity (AE, 121; OB, 75) reinforce such an interpretation.

The metaphor of maternity, however, also signifies in other than these obviously "spatial" terms. Probably a biblical reference is intended in the linking of maternity with the theme of pain and suffering (OB, 79), referring one also to that corporeality of the subject perhaps most insistent in prenatal maternity. Furthermore, the metaphor of maternity connects with, or is the archetype of, the idea of *nourishment* already introduced through the theme of mouth and bread. Again, pre- and postnatal maternity can provide very literal examples of nourishing the other with food that one has enjoyed, but maternity also carries the conventional symbolic signification attached, for example, to the figure of Demeter. Mother of Persephone and the figure of the Mother more generally, Demeter represents the symbolic synthesis of the mother and of the earth as providers of nourishment, a connection that Levinas echoes in the twin tropes of food (feeding) and maternity.

There is a sense in which the choice of the trope of maternity in *Otherwise Than Being* (1974)[6] is an obvious one for Levinas, because of the already established cultural signification of *the maternal* as paradigmatic of care (nourishment) and responsibility. In the particular context of Levinas's philosophy, the trope of the maternal also seems to be more compelling than his previous employment of the notion of *paternity* in, for example, *Totality and Infinity*.[7] Every discussion of fecundity, paternity, and filiality, in which Levinas stresses the originality of the relation in which the son both is and is not the father, would seem to be applicable a fortiori to the mother-child relation. If in the son the father both remains himself and yet becomes other than himself,[8] how much more true this is of the mother's relation to the child when there is, at one level, a sharing of substinence, even substance, such that the child is *of* the mother. How much more meaningful is the notion of 'transubstantiation' (TeI, 301; TI, 269) in this gestation that, in language at least, has confused the distinction between the literal and the metaphorical almost beyond repair. But this being so, what exactly is the connection between the notion of maternity and Levinas's earlier analyses of 'the feminine'? Is the maternal a further elaboration of the feminine, or a supercession of the very distinction masculine/feminine? Is the notion of the maternal consistent with the analyses of the familial terms in the earlier work, or is it introduced as a corrective to the previous discussion of paternity, for example?

Various answers, both laudatory and critical, have been given to these questions. Tina Chanter, for example, sees very little positive in the introduction of the notion of maternity. For Chanter, the category of maternity only underscores the absence of the feminine as eros in *Otherwise Than Being*, with the implication that Levinas therefore fails to think of sexual difference in the Irigarayan-inspired sense that Chanter demands.[9] Catherine Chalier is similarly critical. In "Ethics and the Feminine," she remarks that according to the discussion of *Totality and Infinity*, the feminine would be excluded from ethics.[10] In *Otherwise Than Being* the ultimate meaning of the feminine as maternity does admit the feminine to the ethical realm, but Chalier still finds this restrictive: "[W]e have to take note of the fact that, according to Levinas, ethics in its feminine achievement means to be a mother and nothing else. Can we agree?"[11] Because she cannot agree, Chalier then tries to reinscribe the feminine as ethical against the grain of Levinas's analyses, both in *Totality and Infinity* and *Otherwise Than Being*, through a meditation on the biblical figure of Rebecca.

The positive aspect of Chalier's argument is, however, Levinasian in inspiration, for in several key texts he himself raises the notion of an "effeminization" of the virility of being. In "Judaism and the Feminine Element" (1960), for example, such an effeminization is described in a discussion that prefigures the account of dwelling and the feminine welcome in *Totality and Infinity*. The impersonal world is described as "hard and cold. . . . it neither clothes those who are naked nor feeds those who are hungry. . . . spirit in its masculine existence . . . *lives outdoors*."[12] The "ontological function of the feminine" is then said to be the surmounting of "an alienation which, fundamentally, results from the very masculinity of the universal and conquering logos,"[13] and although the familiar description of her opening of the interiority of the house then follows, in the opposition of the feminine to the universal logos there is also a hinting at a possible *feminization of the ethical*.

If, in *Totality and Infinity*, this hint is not taken, Levinas still speaks there of the effeminization of the virile ego in its relation with the feminine in eros (TeI, 303; TI, 270). The ethical relation, described as an end to the mastery of the subject, could also be read as *implying* a feminization, even if the word is not actually used in this regard. Still later, in 1981, Levinas makes clear what is implied in the notion of feminization; that is, the detachment of the notion of the feminine from the female (the woman) in order to articulate it as a more general concept. In *Ethics and Infinity* he says of his use of the notion of the feminine in *Time and the Other* (1946–47): "Perhaps ... all these allusions to the ontological differences between the masculine and the feminine would appear less archaic if, instead of dividing humanity into two species (or into two genres), they would signify that the participation in the masculine and the feminine were the attribute of every human being."[14] According, one imagines, to such hints, Chalier's reinscription of the feminine in ethics is what she calls "the feminine as the disruption of being by goodness and beyond maternity.... Is this not the meaning of the feminine in the human being?"[15] However, having made such a move, Chalier resists reading the maternal, too, in precisely this way; that is, as a (feminine) model for the disruption of the virility of being, or a (feminine) model for responsibility/substitution; like Chanter, Chalier still objects to the too conventional ascription of feminine excellence to maternity and maternity only.

By contrast, Monique Schneider sees in Levinas's later work a notable attempt to reverse or make good the matricidal impulses of Western thought visible already in Aeschylus's *Oresteia* in Athena's avowal of her purely masculine parentage.[16] In the same way, Schneider suggests that the ancient figure of Baubô bears witness not only to this denegation of maternal origins, but also to a corresponding uneasiness with the mouth as the opening onto "les entrailles," in French both the entrails and the space of gestation. In Greek mythology Baubô is the woman who made the unhappy Demeter laugh by exposing to her her genitals. The few extant sculptured representations of Baubô are somewhat grotesque, in the form of a headless body, the face inscribed on the abdomen to suggest the correlation eyes-breasts and mouth-vulva.[17] According to Schneider, the depiction of Baubô as both obscene and risible, her vulva both hidden and announced (in agreement with the Freudian explanation of the fetish) by the buccal analogue, places the original dwelling place of the human firmly under the sign of derision.[18] It is, then, against this background that Schneider approaches Levinas's work as exceptional, as an extraordinary refusal of this denegation of maternal origins and, concomitantly, a revaluation of the mouth.[19] Having made such a claim, Schneider does not then go on to discuss the Levinasian notion of maternity within the broader context of Levinas's philosophical oeuvre, and nor is she obliged to do so. For others, however, the introduction of the notion of maternity is read as an expiatory gesture with regard to the previous discussions of the feminine in Levinas's work. Bernard

Forthomme's analysis, in *Une philosophie de la transcendance*, is a case in point.[20] Although Forthomme argues that the account of subjectivity in *Totality and Infinity* is essentially "masculine," for him this is not necessarily a criticism of Levinas, for while the virility of Levinas's philosophy does indeed mean that he speaks only as or for "the masculine," this is wholly consonant with the model of the relation to the Other irreducible to any synoptic view or to the indifferent directionality of reciprocity.[21] Later, however, Forthomme's comments would seem to show that the "virility" of *Totality and Infinity*, while perhaps bearing witness to a certain performative enactment of nonreciprocity, is nevertheless inferior to the "femininity" of the model of maternity. Maternity, he says, goes beyond the bipolarity of masculine and feminine, revealing the "neutrality" of an ethical subjectivity beyond sexual difference and surpassing the "masculine" point of view that seems to constrain Levinas in the final section of *Totality and Infinity*.[22] Forthomme's point would seem to be that while the schematism of *Totality and Infinity*, a schematism based on sexual difference, does allow Levinas to open up the phenomenological tradition to "the forgotton horizons of sensibility,"[23] the analysis also remains *trapped within* this schematism. In the model of maternity, however, (ethical) responsibility, what was also called metaphysical desire, is neither masculine nor feminine, and this testifies to a more profound, one might also say more equitable, metaphysic.

Now Forthomme takes it for granted that the notion of maternity in Levinas's philosophical elaboration is not exclusive to the female. If this could not legitimately be deduced from the simple fact that Levinas, as a man, would presumably not want to exclude himself from the possibility of the excellence of responsibility, the text itself would seem to confirm it. Interestingly, Levinas never signals the metaphorical nature of maternity explicitly, never explicitly says, as he so often said of paternity, that maternity is not reducible to its biological signification, but everything suggests this. Thus although the *model* for (ethical) responsibility is in some sense feminine, this is a femininity that can (and ought) to be assumed by the male as well as the female. This, note, is the possibility that Chalier seems not to accept in "Ethics and the Feminine," but that for Forthomme affirms the preeminence of maternity.

John Llewelyn's reading of Levinas, however, seems to encompass the positions of both Chalier and Forthomme. Llewelyn shares with Forthomme the idea that maternity functions effectively as a sort of corrective to the earlier discussion of the feminine, even if Levinas did not consciously intend this. Maternity appears, Llewelyn says, "as though to compensate for the virilization the concept of welcome acquires in [*Totality and Infinity*] and as though to answer or anticipate the objection that the use made in the earlier book of the concepts of gender is indefensibly one-sided, however non-biological and non-sexual that use is claimed to be."[24] Elsewhere, Llewelyn rehearses this same thought within the schema of a more elaborate account of Levinas's philosophy, and if his reading is characterized by a certain generosity, this is because it is less much straightforward commentary, more intellectual engagement and rewriting. When Llewelyn says at the end of the book that the need to escape from the virile, heroic conception of subjectivity demands "[a]nother genealogy, another *parenté* for man,"[25] it is not therefore entirely clear whether he believes Levinas to have succeeded in answering this demand. To the extent that Levinas has not succeeded, Llewelyn "fills in," as it were, but with insights and concepts that he sees as nascent within Levinas's own writings: "Although in this other genealogy theism is identified with what is difficult to refrain from calling the He-ism of illeity, it must be emphasized that the trace of the other passes also through the She-ism and elleity of maternity, so through a non-neutral illelleity."[26]

Llewelyn's argument can be partly reconstructed as follows: if the use of a vocabulary of patrilinearity, for example, *seems* on the surface to affirm a patriarchy that would be wholly consonant with the virility of the domination of the Logos, of Being, or of the One, the analyses of fecundity, paternity, and filiality *in fact* "deconstruct" this. Filiality and so on

> seems to mean the parricide of any phallogocentric idea of the father and the substitution for it of the idea of the mother, of substitution or bearing *par excellence*. This inference of the notion of substitution in which the genealogy of paternity and maternity is unhierarchical but not a neutral androgyny is not unambiguously supported by Levinas's texts.... [T]hey leave the reader with only scattered remarks from which to infer how in Levinas's ethical interpretation of the family sorority and matrilineal filiation, as distinguished from patrilineal filiation, fit in.[27]

It is, then, in Llewelyn's inference of how maternity "fits in," that the generosity of his reading is apparent. Llewelyn would allow patrilineal filiation to signify in a nonpatriarchal way under the influence of the (later) sign of maternity. "Paternity," for Llewelyn, is thus not inevitably compromised by its patriarchal assumptions. Both that argument and Llewelyn's discussion of maternity are dependent on his polysemic notion of *genealogy*. There is, for example, a broadly Nietzschean idea of genealogy signaled in the way Llewelyn's subtitle (*The Genealogy of Ethics*) echoes Nietzsche's *Genealogy of Morals* and is put into play as Llewelyn's tracing of the historical development of Levinas's thinking, where the conditions of possibility for the later works are winkled out of the earlier texts without thereby implying any simple relation of origin or of cause and effect. At the same time, however, the readings of the earlier texts are informed by the demands of the later ones, bearing witness to a certain "reading backwards" in which a hermeneutics of the past (texts) is sacrificed to the exigencies of the present. This methodology is then more specifically applied to the very particular genealogy in Levinas's work described, as Llewelyn says, under the nomenclature of the family tree.[28] Most important for my discussion here, Llewelyn reads in the early texts "traces," both in the common and in the Levinasian senses, of that which is named in *Otherwise Than Being* as maternity. He sees the 1961 discussion of the opening of intimacy by the feminine as just such a precursory moment.[29] Reading backward this also means that the ethical excellence of the maternal rubs off on the seemingly preethical feminine, and Llewelyn thus answers, on Levinas's behalf, to the feminist objections brought against the analysis of the feminine as it appears in *Totality and Infinity*, for example. In essence, the trace of the perfection of maternity passes through the feminine as what Llewelyn calls "elleity."

But as quoted earlier, Llewelyn also coins the term *illelleity*, which expresses the nonbiological nature of the notion of a maternity that is not exclusively female. As he says in *Middle Voice*: "Neither simply active nor simply passive, if the middle voice of responsibility has a gender it is that of the middle sex. The middle sex is not neuter. It is chiasmically bisexual. But what we are talking about here is humanity prior to the sexual difference."[30] This seems not unlike the perhaps utopian thought articulated by Derrida in an interview from 1981:

> [W]hat if we were to approach here (for one does not arrive at this as one would at a determined location) the area of a relationship to the other where the code of sexual marks would no longer be discriminating? The relationship would not be a-sexual, far from

it, but would be sexual otherwise: beyond the binary difference that governs the decorum of all codes, beyond the opposition masculine/feminine, beyond bisexuality as well, beyond homosexuality and heterosexuality which come to the same thing.[31]

In this, Derrida does not envision a discourse in which masculine and feminine would no longer exist, but one in which they would "no longer be discriminating." This is not a commentary on Levinas, but it seems to articulate Llewelyn's position on the latter. In more-conventional terms, Llewelyn expresses the absence of such a discourse (or "genealogy") as one in which "the woman in the man is sacrificed to phallogocentrism. Because man's maternity is passed by, and therefore the closest, the Other in the mother."[32] The other genealogy, the other *parenté*, is also described as another humanism, or a humanism of the other man,[33] and thus Llewelyn's reading joins Chalier's too: "Is this not the meaning of the feminine in the human being?"[34]

Fecundity and Masculine Mothers

From this discussion of the notion of maternity, two major points have arisen. First, and most obvious to any reader of Levinas, the Maternal is not intended to designate something exclusively female, a point that bears importantly on Levinas's previous discussion of fecundity and paternity. Throughout his work Levinas makes reference to the biological *origin* of the notion of fecundity, while emphasizing also, as he says in *Time and the Other*, that this in no way neutralizes the paradox of its ontological and psychological significance (TA, 87; TO, 92).[35] Several such comments are also to be found in *Totality and Infinity*, ostensibly disallowing a purely biological interpretation of the terms,[36] but each time that fecundity is said to overflow its purely biological signification, the biological origin of the concept is nevertheless affirmed. In fact, each of these references could equally be read as an emphasis on the ineluctably biological ground of fecundity, as much as its tendency to signify beyond this.[37] It is only later, after the publication of *Otherwise Than Being*, that the biological aspect of fecundity is decisively denied, as in the 1979 preface to *Time and the Other* (TA, 15; TO, 37), in *Ethics and Infinity* (EeI, 73–74; EI, 70–71), and in *Otherwise Than Being* where, in a passage that leads on to a discussion of fraternity, Levinas speaks of the kinship relation (*relation de parenté*) "outside of all biology" (AE, 138; OB, 87).

This small but significant shift in Levinas's later work is, I would suggest, explicable by the introduction of the notion of maternity in *Otherwise Than Being*, which would also explain the shift in the preceding quotation from *paternity* to *parenté*. Biological origin and signification is played down—or indeed wholly dismissed—after the shift from the paternal to the maternal metaphor because maternity, as the apogean model for responsibility and substitution, must be a universal model. Nothing of the biological must remain in the maternal if it is not to suggest that the female is somehow more capable of the excellence of responsibility than is the male, but in the later work the explicit disavowal of biology is displaced analogously onto discussions of or references to paternity. Retrospectively, paternity signifies nonbiologically in order that it might mirror and at the same time justify or explain the nonbiological status of maternity; in order, that is, that men might be mothers.

Given this, the second point appears as something of a paradox. Important differences notwithstanding, what the readings of Chanter, Chalier, Schneider, Llewelyn, and Forthomme share is a sense of the femininity, however problematic, of the notion of maternity. Even when the last two commentators insist on the "bisexuality" (Llewelyn) of maternity, this amounts to a debiologizing of a notion that nevertheless remains for them "feminine" in origin and in its primary symbolic significations. For Llewelyn, as I have said, this explicitly amounts to a prioritizing of the feminine in the later work. It is perhaps worth considering, then, what relationship the bisexual but feminine notion of maternity could possibly have with the earlier Levinasian notion of the feminine, as at first glance it would seem to be fundamentally incommensurable. The feminine as it appears in Levinas's work up to and including *Totality and Infinity* would seem to be a term parasitic on, or even constitutive of, an idea of sexual difference. It is the very alterity or specificity of the feminine qua feminine that gives any philosophical sense to the part it plays in Levinas's work even if, as Irigaray argues, this specificity or alterity is in fact relentlessly betrayed.[38] As a formal structure it is precisely the radical alterity, specificity, or both, of the feminine that is ostensibly incompatible with the idea of bisexuality raised by Llewelyn. If the maternal is to "belong" to the feminine in this schema, it must belong wholly or not at all; Llewelyn's "bisexuality" would simply mean a compromise in or of sexual difference or alterity. This, it seems to me, is inescapably true with regard to the very specific functioning of "the feminine" in Levinas's work, but to extend the argument to *any* philosophical discussion of maternity would probably be to make a biologistic mistake. For while biologically it is true, so far at least, that gestation and birth in the human being are exclusive to the female, the philosophical elaboration of this fact takes place at the level of the symbolic, in the Lacanian sense. It is possible to fantasize a symbolic order based on a cultural elaboration of the biological experience (which is not only biological) of maternity, and it is this that Llewelyn spells out in his claim that "[a]nother genealogy, another *parenté* for man requires to be found."[39] According to this "other genealogy" the actual and symbolic figure of the mother would be meaningful for both the male and the female apart from biology, that is, would play a symbolically important (privileged) part in founding myths and social structures of all kinds. For this there need not have been matriarchies in the historical past, and one does not necessarily need to postulate the Great Mother or the Goddess. At issue is not the reclamation of an archaic past, but the immediate demands of the present and those of the future. For Llewelyn, for example, the requirement for another genealogy is articulated in the context of deep and sincere ecological concerns.[40] Matriarchal utopias, either past or future, do not come into it. The idea of a maternal genealogy invokes instead the possibility of the very restructuring of thought, which is what makes it a philosophical project.[41] The question is, however, to what extent does the notion of maternity at work in Levinas's text succeed in suggesting, if not effecting, a truly other genealogy?

A comparison with Plato's *Symposium*[42] is instructive. In Diotima's speech—the speech that resonates most profoundly with Levinas's discussions of fecundity and filiality—Plato also introduces the notion of maternity in metaphorical form. And just as for Llewelyn and Forthomme Levinas's notion of maternity signals a move away from the privileging of the masculine in his earlier work, Arlene Saxonhouse argues that the metaphor of birth in the *Symposium*, which she sees as supplanting those of impregnation and ejaculation, constructs the female as the model for humankind, or genders the philosophic eros as feminine.[43] While not agreeing with the details of Saxonhouse's argument, Wendy Brown formulates a similarly sympathetic reading of the *Symposium* in which Plato is seen to engage in "a critique of the socially male modes of thinking, speaking, and acting prevalent in his epoch and milieu."[44] Against the agonistic idea of philosophy in which glory, reputation, and power are at stake, Plato, according to Brown, locates philosophy in the realm of love, nurturance, and procreation, such that "[t]rue being, philosophy, and wisdom are depicted as female just as it is a woman, Diotima, who taught Socrates what he knows about the relationship between eros and wisdom."[45] There are, perhaps, two issues here: the attribution of the source of knowledge to Diotima, a woman; and the metaphor of birth. If Saxonhouse and Brown are right about Plato with regard to either of these two, and if, as I would argue, Levinas's phenomenology of eros and fecundity is heavily indebted to Plato, the metaphor of maternity in Levinas might appear in a new light.

Supposing Diotima to Be a Woman

The "problem" of Diotima seems to break down into three main questions, the last of which is the most curious and the most fascinating: Is she real? Why is she a woman? Is she a woman? The first, the question of her possible historical existence, is usually answered in the negative. Despite the occasional reference to the possibility that Socrates was actually taught by a woman called Aspasia, the idea that a woman might really have been the definitive influence on Socrates—which is, after all, what the *Symposium* suggests—is mooted as a kind of interesting thought experiment, but not really taken seriously.[46] If it is assumed, as it often seems to be, that Diotima was not a historical figure, her presence in the dialogue is then explained as a dramatic device that, for example, allows Plato to add elements to his Socratic heritage that he cannot portray as coming from Socrates himself, allows Socrates to show his rival speech makers that he can match them in imagination and inventive fancy, allows Socrates not to appear to be criticizing the other speakers, and so on.

The second question carries on from the first: If she is a fictional device, why is she a woman? Answers range from the suggestion that Plato deemed it more appropriate that the metaphor of birth should come from the mouth of a woman, to the idea that Diotima represents the mystical element of Platonism and hence the fact of her being a priestess, not a woman, is the determining factor. The possibility is also raised that her reported speech and Socrates' praise for Diotima could be evidence of an incipient feminist element in Plato's thought, but the idea of Plato as an "ancient feminist," as one commentator puts it, seems to me to be too anachronistic to be plausible, female guardians notwithstanding; the suspicion arises that these suggestions are often made with the intention of confounding any feminist critique of Plato.

The more interesting, the more contentious, question, however, asks, Is Diotima a woman at all? Some feminist readings are adamant that she is. Andrea Nye, for example, sees the assumption of Diotima's ficticiousness as completely unwarranted, and elaborates a specifically Diotimean philosophy that she evidently sees shining through any Platonic interference: "She is the spokesperson for ways of life and thought that Greek philosophy feeds on, ways of thought whose authority Plato neutralized and converted to his own purposes."[47] Perhaps alive to the difficulties involved in any historical assertion, Irigaray's reading, on the other hand, needs only to assume the fact of Diotima's sex *within the confines of the fiction* and to elaborate on this symbolically through the metonymic substitution of "Diotima's philosophy" for "feminine philosophy." Socrates, she says, borrows Diotima's wisdom and power,[48] and for the first part of her speech at least, Diotima's "dialectical" teaching on love presents the reader with a model or a method of mediation that resists the dualistic domination of the either/or, neither/nor structure of Socratic dialectic. There was, presumably, a similar strain of thought behind the decision of an important and influential group of Veronese feminist philosophers to take the name Diotima.[49] It is, then, fitting that the most detailed and compelling argument against it should come from a former member of that group, Adriana Cavarero. Like Irigaray, Cavarero resists the discussion of the possibility of Diotima's historical existence; what is important is the fact that Diotima, a woman, is a character in a dialogue convincingly attributed to Plato, a man. It falls to Cavarero, however, to point out something rather obvious that many discussions of Diotima overlook: it is not *unusual* for Plato to dramatize his philosophical discussions through the device of reported speech. Furthermore, it is not contentious to suggest that in the Platonic dialogues it is Plato himself who speaks through the dramatic voice of Socrates, and Cavarero's argument vis-à-vis the *Symposium* is that this is true a fortiori when Socrates reports Diotima's words, which, "far from being original or in some way rooted in the sex of the speaker, are the words of Plato reechoing in a female voice."[50]

Of course, the question still arises of why Plato should choose an ostensibly female mouthpiece, and the key, according to Cavarero, lies in the metaphor of birth. But unlike those of Saxonhouse or Brown, this reading bears witness not to a revaluation of maternity, the feminine, or any of the associated characteristics or values, but, paradoxically, to their erasure. Plato's is "a subtle and ambiguous strategy requiring that a female voice expound the philosophical discourse of a patriarchal order that excludes women, ultimately reinforcing the original matricide that disinvests them."[51] Like Aeschylus's Athena, then, Diotima is a woman made to renounce or denounce the female, and the exquisite irony of Diotima is that she does so through the use of a feminine vocabulary of pregnancy and parturition: "In Diotima's speech maternal power is annihilated by offering its language and vocabulary to the power that will triumph over it, and will build its foundations on annihilation itself."[52] Even so, A. W. Price, for one, has noted that in the *Symposium* there is a certain confusion of the metaphors of begetting and bearing.[53] Plato says, for example, that the procreative impulse that all men have will fuel a natural desire to beget children (of the body and of the soul) (206C), and the relief afforded by contact with beauty is described according to the mechanism of orgasmic release (206D). At the same time, however, the lover is said to "[bring] to birth the children he has long desired to have" (209C). The English translations of Hamilton and Lamb[54] attest to this difficulty in their different renderings of key passages, for example, 206C: "All men, Socrates, have a procreative impulse, both spiritual and physical" (Hamilton); "All men are pregnant, Socrates, both in body and in soul" (Lamb). Furthermore, the well-known metaphor of midwifery, used by Socrates in the *Theaetetus*, for example, cannot but add to the confusion.[55] Against the background of Cavarero's analysis, however, this confusion could be seen as deliberate. In its interweaving of the metaphors of begetting and birthing, the passage for the attribution of the latter to the male is perhaps eased, and the metaphor seems less "unnatural." If begetting is, conventionally, associated with the male,[56] and birthing, more obviously, with the female, the mixed metaphors further serve what Cavarero calls "the mimetic effect of confusing or commingling the male and the female voice."[57]

In the *Symposium* any actual references to women as participants in the procreative process are limited to the biological, the inferior realm of the physical, which the philosopher will have decisively overcome. Spiritual procreation is said to be under the auspices of the Heavenly Aphrodite, whom Pausanias did not just describe, but *defined*, as motherless (180D). Socrates does not disagree; indeed, his argument can be seen to be an elaboration of this very thought. As Cavarero says, the introduction of begetting and birthing is immediately presented with the

distinction between body and soul (206B), and any procreation associated with the woman (actual maternity) is soon dispatched along with
the physical itself.[58] Far from being an introduction of the maternal into
philosophical discourse, then, the *Symposium* effectively dismisses it, and
not through any simple disavowal, but through a complex appropriation
of linguistic images and the puppet character of Diotima.

The promiscuous metaphorical schema, including the intertextual
example of midwifery, allows one final point to be made here. In the
Theaetetus Socrates says that the function of actual midwives is less important than his, and that his "differs from theirs in being practised upon
men, not women, and in tending their souls in labour, not their bodies"
(150B/C). Philosophers beget, they become pregnant, they give birth,
and they assist at birth; it is then a small step to the idea that the philosopher assists at the *rebirth* of his beloved, or even that he is reborn himself,
with a purely masculine parentage. As David M. Halperin remarks, the
occasion of the Symposium on a feast day of Dionysus would itself suggest
this, as Dionysus, in one version of the legend, was born from the thigh
of his father Zeus, not from his mother (Semele).[59] Alternatively, when
Dionysus is identified with Zagreus, he is the twice-born, *reborn* the second time from his father's body and only then immortal. Finally, to risk
an interpretation almost neo-Platonic in its detail, Diotima's Love was
said to have been born in the garden of Zeus, who gave birth to Athena,
his unmothered daughter, from his head. All philosophical, symbolic,
and mythical associations suggest, therefore, that the only maternity that
concerns Plato here is that which can be appropriated for the male, and
for one very obvious reason: the dialogue is about *philosophy*, and as
Cavarero says, "The pregnant birth-giving male, like the male who practices midwifery, stands as the emblematic figure of true philosophy."[60]

The Levinasian Law of the Father

Despite the similarities in the various positive interpretations of Plato and
Levinas with regard to their respective notions of birthing and maternity,
their formulations have very little in common, perhaps nothing at all.
The details of the one account will not illuminate those of the other,
and it would be far-fetched to suggest a constancy in the idea of maternity across two millennia. Their juxtaposition is, however, warranted by

a certain congruence in the *consequences* of an interpretation whose application is not exhausted by the epithet *feminist*. In order to demonstrate this, a fresh interrogation of *Otherwise Than Being* is required.

An increasingly important part comes to be played in Levinas's philosophy by the notion of *le tiers*, the third party or the third person. In *Totality and Infinity*, for example, the trace of *le tiers* in the eyes of the Other is what ensures that the intensity of the ethical relation does not become *injustice* with regard to all the others. The significance of this has been most fully elaborated by Simon Critchley in his claim that the ever present presence of *le tiers* attests to the ultimately political horizon of Levinasian ethics.[61] As Critchley makes clear, *le tiers* does not come to join me in my relation with the Other, or does not follow on from an initial encounter with the Other: "The ethical relation does not take place in an a-political space outside the public realm; rather, ethics is always already political, the relation to the face is always already a relation to humanity as a whole."[62] Furthermore, it is this dimension of the ethical relation that distinguishes it from love understood as eros.[63]

The same move to *le tiers* is, if anything, even more important in *Otherwise Than Being*. The argument there, in section 3 of chapter 5, "From the Saying to the Said, or the Wisdom of Desire," is perhaps a little surprising, in that Levinas makes a return to the notion of the Said in such a way that it seems to be rehabilitated. In a very important sense, the return to the Said is inevitable. The very fact of philosophical discourse, of the very text of Levinas, is itself a return to the Said, or a dependence on the Said, which would then appear to be another betrayal of the Saying even in the very act of trying to redress this betrayal. But this is only a "facile objection," as Levinas says (AE, 242; OB, 155), with no more success than the celebrated refutation of skepticism has had in doing away with skepticism.[64] Besides, as Critchley argues, the Said to which it is necessary to return is not one uninformed or uninterrupted by the trace of the Saying, not an unjustified but a *justified* Said.[65] At the same time, this move is a move to *le tiers*, the opening up of the order of truth and, what seems to be the most important word for Levinas, *justice*. "If proximity ordained me only to the Other," says Levinas,

> there would not have been any problem, even in the most general sense of the term. . . . It is troubled and becomes a problem when a third party enters. . . . What then are the other and the third party for-one-another? What have they done to one another?

Which passes before the other?... It is of itself the limit of re-
sponsability and the birth of the question: What do I have to
do with justice? A question of consciousness/conscience. Justice is
necessary, that is, comparison, coexistence, contemporaneousness,
assembling, order, thematisation. (AE, 245; OB, 157)

That Levinas then aligns this realm, these questions, with philosophy is
perhaps not surprising. What could not have been anticipated, however,
is the extraordinarily suggestive inversion of this love of wisdom into the
wisdom of love: "Philosophy is this measure brought to the infinity of the
being-for-the-other of proximity, it is the wisdom of love" (AE, 251; OB,
161). The love of wisdom by itself, even with the best of intentions,
would court the danger of abstraction, and one thinks, for example, of
the arid formalism of Kant's deontological morality or of Plato's ultimately parthenogenic philosopher-lover in his solitary contemplation of
the realm of Ideas. The love of love, on the other hand, would be the
exclusivity of romantic or erotic love, ultimately not just privileging
the beloved above all others, but also privileging the self, self-indulgent.
When Levinas describes philosophy as "the wisdom of love in the service
of love" (AE, 253; OB, 162), he thus describes the Said said in the service of the Saying, Critchley's "justified Said," in which love has learnt
from wisdom and wisdom has learned from love.[66]

Were it not for the rather awkward fact that "Violence and Metaphysics," Derrida's first essay on Levinas, was written before the publication of *Otherwise Than Being*, one could imagine that it is this field of the
wisdom of love that Derrida refers to when he speaks there of a community of philosophers.[67] Perhaps he was prescient. In any case, the justified
Said (*le tiers*, politics, justice, philosophy) does have something to do
with institutions and, as Critchley says, a community of which I am a citizen and in which I am entitled to call the other to account.[68] But what
community, and what has happened to maternity?

Unfortunately, this community, as elaborated by Levinas in *Otherwise
Than Being*, is still the masculine community of brothers, that apparently
neutral and universal community of "the human fraternity" (TeI, 236;
TI, 215) familiar from *Totality and Infinity*.[69] Once this community, and
the wisdom of love that informs it, appears on the pages of *Otherwise Than
Being*, maternity is not spoken of again, and in the suggestion of an explanation for this, a familar pattern is, perhaps unexpectedly, repeated. Proximity understood as maternity, that is, occupies a position in *Otherwise*

Than Being not wholly dissimilar to that of eros in *Totality and Infinity*. For despite the fact that the proximity of maternity is paradigmatically ethical, the proximity of maternity *by itself* seems to harbor the same problem previously located in eros: a tendency to exclusivity. The intimacy of the ethical couple figuratively based on the mother and child, what Levinas calls "the intimacy of the face to face" (AE, 249; OB, 160), the ethical substitution of the former for the latter, epitomized in maternity, runs the same risk of the exclusion of the third party. And what eros—closely related to the feminine—and maternity lack in both cases will then be elaborated as masculine: *illéité*.[70] The "trace" of *le tiers*, from the alleged neutrality of the pronoun *il* (he/it), it is illeity that makes possible the "ethical universality" of fraternity not fraught with the danger of (maternal) exclusivity.

Now it will be objected that nothing like "proximity by itself" is thinkable within the thinking of *Otherwise Than Being*. Nevertheless, it is Levinas who says that "[t]he relationship with the third party is an incessant *correction* of the asymmetry of proximity" (AE, 246; OB, 158; my emphasis), and it is difficult not to hear the line he quotes from the Song of Songs—"I am sick with love" (AE, 222; OB, 198)—as indicative of a certain *excessive* proximity. And if one were to say, further, indicative of a certain *eroticism*, this would not be the only example. The intense physicality of the passages on sensibility, the almost sadistic/masochistic descriptions of the skin exposed to injury and wound (AE, 83; OB, 49), "pain [that] penetrates into the very heart of the for-oneself" (AE, 94; OB, 56), the almost unbearable "immédiateté à fleur de peau de la sensibilité—sa vulnérabilité" (AE 104),[71] *jouissance* with its connotation of sexual pleasure and, of course, maternity itself (skin, breast, caress) are powerfully erotic images. If, then, nothing like proximity by itself is thinkable within the Levinasian text, it is still the case that the very proximity of proximity invites certain erotic possibilities that stand in need of "correction"; indeed, the fraternal community demands it, for one cannot be "close" to all one's brothers, and one must look beyond the face of one's neighbour. And perhaps the idea of the threat of this purely spectral proximity by itself would not have arisen were it not the case that the notion of maternity was introduced into the text only to disappear after the introduction of *le tiers* and the wisdom of love, and that this disappearance, surely, must be explained. At the very least, it is obvious that maternity does not function like the notion of paternity in the previous texts. Maternity does not *replace* paternity, and the latter survives, somewhat covertly, in the fraternal community that it founds. What, then, is the relationship between the two? Is it possible that the necessity to overcome the duality of erotic coupling, in *Totality and Infinity*, has become, in *Otherwise Than Being*, the necessity to overcome the duality of the asymmetrical ethical relation, epitomized in maternity? To be sure, the idea of *le tiers* was already important in the 1961 text, but Levinas does not speak there of *correction*. In *Otherwise Than Being*, physicality and proximity—the maternal-feminine—must give way to the distance necessary for the abstract relation of fraternity. The universality inherent in the patrilineal genealogy must correct the asymmetry of maternal proximity if that relation is not to be the end of the line.

But a second aspect of the question of the maternal would also demand a consideration of the extent to which the notion of maternity—and perhaps also of the feminine—*could have* contained other possibilities. Otherwise said, was Levinas's betrayal of maternity prefigured *necessarily* in the notion of maternity itself, or could another deployment of the term put maternity to work to much different effect? The generous reading of John Llewelyn would suggest that it could, maybe even that it has already been done, and Catherine Chalier's less forgiving account of Levinas in *Figures du féminin* also does not preclude an attempt to articulate the idea of maternal filiation as resistance to the masculine/patriarchal order of "the proper."[72] As these creative engagements indicate, then, one is not faced with the decision whether to simply accept or reject Levinas's notion of maternity, even if he does not succeed in effecting or installing an alternative feminine genealogy or *parenté* for man. Ultimately, just as in Plato, maternity must and does give way to paternity, that is, to the law of the father. Indeed maternity, for Levinas, is *outside* of any *parenté* when this is understood, as paternity is, as the institution of a universal order of the human, of sociality, community, and philosophy. In the end, as in the beginning, the feminine is made to give way to the masculine; the only reason one bothers to say this, the only reason one *can* say it critically, is that it need not ever be so.

Notes

1. Emmanuel Levinas, *Autrement qu'être ou au-delà de l'essence* (Le Hague: Nijhoff, 1974); *Otherwise Than Being or Beyond Essence*, trans. A. Lingis (The Hague: Nijhoff, 1981). Hereafter referred to as AE/OB.

2. See, for example, "Dieu et la philosophie," in *Le nouveau commerce*, Printemps 1975, Cahier 30–33; "God and Philosophy" (1975), trans. A. Lingis, in *Collected Philosophical Papers* (Dordrecht: Nijhoff, 1987).

3. Levinas, "La trace de l'autre," in *En découvrant l'existence avec Husserl et Heidegger* (Paris: Vrin, 1994), 192; "The Trace of the Other" (1963), trans. A. Lingis, in *Deconstruction in Context*, ed. Mark C. Taylor (Chicago: Chicago University Press, 1986), 349–50.

4. See, for example, AE, 10, 65 n. 2; OB, xliii, 37.

5. "[T]he one for the other in the form of sensibility, or vulnerability, pure passivity or susceptibility, passive to the point of becoming inspiration, that is, precisely, alterity in the same, the trope of the body animated by the soul, psychism as the hand that gives even the bread torn from its own mouth. Psychism as a maternal body" (AE, 109; OB, 67) See also AE, 111; OB, 68 and AE, 114; OB 71.

6. Levinas, *Autrement qu'être*.

7. Emmanuel Levinas, *Totalité et infini: Essai sur l'extériorité* (Paris and Le Hague: Nijhoff, 1971); *Totality and Infinity: An Essay on Exteriority*, trans. A. Lingis (Pittsburgh: Duquesne University Press, 1992). Hereafter referred to as TeI/TI.

8. Emmanuel Levinas, *Le temps et l'autre* (Paris: Presses Universitaires de France, 1994), 85–86; *Time and the Other*, trans. Richard A. Cohen (Pittsburgh: Duquesne University Press, 1987), 91. Hereafter referred to as TA/TO. TeI, 299; TI, 267. TeI, 304–5; TI, 271. TeI, 310; TI, 277.

9. See Tina Chanter, *Ethics of Eros: Irigaray's Rewriting of the Philosophers* (London: Routledge, 1995), 198–99, 208.

10. Catherine Chalier, "Ethics and the Feminine," in *Re-reading Levinas*, ed. Robert Bernasconi and Simon Critchley (London: Athlone, 1991), 123.

11. Ibid., 127. See also *Figures du féminin* (Paris: La Nuit Surveillée, 1982), 45: "And if maternity can be a joy, it is not certain that all women have made their mark or find their forte there. Nor is it certain that, in helping them [to do so] this is their one and only possibility."

12. "Le judaïsme et le féminin," in *Difficile liberté* (Paris: Albin Michel, 1976), 54–55; "Judaism and The Feminine Element" (1960), trans. E. Wyschogrod, *Judaism* 18, no. 1 (1969): 33. Reprinted in the English translation of *Difficult Freedom*.

13. Ibid.

14. *Éthique et infini: Entretiens avec Philippe Nemo* (Paris, Fayard, 1982), 71; *Ethics and Infinity*, trans. Richard A. Cohen (Pittsburgh: Duquesne University Press, 1985), 68. Hereafter referred to as EeI/EI.

15. Chalier, "Ethics and the Feminine," 128. The argument is somewhat different in *Figures du féminin*.

16. Monique Schneider "En deçà du visage," in *Emmanuel Levinas: L'éthique comme philosophie première*, ed. Jean Greisch and Jacques Rolland (Actes du colloque de Cérisy-la Salle, 1986) (Paris: Éditions du Cerf, 1993), 149.

17. Found in 1898 at Priene (on the coast of Asia Minor, facing the island of Samos) in the remains of a temple dedicated to Demeter and Kore. See Maurice Olender, "Aspects of Baubô: Ancient Texts and Contexts," in *Before Sexuality: The Construction of Erotic Experience in the Ancient Greek World*, ed. M. Halperin, J. J. Winkler, and I. Zeitlin (Princeton: Princeton University Press, 1990), 83; Kathleen Freeman, *The Pre-Socratic Philosophers* (Oxford: Basil Blackwell, 1949), 11.

18. Schneider," En deça du visage," 151. In this respect, it is interesting to note the only literary illustration of the word *vulve* given in *Le petit Robert*: "'Singes d'hommes tombés de la vulve des mères,' Rimbaud." A literal translation would read absurdly; Rimbaud implies, however, that the unattractive aspect of "human nature" is of a piece with its maternal origin, reduced here to a crude physical reference. Saint Augustine's well-known phrase expresses much the same thing: *Inter urinam et fasces nascimur*—we are born between piss and shit.

19. Schneider, "En deça du visage," 151. Note, however, that in Schneider's description the abdomen (*ventre*) on which the face of Baubô is inscribed could also mean "belly" or "womb." Thus Levinas's gesture relating maternity (gestation) and eating could also be read as repeating what

Schneider sees as the denegation symbolized in the conflation of mouth and belly in the figure of Baubô.

20. Bernard Forthomme, *Une philosophie de la transcendance:La métaphysique d'Emmanuel Levinas* (Paris: Vrin), 1979.

21. Ibid., 332. Adriaan Peperzak, in *To the Other* (West Lafayette: Purdue University Press, 1993), 195, makes much the same point: "[O]ne might maintain that Levinas's description of love, the beloved and the lover are typically masculine. This would certainly not offend an author who does not swear by the neutrality of 'formal logic.'"

22. Forthomme, *Une philosophie*, 382–83.

23. Ibid., 333.

24. Llewelyn, *The Middle Voice of Ecological Conscience* (Hampshire: Macmillan, 1991), 219.

25. Llewelyn, *Emmanuel Levinas: The Genealogy of Ethics* (London: Routledge, 1995), 208. Llewelyn echoes Levinas here: "[I]l faut trouver à l'homme une autre parenté que celle qui attache à l'être" (AE, 272); "One has to find another kinship relation that that which ties man to being" (OB, 177).

26. Llewelyn, *Emmanuel Levinas*, 208–9.

27. Ibid., 190.

28. Ibid., 1.

29. Ibid., 94. See also Llewelyn, *Middle Voice*, 219: "[T]he idea of maternity, if not the word, was already in the foreground in the second section of *Totality and Infinity* entitled 'Interiority and Economy' which treats of the vulnerability and welcome into the *oikos*." Looking even further back, Llewelyn also suggests that the feminine and the maternal are encountered even before the sections on dwelling where the feminine is mentioned explicitly: "[D]are one ask whether the approach to her is being made already when three times within little more than three pages Levinas refers to the elemental world of earth, sea and sky from which I draw nourishment as the world in which I am *au sein*: in the midst, in the milieu, at the heart, but also maybe at the breast? What nourishment could be more elemental than milk?" Llewelyn, *Emmanuel Levinas*, 93.

30. Llewelyn, *Middle Voice*, 220.

31. Jacques Derrida and Christine V. McDonald, "Choreographies," *Diacritics* 12 (Summer 1982): 76.

32. Llewelyn, *Emmanuel Levinas*, 145.

33. Ibid., 145, echoing the title of Levinas's *Humanisme de l'autre homme* (Paris: Fata Morgana, 1972).

34. Chalier, "Ethics and the Feminine," 128.

35. These lines are repeated almost word for word at TeI, 310; TI, 277.

36. TeI, 309–10; TI, 276/7. TeI, 343; TI, 306.

37. See, for example, TeI, 312; TI, 279: "If biology furnishes us the prototype of all these relations, this proves, to be sure, that biology does not represent a purely contingent order of being, unrelated to its essential production. But these relations free themselves from their biological limitation."

38. Luce Irigaray, "Questions to Emmanuel Levinas," trans. M. Whitford, in Bernasconi and Critchley, *Re-reading Levinas*.

39. Llewelyn, *Emmanuel Levinas*, 208.

40. It is in this way that Llewelyn's *Middle Voice* and *Emmanuel Levinas* can be seen as parts of the same philosophical project.

41. It seems to me that the discussion toward the end of Chalier's *Figures du féminin* would support this view.

42. Plato, *Symposium*, trans. Walter Hamilton (London: Penguin, 1951).

43. Arlene W. Saxonhouse, "Eros and the Female in Greek Political Thought: An Interpretation of Plato's *Symposium*," *Political Theory* 12, no. 1 (February 1984): esp. 21–22.

44. Wendy Brown, "'Supposing Truth Were a Woman': Plato's Subversion of Masculine Discourse," *Political Theory* 16, no. 4 (November 1988): 594.

45. Ibid., 608.

46. See, for example, Daniel E. Anderson, *The Masks of Dionysus: A Commentary on Plato's "Symposium"* (Albany: State University of New York Press, 1993), 51, esp. 163 n. 2.

47. Andrea Nye, "The Hidden Host: Irigaray and Diotima at Plato's Symposium," in *Revaluing French Feminism*, ed. Nancy Fraser and Sandra Lee Bartky (Bloomington: Indiana University Press, 1992), 89.

48. Irigaray, "L'amour sorcier, lecture de Platon (*Le Banquet*, 'Discours de Diotime')," in *Éthique de la différence sexuelle* (Paris: Minuit, 1984), 27; "Sorceror Love: A Reading of Plato's Symposium, Diotima's Speech," trans. Eleanor H, Kuykendall, in *Revaluing French Feminism*, ed. Nancy Fraser and Sandra Lee Bartky (Bloomington: Indiana University Press, 1992), 64.

49. See, for example, Adriana Cavarero, "The Need For a Sexed Thought," in *Italian Feminist Thought: A Reader*, ed. P. Bono and S. Kemp (Oxford: Blackwell, 1991), 181–85; Serena Anderlini-D'Onofrio, "I Don't Know What You Mean by 'Italian Feminist Thought': Is Anything Like That Possible?" in *Feminine Feminists: Cultural Practices in Italy*, ed. Giovanna Miceli Jeffries (Minneapolis: University of Minnesota Press, 1994).

50. Cavarero, *In Spite of Plato*, trans. Serena Anderlini-D'Onofrio and Aine O'Healy (Cambridge: Polity, 1995), 93.

51. Ibid., 94.

52. Ibid., 94; see also 92.

53. A. W. Price, *Love and Friendship in Plato and Aristotle* (Oxford: Clarendon Press, 1988), 15–16.

54. Plato, *Symposium*, trans. W. R. M. Lamb, in *Plato*, vol. 2 (London: Loeb Classical Library, 1987); Plato, *Symposium*, trans. Walter Hamilton (London: Penguin, 1951).

55. "Yes, you are suffering the pangs of labour, Theaetetus, because you are not empty, but pregnant" (148E), says Socrates, who then casts himself as the midwife who is "sterile in point of wisdom . . . ; the god compels me to act as midwife, but has never allowed me to bring forth." (150C/D). Plato, *Theaetetus*, trans. H. N. Fowler, in *Plato*, vol. 7 (London: Loeb Classical Library, 1987).

56. As it certainly is in the Bible, for example, and in the *Collins English Dictionary*, which defines *beget* first and foremost as "to father."

57. Cavarero, *In Spite of Plato*, 93.

58. See Ibid., 98.

59. David M. Halperin, "Why Is Diotima a Woman?" in *One Hundred Years of Homosexuality, and Other Essays on Greek Love* (New York: Routledge, 1990), 144.

60. Cavarero, *In Spite of Plato*, 92.

61. Simon Critchley, *The Ethics of Deconstruction* (Oxford: Blackwell, 1992), 223.

62. Ibid., 226; see also 230.

63. See n. 8.

64. See, for example, AE, 260–61; OB, 167–68.

65. Critchley, *The Ethics of Deconstruction*, 229.

66. On "the wisdom of love," see Chalier, *L'Utopie de l'humain* (Paris: Albin Michel, 1993), 119ff.

67. Jacques Derrida, "Violence et métaphysique," in *L'écriture et la différence* (Paris: Éditions de Seuil, 1967), 118; "Violence and Metaphysics," in *Writing and Difference*, trans. Alan Bass (London: Routledge, 1990), 79–80.

68. Critchley *The Ethics of Deconstruction*, 227, 232.

69. See, for example, AE, 138, 154, 246, 247, 258; OB, 87, 97, 158, 159, 166.

70. See, for example, 'The Trace of the Other," 356 (French, 199).

71. Lingis translates as "the immediacy on the surface of the skin characterised as sensibility, its vulnerability" (OB, 64), which does not capture the implied sensitivity, even hypersensitivity, of the French, but probably no English translation could.

72. Chalier, *Figures du féminin*, esp. 109ff., the chapter titled "La revendication du propre."

9

Levinas and Kant
Maternal Morality and Illegitimate Offspring

Alison Ainley

There are many examples of the power of a mother's imagination in the
literature.... For not only do they give birth to deformed infants but also to
fruits they have wanted to eat, such as apples, pears, grapes and other similar
things. If the mother imagines and strongly desires to eat pears for example, the
unborn, if the foetus is alive, imagines them and desires them just as ardently;
the flow of spirits excited by the image of the desired fruit, expanding rapidly
in a tiny body, is capable of changing shape because of its softness. These
unfortunate infants thus become like the things they desire too ardently.
—Malebranche

[H]uman reason in its weariness ... in a dream of sweet illusions substitutes for
morality a bastard patched up from limbs of very different parentage, which
looks like anything one wishes to see in it, but not like virtue to anyone who
has ever beheld her in her true form.   —Kant

In maternity what signifies is a responsibility for others, to the point of
substitution for the others.   —Levinas

I

In philosophical writing, the imagery of the maternal often appears as
part of an appeal to the legitimacy of the true order, nature reproducing
itself according to a model of similarity, and offering a guarantee of like
following like. The true reflection of the parent in the child is linked to
the possibility of reason's reduplication as uniformity and the consistency
of resemblance. In addition, the symbolism of the maternal as unstinting
care for another is often taken as a paradigm of moral responsibility and
used to point out how a self preoccupied with concern for others might
form a model of moral insight.

In what follows, I will consider the significance of the powerful cap-
abilities assigned to women in the philosophical writings of Kant and

Levinas, insofar as women as mothers appear in some guise as moral exemplars or ideals of the good, but I will also look at the way ideas of creation and reproduction constitute a subversive force in the attempted legitimation of the moral good. I will suggest that the representation of mothers in Kant's and Levinas's texts reveals something about the process of legitimation and creation in each philosopher's writing, as well as something of the relation between the two. This means looking not just at the images of women as such, but also at the way that women are imagined, as mothers and others, into these texts.

The constitution of philosophical images is of particular interest from a feminist perspective when it affects the way that the body is "imagined" into theoretical disciplines and reproduced in specific ways, which also has consequences for the way that moral systems are constructed and subsequently impinge upon the subjects to whom they are addressed.[1] In the context of philosophy, the portrayal of the maternal as standing for the original condition of representation (as legitimate creation or reproduction) and hence as moral ideal or perfection, has repercussions not only for women but also for the "shape" of the discipline of philosophy. The desire for order can often be linked implicitly to a fear of potential chaos, the threat of unlicensed creation and the destabilization of limit and legitimacy. In this respect, the images of women that appear in these texts are the "visible" manifestations of other less evident processes that concern attempts to control or delimit the perceived threat to order. In reading Kant and Levinas in this way, I want to argue that insofar as there are certain Kantian strains to Levinas's thinking, feminist readers of Levinas should be wary of the way in which the maternal appears as the quintessential mark of ethical exemplarity in his texts. I will begin by tracing the maternal as it appears in Kant, in order to show how the maternal works as a principle of legitimation, before exploring the role of the maternal other as Nature and as original condition for representation. I will then go on to link this maternal other with Levinas's discussion of the maternal.

II

In the *Prolegomena*, Kant writes:

> Hume started from a single but important concept in metaphysics, namely that of the connection of cause and effect.... He

challenged reason, which pretends to have generated this concept in her own womb, to answer by what right she thinks anything could be so constituted that if the thing be posited, something else must necessarily be posited (for this is the meaning of
the concept of a cause). He demonstrated irrefutably that it was
perfectly impossible for reason to think *a priori* and by means of
concepts such a combination, for it implies necessity.... From
this he inferred that reason was altogether deluded with reference
to this concept, which she erroneously considered as her own
child, whereas in reality it was nothing but a bastard of imagination impregnated by experience, which subsumed certain representations under the law of association and mistook a subjective
necessity (custom) for an objective necessity arising from insight.
(1988, 158)

In this passage, Reason, as maternal and generative parent, mistakes cause
and effect as necessary (in other words, a legitimate child of hers). However, it may turn out to be in fact not only illegitimate but not even her
own child; born instead of imagination and the experience of custom. If
this is the case, Kant suggests, then Hume was right to question the
objectivity of this notion, and in response he (Kant) will be driven to
find a way to reconstitute its necessity and to reconfigure its legitimacy.
It is interesting that Kant connects the problem of establishing the objective necessity of causation (one thing following another as a matter of
natural course, or issuing "naturally" from it) with the question of establishing a "true" birth, or a legitimate creation. Is this child a natural issue,
or a freak? If Reason *mistakes herself* for the mother (imagines she is the
mother?), whereas it is Imagination who is the true mother of this child,
then the question of legitimacy is not merely contingent upon the birth
of a child under certain authorized conditions, but also on the *proper*
recognition of the child as the mother's own and not a mistaken product
of a contingent (imaginative) encounter with experience.

  If causation needs to be reconfirmed as objective, then Kant's appeal
to the figuratively "natural" imagery of conception, birth, and the child's
legitimacy is not accidental—the subject's need to reconfirm its role as
creative legislator in matters of the material world is echoed in the need
for a mother to recognize her own child properly, when it appears before
her. What is important for Kant is the role of *active recognition*, which
is what makes it possible to establish a gap between mother and child
in which the subject might display its capacity for independence, thus

consciously reconfirming the "natural order" of generative production as legitimate and legitimated. This requirement of active and autonomous selfhood to achieve the necessary separation and distance, is also found in the context of Kant's moral theory.

For Kant, respect (*Achtung*) is expressed as "the moral feeling," produced by reason and directed towards the moral law. In the *Groundwork*, respect for "persons as ends," applying to "persons only, never to things," derives ultimately from the proper attitude of reverence for the law, which entails a rational recognition of one's duty and an autonomous, conscious subjectivity. Although Levinas comments in an interview that he "likes the second formulation of the categorical imperative ... in this formulation ... we are already in the presence of the other" (cited in Critchley 1992, 58), in fact, Kant implies that respect involves *superseding* immediate particularities such as age, race, or class. The common "rational ground" of an objective principle (1948, 91) is what will allow us to raise rational beings to the status of equals, so that respect for the moral law is a higher or more mature form of respect. Only this form of autonomy will permit us to establish the kind of conscious recognition necessary for respect, and the mere experience of the presence of another is not enough to legitimate it.

In *The Metaphysic of Morals*, Kant defines moral respect as "limiting our self-esteem by the dignity of humanity in another person" (1991, 244). This active form of respect entails self-*limitation* and ensures that one human being can never become the means for another. It also suggests distance between humans. The principle of respect demands that humans "keep themselves at a distance from one another", and this is important for Kant, because it is contrasted in this passage and elsewhere with the danger of being *consumed*. If the moral force of distance fails, "then nothingness (immorality), with gaping throat, would drink up the whole kingdom of (moral) beings like a drop of water" (1991, 244). Consuming another is treating another merely as means. However, the contract of marriage establishes an exceptional case to Kant's principle of treating others as ends. Partners in marriage are permitted to mutually exploit each other in "merely animal" intercourse, to make reciprocal use of the sex organs of another (1991, 96–97) for the purpose of procreation. But, Kant warns, "[a]part from this condition, carnal enjoyment is *cannibalistic* in principle even if not always in its effect. Whether something is consumed by *mouth and teeth*, or whether a woman is consumed by pregnancy and the perhaps fatal delivery resulting from it, or the man by exhaustion of his sexual capacity . . . the use by each of the sexual organs of the other, is actually a *consumable* thing" (1991, 166; Kant's emphasis).

Kant has warned of the dangers inherent in the failure to set proper limits, and in a section in "The Doctrine of Virtue" titled "On Defiling Oneself with Lust," he repeats this warning when he argues that a person is also subject to a particular and limiting law of duty with regard to use of his own sexual attributes—which means it is proper to restrain oneself within proper limits. "Lust is *unnatural* if a man is aroused to it not by a real object but by his imagining it, so that he himself creates one contra-purposively; for in this way imagination brings forth a desire contrary to nature's end" (1991, 221). Self-abandonment to lust is more loathsome than suicide, and humans must learn and practice "proper" self-restraint.

However, Kant argues that in fact women *already* possess "natural modesty": by virtue of their sex. As their nature is fitted for beauty, their whole being should be directed toward the cultivation and maintenance of the beautiful. Rather than seeking the active pursuits of masculine intellectual endeavor, they should ensure that any tendency to wish to dominate is only manifest as *charm*. Women's nature is to please, but to do this successfully, they must withdraw, and disguise or cover over any active or dominant tendencies. This capacity is particular to their em-bodied sex: in other words, they can "naturally" distance themselves (1960, 84–85). If distancing is the condition for respect, then women do it without thinking. Kant implies that women are actually capable of the self-regulation that it is men's task to develop and perfect as part of the quest for moral principles, but whereas men must wrench themselves from the realm of Nature in order to grasp the point that respect is dis-tance from others and from Nature as other, women are already in the realm of the naturally other, already distanced from (masculine) subjects. From this position, women can teach men by example and by reproach that it is proper to hold oneself within proper limits (propriety) and not to demean oneself. Self-limitation is withholding oneself, "getting a hold of oneself," or "ruling over oneself" (1991, 208). Thus it appears to be women's chaste passivity that allows respect for them to take place, while men's desire learns the higher duty of restraint. But this also means that women are not in the position of being able to imaginatively or cogni-tively reconfigure a relation to Nature for themselves if they are merely passive and charming. It is only the autonomous masculine subject who can properly practice the self-limitation as self-determination Kant seeks for his actively free self and the intellectual effort that accompanies this requirement. For Kant, women who cultivate this kind of effort are "unsexed" or unnatural.

Elsewhere in Kant's writing, nature and otherness are often linked explicitly and implicitly with symbolic representations of the feminine and maternal, but not always as simply passive. Women are not necessarily always symbolic of "lack, deformity or deficiency" (Gatens 1996, vii), but as nature, appear as "idealised material form, at once intimate and indeterminate, brimming with purposive life yet plastic enough to put up no resistance to the subject's own ends" (Eagleton 1990, 91). Kant's ambivalence about the boundless creativity of nature and the subject's capacity for self-determination and legislation against the "formless form" of nature, suggests he identifies problems about how to draw the limit between subject and nature and how to represent such a limit.

In a section in *Speculum of the Other Woman* titled "Paradox A Priori," Luce Irigaray examines Kant's attempts to orientate a self that could rest on unshakeable laws of self-legislation, in the search for the objective conditions of subjective experience. She quotes from section 287 in the *Prolegomena*, in which Kant reflects on the impossibility of substituting the right-hand glove for the left-hand glove, despite what the image in the mirror may suggest in disordering our sense of which is the original and which the representation or reflection. The right and left hand may *appear* to be reversed in the mirror, but something allows me to separate my mistaken sensation from the understanding's legislation that will show that no such substitution is possible. That this possibility might have been drawn from nature or the sensible world is left behind or forgotten in the quest for mastery and the stable objectivity of the sovereign subject—what was cooperative creation gives way to structured order, and diversity is made to behave. Nature, foreclosed in favor of the ordering of perceptions, can now be rediscovered as relational gap. The otherwise unruly and uncontrollable otherness can now be regulated. "A transcendental property/propriety regulates a horror of the inchoate and unpossessable, as well as a disgust for the misshapen refuse that will be excreted in the form of matter" (Irigaray 1985a, 205).

As Irigaray suggests, Kant's dream of symmetry allows objects to be *properly conceived*. The disgust that brute matter might otherwise excite is made literally respectable, or worthy of respect, by its repudiation. Irigaray indicates the way in which this characterization of matter as other is linked symbolically to figures of the maternal: "Fear and awe of an all-powerful nature forbid man to touch his/the mother and reward his courage in resisting her attractions by granting him the right to judge himself independent" (1985a, 210).

Nature is both mother, as ground and principle of creation; and matter, as sensible. Kant effects this separation in order to create the gap necessary for respect, which appears moral precisely because it contrasts the imperative of duty with feelings, while secretly allowing them (or giving them legitimacy). The moral law excites both repulsion and compulsive fascination—when Kant describes it as "frightening," he appeals to its affective capacity, its power and majesty. This is analogous to the position of the symbolic figure of mother; the other as unknowable origin. The condition of morality, then, is the repudiation of the mother figure, a distancing more "original" than moral respect. Yet Mother Nature continues to invite attention and legislation—on condition that she is left at extreme distance—as Kant illustrates in his image of the statue of Mother Nature in the *Critique of Judgement*. No mortal can lift the veil to expose the figure of Isis in the temple, despite the invitation she extends for mortal knowledge. The inscription below the statue reads, "I am all that is, has been, and will be, and no mortal shall ever lift my veil" (1992, 179). Kant writes, "Perhaps there has never been a more sublime utterance, or a thought more sublimely expressed."

Kant also makes the unrepresentable otherness of nature explicit in his discussion of the sublime. The materiality of nature may reappear as a kind of failure of apprehendable form in the overwhelming excess of the encounter with the sublime. The excess of the sublime is that which the subject cannot successfully represent to itself, as it disorders the senses (1992, 108), but even here the disruption acts as an encouragement to further necessary suffering as part of building onward and upward, apparently confirming the harmonious coincidence of subject and nature. Still, the subject can never be sure that this harmonious unity is actually secured, since the *feeling* of harmony is not the *knowledge* of it, and optimism is tempered with fear.

Respect is due for the "true" maternal, Mother Nature, which inspires awe and fear as the unknown, and respect is occasioned if the moral reconfiguration can allow the unknown to be reappropriated in a co-ordinated way, ensuring that it reminds us of objective validity and the sanctity of the moral law (1992, 105). In the analogous case of aesthetic representation, even when disordered by the extreme experience of the sublime, the imagination can reconfigure the lesson of the lawfulness of the image and spring back to reestablish not only the harmoniousness of the subject's relation to nature, but also its place in nature, albeit negatively. As Irigaray writes:

> [N]o doubt *passion* still went beyond this formal framework; sometimes its enormous pent-up energies burst out and re-projected themselves upon everything in nature that remains unformed or deformed, as if, when faced with the non-specularisable, imagination suffered a violent urge that pushed it to the worst extremities. But, unable to understand it nonetheless, imagination falls back upon itself, marked, as it were, with the negative of its power. (1985a, 209)

The promised objectivity of morality can be created by a negative relation between an active apprehension of the unattainable and unrepresentable moral law and the feeling of respect it subsequently engenders. However, the lack or impossibility of representation does not seem to constitute a real difficulty, as Kant chooses to see the negative effect as a strength. Without representation as a distraction, "the idea of morality is left in possession of the field" (1992, 127). He suggests in fact that Judaism's prohibition of representation and graven images reinforces the negative impact on the imagination, expanding the spiritual powers and elevating the inscrutability of the idea of freedom, to permit the moral law to have its full effect (1992, 127–28). The failure of representation simply gives a stronger motivation to the process of reconfiguring morality or reordering the subject's faculties. The horror occasioned by the extremity of the experience of disordering is rediscovered as a desire to regulate and reestablish legitimate frameworks, legislating in the form of an imperative. The subject must be capable of relinquishing its self-identical relation with nature, driven out of the sheltering security of its "placid feminine enclosure" so that it can re-recognize itself as a moral subject. The child must separate from its mother. "The subject ... is plunged into loss and pain ... yet without this unwelcome violence we would never be stirred out of ourselves, never prodded into enterprise and achievement" (Eagleton 1990, 90).

But as Irigaray suggests, the desire to legitimate moral good and secure the objectivity of such good is a desire that might also harbor a secret pleasure in the dislocation or disordering of the senses, the experience that assails the self with the inscrutability of that which is other and arouses a pain of moral responsibility. In the case of the sublime and aesthetic judgment, Kant is explicit that the feeling of displeasure awakened by the inadequacy of the subject's response is accompanied by "a simultaneously awakened pleasure" (1992, 106). The affective impact of the feeling of moral good is also analyzed in relation to a strange pleasure: the pain of denial is a masochistic self-abasement before the other, nature, and the moral law. But what this also suggests is a necessary distancing or repudiation of such otherness, so that the trauma can be experienced more violently, to impress its ethical effects with sufficient impact.

So far, we have seen Kant appeal to the maternal as a principle of legitimation in his search for a framework of order, but he has also raised the specters of chaos and destablization by making the condition for respect an absolutely unknowable otherness. Nature as mother is both creative and bountiful, but it is the subject who must police his desires with regard to her otherness and ensure that the unregulated bounty does not break forth in a threatening way. However, the subject must be aware of the potential or actual failure of cognition and apprehension to appreciate its ethical vocation. In order to ensure that otherness remains sufficiently awe-inspiring, no representation is guaranteed legitimacy. The question I would now like to pursue is whether, when we turn to Levinas, we find a similar structure in his texts. I will suggest that the Kantian aspects of his quest for ethical responsibility lead him to deploy a notion of the maternal that also demands a derangement of the subject, making the otherness of the other an occasion for a heightened sense of moral obligation.

III

In *Totality and Infinity*, Levinas offers an account of relations with others that stresses both the proximity of beings who are not objects but other human beings, but also the asymmetrical inequality of that relation (1969, 215). There is no reciprocity, no self-consciousness realized through the other and no dialectic of equals. The asymmetry of the other calls to us as ethical demand before we have time to cognize it in familiar ways. The schemes of our habitual thinking have not prepared us for the way the experience of the face of the other disrupts us. It is the immediacy of that appeal, the summons that invokes the need for a response and for responsibility, that is unthematizable. The face-to-face is the ultimate structure that escapes us but that we cannot escape (1969, 81). In this sense, it disorders representation and cognition.

Levinas also insists that the face-to-face relation cannot be neutral. He consistently opens up the question of sexual difference, from his earliest works where he first formulates the connection between le féminin, ethics, and otherness (1989, 48–54) through his discussion of eros, voluptuosity, and fecundity in Totality and Infinity (1969, 256–58), to the section on maternity in Otherwise Than Being (1981, 99–129). He does not intend that this issue should be reduced to a merely thematic concern, a metaphor or a topic, but rather that, from his ethical point of view, it should act as an indispensable perspective that can open up the dimension of the essentially other. Rather than domesticating the feminine, the preservation of difference as other is a prelude to ethical relations that do not seek to reduce, capture, or flatten out the specificity of the other, but maintain a fundamental difference for the other. One of the reasons Levinas characterizes otherness in this way is to reproach Heidegger for what seems to have been forgotten or effaced: the question of sexuality in relation to ontology and thus ethics. Because Levinas identifies ontology with totality, or Being as such, sexuality (or sexual difference) is one way to disrupt the totalizing closure of metaphysics and open up neutrality to ethics.[2]

The equivocal realm of the feminine as other is characterized in terms of a relation of love (éros), an ambiguous and erotic encounter that establishes both vulnerability and the responsibility owed to an other. The caress, the mode of touch that brings two into close contact, does not suggest a prior structure into which the particular instance will fit, but a "fundamental disorder," an immediacy of discovery that engages with the material and carnal existence of an other without exhausting his or her meaning. Levinas's description of such disordering relations, where possession is suspended and the fixity of subject/object transformed, may appear as a possibility of freeing the constrictions of stereotypical sexual roles. As Irigaray puts it, it is "the fecundity of a love whose most elementary gesture, or deed, remains the caress" (1993, 186). Levinas suggests that ethics might arise in the material and carnal encounter, in the "ambiguity of love" (1969, 254). The limitations imposed on self create, as in Kant, a space in which the other is permitted to be unknown, and effect a distance that seems to allow ethics to take place. But unlike in Kant, Levinas's other imposes upon me directly, rather than being duly established as worthy of respect by my distance from him/her and my reverence for the moral law, and it is this directness that apparently makes it capable of ethical disruption.

After *Totality and Infinity*, Levinas acknowledges that his characterization of the other still places it within the grasp of the knowing subject, and that in order to confound representational thinking he must "go back"; that is, make the other even more excessive, more profoundly affecting, to make its impact on the self even more traumatic. This is the only way to secure the other's ethical demand: to make it *more* other. Levinas seeks this possibility for ethics in a past that will be "immemorial and unrecuperable," in order to create the possibility of a different kind of future. As Richard Cohen writes in his introduction to *Time and the Other*: "The radical future of Levinas' earlier works will require the radical past of his later works" (Levinas 1987b, 11). The elusive disappearance of this moment of origin is the very condition of the possibility of Levinasian ethics, and it is explicitly linked to or characterized as the maternal realm, the "birth" of otherness. The disclosure of this absence, the unspeakable or unrepresentable is more other than the light-and-shadow figure in *Totality and Infinity*, with its erotic equivocation of femininity. The maternal is otherness in a state of exposure, where the disorientation of time and self are manifest as discontinuity at its most extreme. To be so exposed is for Levinas the ultimate condition of ethics; the last scraps of selfhood and autonomy are divested before alterity. But the self is neither obliterated (which would leave no future for ethics), nor is it able to offer itself in generosity (which would mean the structure of a self was still retained). Levinas writes of "a tearing from oneself despite oneself," as the self becomes "a hostage to otherness" (1981, 74). This is what it would mean to "respond with responsibility; me, that is, here I am for the others, to lose one's place radically, or one's shelter in being" (1981, 185).

Levinas seeks an inversion of the *conatus essendi*: a fundamental unsettling of the being that strives to persist, which is so severe that he is driven to the language of suffering in its most violent forms in this section. But there is no "cause" for which this suffering is enlisted, its affectivity is meant to be prior to any reason that could be given. "The passivity of wounds, the haemorrhage of the for-the-other, is a tearing away of the mouthful of bread ... one's own mouthful of bread. It is an attack made immediately on the plenitude of the complacency of oneself (the complacency of complacency), on the identity in enjoyment"

(1981, 74). Passivity is "to have the other within one's skin" (1989, 104). The condition of existence that best encapsulates this ultimate state is maternity, which, for Levinas, is "the passivity of passivity."

> It is a writhing in the tight dimensions of pain, the unexpected dimensions of the hither side. It is being torn from oneself, being less than nothing, a rejection into the negative, behind nothing-ness: it is maternity, gestation of the other in the same. Is not the restlessness of someone persecuted but a modification of maternity, the groaning of the wounded entrails by those it will bear or has borne? In maternity what signifies is a responsibil-ity for others, to the point of substitution for the others. (1981, 75–76)

In his attempts to address the other's appeal, Levinas has recourse to a language of pain and suffering, which is meant to mark the quintessential experience of being for another. Maternity is the mark of such an experi-ence because it is a pain of the body, a corporeal undertaking that cannot be disregarded. "The body is not only an image or a figure here, it is the distinctive in-oneself of the contraction of ipseity and its break-up" (1981, 109), Levinas writes, and goes on to say: "The body is neither obstacle opposed to the soul, nor a tomb that imprisons it, but that by which the self is susceptibility itself. Incarnation is extreme passivity; to be exposed to sickness, suffering, death, is to be exposed to compassion, and, as a self, to the gift that costs.... It is the correlate of a persecution, a substitution for the other" (1981, 95).

The pain of maternity confirms the moral requirement of absolute responsibility on the part of the subject, a stark reminder of the need to abase oneself in the service of the other. The pain of suffering and pas-sivity silences the egoity of the subject; here neither reason nor imagina-tion will awaken the subject as productive or reproductive in legislating its autonomy. The maternal is the self "called out of itself" and hence out of the selfishness that both cognition and imaginative creation connote for Levinas. Maternity is an encounter with ethics for an other in the experience of enduring the pain—and there can be no denial or avoid-ance of the other, since it is *within* oneself. This is the moral good in its most embodied form and at its most affective, yet the experience Levinas outlines is one of torment and pain. As he writes in his 1970 essay, "No Identity":

Vulnerability is obsession by the other or an approaching of the other. It is being *for another*, behind the *other* of a stimulus. This approach is not reducible to the representation of the other nor to consciousness of proximity. To suffer from another is to have charge of him, to support him, to be in his place, to be consumed by him. Every love or hatred of a neighbour as a reflected attitude presupposes this prior vulnerability, this mercy, this "groaning of the entrails." (1987a, 146–47)

As Levinas's footnote to the last sentence reveals, this affective capacity is inseparable from maternity. "We are thinking of the Biblical term 'Rakhamin,' which is translated as mercy, but contains a reference to the word 'Rekhem,' uterus; it is a mercy that is like an emotion of the maternal entrails" (1987a, 147).[3]

Levinas does not separate the sensible world of the body from the transcendental claims of ethics, and maternity is the exemplary mode in which this is shown. But if this experience or mode of being is not merely a reflection or representation of a higher court of ethical appeal, then it remains to ask how Levinas can extract himself from the problems that Kant identifies in the nonrepresentability of the moral law. What can legitimate one form of representation over another when the condition for the moral good is its "inscrutability," its unknown otherness? What is the basis of Levinas's claim for the specific and privileged status of maternity?

IV

When it comes to the question of representation, it appears that the nonethical distractions of the aesthetic are a concern for Levinas as much as is the totalizing thought of philosophy. For him, art can appear to be the shadow of another kind of cognitive operation and therefore another kind of reductionism. It is this concern that leads him to declare in "Reality and Its Shadow" that art can be "a dimension of evasion," "essentially disengaged" (1989, 141). Despite his offering a sensuous indeterminacy in place of the quest for objective knowledge, for Levinas the work of art may distort or immobilize the irreducibility of the ethical demand. It also unleashes the potential anarchy of creation without legitimation. As Jean-François Lyotard points out in his essay "Levinas's Logic," Levinas's desire to secure the form of an imperative that allows him to express the possibility of justice, leads him to divide discourses into two sorts: "those placed under the rule of the just/unjust, such as the moral and political, and those of the writer and orator, which draw on an 'aesthetic' value" (Lyotard 1986, 124). Lyotard goes on to write: "Levinas evinces the greatest suspicion concerning the *discursive arts*, which he regularly characterises as techniques of seduction. We know that his wager is on the contrary to succeed in placing the deontic genre at the heart of philosophical discourse. This implies in principle that the latter consists in describing not the rules that determine the truth or falsity of statements but those that determine their justice or injustice" (124).

If representation substitutes distracting images, the ethics that Levinas seeks must find a way of negotiating representational imagery to stress an encounter with the other governed by responsibility. In fact, although Levinas might sound close to Plato in his suspicion of art, further attention to Levinas's diverse writings reveals that certain writers or poets do encapsulate the kind of ethical experience Levinas wants to avow. Those writers, whom Edith Wyschogrod designates "artists of alterity" (Wyschogrod 1995, 139) are ethical in delineating experience of transcendence in the language of immediacy, or else permitting the resonance of otherness to remain. For example, in "The Other in Proust," Levinas writes: "Proustian reflection ... is governed by a sort of refraction," whereby the work of art succeeds in signifying its inability to unify meaning into a whole, and where "success of knowledge would precisely abolish the proximity of the Other" (1989, 164). Hence "[t]he mystery in Proust is the mystery of the other." Equally, Levinas's approval of Blanchot suggests that he thinks Blanchot manages to effect an "exteriorising" of language that is nonintentional, and that this "undoing" of the subject opens up the possibility of ethics (Davies 1995, 95–104). Levinas suggests that it is the "failure" of art to fulfil the task of creating values that opens it up to ethics once again. As Gary Peters makes clear in a recent article, the rhythm of a discontinuous pulse such as that found in modern music, might present sensuous alterity of a kind analogous to Levinas's ethics (1997, 13).

What, then, are we to make of the language of the maternal in Levinas? If there is a possibility of deploying representation in such a way as to awaken ethical response, then what Levinas does is to demand that we read or experience this kind of image in *a different way*. The shock or derangement would have to be akin to the disorder that Kant suggests is the experience of the sublime. The sensuous world (maternal Nature), that cannot be grasped as a unified totality, shocks all conceptual frameworks of judgment. But whereas for Kant the subject is returned to its senses and to cognition, for Levinas, any ability to reconstruct this moment as any kind of recognition or representation, whether aesthetic or conceptual, must be denied. The only register in which it can feature is the ethical, or the just. But Levinas's imperative is established *within* philosophy, to demonstrate the great cost of philosophy's thinking. The images he deploys enact the pain of that cost, demanding an expenditure of the subject's resources, but also manage to suggest that his form of transgression is the *only way* to make this explicit, or that his are the only images that can do this. When he writes of maternity as being "obsessed by the other," it is in order to claim a different order of being and of language for this notion. "Sensible experience as an obsession by the other, or maternity, is already the corporeality which the philosophy of consciousness wants to establish on the basis of it. The corporeality of one's own body signifies, as sensibility itself, a knot or denouement of being" (1981, 77).

But despite Levinas's appeal to "sensibility itself," the level at which this counts as phenomenological description must cease to be recognizable as an experience, if it is to have its effect. To remain unknowable, the otherness of this experience appeals to something that the subject by definition could not recognize. If this appeal is to the essential otherness of sexual difference, it is unclear how women philosophers and readers of Levinas are to situate *themselves* in relation to this feminine or maternal otherness. Do women take up an opposing stance to it, making themselves other to otherness, or identify themselves with the feminine other? In either case, it is unclear that the presence of the feminine and the relation of women to ethics and otherness has been "thought through as such" (Irigaray 1993, 209). As Irigaray writes: "For him, the feminine does not stand for an other to be respected in her human freedom and human identity. The feminine other is left without her own specific face. On this point, his philosophy falls radically short of ethics" (1991, 113).

The revelatory status Levinas demands, which could elevate sensibility to ethical awareness, appears to go beyond the experiential, and toward absolute alterity. If this is the case, then Levinas's evocation of the feminine and the maternal has to face the charge that it is used in a merely instrumental way, used as a reminder of the materiality of lived

existence, but ultimately in service to a larger conception of ethical goodness: the path of metaphysical transcendence. Despite Levinas's insistence that this path is opened through experience and through ethical
relations with others, the images of the feminine and maternal still
seem to "furnish" the possibility of such relations. Irigaray suggests that
although Levinas "opens the feminine in philosophy," he still seems to
"write out" the existence of a point of view for women as such, so that
there is no place for women in what Levinas proposes—as she puts it:
"the caress, that 'fundamental disorder,' does not touch the other" (1991,
110). The divine, which is the incomplete, unfinished promise to come,
glimpsed through the other, is really a promise held out for the male
lover, the male philosopher, and represents another closure of the poten-
tials initially opened up by Levinas. As Irigaray points out, "[T]this ethics
no longer knows its faults" (1991, 112).

By making her objections in this way, Irigaray draws attention to the
political conditions that affect the question of representation. The question of legitimation asks what guarantees the primacy of any particular,
privileged form of representation. Kant does acknowledge the problem of
legitimation: the failure that haunts the limits of reason also obliges us to
act *as if*, and as part of this spontaneous self-legislation a more uncertain
autonomy is generated. Levinas does not allow this kind of freely willed
self-legislation, because his notion of obligation does not emerge out of
reason and duty through the moral law, but through the immediate proximity of the other. For Levinas the legitimacy of representation is not
really a matter of dispute, if the appeal of the other short-circuits the
logic of representational thinking.

V

Both Kant and Levinas wish to inquire whether it is possible for ethical
relations with others to have some guarantee of appeal or absolute legitimacy, so that the good might be made manifest in such a way that ethics
is possible, but neither of them entirely trust philosophical language to
allow such an inquiry to take place. Yet whether this suspicion takes the
form of an ethical reproach to philosophy for its incapacity to answer to
need, suffering, persecution, or oppression, as Levinas suggests, or an inquiry into what might make philosophy *adequate* to the task of "a supreme

principle of morality," as Kant proposes (1948, 57), for both of them there is still a need to try and explicate structures of respect and responsibility *within* philosophy as a discipline and within philosophical language, despite the betrayal this language might ultimately effect. As Levinas says in an interview, "[T]he best thing about philosophy is that it fails" (Cohen 1986, 22)[4] and Kant that we can only fairly ask philosophy to approach its limits of incomprehensibility, as it "presses forward in its principles to the very limit of human reason" (1948, 123).

What makes Levinas's thinking initially appealing for feminist philosophers is the critique it provides of the structure of philosophical thinking. For Levinas, it seems that most or all philosophical thinking is determinate, if it takes others as objects and fixes them under a conceptual category. The identity of the other is thus determined relationally and placed or theorized accordingly. Levinas objects to this primarily because it appears to him to be reductive, making otherness equivalent to "the same," and recuperating alterity under the scope of representational thinking, in a way that, although it may try to make subsequent assertions of ethical legitimacy, is actually denying the possibility of anything other than its own modes of representation and relation. In this respect philosophy is apparently unable to allow for the "otherness" of others, if its thinking is by definition the elaboration of conceptual abstraction and universalizing laws. It is in this regard that Levinas shares some of the concerns of feminist thinking about the "shape" of Western philosophy. Irigaray reflects this mutual concern in her first essay on Levinas in *The Ethics of Sexual Difference*, and elsewhere in her work; for example, in her essay "The Power of Discourse," she writes: "[T]his domination of the philosophical logos stems in large part from its power to *reduce all others to the economy of the Same*. The teleologically constructive project it takes on is always also a project of diversion, deflection, reduction of the other in the Same" (1985b, 74).

But whereas Irigaray insists on making sexual difference the motivating feature of her enquiry, Levinas wants to place ethics, informed by a certain religious sensibility, in a position of priority, to negotiate the otherwise crushing effects of ontology and metaphysics by claiming there is another way to approach the question of the other. In order to do this, he must present an alternative mode of insight, a different kind of relation and in effect a wholly other form of ethical appeal that can somehow wrest itself free of the restrictive logic of metaphysical thinking that, he claims, has dominated philosophical history up to the present. For

Levinas, the only way to permit the other to exist in his or her ethical freedom is to displace the constrictions of conceptual thinking, to unsettle theoretical representational knowledge when this is presented as a totality of identities and relations, and to claim that the difference of others occupies a different realm of experience, corresponding to no previously adequate framework.

The imagery of the maternal highlights some of the Kantian strains in Levinas's thinking, as both thinkers seek to ground a form of imperative, and desire to make the other *other enough* in order to produce ethical effect, capable of demanding awe and responsibility. As maternal nature, moral law, or the sublime, for Kant this otherness is construed as essentially unknowable and yet equivalent to women's essential nature, making it difficult for women to take up the necessary stance of autonomous selfhood that pertains to true moral responsibility. For Levinas, evoking the sensible corporeal experience of maternity as ethical places him in an ambivalent position between, on the one hand, the pathos and affect of descriptive phenomenology, and on the other hand, the imperative of alterity as a revelation of an absolute. This too raises questions about the way in which feminist philosophers can read the figures of women in his texts.

However, philosophically, Kant and Levinas also seem to stand for very different approaches—not only to the troubled history of the Western tradition, but also to what might ground inquiries into morality and so legitimate them. Kant seems to be part of the philosophically optimistic trust in reason that Levinas wishes to oppose—the attempt to legitimate disinterested autonomy, holding others at a distance until duty is established, to make relations with others dependent on the proper clarification and application of the moral law. Conversely, Levinas seeks "unmodern" eschatological horizons and a particular form of phenomenological description of an experience of the other as means to redress what he sees as the indifference of reason. So it might appear that he offers an ethical alternative to the prolongation of crisis at the end of philosophy, and in some ways he does stand for what philosophy has been unable or unwilling to think: the Judaic religious tradition of thought, and the "strangeness" of the feminine other.

But for feminist philosophers, the problem cannot be expressed simply in terms of a preference either for Kantian autonomy and the ethics of self-respect, or Levinas's phenomenology of the eroticized other. The difference between them, if it is a difference, may indicate an *aporia* of the political between Athens and Jerusalem, both holy cities built on the foundations of antinomic or ahistorical absolutes, in which both foundations must fail or falter. Rather than seeking a replacement for the unconditional certainties of an absolute, perhaps feminist philosophers can reinterpret these texts to reflect on the constitution and construction of a tradition, and the images that regenerate and sustain it.

In both Kant and Levinas, the effacement or disturbance of self in favor of an experience unlike any other is also an attempt to reconcile or awaken the self to ethics—a negative jolt of the pain of failure that serves to recall the essential structure of ethical responsibility. The affective pain builds ethics on violent reaction, in which the perverse pleasure of separation is transformed into purity of absolute respect. The monstrous births of these texts indicate not only the deployment of the mother as moral ideal (who else would suffer in the same way as such mothers?), but also warn of the dangers of the overactive imagination that might destabilize the quest for moral legitimation. From a feminist point of view, questioning the imaginative reconfiguration of these images can regenerate or instigate the transgressive effects of women who refuse to remain the matter of the other.

Notes

1. See Gatens 1996 for an excellent discussion of the symbolic representation of bodies in philosophical terms.

2. For example, Levinas writes: "Building directs its building and cultivating ... on a maternal earth. Anonymous, neuter, it directs it, ethically indifferent, as heroic freedom, foreign to all guilt with regard to the other" (1987a, 53).

3. Levinas's connection between "an emotion of the maternal entrails" and "mercy" is inspired by a verse from Jer. 31:20. In the King James Bible this is misleadingly translated as follows: "'Is Ephraim my dear son? Is he a pleasant child? For since I spoke against him I do earnestly remember him still, therefore my bowels are troubled for him, I will surely have mercy upon him,' saith the LORD."

4. Robert Bernasconi, in his essay "Skepticism in the Face of Philosophy," in Re-reading Levinas, ed. Robert Bernasconi and Simon Critchley, 149–61 (Bloomington: Indiana University Press, 1991), points out that in Otherwise Than Being Levinas refers to skepticism as "the legitimate child of philosophy," but that the English translation renders this as "illegitimate" or "bastard" (1981, 7, 192, and 183). Bernasconi writes: "But skepticism is still the legitimate child of philosophy insofar as the question of skepticism is still a question about truth" (160).

References

Cohen, Richard, ed. 1986. *Face to Face with Levinas*. New York: State University of New York Press.

Critchley, Simon. 1992. *Ethics of Deconstruction*. Oxford: Blackwell.

Davies, Paul. 1995. "On Resorting to an Ethical Language." In *Ethics as First Philosophy: The Significance of Emmanuel Levinas for Philosophy, Literature, and Religion*, edited by A. Peperzak, 95–104. London: Routledge.

Eagleton, Terry. 1990. *The Ideology of the Aesthetic*. Oxford: Blackwell.

Gatens, Moira. 1996. *Imaginary Bodies: Ethics, Power, and Corporeality*. London: Routledge.

Hand, Sean. 1996. "Shadowing Ethics: Levinas's View of Art and Aesthetics." In *Facing the Other: The Ethics of Emmanuel Levinas*, edited by Sean Hand, 63–90. London: Curzon Press.

Herman, Barbara. 1993. "Thinking About Kant on Sex and Marriage." In *A Mind of One's Own: Feminist Essays on Reason and Objectivity*, edited by Louise M. Antony and Charlotte Witt, 49–68. Oxford: Westview Press.

Huet, Marie-Hélène. 1993. *Monstrous Imagination*. Cambridge: Harvard University Press.

Irigaray, Luce. 1985a. "Paradox A Priori." In *Speculum of the Other Woman*, translated by G. C. Gill, 203–13. Ithaca: Cornell University Press:

———. 1985b. *This Sex Which Is Not One*. Translated by C. Porter and C. Burke. Ithaca: Cornell University Press.

———. 1991. "Questions to Emmanuel Levinas: On the Divinity of Love." Translated by M. Whitford. In *Re-Reading Levinas*, edited by R. Bernasconi and S. Critchley, 109–18. Bloomington: Indiana University Press. (Reprinted in M. Whitford, ed., *The Irigaray Reader*, 178–89 [Oxford: Blackwell, 1991]).

———. 1993. "The Fecundity of the Caress: A Reading of Levinas, *Totality and Infinity*, "Phenomenology of Eros."" Translated by C. Burke and G. C. Gill. In *The Ethics of Sexual Difference*, 185–217. London: Athlone. (Earlier trans. in R. Cohen, ed., *Face to Face with Levinas*, 231–56. [New York: State University of New York Press, 1986]).

Kant, Immanuel. 1948. *The Moral Law*. Edited by H. J. Paton. London: Hutchinson.

———. 1960. *Observations on the Beautiful and the Sublime*. Berkeley and Los Angeles: University of California Press.

———. 1979. *Lectures on Ethics*. Translated by L. Infield. London: Methuen.

———. 1988. "Prolegomena to Any Future Metaphysics." In *Selections*, edited by Lewis White Beck, 149–234. London: Macmillan..

———. 1991. *The Metaphysic of Morals*. Translated by M. Gregor. Cambridge: Cambridge University Press.

———. 1992. *Critique of Judgement*. Translated by J. Meredith. Oxford: Oxford University Press.

———. 1993. *Critique of Pure Reason*. Translated by V. Politis. London: Everyman.

Kofman, Sarah. 1982. *Le respect des femmes*. Paris: Galillee.

Levinas, Emmanuel. 1969. *Totality and Infinity: An Essay on Exteriority*. Translated by A. Lingis. Pittsburgh: Duquesne University Press.

———. 1981. *Otherwise Than Being or Beyond Essence*. The Hague: Martinus Nijhoff.

———. 1987a. *Collected Philosophical Papers*. Dordrecht: Martinus Nijhoff.

———. 1987b. *Time and the Other*. Pittsburgh: Duquesne University Press.

———. 1989. *The Levinas Reader*. Edited by Sean Hand. Oxford: Basil Blackwell.

Lyotard, Jean-François. 1986. "Levinas's Logic." In *Face to Face with Levinas*, edited by Richard A. Cohen, 117–58. Albany: State University of New York Press.

Mendus, Susan. "Kant: An Honest but Bourgeois Citizen?" In *Women in Western Political Philosophy*, edited by Susan Mendus and Ellen Kennedy, 21–43. Brighton: Harvester Wheatsheaf.

Peters, Gary. 1997. "The Rhythm of Alterity: Levinas and Aesthetics." *Radical Philosophy* 82 (March/April): 9–16.

Wyschogrod, Edith. 1995. "The Art in Ethics: Aesthetics, Objectivity, and Alterity in the Philosophy of Emmanuel Levinas." In *Ethics as First Philosophy: The Significance of Emmanuel Levinas for Philosophy, Literature, and Religion*, edited by Adriaan Peperzak, 137–50. London: Routledge.

10

Paternal Election and the Absent Father

Kelly Oliver

The most well known and comprehensive intellectual discourse on fatherhood is Freud's theory of the Oedipal complex, with its patricidal and
incestuous fantasies. As Freud describes it, the father-son relationship,
and ultimately the sons' murder of their father, is the foundation of civil
society. In *Totem and Taboo* Freud describes the sons eating the corpse
of their father in order to incorporate his authority. It is the act of mur-
dering the father that gives the sons the right and authority to rule;
and it is their guilt that binds them together. On Freud's account the
father-son relationship requires murder, cannibalism, and the ritual and
symbolic repetition of these bloody acts motivated by an irrepressible
guilt for the original murder. The father represents threats and authority
and the son must kill him in order to take his place and his authority.

Paternity is essentially threats and murder, and the time of paternity is a time of repetition of the same violence over and over again in various symbolic forms.

The twentieth-century neo-Freudian Jacques Lacan describes paternity as law. Following Freud, for Lacan, paternity is authority, law, and threats. In addition, because (unlike maternity) paternity is always in question—who is the father?—Lacan maintains that paternity is the effect of a signifier. Paternity is nothing more than the "Name-of-the Father," since it is through the name that fatherhood is designated (Lacan 1977, 199). The paternal function is to propel the infant into the world of names, the world of symbols, through his prohibition or "no" to the infant's symbiotic relationship with its mother. The father demands that the infant give up its original maternal corporeal pleasures and substitute always inadequate paternal symbols. Like the father himself, these symbols are always abstract, always miss their mark, and therefore never satisfy desires born in this space between body and symbol, between need and demand, between maternal and paternal.

In the traditional association between paternity and authority, the association that founds patriarchy, the authority of law demands that the father's body is always absent. The father represents culture, and culture necessarily leaves the body and nature behind. The paternal function that propels the infant into culture requires that the father have no body. Culture is the result of an evolution that leaves the body behind, an evolution that begins in the murderous struggle between father and son for the sake of authority and law. In the traditional story, the father is necessarily an absent father. His authority and his law require his absence.

Emmanuel Levinas gives us an alternative notion of paternity. He rejects the traditional psychoanalytic description of paternity as law and threats. Instead, he holds out the father-son relationship as the model of love. The time of paternity is not the continuous repetition of the same guilt and murder but rather an open time, an infinite time. For Levinas, paternity is a promise of infinity and love. Yet, even as he moves away from the traditional patriarchal notion of paternity, and even as he imagines a corporeal philosophy based on proximity, he too describes a paternity devoid of paternal bodies, which leaves us with an absent father. Ultimately, even his notion of a paternity that gives birth to the other and opens onto infinity is founded in the masculine identity passed down from father to son. In this chapter, I will analyze the promise and the limitations of Levinas's notion of paternity.

Paternity as Promise

Levinas proposes a notion of paternity that cannot be reduced to law or threats but must be a promise. He proposes an ontology of paternity that takes us beyond the Freudian psychoanalysis of paternity, which he claims reduces sexuality and paternity to pleasure and egology. For Levinas, the promise of paternity is not a promise of authority or repetition, but a promise of nonrecognition, of strangeness, of an open future, of what he calls infinity. The promise of paternity is not the Freudian promise that the son will inherit his power. It is not a promise from the past, a promise that returns to itself. Rather, the promise of paternity, as Levinas describes it, is a promise of an open future, the promise that the son is to his father.

Although on Levinas's analysis there is an analogy between death and paternity, fatherhood requires neither Oedipal murder nor Christian sacrifice. Paternity is a special case of alterity that can inform all other relations. For Levinas, it is the only relation in which the self becomes other and survives. In *Time and the Other*, Levinas moves from an analysis of death, through an analysis of fecundity to his analysis of paternity. He maintains that what all of these relations with alterity have in common is that they cannot be thought of in terms of power, especially in terms of the power of an ego. "Sexuality, paternity, and death introduce a duality into existence, a duality that concerns the very existing of each subject. Existing itself becomes double" (Levinas 1982, 92). This doubling of existing brings the subject to time by making it other to itself. Only the relation with the other engenders time; and only where there is infinity is there time.

The relation between time and infinity is necessary not only in the simple sense that we cannot think of not-A without thinking of A or visa versa. Rather, it is the encounter with infinity through the face-to-face relationship that makes time possible. This encounter opens the subject onto itself and separates the subject from the world in a way that makes the counting necessary to time possible. The face-to-face relationship enables subjectivity, and there is no linear time without the subject. The tension between the relationship between time and infinity described in *Time and the Other* (1947) and the relationship between time and infinity described in *Totality and Infinity* (1961) might be explained in terms of the different status of the erotic relationship accorded in these two works. As Tina Chanter points out, in the earlier work, *Time and the*

Other, Levinas describes the erotic relationship as the primary face-to-face—that is, ethical—relationship (Chanter 1994, 196–207). In *Totality and Infinity*, the erotic relationship is beyond the face-to-face, beyond ethics and language. In *Time and the Other*, Levinas emphasizes how time engenders infinity through the erotic relationship, fecundity, and paternity.

In *Totality and Infinity*, the dialectic between time and infinity is more complex than it was in *Time and the Other*. The separation from the world required to experience linear time, the time of subjectivity, is initiated in the face-to-face relationship; this position becomes even more explicit in *Otherwise than Being*, where the subject is described almost as a mere by-product of the relationship with the Other. Yet when the subject experiences his separation from the world as his own enjoyment, he forgets about the relationship with the Other that made it possible. The subject of enjoyment is not the ethical subject, even though the ethical relationship with the Other made the structure of his enjoyment possible. The erotic relationship with the feminine is beyond the ethical relationship; it is paternity that engenders infinity and brings the erotic relationship back within the realm of the ethical. As Chanter points out, within *Time and the Other*, the feminine is an Other who can engage the masculine subject in the ethical relationship, whereas in *Totality and Infinity* she is not an Other capable of an ethical relationship. Paternity rescues the masculine subject from the nonethical, nonsocial, nonlinguistic abyss of the feminine.[1]

For Levinas, paternity begins with eros and fecundity. Yet eros and fecundity are ontologically anchored in paternity. Eros is possible because of sexual difference, which is neither a contradiction between two nor a complementary between two (Levinas 1982, 85). Eros is an event of alterity, a relationship with what is absent in the very moment at which everything is there. Even in an experience that seems to completely fill the universe with itself, the caress seeks something other. The caress is not directed toward another's body; rather the caress is directed toward a space that transcends through the body and a time that Levinas describes as a future never future enough (Levinas 1969, 254). "The seeking of the caress constitutes its essence by the fact that the caress does not know what it seeks ... something other, always other, and always still to come [*à venir*]. The caress is the anticipation of this pure future [*avenir*] without content. It is made up of this increase of hunger, of ever richer promises, opening new perspectives onto the ungraspable" (Levinas 1982, 89). In the erotic relationship, the caress anticipates the always about to come of the Other, of the future, of a future never future enough. In the erotic relationship the caress is directed toward the future, the forever and always of promises of love, a future that is never future enough to fulfill such promises.

The relationship with the Other is such a promise, a promise that cannot be fulfilled, a paradoxical promise whose fulfillment would destroy the promise. And this promise is time. For Levinas, time is not constituted as a series of nows; it is not constituted in the present or by an ego. Rather, time is the absent promise in the relation with the Other; it is the not-yet, the always still to come. It is the time of love, the infinite engendered through finite beings coming together. "Love seeks what does not have the structure of an existent, the infinitely future, what is to be engendered" (Levinas 1969, 266). Love seeks what is beyond any possible union between two. For Levinas, love seeks the "trans-substatiation" that engenders the child (1969, 266). Engendering the child is an inherent element in the structure of the erotic relationship; the erotic relationship is defined as fecundity. The caress and voluptuosity are analyzed within this context of fecundity. Paternity opens the masculine subject onto infinite time and returns him to the ethical relationship.

For Levinas, in the masculine erotic relationship, the Other beyond the subject's control is the feminine other; fecundity necessitates a relationship with a feminine Other. This feminine Other is a prerequisite for moving outside of oneself: "But the encounter with the Other as feminine is required in order that the future of the child come to pass from beyond the possible, beyond projects. This relationship resembles that which was described for the idea of infinity: I cannot account for it by myself, as I do account for the luminous world by myself" (1969, 267). The transsubstantiation of the father by the son is only possible by virtue of the feminine Other. Man needs woman to beget a son. More than this, it would seem, the infinite time opened up between father and son through paternity is possible by virtue of the movement through the cyclical, nonlinear time of the feminine. Paternity moves the (male) subject outside of time through the mediation of another time, the cyclical time of life. Paternity conquers "father time" by moving through the feminine.

Paternity opens the subject onto infinite time in various ways. The discontinuity of generations brings with it inexhaustible youth, each generation replacing the one before it. In addition to this chronology that stretches indefinitely through time, the ontology of paternity sets up the subject within infinite time. The space between the father and the son opens up infinite time. Not only the discontinuity of generations which promises continued youth, but also the transsubstantiation of the father in the son opens the subject to an Other. "[T]he father discovers himself not only in the gestures of his son, but in his substance and his unicity" (Levinas 1969, 267). In this way the father discovers himself in the son and yet discovers that his son is distinct, a stranger.

Through the transsubstantiation of the I, Levinas says that paternity accomplishes desire. It does not satisfy desire, which is impossible, but accomplishes it by engendering it and by engendering another desiring being, the son. Paternity engenders desire, which is the infinite time of the absolutely other. The time of the Other is infinite as compared to the finite time of the self. In the relationship with the child, the subject is opened onto infinity: "The relation with the child—that is, the relation with the other that is not a power, but fecundity—establishes a relationship with the absolute future, or infinite time" (1969, 268). Paternity, with its generation and generations, literally opens onto infinite time, a time beyond death. That future is the infinite desire that is present as a desire for desire itself infinitely extended into a future that is never future enough. What Levinas calls goodness is associated with the infinity of desire engendered by paternity. "In paternity desire maintained as insatiate desire, that is, as goodness, is accomplished" (1969, 272). Paternity is the link between desire and goodness, eros and ethics. Erotic desire is accomplished (since unlike need, it can never be satisfied) in engendering a son, a son who embodies desire. In this sense, desire engenders itself (1969, 269). For Levinas, the desire of the caress in the erotic relationship is ultimately resolved in paternity: "This unparalleled relation between two substances, where a beyond substances is exhibited, is resolved in paternity" (1969, 271). From the beyond—desire—two substances create another desiring substance, the son.

More than the continuation of the substance of the father in the son, as the word "transsubstantiation" might suggest, paternity is a form of transsubstantiation of subjectivity itself. Paternity transforms subjectivity from the subject as "I-can" who sees himself as the center of meaning and values—the constitutor of the world—to a subject beholden to, and responsible for, the other. This form of transsubstantiation takes us beyond substance. The subject or "I" is not a substance, but a response. The paternal subject is not Husserl's or Sartre's virile "I-will" or "I-can" but a response to the other who opens up a radically different time, a time beyond the "I-will" or "I-can." Levinas says that the relationship with the son through fecundity "articulates the time of the absolutely other, an alternation of the very substance of him who can—his trans-substatiation" (1969, 269).

The relationship of paternity is unique in that the I breaks free of itself without ceasing to be I (1969, 278). It is the only relationship in which the self becomes other and survives. The I breaks free of the ego, of what ties it to itself, so that it can reach out to another, even become another, become other to itself. This process of becoming other to itself opens up the possibility of beyond its own possibilities, an openness to an undetermined future. "Fecundity is part of the very drama of the I. The intersubjective reached across the notion of fecundity opens up a place where the I is divested of its tragic egoity, which turns back to itself, and yet is not purely and simply dissolved into the collective. Fecundity evinces a unity that is not opposed to multiplicity, but, in the precise sense of the term, engenders it" (1969, 273).

On Levinas's analysis, the father discovers himself in the gestures, the substance, the very uniqueness of his son. This discovery of himself in the son is not recognition; for Levinas, the father does not recognize himself in his son, but discovers himself, finds himself for the first time. Paternity engenders the father as much as it does the son. Fecundity gives birth not only to the son but also to the father. In relation to his son, who is both himself and not himself, the father discovers his own subjectivity. As he realizes that his son is distinct, a stranger, he discovers that he too is distinct, even a stranger to himself. Paternity challenges what Levinas calls the "virile" subject that always returns to itself, the subject of the "I-can" of traditional phenomenology.[2]

Fecundity engenders the subject as desiring and therefore as an infinite subject who transcends the limits of subjectivity. In fecundity, the I has a different structure from the intentional egotistical virile subject because it has a different relationship to time and it has a different relation to time because it is not the egotistical subject of need but the loving subject of desire. The virile or heroic subject who takes the world as his possession, for his enjoyments, to meet his needs, is a finite subject (cf. Levinas 1969, 306–7). For Levinas, fecundity, associated as it is with paternity, is distinct from virility. Fecundity is "a reversion" of the virile subject (1969, 270).

Whereas fecundity frees the self from its self-enchainment, virility merely returns the self to itself over again. Virility is the experience of the power of the subject, whereas fecundity is the experience of the limit of the mastery of the subject. The virile subject lives in a world of things that it masters through the initiatives of its own power. Out of the anonymity of what Levinas calls the "there is," or raw being, the virile subject designates existents, beings. In this world, however, the subject continually returns to itself and makes even of itself an existent, a thing, which deteriorates and dies. In the world of the virile subject, "[s]elf-possession becomes encumberment with oneself. The subject is imposed upon itself, drags itself along like a possession.... Eros delivers from this encumberment, arrests the return of the I to itself" (Levinas 1969, 270–71). Eros takes the subject outside of itself, outside of the world of its possessions and power. With eros, the very structure of subjectivity changes.

While virility indicates a subject closed in on itself, a subject who is self-sufficient, fecundity necessitates a relation with another. The virile subject relates to its future as the future of its possibilities, possibilities determined by its ego or will; the Sartrean subject projecting itself into the future is a virile subject. From the standpoint of the virile subject, the father-son relationship is a conflict of wills. Freud's notion of paternity makes the father-son relationship a virile struggle for recognition in which the son must kill the father in order to inherit his recognition, designation, and power.

In the relation of fecundity the subject cannot even relate to its own future as the future of its own possibilities. Its future is a future that is not, and cannot be, determined by the ego or will. It is a future that involves relationships with others who cannot be controlled within one's own subjectivity. This future that is not yet calls one out of oneself toward another. Rather than establish the transfer of identity and authority from father to son or the equality of brothers through their shared guilt in the murder of their father à la Freud, Levinas's notion of paternity establishes the uniqueness of the subject in relationship with the Other. The father/son relationship is not one of law-bound repetition, but of outlaw singularity.

Paternal Election and the Abject Father

Levinas holds out paternal love as exemplary: "The love of the father for the son accomplishes the sole relation possible with the very unicity of another; and in this sense every love must approach paternal love" (1969, 279). The father chooses the son after he has had no choice. His love *elects* this particular child in his uniqueness as the loved one, the one meant to be. In this regard, Levinas suggests that all love for another person must approach paternal love insofar as that love elects the loved one from among all others. This love makes the loved one unique and makes this love necessary rather than contingent. This love is not just for a limited time only, but is for all time, for a future never future enough, for infinite time.

Each father-son relationship is unique. In order for the father to love this son, brothers are never equals. The father chooses *this* son from among equal brothers and it is the father's election of this son that makes him unique. Paternity engenders a relationship outside of time, a unique relationship, that cannot be repeated. Unlike Freud's notion of the patriarchal father-son relationship whose authoritarian father and murderous sons guarantee the transfer of patriarchal power and the guilty social pact between brothers, Levinas's image of the father-son relationship breaks the social pact and does away with authority. Neither father nor son has a will or a choice; they choose without authority, power, or choice.

Levinas maintains that just as the lover chooses the beloved when he has no choice, for love is the adventure of what is not chosen, the father chooses or "elects" the son (1969, 254). The father says "I am my child" and yet this child is a stranger to him. At the heart of this identity—the "I am my child"—is otherness. The son's uniqueness comes through paternal election. "He is unique for himself because he is unique for his father" (1969, 279). Yet the father does not possess his child—"I do not have my child, I am my child." Paternity is the transsubstantiation of the I because the father is not in control; he cannot possess either the feminine Other or the child. In these relationships, the father is beyond himself and his will is impotent, even irrelevant.

Paternal election, which chooses from among equals, makes the chosen one unique precisely by recalling the nonuniqueness of the equals from among which this one was chosen:

> The unique child, as elected one, is accordingly at the same time unique and non-unique. Paternity is produced as an innumerable future; the I engendered exists at the same time as unique in the world as brother among brothers. I am I and chosen one, but where can I be chosen, if not from among other chosen ones,

among equals?... If biology furnishes us the prototypes of all these relations, this proves, to be sure, that biology does not represent a purely contingent order of being, unrelated to its essential productions. But these relations free themselves from their biological limitation. (1969, 279)

It seems that contingency is precisely what is at stake in Levinas's notion of paternal election. The child is unique in that he was "chosen," but this choice is not his father's. The father's love that elects the son compensates for the lack of choice or control exercised by the paternal body. It is as if Levinas is saying that just as biology "selects" one sperm cell from among millions, the father (after the fact) selects this child as his son. If biology or paternity does not provide an imaginary selection process, then this child is an accident; he is not unique, is not elected, and cannot image how he could be loved. Levinas's notion of paternal election makes the contingencies of biology irrelevant. All that matters is the father's response to this child; it is his love and not his genetic material that make it determinant and unique. Paternal election seems like an attempt to overcome the contingency and chance of paternity. The notion of paternal election seems an antidote for an abject identification with a father who does not control the products of generation that emanate from his own body.

Through paternal election the child is unique in that he is "chosen," but this choice is not the result of a virile will. The child is unique, not only because it was chosen from among "brothers," as Levinas says, but also because it is its father and yet other to its father. It is the other who calls to its father to recognize it as his unique child. Only after the election has been made does the father respond to the uniqueness of the child. Yet it is the father's response that rescues the child from abject fantasies. He loves this child; he chooses this child even though the choice of this child is not his. He affirms the choice of this child through his love and thereby asserts a paternal election that rescues the child from the contingencies of biology and the paternal body.

Why is the father's body seen as such a threat? As philosophers and psychoanalysts maintain, does the son suffer from the illusion that the father is omnipotent? Or is the substitution of abstractions, law, and symbols for the father's body a screen for the fear that the father is not omnipotent? Without postulating the reign of his will, what is determinant about the father's relationship to child? Behind the Oedipal story and the struggle for authority is the fear of the father's body, not because its omnipotence threatens to kill the son, but because its lack of determinacy threatens the son's very existence; the contingency and chance of its contribution to procreation is a threat to the son. The son becomes an accident of chance, a contingency as precarious as any individual sperm cell once it leaves the father's body. Even more disturbing, in this fantasy, the child may become merely a waste product expelled from the father's body. The fantasy of the father's omnipotence protects the child from a more terrifying fantasy, the fantasy of the father's impotence, which threatens not just the child's death, but the child's coming to be. The threat of what I call an *abject father* is more terrifying than the threat of an omnipotent father. At least the omnipotent father promises omnipotence for the son who one day can take his place. An identification with an abject father, on the other hand, promises indeterminacy and contingency with regard to even life and death. In the end, both the fear of the omnipotent father and the terror of the impotent father operate within the same economy of virility, which trades on the fear of a male body.

In *Powers of Horror*, Kristeva develops a notion of abjection based on Mary Douglas's notion of defilement. In *Purity and Danger*, Douglas describes defilement as the danger to identity constituted by filth, which is always defined in relation to the borders of that very identity. The identity of the subject is tied to the identity of the borders of the body that are threatened by bodily secretions: "Matter issuing from them [the orifices of the body] is marginal stuff of the most obvious kind. Spittle, blood, milk, urine, feces or tears by simply issuing forth have traversed the boundary of the body. . . . It follows from this that pollution is a type of danger which is not likely to occur except where the lines of structure, cosmic or social, are clearly defined" (1969, 113). Notice that Douglas does not mention semen, which for Kristeva becomes a special case.

Kristeva describes those things, which are not quite objects, that threaten the boundaries of our identities, both individual and social, as abject. Following Douglas, she maintains that the abject corresponds to the attempt to clearly delineate borders. In order for borders to be delineated, a line must be drawn between the inside and the outside, between the clean and proper self and the abject other. That which threatens identity must be jettisoned from the borders and placed outside. In this sense, identity is constituted through a process of abjection. As Kristeva describes it, both individual and social identity are constituted by abjecting *maternal* elements. The maternal body threatens the borders of the individual and social subject. It threatens the individual subject who was born out of another body and must deny this in order to establish its own proper identity. It threatens social identity insofar as the maternal body is associated with nature and the social must distinguish itself from the forces of nature. So, those bodily secretions—blood and milk—associated with the maternal body are the most strictly regulated by cultural and religious rituals. Kristeva discusses food prohibitions that revolve around blood and milk, always associated with the maternal.

Although she does not explain why, Kristeva exempts semen from the types of dangerous fluids that call into question the boundaries of identity. Perhaps the exemption of semen stems from Kristeva's premise that it is the fluids associated with the maternal body that are the most dangerous for identity. As I have argued elsewhere, seminal fluids are even more dangerous for identity than those fluids associated with the maternal body, evidenced by the fact that within Western culture the paternal body remains far more repressed than the maternal body.[3] As Freud maintains in his bloody story of the murder and cannibalization of the paternal body that founds society, culture props itself up on the corpse of the paternal body. The maternal body may be denied access to culture because it must remain at the level of body and nature so that culture and paternity can be defined in opposition to the maternal, natural realm. But, the paternal body is evacuated from both culture and nature. There is no paternal body in this imaginary economy between nature and culture, between maternal and paternal. The paternal is an abstract symbolic function that seals the social pact only when the paternal body is absent.

The paternal body threatens identity because seminal fluids are out of control, accidental, chancy. Paternity is indeterminate. If the child identifies with the paternal body, then the very possibility of identity becomes indeterminate, because the patriarch's authority and laws cannot explain why one sperm cell was chosen over all others. Why *this* child? What is at stake is not only the question of why this child rather than another child, but also the more ominous question of why this child rather than nothing, why life rather than death? The paternal body reminds us of the precariousness of life. It reminds us that ultimately we have no control over life. Levinas's notion of paternal election is an attempt to counterbalance the abject father, the indeterminacy of the paternal body, and the paternal contribution to procreation.

In the traditional psychoanalytic account, it is the father's authority and virility that counterbalance the abject father. The father is disassociated from indeterminacy or chance through his virile will and the authority of his law. The virility of his will and the authority of his law are based on the complete evacuation of his body and its uncontrollable seminal fluids. The repressed fantasy of the abject paternal body—a body out of control—threatens virile subjectivity. Yet it is only because of the notion of virile subjectivity, and the opposition between body and mind or nature and culture, that the father's body can be reduced to the abject provider of chance fertilization. The fantasy of the abject father is both maintained and repressed by a culture that has no antidote or counterweight for such a fantasy. The antidote is an image of paternal eros—a paternal eros that is embodied, passionate, and that is not just channeled through the maternal body.[4]

Although Levinas opens up the possibility of an alternative to this virile and authoritarian father, he too evacuates the paternal body from the father-son relationship. In Levinas we see once again the body identified with maternity and the social identified with paternity at the expense of the body. As we will see, although the erotic relationship with the feminine is necessary in order to engender the father-son relationship, which is the essential love relation, the erotic relationship is not a properly social relationship, because it is the union of two bodies. At its most divine, the erotic relationship aims at something beyond the body, which ultimately must be left behind; the caress itself aims at something other than the body.

Following the tradition of disembodied paternal elements, in spite of his attempts to insist on the body in philosophy, bodies are once again evacuated from Levinas's analyses of love and paternity. The paternal body is irrelevant to paternal love; paternal election replaces the father's bodily contributions to procreation. Here, Levinas's theory is at the threshold of the belief that *embodied eros* is a contradiction, that feelings and passions are associated with the body that must be overcome for pure eros. Levinas's notion of paternal election allows for paternal love *in spite of*, and not *through*, the body. For Levinas, even though the father is not the virile subject, his love is not embodied. The body of the father is still absent from paternity and the father's love is still abstract.

Levinas's notion of paternal eros, with its paternal election, merely replaces the virile attempts to control the paternal body by replacing it with reason, with an abstract disembodied paternal love that like Platonic eros transcends the body for the sake of infinity. Even while Levinas works against the traditional association between paternity and law or authority, he retains from that tradition the evacuation of the paternal body motivated by a fear of the contingency and chance of that body. Like the traditional notions of paternity that link father and law through virile struggles, Levinas's notion of paternal election masks a fear of an abject paternal body. Like the traditional notions of paternity that evacuate the paternal body, Levinas's notion of paternity presents us with another version of the patriarchal story of an absent father.

The real or embodied father is necessarily absent from traditional patriarchal accounts of the father's authority. So, too, the real or embodied father is absent from Levinas's account of paternal election, which turns the father-son relationship into an act of the father's will about that which he has no will, an act of the father's choice about that which he has no choice. Realizing his impotence, the father makes a choice; he wills this son. Like the virile eros that Levinas rejects, the strength of paternal eros is ultimately the father's potency in the face of his impotence. He must respond to his impotence like a man and choose his son in spite of himself.

Could the Future Be a Daughter?

At this point, we might wonder why the relationship with the feminine lover does not provide the same kind of uniqueness as the father-son relationship. Strangely enough, it seems that for Levinas the feminine lover is *neither* radically other *nor* the same, and *both* are required for the uniqueness of the father-son relationship. While the feminine lover may be unique and chosen by the father, she is neither other nor the same, because she is not fully human. And it turns out that it is the son's *sameness* that engenders the uncanny otherness experienced by the father in this unique relationship.

For Levinas, the fecund relationship with a woman has its goal in the child, more particularly, a son. The paternal relationship, however, is higher than the lover's relationship because it is social. The lovers' relationship takes place at the level of laughter and caresses and not language proper. Levinas describes the beloved woman as "silly" and "infantile," her face fading into animality; making love with her is like playing with a "young animal" (1969, 263). While the woman's animality is necessary to engender the father-son relationship and with it love and sociality, it is also what makes the woman inadequate for a properly social love relationship. The woman's animality protects the man from his own animality. By absorbing animality, the woman allows the man to escape from animality and nature in order to enter the social. She gives birth to the father and the son so that they can discover true love through each other.

Levinas always describes paternity as a relationship between a father and a son. But, if fatherhood is a promise for the future, could this future be a daughter? Or does it have to be a son? Recall that for Levinas the father discovers himself in the son, who is both himself and a stranger. Through the son, the father becomes other and yet survives as himself. He discovers himself in his son's gestures, substance, and uniqueness. His subjectivity itself is transformed through this relationship with an other who is him and not him. Levinas emphasizes that it is the otherness of the son that pulls the father out of himself toward infinity. Yet it is the sameness of the son that allows the movement without shattering the father's subjectivity altogether. Ultimately, it is the sameness between father and son that allows for the father to discover himself and his uniqueness through his son. The father identifies with his son. And paternal love is the father's election of this son from among equal "brothers." Paternal election makes biology irrelevant. So it is not just the biological substance of the son that makes him like and unlike his father; it is something about the son qua son. The father chooses this son and that election makes him unique; in turn the son's uniqueness makes the father unique. Through their relationship, they both are singular. Yet the discovery of their singularity has its basis in their sameness.

Levinas suggests that paternity opens onto infinity because it is a relationship with an absolute other in which the I survives. The I survives because paternity is also a relationship with the same. The father is his son and yet the son is a stranger to the father and the paternal relationship makes him a stranger to himself. Yet how can the son be an absolute other if he is also the same? Is it the son's difference or his sameness that restructures the I through paternity? Wouldn't a daughter be a stranger child? Because of sexual difference and the antidotal effects of feminine time, wouldn't the daughter be other enough to open up an infinite future? For Levinas desire is possible only in a relationship with an absolute other. Paternity engenders desire and thereby returns the erotic relationship to the ethical. And, yet, doesn't this paternal desire fall back into need if the son returns the father always to himself?

If, however, it is otherness that opens onto infinity and the possibility of radical surprise and the rupture of linear time, then couldn't, shouldn't, the future be a daughter? If paternal election is what makes the son unique and in turn, therefore, what makes the father unique, then could the father choose a daughter? Should we interpret Levinas literally in his discussion of the paternal election of a son? If so, paternal election not only provides an image of the father's choice of this particular child, but it also provides the image of the father's choice of a son in particular. Unless the daughter cannot be other because like the feminine in the erotic relationship she is subhuman, more like an animal, then the paternal discovery in her *could* be based on the otherness that opens the future to possibility.

For Levinas, it seems to go without saying that the father chooses a son rather than a daughter. The fact that he is a son is not what makes him unique; he is unique because he is *this* son chosen from among *brothers*. All children are brothers, but only this one is my son. Could the trans-substantiation of the father take place in relation to a daughter? Would the father discover himself in his daughter's substance, gestures, and uniqueness? And, if the father does not, or cannot, elect a daughter, then doesn't the fantasy that she is unwanted, an accident, unloved, should-have-been-otherwise, become devastating for her? Isn't she forced into an identification with an abject father who refuses to love *her*?

For Levinas, the future that paternity engenders is masculine. Insofar as it is masculine, it is limited. Insofar as it is limited, it is not open to radical alterity. And, insofar as it is not open to radical alterity, the future is finite and must come to an end. If there are no daughters, then there will be no more sons.

Notes

1. Some of his contemporaries have criticized Levinas for sacrificing the feminine for the mas-culine subject's ascent into the ethical relationship through paternity. See Catherine Chalier, *Figures du féminin: Lecture d'Emmanuel Levinas* (Paris: La Nuit Surveillée, 1982); Luce Irigaray, "The Fecun-dity of the Caress" (1984), in *An Ethics of Sexual Difference*, trans. Carolyn Burke and Gillian Gill (Ithaca: Cornell University Press, 1993) and "Questions to Emmanuel Levinas," in *The Irigaray Reader*, ed. Margaret Whitford (Cambridge, Mass.: Basil Blackwell, 1991).

2. Levinas reads the history of phenomenology from Husserl through Sartre as the history of a notion of the subject as the center or meaning and value. The subject gives meaning to experience; the subject constitutes meaning. Levinas calls the subject as meaning giver the subject as "I-can."

3. See my *Family Values: Subjects Between Nature and Culture* (New York: Routledge, 1997).

4. In *Family Values*, I analyze several philosophical and psychoanalytic conceptions of paternity to expose the ways in which they are disembodied and the ways in which paternal embodiment is absorbed into the maternal body, which becomes the only body and as such is excluded from culture. In addition, I suggest ways to conceive of paternity as embodied and passionate.

References

Chalier, Catherine. *Figures du féminin: Lecture d'Emmanuel Levinas*. Paris: La Nuit Surveillée, 1982.

Chanter, Tina. *Ethics of Eros: Irigaray's Rewriting of the Philosophers*. New York: Routledge, 1994.

Douglas, Mary. *Purity and Danger*. New York: Routledge, 1969.

Freud, Sigmund. *Totem and Taboo*. Vol. 13 of *The Standard Edition of the Complete Psychological Works of Sigmund Freud*, translated and edited by James Strachey. London: Hogarth Press, 1913.

Irigaray, Luce. "Love of Same, Love of Other." In *An Ethics of Sexual Difference*, translated by Carolyn Burke and Gillian Gill. Ithaca: Cornell, 1993.

———. *Marine Lover of Friedrich Nietzsche*. Translated by Gillian Gill. New York: Columbia University Press, 1991.

———. "Questions to Emmanuel Levinas." In *The Irigaray Reader*, edited and translated by Margaret Whitford. Cambridge, Mass.: Basil Blackwell, 1991.

———. *Sexes and Genealogies*. Translated by Gillian Gill. New York: Columbia, 1993.

———. *This Sex Which Is Not One*. Translated by Catherine Porter. Ithaca: Cornell University Press, 1985.

Kristeva, Julia. *Powers of Horror*. Translated by Leon Roudiez. New York: Columbia University Press, 1982.

Lacan, Jacques. *Écrits: A Selection*. Translated by Alan Sheridan. New York: Norton, 1977.

———. "The Neurotic's Individual Myth." *Psychoanalytic Quarterly* 48, no. 3 (1979): 422–23.

Levinas, Emmanuel. *Autrement qu'être ou au-dela de l'essence*. The Hague: Martinus Nijhoff, 1974.

———. *Ethics and Infinity*. Translated by Richard Cohen. Pittsburgh: Duquesne University Press, 1985.

———. "Language and Proximity." In *Collected Philosophical Papers*, translated by Alphonso Lingis. Boston: Kluwer, 1993.

———. *Otherwise Than Being or Beyond Essence*. Translated by Alphonso Lingis. Boston: Kluwer, 1991.

———. *Time and the Other*. Translated by Richard Cohen. Pittsburgh: Duquesne University Press, 1982.

———. *Totality and Infinity*. Translated by Alphonso Lingis. Pittsburgh: Duquesne University Press, 1969.

Oliver, Kelly. *Family Values: Subjects Between Nature and Culture*. New York: Routledge, 1997.

Bibliography

For a more comprehensive bibliography, see Roger Burggraeve, *Emmanuel Levinas: Une bibliographie primaire et secondaire (1929–1989)* (Leuven: Peeters, 1990). See also Henrik Petersen's bibliography in *Philosophy and Social Criticism* (special issue on Emmanuel Levinas) 23, no. 6 (1997); Joan Nordquist, ed., *Emmanuel Levinas: A Bibliography* (Santa Cruz, Calif.: Reference and Research, 1997). In the bibliography below, I have focused mainly on English-language works, but I have also included some works in French. I am grateful to Robert Bernasconi for sharing with me his bibliography, which was indispensable. The following bibliography is an updated version, organized into four sections: works by Levinas, single-authored books on Levinas, collections on Levinas, and articles on Levinas. While there is some overlap between sections 3 and 4, I have not always listed independently all the essays that appear in collected editions on Levinas (although I identify, in parentheses, the authors of contributors to such volumes in section 3).

I: Works by Levinas

"About Blanchot: An Interview." Translated by Garth Gillan. *Sub-Stance* 14 (1976): 54–57.
Alterity and Transcendence. Translated by Michael B. Smith. New York: Columbia University Press, 1999. *Altérité et Transcendence*. Paris: Fata Morgana, 1995.
"As If Consenting to Horror." Translated by Paula Wissing. *Critical Inquiry* 15 (Winter 1989): 485–88.
"Bad Conscience and the Inexorable." Translated by Richard Cohen. In *Face to Face with Levinas*, edited by R. Cohen, 35–40. Albany: State University of New York Press, 1986.
"Balance Sheet." In *American Jewish Year Book 1977*, edited by Morris Fine and Milton Himmelfarb. Vol. 77, 383–84. New York: American Jewish Committee; Philadelphia: Jewish Publication Society of America, 1976.
"Beyond Intentionality." Translated by Kathleen McLaughlin. In *Philosophy in France Today*, edited by A. Montefiore, 100–115. Cambridge: Cambridge University Press, 1983.
Beyond the Verse: Talmudic Readings and Lectures. Translated by Gary D. Mole. London: Athlone Press; Bloomington: Indiana University Press, 1994. *L'Au-Delà du Verset: Lectures et discours talmudiques*. Paris: Éditions de Minuit, 1982.

Collected Philosophical Papers. Translated by A. Lingis. The Hague: Martinus Nijhoff, 1987. *Humanisme de l'autre homme.* Paris: Fata Morgana, 1972. (Also includes other essays).

"The Contemporary Criticism of the Idea of Value and the Prospects for Humanism." In *Value and Values in Evolution,* edited by Edward A. Maziarz, 179–87. New York: Gordon and Breach, 1979.

De l'évasion. Paris: Fata Morgana, 1982.

Dieu, la mort, et le temps. Edited by Jacques Rolland. Paris: Éditions Grasset et Fasquelle, 1993. (Lectures; includes a reprint of *La Mort et le temps* [Paris: Éditions de l'Herne, 1991]).

Difficult Freedom: Essays on Judaism. Translated by Seán Hand. Baltimore: John Hopkins University Press, 1990. *Difficile liberté: Essais sur le judaïsme.* Paris: Albin Michel, 1963 and 1976.

Discovering Existence with Husserl. Translated by Richard A. Cohen and Michael B. Smith. Evanston: Northwestern University Press, 1998. (Includes five chapters from *En découvrant l'existence avec Husserl et Heidegger*).

Emmanuel Levinas: Basic Philosophical Writings. Edited by Adriaan Peperzak, Simon Critchley, and Robert Bernasconi. Bloomington: Indiana University Press, 1996.

En découvrant l'existence avec Husserl et Heidegger. Paris: Vrin, 1949; 2d exp. ed., 1967, 1974.

Entre Nous: Thinking of the Other. Translated by Michael B. Smith and Barbara Harshav. New York: Columbia University Press, 1998. *Entre nous: Essais sur le penser-à-l'autre.* Paris: Grasset et Fasquelle, 1991.

"Entretiens." In *Emmanuel Levinas: Qui êtes-vous?* Edited by François Poiré, 63–136. Lyon: La Manufacture, 1987. Interview with François Poiré, translated by J. Robbins and M. Coelen, with T. Loebel. In *Is It Righteous to Be? Interviews.* Edited by Jill Robbins. Forthcoming.

"Emmanuel Levinas." In *French Philosophers in Conversation,* edited by Raoul Mortley, 11–23. New York: Routledge, 1991.

Ethics and Infinity: Conversations with Philippe Nemo. Translated by R. Cohen. Pittsburgh: Duquesne University Press, 1985. *Éthique et infini: Dialogues avec Philippe Nemo.* Paris: Arthème Fayard et Radio-France, 1982.

"Ethics of the Infinite." In *Dialogues with Contemporary Continental Thinkers,* by Richard Kearney, 47–69. Manchester: Manchester University Press, 1984. Reprinted in *Face to Face with Levinas,* edited by R. Cohen, 13–33. Albany: State University of New York Press, 1986.

Existence and Existents. Translated by A. Lingis. The Hague: Martinus Nijhoff, 1978. *De l'existence à l'existant.* Paris: J. Vrin, 1984.

Foreword to *System and Revelation: The Philosophy of Franz Rosenzweig,* by Stéphane Mosès, translated by Catherine Tihanyi, 13–22. Detroit: Wayne State University Press, 1992.

"Franz Rosenzweig." Translated by R. Cohen. *Midstream* 29, no. 9 (1983): 33–40. (Abbreviated version of an essay that can be found complete in *Difficult Freedom* under the title "Between Two Worlds").

"God and Philosophy." Translated by R. Cohen. *Philosophy Today* 22 (1978): 127–45. (Revised version in *Collected Philosophical Papers*).

"Ideology and Idealism." In *Modern Jewish Ethics,* edited by Marvin Fox, 121–38. Columbus: Ohio State University, 1975.

In the Time of Nations. Translated by Michael B. Smith. London: Athlone Press; Bloomington: Indiana University Press, 1994. *A l'heure des nations.* Paris: Éditions de Minuit, 1988.

"Interrogation of Martin Buber Conducted by Maurice S. Friedman." In *Philosophical Interrogations*, edited by Sydney and Beatrice Rome, 23–26. New York: Harper & Row, 1970.

"Intersubjectivity: Notes on Merleau-Ponty." Translated by Michael B. Smith. In *Ontology and Alterity in Merleau-Ponty*, edited by Galen A. Johnson and Michael B. Smith, 55–60. Evanston: Northwestern University Press, 1990. (A slightly different version appears in *Outside the Subject*).

"Intervention by Levinas." In *A Short History of Existentialism*, by Jean Wahl, translated by Forrest Williams and Stanley Maron, 47–53. New York: Philosophical Library, 1949.

"Interview." In *Conversations with French Philosophers*, edited by Florian Rötzer, translated by Gary Aylesworth, 57–65. Atlantic Highlands, N.J.: Humanities Press, 1995.

"Interview with Emmanuel Levinas: December 31, 1982." Conducted and translated by Edith Wyschogrod. *Philosophy and Theology* 4, no. 2 (1989): 105–18.

"Intuition of Essences." Translated by Joseph Kockelmans. In *Phenomenology: The Philosophy of Edmund Husserl and Its Interpretation*, edited by J. Kockelmans, 83–105. Garden City, N.Y.: Doubleday Anchor, 1967. (A translation of chap. 6 of the subsequently translated *The Theory of Intuition in Husserl's Phenomenology*).

Is It Righteous to Be? Interviews. Edited by Jill Robbins. Stanford: Stanford University Press, forthcoming.

"Is Ontology Fundamental?" Translated by Peter Atterton. *Philosophy Today* 33, no. 2 (1989): 121–29. Reprinted in *Emmanuel Levinas: Basic Philosophical Writings*.

"The Jewish Understanding of Scripture." Translated by Joseph Cunnean. *Cross Currents* 66 (1994): 488–504.

"Judaism and the Feminine Element." Translated by E. Wyschogrod. *Judaism* 18, no. 1 (1969): 30–38. (Another version appears in *Difficult Freedom*).

"A Language Familiar to Us." Translated by Douglas Collins. *Telos* 44 (1980): 199–201.

The Levinas Reader. Edited by Seán Hand. Oxford: Basil Blackwell, 1989.

"Martin Buber, Gabriel Marcel, and Philosophy." Translated by Esther Kameron. In *Martin Buber: A Centenary Volume*, edited by Haim Gordon and Jochanan Bloch, 305–21. New York: Ktav, for the Faculty of Humanities and Social Sciences, Ben Gurion University of the Negev, 1984. (Another version appears in *Outside the Subject*).

"Martin Buber and the Theory of Knowledge." In *The Philosophy of Martin Buber*, edited by Paul Schilpp and Maurice Friedman, 133–50. La Salle, Ill.: Open Court, 1967.

New Talmudic Readings. Translated by Richard A. Cohen. Pittsburgh: Duquesne University Press, 1999. *Nouvelles lectures tamludiques.* Paris: Éditions de Minuit, 1996.

Nine Talmudic Readings. Translated by Annette Aronowicz. Bloomington: Indiana University Press, 1990. *Quatre lectures talmudiques*, Paris, Éditions de Minuit, 1968; and *Du sacre au saint: Cinq nouvelles lectures talmudiques*. Paris: Éditions de Minuit, 1977.

Of God Who Comes to Mind. Translated by Bettina Bergo. 2d ed., with a new preface. Stanford, Stanford University Press, 1998. *De Dieu qui vient a l'idée.* Paris: Librairie Philosophique J. Vrin, 1982.

"On the Trail of the Other." Translated by Daniel J. Hoy. *Philosophy Today* 10, no. 1

(1966): 34–46. (See "The Trace of the Other" for a new translation that supersedes this one).

Otherwise Than Being or Beyond Essence. Translated by Alphonso Lingis. The Hague: Martinus Nijhoff, 1981. *Autrement qu'être ou au-delà de l'essence.* The Hague: Martinus Nijhoff, 1974. 2d ed., 1978, 1981.

Outside the Subject. Translated by Michael B. Smith. Stanford: Stanford University Press, 1993. *Hors sujet.* Paris: Fata Morgana, 1987.

"The Paradox of Morality: An Interview with Emmanuel Levinas." Conducted by Tamra Wright, Peter Hughes, and Alison Ainley. In *The Provocation of Levinas: Rethinking the Other,* edited by R. Bernasconi and D. Wood, 168–80. New York: Routledge & Kegan Paul, 1988.

"Phenomenology and the Non-Theoretical." Translated by J. N. Kraay and A. J. Scholten. In *Facts and Values,* edited by M. C. Doeser and J. N. Kraay, 109–19. Dordrecht: Martinus Nijhoff, 1986.

"Philosophy and Awakening." Translated by Mary Quaintance. In *Who Comes After the Subject?* edited by Eduardo Cadava, Peter Connor, and Jean-Luc Nancy, 206–16. New York: Routledge, 1991.

"Present Problems of Jewish Education in Western Lands." *Community* 12 (November 1960): 1–6.

"The Primacy of Pure Practical Reason." Translated by Blake Billings. *Man and World* 27 (1994): 445–53.

Proper Names. Translated by Michael B. Smith. Stanford: Stanford University Press, 1996. *Noms propre.* Paris: Fata Morgana, 1976; and *Sur Maurice Blanchot.* Paris: Fata Morgana, 1975.

Que dirait Eurydice? What Would Eurydice Say? Emmanuel Levinas en/in conversation avec/with Bracha Lichtenberg-Ettinger. Paris: BLE Atelier, 1977.

"Reflections on the Philosophy of Hitlerism." Translated by Séan Hand. *Critical Inquiry* 17 (1990): 62–71. *Quelques réflexions sur la philosophie de l'hitlérisme.* Paris: Éditions Payot & Rivages, 1997.

"Sensibility." Translated by Michael B. Smith. In *Ontology and Alterity in Merleau-Ponty,* edited by Galen A. Johnson and Michael B. Smith, 60–66. Evanston: Northwestern University Press, 1990. (A slightly different version appears in *Outside the Subject*).

"Signature." Translated by Mary Ellen Petrisko. Edited by Adriaan Peperzak. *Research in Phenomenology* 8 (1978): 175–89. (Replaces "Signature," trans. William Canavan, *Philosophy Today* 10, no. 1 [1966]).

"Simulacra." Translated by David Allison. In *Writing the Future,* edited by David Wood, 11–14. London: Routledge & Kegan Paul, 1990.

The Theory of Intuition in Husserl's Phenomenology. Translated by André Orianne. 2d ed., with a new foreword by Richard Cohen, 1995. Evanston: Northwestern University Press, 1973.

Time and the Other. Translated by Richard Cohen. Pittsburgh: Duquesne University Press, 1987. (Also includes "The Old and the New" and "Diachrony and Representation.") *Le temps et l'autre.* Paris: Fata Morgana, 1979.

"To Love the Torah More Than God." Translated by Helen A. Stephenson and Richard I. Sugarman. *Judaism* 28, no. 2 (1979): 216–23. (See also the translation by Frans Jozef van Beeck in *Loving the Torah More Than God* [Chicago: Loyola University of Chicago, 1989], 36–40; and by Seán Hand in *Difficult Freedom*).

Totality and Infinity: An Essay on Exteriority. Translated by Alphonso Lingis. The Hague: Martinus Nijhoff, 1979. First published with Martinus Nijhoff in assocation with Duquesne University Press, 1969. *Totalité et infini: Essai sur l'extériorité.* The Hague: Martinus Nijhoff, 1961.

"The Trace of the Other." Translated by Alphonso Lingis. In *Deconstruction in Context,* edited by Mark Taylor, 345–59. Chicago: University of Chicago Press, 1986.

"Transcendence and Evil." Translated by A. Lingis. In *The Phenomenology of Man and of the Human Condition,* edited by A-T. Tymieniecka, 153–65. Analecta Husserliana, vol. 14. Dordrecht: D. Reidel, 1983. (Reprinted in *Collected Philosophical Papers*).

"Transcending Words." Translated by Didier Maleuvre. *Yale French Studies* 81 (1992): 145–50. (Alternative version in *The Levinas Reader*).

"The Understanding of Spirituality." Translated by Andrius Valevicius. *Man and World* 31 (1998): 1–10.

"Useless Suffering." Translated by R. Cohen. In *The Provocation of Levinas,* edited by R. Bernasconi and D. Wood, 156–67. New York: Routledge & Kegan Paul, 1988.

"Wholly Otherwise." Translated by Simon Critchley. In *Re-reading Levinas,* edited by R. Bernasconi and S. Critchley, 3–10. Bloomington: Indiana University Press, 1991. (Also appears in *Proper Names*).

II: Monographs on Levinas

Benso, Silvia. *The Face of Things: A Different Side of Ethics.* Contemporary Continental Philosophy. Albany: State University of New York, 2000.

Burggraeve, Roger. *From Self-Development to Solidarity: An Ethical Reading of Human Desire in Its Socio-Political Relevance According to Emanuel Levinas.* Translated by C. Vanhove-Romanik. Louvain: Centre for Metaphysics and Philosophy of God, 1985.

Chalier, Catherine. *Figures du féminin.* Paris: La Nuit Surveillée, 1982.

Champagne, Ronald A. *The Ethics of Reading According to Emmanuel Levinas.* Amsterdam: Editions Rodopi, 1998.

Chanter, Tina. *Time, Death, and the Feminine: Levinas with Heidegger.* Stanford: Stanford University Press, 2001.

Cohen, Richard A. *Elevations.* Chicago: University of Chicago Press, 1994.

Critchley, Simon. *The Ethics of Deconstruction: Derrida and Levinas.* Oxford: Blackwells, 1992.

Critchley, Simon. *Very Little . . . Almost Nothing,* 31–38. London: Routledge, 1997.

Critchley, Simon. *Ethics, Politics, Subjectivity,* esp. chaps. 3, 9, 10. London: Verso, 1999.

Davis, Colin. *Levinas: An Introduction.* Cambridge: Polity Press, 1996.

Derrida, Jacques. *Adieu.* Translated by Pascale-Anne Brault and Michael Naas. Stanford: Stanford University Press, 1999.

Eaglestone, Robert. *Ethical Criticism: Reading After Levinas.* Edinburgh: Edinburgh University Press, 1997.

Finkielkraut, Alain. *La sagesse de l'amour.* Paris: Gallimard, 1984. *The Wisdom of Love.* Translated by K. O'Neill and D. Suchoff. Lincoln: University of Nebraska Press, 1997.

Forthomme, Bernard. *Une philosophie de la transcendance: La métaphysique d'Emmanuel Levinas.* Paris: Vrin, 1979.

Gibbs, Robert. *Correlations in Rosenzweig and Levinas*. Princeton: Princeton University Press, 1992.

Handelman, Susan A. *Fragments of Redemption: Jewish Thought and Literary Theory in Benjamin, Scholem, and Levinas*. Bloomington: Indiana University Press, 1991.

Keenan, Dennis. *Death and Responsibility*. Albany: State University of New York Press, 1999.

Libertson, Joseph. *Proximity: Levinas, Blanchot, Bataille, and Communication*. Phaenomenologica 87. The Hague: Martinus Nijhoff, 1982.

Llewelyn, John. *Emmanuel Levinas: The Genealogy of Ethics*. London: Routledge, 1995.

————. *The Middle Voice of Ecological Conscience*. London: Macmillan, 1991.

Manning, Robert John Sheffler. *Interpreting Otherwise Than Heidegger*. Pittsburgh: Duquesne University, 1993.

Mole, Gary D. *Lévinas, Blanchot, Jabès: Figures of Estrangement*. Crosscurrents: Comparative Studies in European Literature and Philosophy. Gainesville: University Press of Florida, 1997.

Nealon, Jeffrey T. *Alterity Politics: Ethics and Performative Subjectivity*. Durham: Duke University Press, 1998.

Ouaknin, Marc-Alain. *Méditations érotiques*. Paris: Balland, 1992.

Peperzak, Adriaan. *To the Other: An Introduction to the Philosophy of Emmanuel Levinas*. West Lafayette: Purdue University Press, 1993.

Poiré, François. *Emmanuel Levinas: Qui êtes-vous?* Lyon: La Manufacture, 1987

Robbins, Jill. *Altered Reading: Levinas and Literature*. Chicago: University of Chicago Press, 1999.

Rosmarin, Leonard. *Emmanuel Levinas: Humaniste de l'autre homme*. Toronto: Éditions du GREF, 1991.

Sandford, Stella. *The Metaphysics of Love: Gender and Transcendence in Levinas*. London: Athlone Press, 2000.

Schroeder, Brian. *Altered Ground: Levinas, History, and Violence*. New York: Routledge, 1996.

Smith, Steven G. *"The Argument to the Other: Reason Beyond Reason in the Thought of Karl Barth and Emmanuel Levinas."* American Academy of Religion Academy Studies, no. 42. Chico, Calif.: Scholars Press, 1983.

Srajek, Martin, C. *In the Margins of Deconstruction: Jewish Conceptions of Ethics in Emmanuel Levinas and Jacques Derrida*. Dordrecht: Kluwer, 1998.

Vasseleu, Catherine. *Textures of Light: Vision and Touch in Irigaray, Levinas, and Merleau-Ponty*. New York: Routledge, 1998.

————. *Emmanuel Levinas: The Problem of Ethical Metaphysics*. The Hague: Martinus Nijhoff, 1974.

Wright, Tamra. *The Twilight of Jewish Philosophy: Emmanuel Levinas's Ethical Hermeneutics*. Amsterdam: Harwood, 1999.

III: Collections on Levinas:
Books, Special Issues of Journals, and Proceedings

Bernasconi, Robert, and Simon Critchley. *Re-reading Levinas*. Bloomington: Indiana University Press, 1991. (Essays by Levinas, Derrida, Greisch, Ciaranelli, Irigaray,

Chalier, Chanter, Bernasconi,. Critchley, Berezdivin, Davies, O'Connor, and Llewelyn).

Bernasconi, Robert, and David Wood. *The Provocation of Levinas.* New York: Routledge & Kegan Paul, 1988. (Essays by Heaton, Boothroyd, Chanter, O'Connor, Ainley, Gans, Howells, Bernasconi, Llewelyn, and Levinas).

Bloechl, Jeffrey, ed. *The Face of the Other and the Trace of God: Essays on the Philosophy of Emmanuel Levinas.* New York: Fordham University Press, 2000.

Chalier, Catherine, and Miguel Abensour, eds. *Emmanuel Lévinas.* Paris: Cahier de l'Herne, 1991. (Including contributions by Levinas, Lingis, Wenzler, de Fontenay, David, Richir, Chrétien, Taminiaux, Trotignon, Petitdemange, Marty, Collin, Bernasconi, Cohen, Bernheim, Aronowicz, Mopsik, Chalier, Banon, Faessler, Peperzak, Schneider, Haar, Weber, Finkielkraut, Abensour, Armengaud).

Cohen, Richard A., ed. *Face to Face with Levinas.* Albany: State University of New York Press, 1986. (Essays by Levinas, Blanchot, Smith, Reed, de Boer, Lyotard, de Greef, Bernasconi, Peperzak, Lingis, and Irigaray).

Dupuis, Michel, ed. *Levinas en contrastes.* Brussels: Le Point Philosophique, 1994. (Contributions by Ricœur, Dupuis, Lannoy, De Greef, Baum, Feron, Delhez and Frogneux, Mies, Ruol, De Bauw, Lisse).

Greisch, Jean, and Jacques Rolland, eds., *Emmanuel Lévinas: L'éthique comme philosophie première.* Actes du colloque de Cerisy-la-Salle 23 août–2 septembre 1986. Paris: Éditions du Cerf, 1993. (Essays by Greisch, Marion, Chalier, Mosès, Petrosino, Schneider, Jandin, Kovac, Hisashige, Banon, Dupuy, Faessler, Casper, David, Mongin, Petitdemange, Kearney, Valavandis-Wybrands, Wiemer, Aubay, Rolland, Levinas).

Hand, Seán. ed. *Facing the Other: The Ethics of Emmanuel Levinas.* Richmond, Surrey: Curzon, 1996. (Papers by Ainley, Ford, Gans, Hand, Holland, Hutchens, Leonard, Lesser, Ward).

Harasym, Sarah, ed. *Levinas and Lacan: The Missed Encounter.* Albany: State University of New York, 1998. (Papers by Chanter, Gondek, Brody, Assoun, Van Haute, Juranville, Cornell, Visker).

In Memoriam: Emmanuel Levinas. Special issue, *Research in Phenomenology* 28 (1998). (Papers by Bernasconi, Derrida, Llewelyn, Lingis, Critchley, Chanter, Peperzak, Davies, Sallis, Raffoul).

Levinas: The Face of the Other. Proceedings of the fifteenth annual symposium of the Simon Silverman Phenomenology Center, Duquesne University, Pittsburgh, 1998. Pittsburgh: Duquesne University Press, 1998. (Papers by Caputo, Chanter, Peperzak, Visker).

Levinas's Contribution to Contemporary Philosophy. Special issue, *Graduate Faculty Philosophy Journal,* vol. 20, no. 2–vol. 21, no. 1 (1998). (Papers by Levinas, Mosès, Marion, Greisch, Lingis, De Vries, Bailhache, De Greef, Richir, Guibal, Scott, Faulconer, Abensour, Chalier, Westphal, Anderson, Cohen, Marty, Labarrière, Manning, Ciaramelli, Wenzler, Tauber, Rolland, Trotignon, Chanter).

Les nouveaux cahiers: Emmanuel Levinas 82 (Autumn 1985). (Contributions by De Fontenay, Chalier, Sarfati, Kessler, Banon, Anissimove, Dupuy, Bouganim, Walter, Rolland, Jessua, Levinas, Kessler).

Olthius, James H. *Knowing Other-wise: Philosophy at the Threshold of Spirituality.* Edited by James H. Olthius. New York: Fordham University Press, 1997.

Peperzak, Adriaan, ed. *Ethics as First Philosophy: The Significance of Emmanuel Levinas for*

Philosophy, Literature, and Religion. New York: Routledge, 1995. (Chalier, Gibbs, Scott, Waldenfels, Miller, Werhane, Weber, Bernasconi, Ciaramelli, Davies, Tallon, Richardson, Wyschogrod, Westphal, De Boer, Robbins, Peperzak, Tracy, Llewelyn, De Vries, Comay).

Philosophy Today 43, no. 2/4 (1999). Edited and with an introduction by Caroline Bayard and Joyce Bellous. (G. Hansel, Dussel, Sussin, Sokol, Bauman, J. Hansel, Cohen, Larochelle, Sikka).

IV: Articles on Levinas

Abensour, Miguel. "Le mal élemental." In *Quelques réflexions sur la philosophie de l'hitlérisme*, by Emmanuel Levinas, 27–103. Paris: Éditions Payot & Rivages, 1997.

Anderson, Travis. "Drawing upon Levinas to Sketch Out a Heterotopic Poetics of Art and Tragedy." *Research in Phenomenology* 24 (1994): 69–96.

Aquino, Ranhilo C. "Beyond the Clutches of Parmenides? Some Questions Asked Levinas—Face to Face," *Colloquia Manilana*, no vol. no. (n.d.): 34–48.

Atterton, Peter. "Levinas and the Language of Peace: A Response to Derrida." *Philosophy Today* 36, no. 1 (1992): 59–70.

———. "Levinas's Skeptical Critique of Metaphysics and Anti-Humanism." *Philosophy Today* 41 (Winter 1997): 491–506.

Awerkamp, Don. *Emmanuel Leyinas: Ethics and Politics.* New York: Revisionist Press, 1977.

Barber, Michael D. "Emmanuel Levinas and the Philosophy of Liberation." *Laval Theologique et Philosophique* 54, no. 3 (1998): 473–81.

———. "Virtue of Virtues: Levinas and Virtue-Ethics." *International Philosophy Quarterly* 38 no. 2 (1998): 119–26.

———. "The Vulnerability of Reason: The Philosophical Foundations of Emmanuel Levinas and K. O. Apel." In *The Prism of the Self: Philosophical Essays in Honor of Maurice Natanson*, edited by Steven Galt Crowell. Dordrecht: Kluwer, 1995.

Baum, Mylène. "Visage Versus Visages." *Philosophy and Theology* 4, no. 2 (1989): 187–205.

Bauman, Zygmunt. *Postmodern Ethics*, chaps. 2, 3, 4, pp. 47–52, 69–77, 84–97. Oxford: Blackwell, 1993.

Beavers, Anthony F. *Levinas Beyond the Horizons of Cartesianism.* New York: Peter Lang, 1995.

Benso, Silvia. "The Face of Things: Heidegger and the Alterity of the Fourfold." *Symposium* 1, no. 1 (1997): 5–15.

———. "Levinas—Another Ascetic Priest." *Journal of the British Society for Phenomenology* 27, no. 2 (1996): 137–56.

———. "Of Things Face-To-Face with Levinas Face-to-Face with Heidegger: Prolegomena to a Metaphysical Ethics of Things. *Philosophy Today* 40, no. 1 (1996): 132–41.

Bergo, Bettina. "A Reading of Emmanuel Levinas's 'Dieu et la philosophie.'" *Graduate Faculty Philosophy Journal* 16, no. 1 (1993): 113–64.

Bernasconi, Robert. "Deconstruction and the Possibility of Ethics." In *Deconstruction and Philosophy*, edited by John Sallis, 122–39. Chicago: University of Chicago Press, 1987.

————. "Different Styles of Eschatology: Derrida's Take on Levinas's Political Messianism." *Research in Phenomenology* 28 (1998): 3–19.

————. "The Ethics of Suspicion." *Research in Phenomenology* 20 (1990): 3–18.

————. "Fundamental Ontology, Metontology, and the Ethics of Ethics." *Irish Philosophical Journal* 4, nos. 1 and 2 (1987): 76–93.

————. "Hegel and Levinas: The Possibility of Reconciliation and Forgiveness." *Archivio di Filosofia* 54 (1986): 325–46.

————. "Levinas Face to Face—with Hegel." *Journal of the British Society for Phenomenology* 13, no. 3 (1982): 267–76.

————. "Levinas on Time and the Instant." In *Time and Metaphysics*, edited by D. Wood and R. Bernasconi, 199–217. Coventry, U.K.: Parousia Press, 1982.

————. "Levinas: Philosophy and Beyond." In *Continental Philosophy*, vol. 1, 232–58. New York: Routledge & Kegan Paul, 1987.

————. "One-Way Traffic: The Ontology of Decolonization and Its Ethics." In *Ontology and Alterity in Merleau-Ponty*, edited by Galen A. Johnson and Michael B. Smith, 67–80. Evanston: Northwestern University Press, 1990.

————. "Rereading *Totality and Infinity*." In *The Question of the Other: Essays in Contemporary Continental Philosophy*, edited by A. Dallery and C. Scott, 23–34. New York, State University of New York Press, 1989.

————. "The Silent Anarchic World of the Evil Genius." In *The Collegium Phaenomenologicum: The First Ten Years*, edited by G. Moneta, J. Sallis, and J. Taminiaux, 257–72. Dordrecht: Kluwer, 1988.

————. "The Third Party." *Journal of the British Society for Phenomenology* 30, no. 1 (1999): 76–87.

————. "The Trace of Levinas in Derrida." In *Derrida and Difference*, edited by D. Wood and R. Bernasconi, 13–29. Evanston: Northwestern University Press, 1988.

————. "The Violence of the Face: Peace and Language in the Thought of Levinas." *Philosophy and Social Criticism* 23, no. 6 (1997): 81–93.

————. "Who Is My Neighbor? Who Is the Other?" *Ethics and Responsibility in the Phenomenological Tradition* (Simon Silverman Phenomenology Center, Duquesne University) (1992): 1–31.

Blanchot, Maurice. *The Infinite Conversation.* Translated by Susan Hanson, esp. 49–58. Minneapolis: University of Minnesota Press, 1993.

————. *The Writing of the Disaster.* Translated by Ann Smock, esp. 13–30. Lincoln: University of Nebraska Press, 1986.

Bloechl, Jeffrey. "How Best to Keep a Secret? On Love and Respect in Levinas's 'Phenomenology of Eros.'" *Man and World* 29, no. 1 (1996): 1–17.

————. "Levinas, Daniel Webster, and Us: Radical Responsibility and the Problem of Evil." *International Philosophical Quarterly* 38, no. 3 (1998): 259–73.

Blum, Roland Paul. "Deconstruction and Creation." *Philosophy and Phenomenological Research* 46, no. 2 (1985): 293–306.

————. "Emmanuel Levinas's Theory of Commitment." *Philosophy and Phenomenological Research* 44, no. 2 (1983): 145–68.

Boothroyd, David. "Foucault's Alimentary Philosophy: Care of the Self and Responsibility for the Other." *Man and World* 29 (1996): 361–86.

————. "Levinas and Nietzsche: In Between Love and Contempt." *Philosophy Today* 39, no. 4 (1995): 345–57.

Bouckaert, Luk. "Ontology and Ethics: Reflections on Levinas's Critique of Heidegger." *International Philosophical Quarterly* 10 (1970): 402–19.

Bracher, Nathan. "Facing History: Mauriac and Levinas on Nazism." *Journal of European Studies* 23 (1993): 159–77.

Brody, D. H. "Emmanuel Levinas: The Logic of Ethical Ambiguity in *Otherwise Than Being or Beyond Essence*." *Research in Phenomenology* 25 (1995): 177–203.

Bruns, Gerald L. "Blanchot/Levinas: Interruption (On the Conflict of Alterities)." *Research in Phenomenology* 26 (1996): 132–54.

———. "Dialogue and the Truth of Skepticism." *Religion and Literature* 22, nos. 2–3 (1990): 85–92.

Burggraeve, Roger. "Emmanuel Levinas, Thinker Between Jerusalsem and Athens: A Philosophical Biography." *Journal of Social Philosophy* 28, no. 1 (1997): 110–26.

———. "The Ethical Basis for a Humane Society According to Emmanuel Levinas." Translated by C. Vanhove-Romanik. In *Emmanuel Levinas*, 5–57. Louvain: Centre for Metaphysics and Philosophy of God, 1981.

Burke, John Patrick. "The Ethical Significance of the Face." *Proceedings of the American Catholic Philosophical Association* 56 (1982): 194–206.

———. "Listening at the Abyss." In *Dialogue and Alterity in Merleau-Ponty*, 81–97. Evanston: Northwestern University Press, 1990, pp.

Busch, Thomas W. "Ethics and Ontology: Levinas and Merleau-Ponty." *Man and World* 25 (1992): 195–202.

Caputo, John D. "Hyperbolic Justice: Deconstruction, Myth, and Politics." *Research in Phenomenology* 21 (1991): 3–20.

———. "Hyperbolic Names." In *Against Ethics*, 79–85. Bloomington: Indiana University Press, 1993.

Carey, Seamus. "Embodying Original Ethics: A Response to Levinas and Caputo." *Philosophy Today* 41, nos. 3–4 (1997): 446–59.

Caruana, John. "The Catastrophic 'Site and Non-Site' of Proximity: Redeeming the Disaster of Being." *International Studies in Philosophy* 30, no. 1 (1998): 33–46.

Casey, E. "Levinas on Memory and Trace." In *The Collegium Phaenomenologicum: The First Ten Years*, edited by G. Moneta, J. Sallis, and J. Taminiaux, 241–55. Dordrecht: Kluwer, 1988.

Chalier, Catherine. "Emmanuel Levinas: Responsibility and Election." *Ethics*, Royal Institute of Philosophy supp. 35, edited by A. Phillips Griffiths, 63–76. Cambridge: Cambridge University Press, 1993, pp.

———. "Ethics and the Feminine." In *Re-reading Levinas*, edited by R. Bernasconi and S. Critchley, 119–29. Bloomington: Indiana University Press, 1991.

Chanter, Tina. "The Alterity and Immodesty of Time: Death as Future and Eros as Feminine in Levinas." In *Writing the Future*, edited by David Wood, 137–54. London: Routledge & Kegan Paul, 1990.

———. "Antigone's Dilemma." In *Re-reading Levinas*, edited by R. Bernasconi and S. Critchley, 132–48. Bloomington: Indiana University Press, 1991.

———. "The Betrayal of Philosophy: Emmanuel Levinas's *Otherwise Than Being*." *Philosophy and Social Criticism* 3, no. 6 (1997): 65–79.

———. *Ethics of Eros: Irigaray's Rewriting of the Philosophers*, chap. 5, 170–224. New York: Routledge, 1994.

———. "Feminism and the Other." In *Provocation of Levinas: Thinking the Other*, edited by R. Bernasconi and D. Wood, 32–56. New York: Routledge & Kegan Paul, 1988.

———. "Giving Time and Death: Levinas, Heidegger, and the Trauma of the Gift." In *Levinas: The Face of the Other*, 37–56. Proceedings of the fifteenth annual symposium of the Simon Silverman Center for Phenomenology Center, Pittsburgh, Duquesne University, 1998. Pittsburgh: University of Duquesne Press, 1998.

———. "Levinas and Impossible Possibility: Thinking Ethics with Rosenzweig and Heidegger in the Wake of the Shoah." *Research in Phenomenology* 38 (1998): 91–109.

———. "Neither Materialism nor Idealism: Levinas's Third Way." In *Postmodernism and the Holocaust*, edited by Alan Milchman and Alan Rosenberg, 137–54. Value Inquiry Book Series. Amsterdam: Rodopi, 1997.

———. "The Ontological Status of Sexual Difference." In *A Dieu: Theology and Philosophy in Heidegger, Derrida, Levinas*, edited by Jill Robbins. Albany: State University of New York Press, forthcoming.

———. "The Question of Death: The Time of the I and the Time of the Other." *Irish Philosophical Journal* 4, nos. 1 and 2 (1987): 94–119.

———. "Reading Hegel as a Mediating Master: Lacan and Levinas." In *The Missed Encounter: Lacan and Levinas*, edited by Sarah Harasym, 1–21. Albany: State University of New York Press, 1998.

———. "The Temporality of Saying: Politics Beyond Ontological Difference." In *Levinas's Contribution to Contemporary Philosophy*. Special issue, *Graduate Faculty Philosophy Journal*, vol. 20, no. 2–vol. 21, no. 1 (1998): 503–28.

———. "Traumatic Response: Levinas's Legacy." *Philosophy Today* 41, supp. (1997): 9–27.

Chapman, Helen. "Levinas and the Concept of the Feminine." *Warwick Journal of Philosophy* 1, no. 1 (1988): 65–83.

Ciaramelli, Fabio. "The Circle of the Origin." In *Reinterpreting the Political: Continental Philosophy and Political Theory*, edited by Leonore Langsdorf. Albany: State University of New York Press, 1998.

———. "The Inner Articulation of Origin and the Radical Problem of Democracy." In *Dissensus Communis*, edited by Philippe van Haute and Peg Birmingham, 52–73. Kamper, The Netherlands: Kok Pharos, 1995.

———. "The Riddle of the Pre-original." In *Ethics as First Philosophy: The Significance of Emmanuel Levinas for Philosophy, Literature, and Religion*, edited and with an introduction by Adriaan Peperzak, 87–94. New York: Routledge, 1995.

Clark, Timothy. *Derrida, Heidegger, Blanchot*, chaps. 2, 4; postscript. Cambridge: Cambridge University Press, 1992.

Cohen, Richard A. "Absolute Positivity and Ultrapositivity: Husserl and Levinas." In *The Question of the Other: Essays in Contemporary Continental Philosophy*, edited by A. Dallery and C. Scott, 35–43. Albany: State University of New York Press, 1989.

———. "Emmanuel Levinas: Happiness is a Sensational Time." *Philosophy Today* 25, no. 3 (1981): 196–203.

———. "The Face of Truth in Rosenzweig, Levinas, and Jewish Mysticism." *Phenomenology of the Truth Proper to Religion*, edited by Daniel Guerrière, 175–201. Albany: State University of New York Press, 1990.

———. "Justice and the State in the Thought of Levinas and Spinoza." *Epoché* 4, no. 1 (1996): 55–70.

———. "Levinas, Rosenzweig, and the Phenomenologies of Husserl and Heidegger." *Philosophy Today* 32, no. 2 (1988): 165–78.

———. "Non-In-Difference in the Thought of Emmanuel Levinas." *Graduate Faculty Philosophy Journal* 13 (1988): 141–53.

———. "The Privilege of Reason and Play: Derrida and Levinas." *Tijdschrift voor Filosofie* 45, no. 2 (1983): 242–55.

———. "Review of Existence and Existents." *Man and World* 12 (1979): 521–26.

Cornell, Drucilla. "Post-Structuralism, the Ethical Relation, and the Law." *Cardozo Law Review* 9 (1988): 1587–628.

Critchley, Simon. "The Chiasmus: Levinas, Derrida, and the Ethical Demand for Deconstruction." *Textual Practice* 3, no. 1 (1989): 91–106.

———. "'Das Ding:' Lacan and Levinas." *Research in Phenomenology* 28 (1998): 72–90.

———. "*Il y a*—A Dying Stronger Than Death (Blanchot with Levinas)." *Oxford Literary Review* 15, no. 1–2 (1993): 81–131.

Crowell, Steven Galt. "Being Truthful." In *The Truthful and the Good*, edited by John J. Drummond. Dordrecht: Kluwer, 1996.

Daly, James. "Totality and Infinity in Marx." *Irish Philosophical Journal* 4, nos. 1 and 2 (1987): 120–44.

Davidson, Arnold. "1933–1934: Thoughts on National Socialism." *Critical Inquiry* 17, no. 1 (1990): 35–45.

Davies, Paul. "Difficult Friendship." *Research in Phenomenology* 18 (1988): 149–72.

———. "The Face and the Caress: Levinas's Ethical Alterations of Sensibility." In *Modernity and the Hegemony of Vision*, edited by David Michael Levin, 252–72. Berkeley and Los Angeles: University of California Press, 1993.

———. "A Linear Narrative? Blanchot with Heidegger in the Work of Levinas." In *Philosophers' Poets*, edited by David Wood, 37–69. London: Routledge, 1990.

———. "On Resorting to Ethical Language. In *Ethics as First Philosophy: The Significance of Emmanuel Levinas for Philosophy, Literature, and Religion*, edited and with an introduction by Adriaan Peperzak, 95–104. New York: Routledge, 1995.

———. "Sincerity and the End of Theodicy: Three Remarks on Levinas and Kant." *Research in Phenomenology* 28 (1998): 126–51.

De Boer, Theo. "Beyond Being: Ontology and Eschatology in the Philosophy of Emmanuel Levinas." *Philosophia Reformata* 38 (1973): 17–29.

———. "Judaism and Hellenism in the Philosophy of Levinas and Heidegger." *Archivio di Filosofia* 53 (1985): 197–215.

De Greef, Jan. "The Irreducible Alienation of the Self." In *The Self and the Other*, edited by A-T. Tymieniecka. Analecta Husserliana, vol. 6, 27–30. Dordrecht: D. Reidel, 1983.

Degnin, Francis Dominic. "Laughter and Metaphysics: Interruptions of Levinas and Nietzsche." *Philosophy Today* 39, no. 1 (1995): 31–46.

Diehm, Christian. "Facing Nature: Levinas Beyond the Human." *Philosophy Today* 44, no. 1/4 2000: 51–59.

Derrida, Jacques. "At This Very Moment in This Work Here I Am." Translated by Ruben Berezdivin. In *Re-Reading Levinas*, edited by Robert Bernasconi and Simon Critchley, 11–48. Bloomington: Indiana University Press, 1991.

———. "Violence and Metaphysics." In *Writing and Difference*, translated by Alan Bass, 79–153. Chicago: University of Chicago Press; London: Routledge & Kegan Paul, 1978.

Desmond, William. "Philosophies of Religion: Marcel, Jaspers, Levinas." In *Twentieth Century Continental Philosophy*, edited by Richard Kearney, 131–74. London: Routledge, 1994.

Dhondt, Urbain, "Ethics, History, Religion: The Limits of the Philosophy of Religion." In

Eros and Eris, edited by Paul van Tongeren, Paul Sars, Chris Bremmers, and Koen Boey, 273–80. Dordrecht: Kluwer, 1992.

Drabinski, John, "Between Representation and Being: Levinas and Transcendental Thought." *Skepteo* 1, no. 1 (1993): 57–72.

———. "The Hither-Side of the Living Present in Levinas and Husserl." *Philosophy Today* 41, no. 1 (1996): 142–50.

———. "Sense and Icon: The Problem of Sinngebung in Levinas and Marion." *Philosophy Today* 42, supp. (1998): 47–58.

———. "The Status of the Transcendental in Levinas's Thought." *Philosophy Today* 38, no. 1 (1994): 149–58.

Durfee, Harold A. "Emmanuel Levinas's Philosophy of Language." In *Explanation: New Directions in Philosophy*, 89–120. The Hague: Martinus Nijhoff, 1973.

———. "War, Politics, and Radical Pluralism." *Philosophy and Phenomenological Research* 35 (1975): 549–58.

Durie, Robin. "Indication and the Awakening of Subjectivity." In *Critical Studies: Ethics and the Subject*, edited by Karl Simms. Amsterdam: Rodopi, 1997.

———. "Speaking of Time ... Husserl and Levinas on the Saying of Time." *Journal of the British Society for Phenomenology* 30, no. 1 (1999): 35–58.

Dykeman, Cass. "Encountering the Face of the Other: The Implications of the Work of Emmanuel Levinas for Research in Education." *Journal of Thought* 28 (1993): 5–15.

Ehman, Robert R. "Emmanuel Levinas: The Phenomenon of the Other." *Man and World* 8, no. 2 (1975): 141–45.

Farley, Wendy, "Emmanuel Levinas: Ethics as Domination or Desire." In *Transitions in Continental Philosophy*, edited by A. Dallery, S. Watson, and E. M. Bower, 273–81. Albany: State University of New York Press, 1994.

———. *Eros for the Other*. University Park: Pennsylvania State University Press, 1996.

———. "Ethics and Reality: Dialogue Between Caputo and Levinas." *Philosophy Today* 36, no. 3 (1992): 210–20.

Floyd, Wayne. "To Welcome the Other: Totality and Theory in Levinas and Adorno." *Philosophy and Theology* 4, no. 2 (1989): 145–70.

Foshay, Toby. "Resentment and Apophansis: The Trace of the Other in Levinas, Derrida, and Gans." In *Shadow of Spirit*, edited by Philippa Berry. New York: Routledge, 1992.

Friedlander, Judith. "The Lithuanian Jewish Enlightenment in French Translation: Emmanuel Levinas and His Disciple Alain Finkielkraut." In *Vilra on the Seine*, 80–106. New Haven: Yale University Press, 1990.

Furrow, Dwight. "Levinas: Ethics Without a Limit." In *Against Theory*, 139–60. New York: Routledge, 1995.

Gans, Steven. "Ethics or Ontology." *Philosophy Today* 16, no. 2 (1972): 117–21.

———. "Lacan and Levinas: Towards an Ethical Psychoanalysis." *Journal of the British Society for Phenomenology* 28, no. 1 (1997): 30–48.

Garcia, Leorino. "Infinite Responsibility for the Other: The Ethical Basis of a Humane Society According to Emmanuel Levinas." In *Philippines After 1972: A Multidisciplinary Perspective*, edited by Ramon C. Reyes, 148–65. Budhi Papers 6. Quezon City, Philippines: Ateneo de Manila University, 1985.

Gerber, Rudolph J. "Totality and Infinity: Hebraism and Hellenism—the Experiential Ontology of Emmanuel Levinas." *Review of Existential Psychology an Psychiatry* 7, no. 3 (1967): 177–88.

Gibbs, Robert. "Asymmetry and Mutuality: Habermas and Levinas." *Philosophy and Social Criticism* 23, no. 6 (1997): 51–63.

———. "Blowing on the Embers: Two Jewish Works of Emmanuel Levinas, a Review Essay." *Modern Judaism* 14 (1994): 99–113.

———. "'Greek' in the 'Hebrew' Writings of Emmanuel Levinas." *Studies in Jewish Philosophy* 2, forthcoming.

———. "The Other Comes to Teach Me: A Review of Recent Levinas Publications." *Man and World* 24 (1991): 219–233.

———. "Substitution: Marcel and Levinas." *Philosophy and Theology* 5, no. 2 (1984): 171–86.

Gilkey, Langdon. "Comments on Emmanuel Levinas's *Totalité et Infin*." *Algemee Nederlands Tijdschrift voor Wijsbegeerte* 64 (1972): 26–38.

Goicoechea, David. "Levinas: The Sorrow of the Other That Claims Me Morally." *Joyful Wisdom* 2 (1992): 102–23.

Gottlieb, Roger. "Levinas, Feminism, Holocaust, Ecocide." In *Artifacts, Representations, and Social Practice*, edited by Carol C. Gould. Dordrecht: Kluwer, 1994.

Greisch, Jean. "Ethics and Ontology." *Irish Philosophical Journal* 4, nos. 1 and 2 (1987): 64–75.

———. "Ethics and Ontology: Some 'Hypocritical' Considerations." Translated by Leonard Lawlor. In *Levinas's Contribution to Contemporary Philosophy*. Special issue, *Graduate Faculty Philosophy Journal*, vol. 20, no. 2–vol. 21, no. 1, (1998): 41–69.

Handelman, Susan. "Facing the Other: Levinas, Perelman, and Rosenzweig." *Religion and Literature* 22, nos. 2–3 (1990): 61–84.

Hannay, Alastair. "What Can Philosophers Contribute to Social Ethics?" *Topoi* 17, no. 2 (1998): 127–36.

Hatley, James. "The Sincerity of Apology: Levinas's Resistance to the Judgment of History." In *Phenomenology, Interpretation, and Community*, edited by Lenore Langsdorf. Albany: State University of New York Press, 1996.

Hendley, Steven. "Autonomy and Alterity: Moral Obligation in Sartre and Levinas." *Journal of the British Society for Phenomenology* 27, no. 3 (1996): 246–66.

Hooke, Alexander E. "An Ethic of Accompanying the Dying: Reflections on the Work of Alphonso Lingis." *Philosophy Today* 41, supp. (1997): 153–60.

Hughes, Cheryl L. "The Primacy of Ethics: Hobbes and Levinas," *Continental Philosophy Review* 31, no. 1 (1998): 79–94.

Ince, Kate. "Questions to Luce Irigaray." *Hypatia* 11, no. 2 (1996): 122–40.

Irigaray, Luce. "The Fecundity of the Caress: A Reading of Levinas, *Totality and Infinity*, 'Phenomenology of Eros,'" *An Ethics of Sexual Difference*. Translated by Carolyn Burke and Gillian Gill, 185–217. Ithaca: Cornell University Press, 1993.

———. "Questions to Emmanuel Levinas: On the Divinity of Love." Translated by Margaret Whitford. In *Re-reading Levinas*, edited by R. Bernasconi and S. Critchley 109–18. Bloomington: Indiana University Press, 1991, pp.

Izzi, John. "Proximity in Distance: Levinas and Plotinus." *International Philosophy Quarterly* 38 (1998): 5–16.

Jacques, Francis. "Primum Relationis." In *Difference and Subjectivity*, translated by Andrew Rothwell, 115–61, esp. 127–46. New Haven: Yale University Press, 1991.

Jay, Martin. "Hostage Philosophy: Levinas's Ethical Thought." *Tikkun* 5, no. 6 (1990): 85–87.

Jedraszewski, Marek. "On the Paths of Cartesian Freedom: Sartre and Levinas." *Analecta Husserliana*, vol. 27, 671–83. Dordrecht: D. Reidel, 1989.

Jopling, David. "Levinas on Desire, Dialogue and the Other." *American Catholic Philosophical Quarterly* 65, no. 4 (1991): 405–27.

———. "Levinas, Sartre, and Understanding the Other." *Journal of the British Society for Phenomenology* 24, no. 3 (1993): 214–31.

Jowett, Donna. "Origins, Occupations, and the Proximity of the Neighbour." In *Who Is This "We"?* edited by Eleanor M. Godway and Geraldine Finn, 11–30. Montreal: Black Rose Books, 1994.

Joy, Morny. "Levinas: Alterity, the Feminine, and Women—a Meditation." *Studies in Religion* 22, no. 4 (1994): 463–85.

Kantor, Alon. "Time of Ethics: Levinas and the 'Eclectement' of Time." *Philosophy and Social Criticism* 22, no. 6 (1996): 19–53.

Keenan, Dennis King. "Reading Levinas Reading Descartes' 'Meditations.'" *Journal of the British Society of Phenomenology* 29, no. (1998): 63–74.

———. "Responsibility and Death." *Philosophy Today* 42, no. 1 (1998): 6–15.

———. "Skepticism and the Blinking Light of Revelation." *Epoché* 4 (1996): 33–53.

Keifert, Patrick. "The Other: Hospitality to the Stranger, Levinas, and Multicultural Mission." *Dialog* 30, no. 1 (1991): 36–43.

Kelbley, Charles A. "An Introduction to Emmanuel Levinas." *Thought* 49, no. 192 (1974): 81–86.

Kelly, Andrew. "Reciprocity and the Height of God: A Defence of Buber Against Levinas." *Sophia* 34, no. 1 (1995): 65–73.

Kemp, Peter. "Another Language for the Other: From Kierkegaard to Levinas." *Philosophy and Social Criticism* 23, no. 6 (1997): 5–28.

———. "Ricoeur Between Heidegger and Levinas: Original Affirmation Between Ontological Attestation and Ethical Injunction." *Philosophy and Social Criticism* 21, nos. 5/6 (1995): 41–61.

Keyes, C. D. "An Evaluation of Levinas's Critique of Heidegger." *Research in Phenomenology* 2 (1972): 121–42.

Klemm, David. "Levinas's Phenomenology of the Other and Language as the Other of Phenomenology." *Man and World* 22 (1989): 403–26.

Kosky, Jeffrey. "The Disqualification of Intentionality: The Gift in Derrida, Levinas, and Michel Henry." *Philosophy Today* 41, supp. (1997): 186–97.

Kovacs, George. "The Question of Ultimate Meaning in Emmanuel Levinas." *Ultimate Reading and Meaning* 14, no. 2 (1991): 99–108.

Kuipers, Ronald A. "Singular Interruptions: Rortyan Liberalism and the Ethics of Deconstruction." *International Studies in Philosophy* 28, no. 1 (1996): 11–27.

Large, William. "On the Meaning of the Word Other in Levinas." *Journal of the British Society for Phenomenology* 37, no. 1 (1996): 36–52.

Lawton, Philip. "A Difficult Freedom: Levinas's Judaism." *Tijdschrift voor Filosofie* 37, no. 4 (1975): 681–91.

———. "Levinas' Notion of the 'There Is.'" *Tijdschrift yoor Filosofie* 37, no. 3 (1975): 477–89. (Also published in *Philosophy Today* 29, no. 1 [1976]: 67–76).

———. "Love and Justice: Levinas's Reading of Buber." *Philosophy Today* 20, no. 1 (1976): 77–83.

Levin, David Michael. "Tracework: Myself and Others in the Moral Phenomenology of Merleau-Ponty and Levinas." *International Journal of Philosophical Studies* 6, no. 3 1998: 345–92.

Levy, Ze'ev. "Hermann Cohen and Emmanuel Levinas." In *Hermann Cohen's Philosophy of*

Religion, edited by Stéphane Moses and Hartwig Wiedebach, 133–43. Hildesheim: Georg Olms, 1997.

Libertson, J. "Levinas and Husserl: Sensation and Intentionality." *Tijdschrift voor Filosofie* 41, no. 3 (1979): 485–502.

Librett, Jeffrey S. "The Practice of the World: Jean-Luc Nancy's Liminal Cosmology Between Theory and History." *International Studies in Philosophy* 28, no. 1 (1996): 29–44.

Lichtigfeld, Adolph. "Jaspers's Cipher and Levinas's Trace." In *Karl Jaspers: Philosopher Among Philosophers*, edited by Richard Wisser and Leonard Ehrlich, 186–89. Würzburg: Königshausen and Neumann, 1993.

———. "On Infinity and Totality in Hegel and Levinas." *South African Journal of Philosophy* 2 (1983): 31–33.

Lingis, Alphonso. "The Elemental Imperative," *Research in Phenomenology* 18 (1988): 3–21.

———. "Emmanuel Levinas and the Intentional Analysis of the Libido." *Philosophy in Context* 8 (1978): 60–69.

———. "Face to Face." In *Deathbound Subjectivity*, chap. 6, 135–55. Bloomington: Indiana University Press, 1989.

———. "Face to Face: A Phenomenological Meditation." *International Philosophical Quarterly* 19, no. 2 (1979): 151–63.

———. "Fateful Images." *Research in Phenomenology* 28 (1998): 55–71.

———. "Intuition of Freedom, Intuition of Law." *Journal of Philosophy* 79, no. 10 (1982): 588–96. Reprinted in *Phenomenological Explanations*, 103–12. Phaenomenologica 96. Dordrecht: Martinus Nijhoff, 1986.

———. *Libido: The French Existential Theories*, 58–73, 103–20. Bloomington: Indiana University Press, 1985.

———. "A Phenomenology of Substance." *American Catholic Philosophical Quarterly* 71 no. 4 (1997): 505–22.

Llewelyn, John. "Approaches to Semioethics" In *Cultural Semiosis: Tracing the Signifier*, edited by Hugh Silverman, 196–218. Continental Philosophy 6. New York: Routledge, 1998.

———. "In the Name of Philosophy." *Research in Phenomenology* 28 (1998): 37–54.

———. "Levinas, Derrida, and Others Vis-à-Vis." In *Beyond Metaphysics*, 185–206. Atlantic Highlands, N.J.: Humanities Press, 1985.

———. "Levinas's Critical and Hypocritical Diction." *Philosophy Today* 41, supp. (1997): 28–40.

———. "Jewgreek or Greekjew." *The Collegium Phaenomenologicum: The First Ten Years*, edited by G. Moneta, J. Sallis, and J. Taminiaux, 273–87. Dordrecht: Kluwer, 1988.

———. "Meanings Reserved, Re-served and Reduced." *Southern Journal of Philosophy*, 32, supp. (1994): 27–54.

———. "Selection." In *Postmodernism and the Holocaust*, edited by Alan Milchman and Alan Rosenberg. Value Inquiry Book Series. Amsterdam: Rodopi, 1998.

Long, Christopher Philip. "Reluctant Transcendence: The Face to Face in Levinas' *Totality and Infinity*." *Conference* (New York) 5, no. 1 (1994): 1934.

Lorenc, Iwona. "Philosophical Premises of Levinas's Conception of Judaism." *Dialectics and Humanism* 16 (1989): 157–70.

Lyotard, Jean-François. *The Differend*. Translated by Georges van Den Abbeele, esp. 110–15. Minneapolis: University of Minnesota Press, 1988.

————. "Jewish Oedipus." In *Driftworks*, 35–55. New York: Semiotext(e), 1984.

McCollester, Charles. "The Philosophy of Emmanuel Levinas." *Judaism* 19 (1970): 344–54.

McDonald, Dana Noelle. "Moving Beyond the Face Through Eros: Levinas and Irigaray's Treatment of the Woman as an Alterity." *Philosophy Today* 42, supp. (1998): 71–75.

MacDonald, Michael J. "Jewgreek and Greekjew": The Concept of the Trace in Derrida and Levinas." *Philosophy Today* 35, no. 3 (1991): 215–27.

McGuirk, Bernard. "On the Trajectory of Gnosis: St. John of the Cross, Reverdy, Derrida, Levinas." *Nottingham French Studies* 28, no. 2 (1989): 93–107.

Maloney, Philip J. "Levinas, Substitution, and Transcendental Subjectivity." *Man and World* 30, no. 1 (1997): 49–64.

Manning, Robert John Sheffler. "Thinking the Other Without Violence? An Analysis of the Relation Between the Philosophy of Emmanuel Levinas and Feminism." *Journal of Speculative Philosophy* 5, no. 2 (1991): 132–43.

Mansbach, Abraham. "Strange Epoch!" *South African Journal of Philosophy* 17, no. 3 (1998): 226–38.

Marquez, César A. Moreno. "The Curvature of Intersubjective Space: Sociality and Responsibility in the Thought of Emmanuel Levinas." *Analecta Husserliana*, vol. 22, 343–52. Dordrecht: D. Reidel, 1987.

Masterson, Patrick. "Ethics and Absolutes in the Philosophy of E. Levinas." *Neue Zeitschrift für Systematische Theologie und Religionsphilosoghie* 25 (1983): 211–23.

Meskin, Jacob. "From Phenomenology to Liberation: The Displacement of History and Theology in Levinas's *Totality and Infinity*." *Philosophy and Theology* 4, no. 2 (1989): 119–44.

Miller, Hugh. "Phenomenology, Dialectic, and Time in Levinas's *Time and the Other*." *Philosophy Today* 40, no. 2 (1996) 219–34.

Miller, Jerome. "Intelligibility and the Ethical." *American Philosophical Quarterly* 71, no. 1 (1997): 101–12.

Molesworth, Charles. "Facing the Middle: Alan Wilde, Levinas, and the Poetics of Fiction." *Boundary 2* 16, no. 2 (1989): 391–400.

Norris, Christopher. *Truth and the Ethics of Criticism*, 47–65. Manchester: Manchester University Press, 1994.

O'Connor, Noreen. "Being and the Good: Heidegger and Levinas." *Philosophical Studies* (National University of Ireland) 27 (1980): 212–20.

————. "Exile and Enrootedness." *Seminar* (Journal of the Philosophical Seminar, University College, Cork) 2 (1978): 53–57.

————. "Intentionality Analysis and the Problem of Self and Other." *Journal of the British Society for Phenomenology* 13, no. 2 (1982): 186–92.

————. "The Meaning of 'Religion' in the Work of Emmanuel Levinas." *Proceedings of the Irish Philosophical Society*, 1977.

Ogletree, Thomas W. "Hospitality to the Stranger: The Role of the 'Other' in Moral Experience." In *Hospitality to the Stranger: Dimensions of Moral Understanding*, 35–63. Philadelphia: Fortress Press, 1985.

Oliver, Kelly. "Fatherhood and the Promise of Ethics." *Diacritics* 27, no. 1 (1997): 45–57.

Oppenheim, Michael. "Franz Rosenzweig and Emmanuel Levinas: A Midrash or Thought-Experiment." *Judaism* 42, no. 2 (1993): 177–92.

Peperzak, Adriaan. "Beyond Being." *Research in Phenomenology* 8 (1978): 239–61.

——. "Emmanuel Levinas: Jewish Experience and Philosophy." *Philosophy Today* 27, no. 4 (1983): 297–306.

——. "From Intentionality to Responsibility: On Levinas's Philosophy of Language." In *The Question of the Other: Essays in Contemporary Continental Philosophy*, edited by A. Dallery and C. Scott, 3–21. New York: State University of New York Press, 1989.

——. "*Illeity* According to Levinas," *Philosophy Today* 42, supp. (1998): 41–46.

——. "Levinas on Technology and Nature." *Man and World* 25 (1992): 469–82.

——. "Levinas's Method." *Research in Phenomenology* 28 (1998): 110–25.

——. "The One for the Other: The Philosophy of Emmanuel Levinas." *Man and World* 24 (1991): 427–59.

——. "The Other, Society, People of God." *Man and World* 29 (1996): 109–18.

——. "Phenomenology—Ontology—Metaphysics: Levinas' Perspective on Husserl and Heidegger." *Man and World* 16 (1983): 113–27.

Perpich, Diane. "A Singular Justice: Ethics and Politics Between Levinas and Derrida." *Philosophy Today* 42, supp. (1998): 59–70.

Peters, Gary. "The Rhythm of Alterity: Levinas and Aesthetics." *Radical Philosophy* 82 (1997): 9–16.

Pier, Joanne M. "Sartre/Levinas: An Is/Ought Gap of Ethics?" *Dialog* (Milwaukee) 31 (1989): 52–57.

Powell, Jeffrey. "Levinas Representing Husserl on Representation: An Ethics Beyond Representation." *Philosophy Today* 39, no. 2 (1995): 185–97.

Protevi, John. "Repeating the Parricide: Levinas and the Question of Closure." *Journal of the British Society for Phenomenology* 23, no. 1 (1992): 21–32.

Purcell, Michael. "Divine and Human Service." *Heythrop Journal* 38, no. 2 (1997): 144–64.

——. "The Ethical Significance of Illeity." *Heythrop Journa* 37, no. 2 (1996): 125–38.

——. "For the Sake of Truth … The Demand of Discontinuity in Foucault, Blanchot, and Levinas." *American Catholic Philosophical Quarterly* 71, no. 2 (1997): 237–58.

——. "Quasi-Formal Causality, or the Other-in-Me: Rahner and Levinas." *Gregorianum* 78, no. 1 (1997): 79–93.

Raffoul, François. "On Hospitality, Between Ethics and Politics: Review of *Adieu à Emmanuel Levinas* by Jacques Derrida." *Research in Phenomenology* 28 (1998): 274–82.

——. "Responsibilité et alterité chez Heidegger et Levinas." *Symposium* 1, no. 1 (1997): 49–64.

——. "The Subject of the Welcome: On Jacques Derrida's *Adieu à Emmanuel Levinas*," *Symposium* 2 no. 2 (1998): 211–22.

Rapaport, Herman. "Face to Face with Ricoeur and Levinas." In *Meanings in Texts and Actions: Questioning Paul Ricoeur*, edited by David E. Klemm and William Schweiker, 226–33. Charlottesville: University Press of Virginia, 1993.

Reinhard, Kenneth. "Kant with Sade, Lacan with Levinas," *Modern Language Notes* 110 (1995) 785–808.

Richard, Lucien. "The Possibility of the Incarnation According to Emmanuel Levinas." *Studies in Religion* 17 (1988): 391–405.

Ricoeur, Paul. "What Ontology in View." In *Oneself as Another*. Translated by Kathleen Blarney, 297–356, esp. 329–56. Chicago: Chicago University Press, 1992).

Robbins, Jill. "Aesthetic Totality and Ethical Infinity: Levinas on Art." *L'Esprit Créateur* 35, no. 3 (1995): 66–79.

———. "Alterity and the Judaic: Reading Levinas." In *Prodigal Son/Elder Brother: Interpretation and Alterity in Augustine, Petrarch, Kafka, Levinas*, 100–132. Chicago: University of Chicago Press, 1991.

———. "Facing Figures: Levinas and the Claims of Figural Interpretation." In *Transitions in Continental Philosophy*, edited by A. Dallery, S. Watson, and E. M. Bower, 283–91. Albany: State University of New York Press, 1994.

———. "An Inscribed Responsibility: Levinas's *Difficult Freedom*," *Modern Language Notes* 106 (1991): 1052–62.

———. "Visage, Figure: Reading Levinas's *Totality and Infinity*." *Yale French Studies* 79 (1991): 135–49. (Revised version in *Critical Encounters: Reference and Responsibility in Deconstructive Writing*, edited by Cathy Caruth and Deborah Esch, 275–98. [New Brunswick: Rutgers University Press, 1994]).

Rose, Gillian. "Angry Angels: Simone Weil and Emmanuel Levinas." *Judaism and Modernity*, 211–23. Oxford: Blackwell, 1993

Rosmann, Léonard. "Joy Through Commitment to the Other in the Works of Emmanuel Levinas." *Joyful Wisdom: A Post-Modern Ethics of Joy*, edited by M. Zlomislic, Gerard Grand, and David Goicoechea, 57–68. St. Catherines, Ontario: Brock University, 1991.

Salemohamed, George. "Levinas: From Ethics to Political Theology." *Economy and Society* 21, no. 2 (1992): 192–206.

Sallis, John. "Levinas and the Elemental." *Research in Phenomenology* 28 (1998): 152–59.

Sandford, Stella. "Writing as a Man: Levinas and the Phenomenology of Eros." *Radical Philosophy* 87 (January/February, 1998): 6–17.

Schrag, Calvin O. "The Recovery of the Phenomenological Subject: In Conversation with Derrida, Ricoeur, and Levinas." *Journal of the British Society for Phenomenology* 28, no. 3 (1997): 228–35.

Schroeder, Brian. "Reversibility and Irreversibility: Paradox, Language, and Intersubjectivity in Merleau-Ponty and Levinas." *Symposium* 1, no. 1 (1997): 65–79.

Sikka, Sonia. "Questioning the Sacred: Heidegger and Levinas on the Love of Divinity." *Modern Theology* 14, no. 3 (1998): 299–323.

Simmons, William Paul. "The Third: Levinas's Theoretical Move from An-archical Ethics to the Realm of Justice and Politics." *Philosophy and Social Criticism* 25, no. 6 (1999): 83–104.

Smith, Michael, B. "Philosophy and Inspiration: Chalier's Levinas." *Bulletin de la Société Américaine de Philosophie de Langue Françoise* 9, no. 1 (1997): 22–30.

Smith, Steven G. "Reason as One for Another: Moral and Theoretical Argument in the Philosophy of Levinas." *Journal of the British Society for Phenomenology* 12, no. 3 (1981): 231–44.

Steiner, David M., and Krzysztof L. Helminski. "The Politics 'of' Relationality: From the Postmodern to Post-Ontology." *Philosophy and Social Criticism* 24, no. 4, (1998): 1–21.

Stoll, Donald. "Heidegger, Levinas, Derrida: Forgetting and Remembering the Jews." *Philosophy Today* 43, no. 4 (1999): 336–47.

Strasser, Stephan. "The Concept of 'Phenomenon' in Levinas and Its Importance for Religious Philosophy." In *Clefts in the World*, edited and translated by Richard Rojcewicz, 41–57. Pittsburgh: Simon Silverman Phenomenology Center, Duquesne University, 1986.

———. "Emmanuel Levinas (Born 1906): Phenomenological Philosophy." In *The*

Phenomenological Movement, edited by Herbert Spiegelberg, 612–49. 3d revised and enlarged edition. Phaenomenologica 5/6. The Hague: Martinus Nijhoff, 1982.

———. "The Unique Individual and His Other." In *The Self and the Other*, edited by A-T. Tymieniecka. Analecta Husserliana, vol. 6, 9–26. Dordrecht: D. Reidel, 1983.

Strolz, Walter. "The Humanism of the Other: On the Philosophy of Emmanuel Levinas." *Studies in Interreligious Dialogue* 2, no. 1 (1992): 51–64.

Surber, Jere Paul. "Kant, Levinas, and the Thought of the 'Other.'" *Philosophy Today* 38, no. 3–4 (1994): 294–316.

Tallon, Andrew. "Editor's Page." *Philosophy and Theology* 5, no. 2 (1989): 206–18.

———. "Emmanuel Levinas and the Problem of Ethical Metaphysics." *Philosophy Today* 20, no. 1 (1976): 53–66.

———. "Intentionality, Intersubjectivity, and the Between: Buber and Levinas on Affectivity and the Dialogical Principal." *Thought* 53, no. 210 (1978): 292–309.

———. "Review of *Autrement qu'être ou au-delà de l'essence*." *Man and World* 9 (1976): 451–62.

Taminiaux, Jacques. "The Early Levinas's Reply to Heidegger's Fundamental Ontology." *Philosophy and Social Criticism* 23, no. 6 (1997): 29–49.

Taylor, Mark C. "Infinity." In *Altarity*, 185–216. Chicago: University of Chicago, 1987.

Thoné, Astrid. "A Radical Gift. Ethics and Motherhood in Emmanuel Levinas's *Otherwise Than Being*." *Journal of the British Society for Phenomenology* 29, no. 2 (1998): 116–31.

Tiemersma, Douwe. "Ontology and Ethics in the Foundation of Medicine and the Relevance of Levinas's View." *Theoretical Medicine* 8 (1987): 127–33.

Treanor, Brian. "Marcel and Levinas: 'Disponsibilité' and Responsibility." *Dialogue* 41, no. 1 (1998): 12–19.

Trey, George. "Communicative Ethics in the Face of Alterity: Habermas, Levinas, and the Problem of Post-Conventional Universalism." *Praxis International* 11, no. 4 (1992): 412–27.

Udoff, Alan. Introduction to *The Knowledge of Man*, by Martin Buber, edited by Maurice Friedman, viii–xxii. New ed. Atlantic Highlands, N.J.: Humanities Press, 1988.

Valevicius, Andrius. "Afterword: Emmanuel Levinas, the Multicultural Philosopher." *Continental Philosophy Review* 31, no. 1 (1998): 11–14.

———. "Emmanuel Levinas: Some Basic Facts." *Lituanus* 33, no. 1 (1987): 18–26.

———. *From the Other to the Totally Other*. New York: Peter Lang, 1988.

Van Beeck, Frans Jozef. *Loving the Torah More Than God?* Chicago: Loyola University Press, 1989.

Vasey, Craig R. "Emmanuel Levinas: From Intentionality to Proximity." *Philosophy Today* 25, no. 3 (1981): 178–95.

———. "Faceless Women and Serious Others: Levinas, Misogyny, and Feminism." In *Ethics and Danger*, edited by Arleen B. Dallery and Charles E. Scott with P. Holley Roberts, 317–30. Albany: State University of New York Press, 1992.

———. "Review of *Existence and Existents*." *Thought* 44 (1980): 466–73.

Vetlesen, Arne Johan. "Relations with Others in Sartre and Levinas: Assessing Some Implications for an Ethics of Proximity," *Constellations* 1, no. 3 (1995): 358–82.

———. "Worlds Apart? Habermas and Levinas." *Philosophy and Social Criticism* 23, no. 1 (1997): 1–20.

Visker, Rudi. "Dis-possessed: How to Remain Silent 'After' Levinas." *Man and World* 29, no. 2 (1996): 119–46.

Walsh, Robert D. "Action, Passion, and Responsibility: Levinas's Circumcision of Consciousness." In *Reinterpreting the Political: Continental Philosophy and Political Theory*, edited by Leonore Langsdorf. Albany: State University of New York Press, 1998.

Ward, Graham. "The Revelation of the Holy Other as the Wholly Other: Between Barth's Theology of the Word and Levinas's Philosophy of Saying." *Modern Theology* 9, no. 2 (1993): 159–80.

Watson, Stephen. "The Face of the Hibakusha: Levinas and the Trace of Apocalypse." In *Writing the Future*, edited by David Wood, 155–73. London: Routledge & Kegan Paul, 1990.

———. "Levinas, the Ethics of Deconstruction, and the Remainder of the Sublime." *Man and World* 21 (1988): 35–64.

———. "Reason and the Face of the Other." *Journal of the America Academy of Religion* 54, no. 1 (1986): 33–57.

Webb, Mark. "The Rape of Time." *Southwest Philosophical Studies* (San Marcos, Tex.) 7 (1982): 147–54.

Westphal, Merold. "Levinas, Kierkegaard, and the Theological Task." *Modern Theology* 8, no. 3 (1992): 241–61.

———. "The Transparent Shadow: Kierkegaard and Levinas in Dialogue." In *Kierkegaard in Post/Modernity*, edited by Martin J. Matustik. Bloomington: Indiana University Press, 1995.

Williams, Robert R. "Hegel and Phenomenology: Husserl, Sartre, and Levinas." In *Recognition: Fichte and Hegel on the Other*, 285–307. Albany: State University of New York, 1992

Wingenbuch, Ed. "Liberating Responsibility: The Levinasian Ethic of *Being and Time*." *International Philosophical Quarterly* 36, no. 141 (1996): 29–45.

Wirzba, Norman. "From Maieutics to Metanoia: Levinas's Understanding of the Philosophical Task." *Man and World* 28, no. 2 (1995): 129–44.

———. "Teaching as Propaedetuic to Religion: The Contribution of Levinas and Kierkegaard." *International Journal for Philosophy of Religion* 39, no. 2 (1996): 77–94.

Wolosky, Shira. "Derrida, Jabés, Levinas: Sign-Theory as Ethical Discourse." *Prooftexts: Journal of Jewish Literary History* 2 (1982): 283–302.

Woods, Tim. "The Ethical Subject: The Philosophy of Emmanuel Levinas." In *Critical Studies: Ethics and the Subject*, edited by Karl Simms. Amsterdam: Rodopi, 1997.

Wyschogrod, Edith. "Derrida, Levinas, and Violence." In *Derrida and Deconstruction*, edited by Hugh J. Silverman, 182–200. London: Routledge, 1989

———. "Does Continental Ethics Have a Future?" In *Ethics and Danger*, edited by Arleen B. Dallery and Charles E. Scott with P. Holley Roberts, 229–41. Albany: State University of New York Press, 1992.

———. "Doing Before Hearing: On the Primacy of Touch." In *Textes pour Emmanuel Levinas*, edited by François Laruelle, 179–203. Paris: Jean-Michel Place, 1980.

———. "Elementary Individuals: Toward a Phenomenological Ethics." *Philosophy and Theology* 1, no. 1 (1986): 9–31.

———. "Emmanuel Levinas and the Problem of Religious Language." *Thomist* 26, no. 1 (1972): 1–38.

———. "From the Disaster to the Other: Tracing the Name of God in Levinas." In *Phenomenology and the Numinous*, 67–86. Pittsburgh: Simon Silverman Phenomenology Center, Duquesne University, 1988.

————. "From Ethics to Language: The Imperative of the Other." *Semiotica* 97, no. 1 (1993): 163–76.

————. "God and 'Being's Move' in the Philosophy of Emmanuel Levinas." *Journal of Religion* 62, no. 2 (1982): 145–55.

————. "The Moral Self: Emmanuel Levinas and Hermann Cohen." *Daat: A Journal of Jewish Philosophy* 4 (1980): 35–58.

————. "Review of *Totality and Infinity.*" *Human Inquiries* 10 (1971): 185–92.

Young, Iris Marion. "Asymmetrical Reciprocity: On Moral Respect, Wonder, and Enlarged Thought. *Constellations* 3, no. 3 (1997): 340–63.

Ziarek, Ewa. "Kristeva and Levinas: Mourning, Ethics, and the Feminine." In *Ethics, Politics, and Difference in Julia Kristeva's Writing*, edited by Kelly Oliver, 62–78. New York: Routledge, 1993.

Ziarek, Ewa Płonowska. "The Rhetoric of Failure and Deconstruction." *Philosophy Today* 40, no. 1 (1996): 80–90.

Ziarek, Krzysztof. *Inflected Language: Toward a Hermeneutic of Nearness, Heidegger, Levinas, Stevens, Celan*, esp. chaps. 3, 65–102. Albany: State University of New York Press, 1994.

————. "The Language of Praise: Levinas and Marion." *Religion and Literature* 22, no. 2–3 (1990): 93–108.

————. "Semantics of Proximity: Language and the Other in the Philosophy of Emmanuel Levinas." *Research in Phenomenology* 19 (1989): 213–17.

Index

Notes on Contributors

Alison Ainley is senior lecturer in philosophy and field leader of European philosophy and literature at Anglia Polytechnic University in Cambridge, England. She has published essays in various edited collections and articles in journals on Levinas, Heidegger, Nietzsche, and Merleau-Ponty and related topics in phenomenology, psychoanalysis, and feminist philosophy.

Bettina Bergo is assistant professor of philosophy at Loyola College, Maryland. She is translator of Levinas's *Of God Who Comes to Mind* (Stanford University Press, 1998) and *God, Death, and Time* (Stanford University Press, forthcoming). She is the coeditor, with Diane Perpich, of a special issue of the *Graduate Faculty Philosophy Journal* (1998), *Levinas's Contribution to Contemporary Philosophy*. She is author of *Levinas Between Ethics and Politics: For the Beauty That Adorns the Earth* (Kluwer, 1998).

Donna Brody has a doctorate in philosophy from the University of Essex, England. She is author of "Emmanuel Levinas: The Logic of Ethical Ambiguity in *Otherwise Than Being or Beyond Essence*," published in *Research in Phenomenology* (1995).

Catherine Chalier is the author of a number of books, including *Figures du féminin* (1982), *Judaisme et altérité* (1982), *Les matriarches* (1985), *La persévéance du mal* (1987), and *L'alliance avec la nature* (1982).

Tina Chanter is professor of philosophy at DePaul University. She is author of *Ethics of Eros: Irigaray's Rereading of the Philosophers* (Routledge, 1995) and *Time, Death, and the Feminine: Levinas with Heidegger* (Stanford University Press, forthcoming), as well as articles on figures such as Beauvoir, Derrida, Kofman, Kristeva, Hegel, Heidegger, Irigaray, Lacan, Levinas, and Merleau-Ponty and on topics such as theory and tragedy, sex and gender, time and temporality, and film theory. She has contributed to such journals as *Differences, Signs, Philosophy and Social Criticism, Graduate Faculty Philosophy Journal, Philosophy Today*, and *Research in Phenomenology*. Her current book project is on abjection and film.

Luce Irigaray is author of numerous books, among them *Speculum of the Other Woman, This Sex Which Is Not One, An Ethics of Sexual Difference*, and *Sexes and Genealogies*.

Claire Katz is an assistant professor of philosophy and Jewish studies at Pennsylvania State University. In her work she addresses issues in Jewish philosophy, feminist theory, and continental Philosophy. She is currently completing a manuscript on Levinas and the feminine.

Diane Perpich is assistant professor of philosophy at Vanderbilt University. She is coeditor of a special issue of the *Graduate Faculty Philosophy Journal* dedicated to Emmanuel Levinas. She teaches and researches in the areas of phenomenology, ethics, and feminism.

Sonia Sikka teaches philosophy at the University of Ottawa, Canada. She is the author of *Forms of Transcendence: Heidegger and Medieval Mystical Theology* (State University of New York Press, 1997). She has also published numerous articles on continental philosophy, including, on Levinas: "Questioning the Sacred: Heidegger and Levinas on the Locus of Divinity" (*Modern Theology*, 1998) and "How Not to Read the Other: 'All the Rest Can be Translated'" (*Philosophy Today*, 1999).

Kelly Oliver is professor of philosophy and women's studies at the State University of New York, Stony Brook. Her books include *Beyond Recognition: Toward a Theory of Othered Subjectivity* (University of Minnesota Press, forthcoming), *Subjectivity Without Subjects: From Abject Fathers to Desiring Mothers* (Rowman and Littlefield, 1998), *Family Values: Subjects Between Nature and Culture* (Routledge, 1997), *Womanizing Nietzsche: Philosophy's Relation to "the Feminine"* (Routledge 1995), and *Rereading Kristeva: Unraveling the Double-Bind* (Indiana University Press, 1993).

Stella Sandford is lecturer in modern European philosophy at Middlesex University, London. She is the author of *The Metaphysics of Love: Gender and Transcendence in Levinas* (Athlone, 2000).

Ewa Płonowska Ziarek is associate professor of English and gender studies at the University of Notre Dame. She is the author of *The Rhetoric of Failure: Deconstruction of Skepticism, Reinvention of Modernism* (State University of New York Press, 1995), *Gombrowicz's Grimaces: Modernism, Gender, Nationality* (State University of New York Press, 1998) and *An Ethics of Dissensus: Feminism, Postmodernity, and the Politics of Radical Democracy* (Stanford, 2001). She has published numerous articles on Kristeva, Irigaray, Derrida, Levinas, Foucault, Fanon, and literary modernism.